WORKFORCE INTERMEDIARIES FOR THE TWENTY-FIRST CENTURY

WORKFORCE INTERMEDIARIES

FOR THE

TWENTY-FIRST CENTURY

EDITED BY

ROBERT P. GILOTH

*Published in association with The American Assembly,
Columbia University*

Temple University Press   Philadelphia

Temple University Press, Philadelphia 19122
Copyright © 2004 by The American Assembly, Columbia University
Published 2004
Printed in the United States of America

∞ The paper used in this publication meets the requirements of the American National Standard for Information Sciences—Permanence of Paper for Printed Library Materials, ANSI Z39.48-1984

Library of Congress Cataloging-in-Publication Data

Workforce intermediaries for the twenty-first century / edited by Robert P. Giloth.
   p. cm.
  Includes bibliographical references and index.
  ISBN 1-59213-204-9 (cloth)
   1. Hard-core unemployed—Services for—United States.   2. Hard-core unemployed—Services for—United States—Case studies.   3. Welfare recipients—Employment—Government policy—United States.
  4. Occupational training—Government policy—United States.
  5. Employment agencies—United States.   I. Title: Workforce intermediaries for the 21st century. II. Giloth, Robert.

HD5708.85.U6W67 2004
331.25'92'0973—dc22   2003060363

2 4 6 8 9 7 5 3 1

CONTENTS

IV   CUSTOMER VOICES

V   BUILDING WORKFORCE INTERMEDIARIES

VI   CONCLUSION

APPENDIX

FOREWORD

THE AMERICAN ECONOMY AND SOCIETY ARE CONFRONTED WITH THE major challenge of how to improve the system of training and job placement. This includes self-sufficiency and career progression for low-skilled and hard-to-employ workers while also providing employers with a workforce that allows them to remain globally competitive. Over the past decade, there has been progress in addressing this "dual customer" orientation. During this period, the field of workforce development has become entrepreneurial and opportunistic, and a recent convergence of strategies, which knits together many policies, procedures, and efforts, and simplifies the workforce field for both employer and jobseeker customers, has emerged in the development of the workforce intermediary approach.

Workforce intermediaries bring together a set of key players to create long-term pathways to careers for low-skilled workers and value-added productivity for employers. They have the ability to assemble the right mix of targeted good jobs, combine pre-employment and hard-skills training, assess skills and career directions, case manage human services, and provide social supports in the workplace and on the job. A central issue for workforce intermediaries is how best to build an infrastructure to support their growth and impact, and to augment and improve on the current workforce system in ways that will allow their capacity, performance, and scale to develop for the economic betterment of the nation.

Since its founding in 1950 The American Assembly has often explored aspects of the nation's workforce. The examination of workforce intermediaries fits this legacy and fits with founder Dwight D. Eisenhower's mandate for the institution "to illuminate issues of national policy." The Assembly undertook this project and commissioned this volume as part of a project to develop a consensus on the role of workforce intermediaries in the twenty-first century and to identify policy guidelines for the challenges ahead.

The chapters in this volume were first used as background for an American Assembly held at Arden House, Harriman, New York, on February 6–9, 2003. A distinguished group of authorities and representatives of business, government, workforce intermediaries, labor, law, academia, and non-profit organizations convened to make recommendations and to help define an agenda to advance the workforce delivery system through the use of workforce intermediaries. Their names, affiliations, and report of findings are included in this volume.

This American Assembly was co-directed by John Colborn, deputy director, Economic Development Unit, the Ford Foundation; Betsy Biemann, associate director, Working Communities, the Rockefeller Foundation; and the editor of this book, Robert Giloth, director of family economic success, the Annie E. Casey Foundation. This project was also ably assisted by advisors and a steering committee, whose names and affiliations are also listed in the appendix.

We gratefully acknowledge support for this book and for the Arden House Assembly from the Ford Foundation, the Annie E. Casey Foundation, the Rockefeller Foundation, the John D. and Catherine T. MacArthur Foundation, and the Open Society Institute, Baltimore.

These organizations, as well as The American Assembly, take no position on the subject presented here in public discussion.

DAVID H. MORTIMER
The American Assembly

I
INTRODUCTION

1

Introduction:
A Case for Workforce Intermediaries

ROBERT P. GILOTH

Government needs to offer greater public support
to non-profit organizations and other intermediaries
to create training and job-ladder strategies.
—DAVID T. ELLWOOD, September 2002

THE LABOR AND SKILL SHORTAGES OF THE 1990S FORESHADOWED the coming workforce crisis of the decades ahead. Recent news accounts of global labor recruiting for trained nurses for our hospitals are reminders of labor shortage desperation, even in these harder times. The near future will bring more retirements of skilled workers, fewer new workers, and minimal growth in new skills. The workforce will become more diverse. Companies and regions are likely to suffer because a skilled workforce is indispensable to local growth. Tight labor markets are good for low-skilled, low-income workers, but opportunities will be lost without adequate training and education systems in place.

What is needed is a concerted and sustained public and private effort to address both the needs of business for job ready, skilled workers who can help companies grow and the needs of workers and jobseekers to navigate the pathway to careers and family-supporting earnings and benefits. There are good examples of how this can be done for different types of businesses, different levels of skilled workers, and in different regions. But there are far too few examples to meet the long-term needs and aspirations of business and workers.

Public workforce development systems have embraced and advocated for many of these new ideas and practices as well, going back to the path breaking *America's Choice* report in 1990. But top down, federal reform of workforce development systems has not fully solved a basic problem for employers and workers/jobseekers. The Regional Workforce Partnership of Philadelphia, for example, recently released a revealing map of the approximately $1.3 billion of state and federal resources spent on workforce development in Pennsylvania in 2001 through 49 different programs and 22 Workforce Investment Boards (WIBs), but with few common and explicit outcome measures. Estimates of the number of federal workforce related programs are in the range of 163 largely disconnected programs and $20 billion (Regional Workforce Partnership, 2002; Grubb, 1996). This picture of fragmented workforce programs shows how much disconnection remains in a time in which workforce development is grappling with long-term "worker, skill, and wage gaps" (Aspen Institute, 2002).

This book presents an approach for advancing these promising workforce development ideas and practices that complements the reform of public workforce development systems. It involves a new breed of workforce organization that we have named workforce intermediaries (WIs), but that go under other names as well, such as employer intermediaries, sectoral initiatives, and community college bridge programs. They are a part of a larger family of labor market intermediaries (LMIs) that have become more prominent in today's labor market. LMIs include staffing and temporary service firms as well as proprietary schools and labor market exchanges like the employment services of monster.com. Workforce intermediaries also are part of a larger group of workforce development organizations, usually nonprofit, that provides an array of workforce services.

The 1990s economic boom in conjunction with policy changes and accumulated learning produced new and promising ways to think about workforce development for low-skilled workers in the United States. Although today's economy has put a damper on some of this innovation, and workforce development in general remains underfunded, the coming labor shortages of the twenty-first century underscore the importance of understanding these approaches. Employers still need reliable sources of productive employees, and workers/jobseekers still need investment in their lifelong learning and career advancement for family-supporting employment.

What seemed path breaking in the early 1990s is now common sense, although a substantial gap in achievement remains. Workforce development focuses on long-term job retention and career advancement, not just job training or job placement. Workforce development is pursued in the context of family self-sufficiency, a realistic understanding of what it takes a family to prosper. This understanding leads to knitting together the public, private, and family resources required as families move along the path of career advancement. Workforce development strategies are dual customer—serving employers and workers/jobseekers—and focus on regions and economic sectors/clusters. The most effective workforce strategies target higher wage jobs, mix job readiness and contextualized skill training, provide post employment services and supports, and provide upgrade training in the context of identified career pathways. Cookie cutter approaches don't work for employers or jobseekers. And new partnerships have grown up—what we call workforce intermediaries—to implement these effective practices, in conjunction with other public and private institutions, in an entrepreneurial, dynamic, results oriented fashion.

Workforce intermediaries are homegrown, local partnerships that bring together employers and workers, private and public funding streams, and relevant partners to fashion and implement pathways to career advancement and family-supporting employment for low-skilled workers. Their explicit focus on career advancement for low-skilled workers is what distinguishes them from other labor market intermediaries (see chapter 11). They come in all shapes and sizes, as the late Bennett Harrison, of MIT and New School University, showed us in his research on workforce networks, but have together demonstrated their ability to navigate public and private systems to attain important and distinctive results for employers and workers (Harrison and Weiss, 1998). The 1990s witnessed a growth in their number from a handful to at least 250; many more if we count the efforts of our 1,000 community colleges (see chapter 4).

WIs have frequently emerged and grown in spite of public workforce systems. Not surprisingly, some public system advocates see them as duplicative competitors that consume limited resources and contribute to system fragmentation. Yet it is the uneven performance of the public workforce system and institutions, despite a number of exceptional WIBs, that has given impetus to their formation. Indeed, WIs' promising results in serving low-skilled workers and engaging employers have demonstrated the career advancement potential of workforce development, while generating many of the workforce innovations that now define the cutting edge of the workforce development field.

This book was assembled as a starting point and common framework to spur discussions at the 102nd American Assembly, a four-day nonpartisan dialogue about the future of workforce intermediaries. Given the lack of sustained public and private attention to WIs, it was essential to provide background readings for the Assembly that would capture the current state of knowledge about them. This book has commissioned an array of new research and analysis with a focus on WIs. Research includes surveys, ethnographies, focus groups, key informants, and case studies as well as economic and demographic analysis. While the research documents the role and activities of WIs, it does so always in the context of WIs furthering the career advancement prospects of low-skilled workers/jobseekers.

This volume includes chapters that discuss the career advancement challenge for low-income, low-skilled workers, the definition, functions, evaluation evidence, and population of WIs, the economic and policy rationales for WIs, employer and worker perspectives on workforce needs and career advancement, how to build the capacity of WIs, and promising financing mechanisms for career advancement and WIs. There is also much to be learned from the community development field and the proliferation of Community Development Corporations (CDCs) as producers of affordable housing in the past several decades. In many respects, WIs are at the same stage as CDCs were in the early 1980s (see chapter 14).

This chapter provides an overview of the volume. It defines WIs and provides four brief examples of WIs in action. It summarizes the economic, demographic, and policy rationales for WIs. The chapter then presents five counterarguments about the efficacy of WIs and workforce development in general, such as skepticism about the contribution of job training for poverty alleviation. Several examples of policy and financing tools for supporting WIs are then presented as a way of suggesting the infrastructure needed to support WIs. Finally, the chapter concludes by summarizing the major themes of the volume chapters.

The goal of this book is to make a plausible case for the viability of WIs as an important complement and implementing mechanism for public workforce development systems. Moreover, the book goes beyond just making a plausible case to suggesting practical ways to strengthen the capacity and effectiveness of WIs through more adequate financing, capacity building investments, and other public and private policies. In the end, there is a strong case that WIs serve both employers and workers/jobseekers in new ways, and that they represent a promising mechanism for helping working families achieve family-supporting incomes through career advancement.

WHAT ARE WORKFORCE INTERMEDIARIES?

An eclectic group of organizations has emerged during the past 20 years, more rapidly in the 1990s, that has achieved remarkable results for both employers and jobseekers/workers. Named workforce intermediaries, these local organizations are deeply connected or "embedded" in low-income communities and in networks of employers, workforce providers, and community organizations (Fitzgerald, 2000; New Deal Task Force, 1999).

Making connections is an important part of what WIs do, but it is only one part. They implement strategies that help employers grow, articulate labor demand, and define occupational specifications, while building networks of service providers and measuring progress. In some cases WIs serve as a "buffer" or interpreter between employers and workers, frequently overcoming distrust, misperceptions, and even hostility (see chapter 9). They are fundamentally brokers, integrators, and learners who entrepreneurially enact workforce development rather than simply "meeting the market" or conforming to a publicly mandated set of roles and responsibilities. Finally, WIs are quite diverse. They have grown out of community organizations, employer associations, labor unions, and community colleges. Whatever their origin, however, they are partnerships comprising employers, community organizations, community colleges, and human service providers (see chapter 3).

One challenge in discussing WIs is that they represent such a broad range of institutions and approaches. For the purposes of this book, WIs are understood to embody five attributes in the context of implementing workforce strategies:

- WIs take a dual *customer approach* by addressing the needs of employers and low-income and less-skilled workers and jobseekers. WIs measure their effectiveness by outcomes that relate to both customers.
- WIs go *beyond job matching*. Connecting jobseekers and employers is usually at the heart of WIs, but successful WIs offer a host of interventions. Most seek to change the supply side of the labor market by providing training or by working to improve the way jobseekers and employers are served by a variety of partners. A demand side strategy of WIs is to work with employers to improve their human resource systems, career ladders, job quality, and overall competitiveness.
- WIs act as *integrators* of funding streams, public and private sector services and programs, and information sources to better serve the needs of jobseekers, workers, and employers. In performing this role, successful WIs act as a "center of gravity" in developing relationships, enforcing accountability, and leveraging resources.
- WIs are generators of *ideas and innovations* about what workers, firms, and communities need in order to prosper. Lifelong learning, worker advancement, regional competitiveness, environmental sustainability—these and many other ideas guide their work.
- WIs are not *single purpose or function* organizations, such as community based organizations that operate a stand-alone training program or trade associations of training providers that advocate for policy changes. Many training providers are the reflections of fragmented public funding systems and priorities.

This definition of workforce intermediary embodies distinctive strategy elements as well as organizational characteristics. The intermediary approach is dual customer, brokering partners, and integrating resources for the purposes of meeting employer and worker needs. The intermediary organization has to be entrepreneurial, results oriented, and an adaptive learner. Both components are essential for what we are calling workforce intermediaries.

But is it fair to ask whether the Workforce Investment Boards of the Workforce Investment Act (WIA) system (1998 workforce legislation that places emphasis on involving the private sector and responding to the demands of employers) share these attributes as well? At one level they do: these are the common sense ideas of effective workforce development.

There are important role and function differences, however. WIBs address governance and system integration and accountability at the policy and strategy levels. WIs are neither substitutes nor competitors of WIBs for this role. Rather, WIs are on-the-ground partnerships that pursue results for specific groups of employers and workers/jobseekers. The focus of WIs on career advancement and business development stands in contrast to the "Work First" and universal access approach of WIA. Moreover, WIs have demonstrated the ability to aggregate employer and jobseeker/worker interests, flexibly redesign training approaches as circumstances change, and produce important workforce innovations on behalf of achieving practical results.

Four contemporary WIs illustrate the partnerships, strategies, and projects that they have undertaken to promote career advancement for low-skilled workers/jobseekers.

Wisconsin Regional Training Partnership (WRTP)

WRTP is a union-employer partnership of 125 firms and 100,000 workers in southeastern Wisconsin (Parker, 2000; Fleischer, 2001). It was formed to organize firms by sectors and to engage in cooperative labor market planning and modernization. WRTP works in manufacturing, hospitality, construction, healthcare, finance, and technology.

Starting with upgrade training of incumbent workers, WRTP has trained 6,000 workers, and employers have invested $25 million in training production workers. WRTP has extended its training efforts to entry-level workers from inner city Milwaukee placing 1,400 jobseekers by 2002 in entry-level jobs paying more than $10 per hour during the past three years. WRTP has worked with the Milwaukee Area Technical College, the Private Industry Council, and an array of community based organizations and social service agencies to make this happen. WRTP has developed union based mentoring programs in plants as well as diversity training in order to overcome workplace barriers and increase retention.

Project QUEST

COPS/Metro, a church based community organizing network in San Antonio, incorporated Project QUEST in 1992, a WI that trains local residents for family-supporting jobs (Campbell, 1994). It was the grassroots power and relationships of COPs/Metro that successfully negotiated jobs from employers, resources from local and state governments, and new ways of teaching and supporting students from the local community college.

Since 1992, Project QUEST has placed over 1,400 people in jobs with an average wage of $10 per hour, 90 percent of the jobs including health benefits. These jobs are in the fields of healthcare, finance, and manufacturing (Project Quest, 2000). An evaluation of QUEST found that participants gained an average of $7,000 in annual income because of their training and support (Lautsch and Osterman, 1998). More recent tracking of QUEST participants shows an average increase of $4.03 per hour compared to jobs before training (Aspen Institute, 2001).

Seattle Jobs Initiative (SJI)

SJI is a public sector led WI started by the city of Seattle's Office of Economic Development, which grew up under the leadership of former Mayor Norman Rice (AECF, 2000; Fleischer, 2001; Smith and Davis, 2003). It combines short-term training and placement programs, sector based partnerships, human service integration, a network of culturally diverse community based organizations, and an ambitious policy agenda. Since operational startup in 1997, SJI has placed 3,000 jobseekers and has leveraged an additional $25 million in workforce investments. SJI developed a strategic plan with an inner city community college, Seattle Vocational Institute, to expand its capacity and worked with community based organizations to develop case management standards for job retention and advancement.

What makes SJI remarkable, in addition to its scale, is its ability to experiment, adapt, and grow innovations within the public sector environment. Moreover, this ability has survived three mayors and the downsizing of Boeing and its suppliers, and now the overall economic slump. SJI has embraced change during its short life, reinventing its employer relationships, relationship to City Hall, and portfolio of projects. As of January 1, 2003, SJI became an independent nonprofit so that it can take on new roles and build stronger relationships with employers, community organizations, and other workforce players.

Cleveland Jobs and Workforce Initiative

The Cleveland Jobs and Workforce Initiative is a project of the Cleveland Growth Association, one of the largest regional Chambers of Commerce with nearly 17,000 members. Started by the former associate director of the George Gund Foundation in Cleveland, the role of the initiative is to make catalytic investments in changing the workforce systems to become more focused, particularly from the employer's point of view (Berry, 1998). Its purpose as an intermediary is change, not operating programs, and identifying the public, private, and civic supports needed to sustain these changes.

Accomplishments include setting up a successful Center for Employment Training (CET) program, promoting sectoral initiatives in healthcare and telecommunications, successful advocacy for new employer based tax credits for training, and organizing a workforce consortium for manufacturing in Cleveland. These efforts have resulted in more than 1,000 people receiving skills training and jobs with starting wages of $8 to $9.50, 300 obtaining basic skills training, and 150 people placed in jobs after job readiness training. Twenty-five million dollars in tax credits leveraged an additional $25 million and supported skill upgrade training for 3,000 workers in 145 companies (Greater Cleveland Growth Association, 2002). (See chapter 8.)

THE ARGUMENTS
FOR WORKFORCE INTERMEDIARIES

The economic and policy landscape in which workforce development is occurring presents daunting challenges. Labor market, organization, and systems change barriers make accessing these jobs and career advancement difficult for both employers and workers/jobseekers.

The overarching workforce development challenge is to build a system of opportunities and pathways for low-skilled workers to reach family self-sufficiency. This is not a small problem. Family self-sufficiency, in real terms, may be defined as $25,000 to $30,000 for a mother and two school-age children (Pearce and Brooks, 1999). Minimum wage jobs, however, only produce $10,000 to $12,000 in annual income. On the one hand, "making work pay" strategies, combining tax incentives, childcare, and other subsidies, may fill the gap in the short run. On the other hand, career advancement strategies that move people from minimum wage to $15 per hour may require upwards of 1,000 hours of training (Carnevale and Reich, 2000; Jenkins, 1999). This scenario presents a double dilemma: how can families afford the time and cost of this training; and how can training systems deliver this skill upgrading and technical training in an effective manner (see chapter 10).

The Labor Market Problem

Characteristics of firms and jobseekers make the matching process for good jobs difficult beyond the expected uncertainties of market processes. On the firm side, many established companies have closed their human resource departments, outsourced entry-level jobs to contingent workers, flattened job ladders in the search of lowering costs and higher productivity, and de-skilled jobs at the same time they adopt new technologies. Cutbacks and aging workforces have left them unprepared to incorporate new workers, many of whom come from more diverse backgrounds than their current workforce. Smaller firms, particularly those undergoing growth, share similar problems, but with fewer resources and frequently without a history of hiring entry-level workers (Osterman, 1999). (See chapter 6.)

Many low-skilled jobseekers do not have the basic skills, job readiness skills, or informal network connections required to navigate today's labor market. While many workers move up over time, many do not and remain at the margins of self-sufficiency. Indeed, many inner city residents do not have the necessary skills, role models for advancing in the labor market, nor faith in training institutions and in the payoff of investing in their own human capital (Wilson, 1998). The pressures of supporting a family, the current policy environment of reducing social welfare supports, and the inflexibility of many training institutions reinforce the unwillingness of many working poor families to seek higher paying skilled employment.

Both firms and jobseekers are further inhibited by their sheer spatial separation—firms in the suburbs and jobseekers in inner city neighborhoods. Low levels of car ownership, driver's license revocations and penalties, inflexible and time intensive public transportation, and the necessities of childcare and family support make the matching of good jobs and low-skilled jobseekers more difficult, even for the many job openings in central cities.

This labor market problem will grow worse in the next several decades as baby boomers retire and a smaller, more diverse workforce takes their place. How will the United States remain globally competitive in this context (Aspen Institute, 2002)? (See chapter 7.)

The Organization Problem

Workforce intermediaries do three important things. They have an entre-preneurial focus on outcomes like long-term job retention, wage progres-sion, and career mobility; they network and partner across the supply, demand, educational, financing/funding, and spatial dimensions of regional labor markets; and they have the ability to learn and adapt as market con-ditions and opportunities change. Most employment training projects, including much of the public workforce development system, are not adept at one or several of these capacities.

Outcomes

Most employment and training programs do not commit to results. They focus on program inputs like "classroom time" rather than outcomes, change workforce goals when encountering difficulties rather than modify strategies, fail to set ambitious goals related to job retention and advance-ment, and exclude meaningful outcomes for employers (Giloth and Phillips, 2000). The public workforce system has compounded these problems by its narrow use of performance based contracts.

Without a long-term focus on ambitious outcomes, workforce devel-opment contributes little to family self-sufficiency because the pathway to good jobs and careers is often long and not necessarily linear. With com-mitment to ambitious employment outcomes, it is then possible to push other labor market players to focus their energies and resources on pro-ducing common results.

WIs are also focused on business results that involve reducing the costs of recruitment and turnover as well as enhancing productivity. Frequently, WIs become involved with firms around issues of modernization and busi-ness development. More broadly, many WIs focus on sectors or clusters of the economy; their interventions often lead to better industry practices and investments related to workforce development.

Networks

Many employment and training efforts have relied on the "we do it all" approach to program design as well as upon the formal service delivery par-adigm. What this has meant is that many employment programs, because of limited skills and resources, are disconnected from important labor mar-ket players and informal networks that connect people and employers.

The alternative approach requires working in the worlds of interorga-nizational collaboration, co-investment, and of community based networks

(Harrison and Weiss, 1998). Neither of these worlds is easy to navigate, although a growing literature on the experiences and best practices of such partnerships is emerging (Kanter, 1995). Partners are brought together with the right mixture of incentives and leadership.

Learning

Effective workforce providers rapidly adapt to changes in the labor market, measure outcomes and collect relevant data, adopt innovations and undertake redesign, and promote learning as an organizational priority. Two problems result when workforce learning does not occur. First, stagnant programs cease to work as the economic and policy environments change. This can even happen to the replication of best practice workforce projects, which transplant all the key ingredients except for a learning culture (Kato, 1999). Second, long-term retention and advancement outcomes have created knowledge gaps about what works (Strawn and Martinson, 2000). Redesign based upon learning is a must if we are to learn how to reach these outcomes.

The Systems Problem

Workforce development can be a system, systems, or nonsystem depending on the conversation. The public workforce development system, as constituted over the last 50 years, has increasingly tried to remedy the problems of fragmentation, funding silos, lack of employer voice, and poor performance. Devolution of governance, consolidation of programs, and performance contracting are the tools that have been used. Progress has been made, but it has been slow, and the rhetoric exceeds the achievement.

First Chance/Second Chance

A first complication is that the system works very well for some individuals and communities. K–12 schools perform. Young people graduate. Financing is available for post secondary education. Employers invest in skilled workers. And lifelong learning is becoming a way of life. This is often called the first chance system.

The second chance system serves those the first chance system has failed or failed to reach. Approximately 15–50 million people require these additional workforce services. It includes GED, ESL, adult and vocational education, job training, and many programs targeted to special populations. A wide array of underfunded and underperforming organizations makes up the second chance system. Although there are many exceptions, the second chance system is second rate.

A major challenge is how to connect these two systems to each other and to the labor market. This will require that second chance programs improve their quality and their partnerships, and that the first chance system commits to making second chance systems a preparation stage for their programs. One Stop Centers are designed, in part, to bring these services and public benefits together.

Business/Workers/Jobseekers

Business remains largely disengaged from workforce development for low-skilled workers. Public systems regularly recruit business leaders for governance roles, but rarely are employers engaged in ongoing program design and improvement. For their part, businesses are heterogeneous, unorganized, skeptical about programs and training, too busy to get involved, and primarily focused on business growth. And there remain employers who either discriminate against or who hesitate before hiring inner city minority workers (see chapter 9).

Workers/jobseekers are equally heterogeneous, with diverse skills, aspirations, barriers, family circumstances, support networks, and economic assets. Navigating a more complex labor market is confusing and frequently poses conflicts between family and work that seem irreconcilable. Workers/jobseekers are also skeptical about public programs, and have dropped out, not even taking advantage of public benefits for which they are qualified because of time constraints and poor treatment (Howard, Miller, and Molina, 2002). Many of these jobseekers are isolated from networks that could connect them to the mainstream economy and lack knowledge about business culture (see chapters 10 and 11).

Both business and low-skilled workers/jobseekers are isolated from each other, perpetuating this disconnection and lack of trust.

Institutional Fragmentation

Can an effective workforce system be built from separate and competing parts and geographic divisions? Under the Job Training Partnership Act (the former federal employment and training act prior to the Workforce Investment Act of 1998), metropolitan areas contained as many as six to eight Service Delivery Areas (SDAs), each of which—in today's parlance—contained a Workforce Investment Board. In many instances, cooperative planning among SDAs was not a top priority, even though local economies and labor markets function on a regional basis (Hughes, 1996). Other elements of the workforce system include community colleges, adult basic education, K–12 schools, English as a second language, vocational rehabilitation, welfare-to-work programs, proprietary training schools, and many others. The Workforce Investment Act of 1998 provides an opening for metro areas that want to pursue coordinated workforce planning and implementation.

Civic Capacity

Changing workforce systems to function more effectively on behalf of business and low-skilled, low-income workers/jobseekers will not be easy. At the national level, a new public commitment is needed between employers, the federal government, and community representatives to invest in creating a skilled workforce. At the local level, investment in human capital development for low-income jobseekers has not galvanized the interest of economic stakeholders, political coalitions, or public administrators. The local development imperative of the past several decades has been to re-establish viable economic engines for central cities and regions, whether they be downtown development, tourism, transportation infrastructure, or "smokestack" chasing. At the same time, workforce programs ironically served the function, similar to school systems, of creating an "employment regime" of jobs for professionals and patronage workers (Stone, 1998).

What is needed is a durable coalition of civic actors to advocate for workforce development. Such civic capacity requires extraordinary leadership, leaders inside and outside of public systems, and networks and relationships based upon common beliefs and strategies for action.

Some workforce policy makers believe that WIBs can be the vehicle to bring together all aspects of the public workforce system. This "ideal" while praiseworthy in many respects is unrealistic for at least four reasons. First, the WIA and WIBs neither embody sufficient authority or resources to bring all the key actors to the table—community colleges, adult education, welfare-to-work, and vocational education (O'Shea and King, 2001). Indeed, the WIA may serve less than 5 percent of the eligible employer and jobseeker population in need of its services (Lafer, 2002). A recent business survey indicated that 95 percent of the 1,800 surveyed businesses did not use One Stop Centers for employee recruitment, training, or retention services (Center for Workforce Preparation, 2001). More recent surveys show more name recognition of One Stop Centers. Second, compared to the incentives governing participation in downtown development, workforce development offers meager incentives to business and other workforce actors to come to the table and to stay at the table. The payoffs of workforce development are long term and uneven. Third, the scale and diversity of local labor markets call into question the limits of centralized planning in WIBs to understand the nuances and scope of specific business and sector niches and to have the savvy to put together partnerships to address specific opportunities. As Dan Berry argues in chapter 8, there is a need for multiple "mediating" institutions in local labor markets. Fourth, WIBs face the reinventing government problem of whether they should steer or row; many public organizations fail when they try to both set policy directions and deliver services. WIBs and their predecessor PICs are mostly thumbs, not innovators. In part, this is one reason why entrepreneurial charter schools, community development corporations, and WIs have formed to break through the bureaucracy and paralysis typical of public systems to serve specific customer groups (Grogan and Proscio, 2001).

One starting point for building and expanding civic capacity, in addition to public workforce planning, is with WIs, who bring together key actors, draw upon important networks, and focus on important outcomes. They have demonstrated civic capacity in the ways they have built partnerships, brought together new and underutilized workforce resources, and obtained results.

COUNTERARGUMENTS AND RESPONSES

The proposition that WIs are a plausible mechanism for serving employers and for enhancing career advancement opportunities for low-skilled workers is not universally embraced. Indeed, strong counterarguments have been made, or can be made, that call this proposition into question. In several cases, skepticism concerns workforce development more generally, not just WIs. This section summarizes these counterarguments, articulating their strongest version, and then offers responses. Five counterarguments are most compelling:

- WIA, WIBs, and One Stop Centers already integrate services and funding streams, engage employers, and map pathways to self-sufficiency. Insufficient public and private resources cannot support duplicative efforts.
- Work First and work supports are more effective contributors to poverty alleviation than job training. Evaluation studies show that job training produces modest effects, at best.
- WIs serve the more job ready rather than the hardest to employ.

- WIs do not provide real and substantial economic benefits for employers. If they did, employers would pay for a larger portion of WI activities and training.
- Too few family-supporting jobs exist within reach of low-skilled workers/jobseekers. More training is not the answer.

The "We Already Do It" Argument

The WIA is a federal attempt to integrate disconnected workforce programs, support local decision making, and make workforce systems more accountable and customer driven. Workforce Investment Boards are supposed to represent employers and other key workforce players. The state option for unified plans provided an opportunity to bring together workforce, welfare, and other programs. And One Stop Centers are a mechanism to provide universal access to a variety of workforce services.

It is simplistic to say that the rigors of implementation have interfered with WIA's good intentions. Progress, however, has been slow in meeting WIA integration objectives. But available evidence suggests important progress has been made. Upcoming WIA reauthorization offers another opportunity to strengthen and fine-tune this approach.

A stronger response argues that WIBs and WIs represent two different but complementary and synergistic forms of integration (see chapter 3). WIBs set policy directions, identify economic opportunities and strategies, and build a system of access to services. A recent survey of WIBs across the country suggests that their primary focus is on policy issues and strategic planning, not on operational details (National Leadership Institute for Workforce Excellence, 2002).

WIs, in contrast, are several steps closer to implementation. They build on-the-ground partnerships, design and implement specific pathways and supports to careers, integrate a wide variety of resources on behalf of employers and workers, build partnerships with other providers, and focus on achieving ambitious outcomes. In many cases, WIs bring new resources to the table, in the forms of public, private, and philanthropic investments.

It would be incorrect to lump WIs with all other workforce development organizations. WIs are different; they are specific partnerships that engage business and obtain new and promising results. WIBs may play this role as well, but more often they will set the policy and strategic conditions for WIs as well as play the important role of investor. Workforce investors build the capacity of WIs and other parts of the workforce system to be high performing.

There is an important case to be made that WIBs and WIs can strengthen each other's performance. WIs require a pipeline of workers/jobseekers for particular training opportunities. One Stop Centers are a source of such workers as well as other relevant support services. WIBs require implementing organizations to put together the partnerships needed on the ground to serve multiple customers and bring together different funding sources.

Job Training Doesn't Work

The resounding summary conclusion of the Job Training Partnership Act (JTPA) evaluations of the early 1990s was that job training did not work (Orr, Bloom, and Bell, 1995). It was costly and did not deliver substantial and long lasting positive income effects for low-income workers/jobseekers.

An alternative approach gained credibility in the same period, and became embodied in the Personal Responsibility and Work Opportunity Reconciliation Act (PRWORA) of 1996 and the WIA of 1998. "Work First" places people into jobs sooner than later, and it reinforces work attachment with income supports, Earned Income Tax Credits (EITC), and childcare, transportation, and other subsidies. An assumption of Work First is that people learn about work from working, and that labor force attachment eventually leads to economic mobility as low-income workers find ways to move up. Some evaluation evidence exists that Work First and work supports have lowered poverty and child poverty (Riedl and Rector, 2002).

A left of center version of this argument claims that job training places the onus of bad labor market outcomes on the deficiencies of people rather than on the paucity of good job opportunities that can support families and communities. Moreover, the implementation of job training programs distracts real community attention from the fundamental problem of good jobs (Lafer, 2002).

Several responses can be made to these criticisms. First, hidden in the JTPA evaluations of the early 1990s was the example of the Center for Employment Training, which achieved substantial income impacts through short-term, employer driven training, job placement in better jobs, and integration with other supports. This is the WI model. A number of nonexperimental evaluations of other WIs in the 1990s have confirmed these impacts (Smith, Wittner, Spence, and Van Kluenen, 2002). (See chapters 2 and 5.)

Second, research shows, in spite of vigorous debates about extent of the "skills gap," that increased education produces substantial returns, particularly post secondary training. With heightened skill requirements and multiple career changes, lifelong learning and the acquisition of new skills are a prerequisite for moving up. The question is how to make this work for low-skilled workers who have been relegated to second chance systems and low-skilled jobs (Aspen Institute, 2002). (See chapter 7.)

Third, recent evaluations show that Work First and skills training can be compatible, not opposites. Some of the most effective welfare-to-work programs combine job readiness, work experience, employer driven skills training, and work supports (see chapter 2). Finally, emerging evidence shows that Work First, without skills upgrading, job targeting, and other supports, may not lead to sustained economic mobility.

WIs Don't Serve the Hardest to Employ

A common criticism of WIs is that they primarily serve a more job ready population. Not surprisingly, those with more basic skills, job experiences, and support networks do better, stay in jobs longer, and move up when possible. Those with multiple barriers are left behind.

In some sense, the more a workforce project is dual customer and focused on higher wage jobs the more discriminating it has to be in selecting participants. For many years, for example, Project QUEST required participants to have high school diplomas.

In many cases, WIs do not serve those jobseekers who face multiple barriers to work and life. They require supply side interventions, like Project Match, or transitional work opportunities with support services attached that stay with them for years after that work assignment has been completed to help stabilize family life and employment.

But this is only a part of the picture. WIs are quite diverse, serving very different employers and workers/jobseekers. A number of WIs build on temporary work or support work models, for example. And evidence exists that many WIs serve a harder-to-employ population than many typical workforce development programs (Fleischer, 2001). At the same time, many WIs build and support a pipeline of preparation and readiness training so that eventually a harder-to-employ population can take advantage of WI training and jobs. Ultimately, the most effective welfare-to-work programs target higher paying jobs, mix readiness and skills training, and provide ongoing post employment supports.

There is a larger debate about whether the focus of the workforce development system should be universal or targeted. WIs, as we have defined them, focus on low-skilled, low-income workers/jobseekers. Some critics argue that a division of services stigmatizes these workers; and business and unions are reluctant to treat some workers different than others. On the other hand, many low-income workers/jobseekers are voting with their feet and not taking advantage of available workforce services because they are not customized, consume limited family time, and are out of the way (Howard, Miller, and Molina, 2002).

The disconnection between the hardest to employ and the mainstream economy is so substantial that job training alone is not enough. This disconnection has been characterized as the "two worlds" problem. One world is made up of business culture and expectations that hard work is rewarded. The other world is made up of people who have been marginalized by the mainstream over generations and face the labor market with cynicism, loss of hope, and few positive expectations. Bridging these two worlds is an enormous challenge (Stone and Worgs, 2003).

If It Works, Why Don't Employers Pay?

If WIs really produced tangible benefits for business, such as increasing productivity and reducing turnover, they would pay for training. Since employer investment in entry-level workers is relatively low, it is fair to assume that these benefits are negligible or nonexistent.

United States employers underinvest in entry-level workers compared to employers in other advanced economies. Although their investments may have modestly increased during the tight labor markets of the 1990s, entry-level training by employers remains small; employers, however, do invest in their other, more skilled employees at much higher levels.

Several qualifications on the issue of business investment in training are worth noting at the outset. Lean management approaches combined with heightened occupational skill requirements, even for some entry-level jobs, have made it more difficult for many businesses to obtain employees. This situation is exacerbated because available workers are less prepared in terms of basic skills, job readiness, and work experience. Employers have been more willing to pay for training in specific job skills rather than general skills, which they expect schools, families, and communities to produce. Employers have also expressed a lack of confidence that the public workforce development system can understand their needs and provide the training and referrals that really can serve them. Finally, the fragmentation of businesses in specific regions, even businesses in the same general sector, still gives power to the "free rider" dilemma, in which employers fear that the benefits from their investments in training will be reaped by competitor firms down the street who lure away training employees with marginal wage enhancements.

Businesses do, in fact, invest in the efforts of WIs (see chapter 8). Their investments comprise release time for employees, workplace learning centers, involvement in curriculum development and training, and oversight of training and brokering efforts. Apprenticeship programs and other joint employer/union collaborations remain some of the best examples of how employers invest on an ongoing basis in job training. Recent experiments in Lifelong Learning Accounts and tuition reimbursements are further evidence of employer willingness to invest jointly in job training for low-skilled workers when the payoffs are clear.

But the most powerful response to this argument is about the future, not the past. Retirement of skilled workers and the shrinking of the available labor force create new opportunity to build partnerships with business around training, skill upgrading, and economic development. The question is whether an appropriate mix of effective training programs, employer investments, and public incentives can be put together. Enough current examples exist to make us believe that this can be done on a broader scale.

There Aren't Enough Good Jobs

A number of workforce development critics argue that job training is a diversion from the real problem—the lack of available family-supporting jobs (Lafer, 2002). One form of this analysis, based on jobs gap studies, concludes that in many states there are 25 or more workers seeking every family-supporting job that requires less than one year of training. Another approach has estimated that there is an absolute need for 5 million to 9 million new jobs in the United States (Bartik, 2002). Gordon Lafer in *Job Training Charade* estimates that 19 million jobs are needed. Still another perspective calls attention to the growth of contingent jobs, seasonal work, and outsourced temp work as opposed to family-supporting jobs.

These are important debates about economic development and the creation of high-wage, high-skilled jobs. Contrary perspectives exist. These debates, however, do not take away from the fact that shortages exist in skilled occupations, such as healthcare, manufacturing, construction, and information technology. While some of these shortages have diminished in today's economic environment, others have remained and grown, such as in healthcare occupations.

WIs focus on skill and labor shortages that exist in the present that provide opportunities for specific career pathways and business partnerships. There are examples of WIs turning temp jobs into permanent high-wage jobs. WIs that work in the low-wage sector have to develop strategies to improve job quality if they are to make a difference.

This does not take away from larger regional and national economic development challenges for creating high-wage jobs; but employment opportunities exist with which to build many more WIs.

At the same time, this counterargument gives credence to the need for creating many more publicly supported, transitional jobs targeted to job-seekers with significant barriers or with little job experience. This is particularly relevant for the re-entry of ex-offenders and for welfare recipients facing multiple barriers. Transitional jobs represent a steppingstone into the private labor market.

LESSONS AND PROSPECTS

WIs are impressive in different ways and collectively demonstrate how labor market, organization, and systems problems on behalf of low-skilled workers may be overcome to achieve improvements in career advancement and business prosperity. What is their realistic potential as a vehicle to increase career advancement? Can we easily expand their number? How large should a WI become? Who will pay for this expansion—local, state, or federal resources? Who will be the leaders and conveners of these new partnerships? Can WIs and the formal public workforce development system reach agreement on roles, alignment, partnerships, and financing?

What stands out in the stories of existing WIs is the breadth and strength of partners, social entrepreneurs, scale of operations, geography, and ongoing program improvements. They have complicated webs of partners and resources. At the same time, they have reached a level of organizational capacity in which they can broker strong partnerships, negotiate for and integrate a wide array of resources, and advocate in the public policy arena. They persist and grow as they fine-tune and adapt their programs.

The recent growth of WIs has been a chaotic and entrepreneurial process encouraged by our recent tight labor markets and major workforce/welfare policy changes. WIs have grown out of special initiatives, demonstrations, or partnerships that provided flexible dollars and resources for start up. This core of resources has leveraged other, more categorical, dollars and partnerships for program operations. Yet WIs are perceived in many arenas as competitors or duplicators of the public workforce development system.

These resources continue to shape the field of WIs, but they are not enough. Great need exists to build regional and national infrastructures to support the development and expansion of WIs, including venture funding for growth, benchmarking, human resource development, ongoing learning, and public policy. This infrastructure must be aligned with the goals and strategies of public workforce development systems.

Strengthening WIs, moreover, requires significant additional resources. The upcoming reauthorization process for the Workforce Investment Act, Higher Education Act, and PWRORA offers significant opportunities for explicitly addressing the needs of WIs in the context of creating better supports for low-skilled workers to advance in the labor market (see chapters 2, 3, and 14).

Lack of capacity and significant entry barriers limit the absolute growth of WIs. And the broader policy environment, although providing niche funding, is not explicitly supportive of this strategy. Indeed, many in the public workforce development system are skeptical about WIs. Alternatively, an existing infrastructure exists of thousands of employer associations, community colleges, labor unions, and community organizations that could adopt the workforce intermediary approach to become or strengthen their capacity as intermediary organizations. Supporting the institutional transformation of these organizations to workforce intermediaries offers a challenging but practical approach to increasing the scale and impacts of WIs.

Three alternative pathways address these barriers for WI adoption and growth and offer plausible potential for strengthening WIs. These pathways are speculative possibilities, in many respects, but also build upon real opportunities that now exist (see chapter 14). More specific recommendations, developed at the recent American Assembly, are presented in chapter 15 and in the Final Report.

Sectoral Approach

In their most ambitious form, sectoral partnerships go beyond industrial targeting to organizing and connecting supply and demand elements for a cluster of firms, such as in the case of WRTP. Sectoral partnerships represent an important type of WI, and indeed the deep knowledge of the economy that characterizes sectoral projects is also a defining characteristic of the best of WIs. At some point, these business, union, community, and public sector relationships create the civic capacity to advocate for pieces of multiple workforce funding streams, credentialing and standards, and resources priorities. These sectoral partnerships frequently establish linkages to economic development initiatives that focus on business modernization, venture capital, job creation, and improving job quality (see chapter 4).

The work of Michael Porter and colleagues on economic clusters—the Regional Skills Alliances of the Department of Labor, employer intermediaries connected with the U.S. Chamber and the National Association of Manufacturers, Working for America Institute, National Sector Partners, and Manufacturing Technology Centers—suggests the building blocks for such a strategy. Additional resources and attention should be focused on this promising strategy.

Community College Approach

The greatest underutilized resources for WIs are community colleges and technical schools. There are 1,000 of these colleges in the United States serving millions of student and representing billions of dollars in educational investments. This infrastructure, at its best, combines adult education, vocational training, connections to community organizations, and case management and college-level certification/articulation with a variety of business responsive training and development services. Bridge programs that create a pipeline for community colleges and career pathway programs that create a transparent map of how to advance in the labor market toward family-supporting jobs illustrate the potential of community colleges (Golanka and Matus-Grossman, 2001; Workforce Strategy Center, 2002).

But many community colleges, especially in large cities, are unresponsive to business and community partners and are unwilling to change old ways of teaching and training. Many also continue to see themselves as primarily a training ground for four-year colleges. On the other hand, community colleges and technical schools are key partners with many WIs, as in the case of WRTP and Project QUEST, and potentially could serve as a vehicle for scaling up and spreading these best practices. To do this, they require supportive state policies, new financing mechanisms for low-income students, and college-level leadership to make employment, career progression, and business partnerships high priorities (see chapters 2 and 14).

WI Venture Capital Approach

One of the key lessons of the Community Development Corporation movement for affordable housing and neighborhood economic development is that venture funds and capacity building intermediaries brought CDCs to scale. Over the years, foundations in partnerships with government have created entities such as the Enterprise Foundation, the Local Initiatives Support Corporation, the National Community Development Initiative (now renamed Living Cities), and a host of local funding collaboratives to support CDCs (see chapter 12).

The bottom up process of social entrepreneurs or the special demonstrations of national foundations are simply too small, short term, and uncertain to create the number, density, and capacity of WIs that are needed. Moreover, government workforce policy, alone, is not likely to focus on building WIs, although recent funding for Regional Skills Alliances, sectoral partnerships, and employer intermediaries shows the potential of federal partnerships. What is needed is a partnership of national and regional foundations and federal agencies to design and assemble one or several venture funds for the purposes of building the capacity of WIs. At the same time, these entities could assemble best practices, technical assistance providers, benchmarking information, and learning technologies to enhance the continuous improvement of WIs in supporting the career advancement of low-skilled workers (see chapters 4, 5, 13, and 14).

THE CHAPTERS AHEAD

This introductory chapter has provided a summary version of the argument on behalf of WIs as an important vehicle for furthering the career advancement of low-skilled workers/jobseekers while producing important benefits for business. WIs require more concerted attention and investment as a complement to our public workforce development system. This chapter has introduced WIs, given a sense of what they look like, explored multiple rationales for WIs, offered counterarguments and responses to the WI proposition, and portrayed three broad approaches for supporting and investing in WIs.

The following chapters provide a much more in-depth version of these arguments and proposals. All the chapters adopt the term and definition of WIs introduced in this chapter. But depending upon the topic and lens of the authors, they may situate WIs as a part of the broader group of labor market intermediaries or as a segment of all nonprofit, workforce development organizations. This may seem inconsistent. Wherever possible chapter authors have attempted to be quite explicit about their terminology in the context of this book's focus on WIs.

Chapter 2 in this Introductory Section, by Nan Poppe, Julie Strawn, and Karin Martinson, provides a detailed review of what we have learned about career advancement for low-skilled workers from the most rigorous evaluation studies, including community college and community organization examples of WIs

The Background Section contains three chapters that provide in-depth information about WIs. Richard Kazis, in chapter 3, defines WIs, portrays what they do through the voices of WI practitioners, and highlights a number of key issues about WI practice. Cindy Marano and Kim Tarr, in chapter 4, report on a just-completed survey of 243 WIs that provides more information on what WIs look like, how old they are, what they do, how they are funded, and from where they obtain help and support. Richard

McGahey, in chapter 5, synthesizes available research and evaluation studies about WIs to give a better sense of the kinds of results WIs are achieving, how these compare with other workforce interventions, and the next generation of WI research questions.

The Rationale Section contains two chapters that explore the underlying forces that support the role and activities of WIs. In chapter 6, Paul Osterman examines changing labor market institutions and employer practices and how leaner firms and a more turbulent, less transparent labor market require new forms of labor market intermediation. Anthony Carnevale and Donna Desrochers, in chapter 7, document the limits of economic mobility, the number of Americans in need of career services, and the coming demographic crisis.

The Customer Section contains four chapters that document perspectives of employers and workers/jobseekers. In chapter 8, Daniel Berry recounts in some detail the story of the Jobs and Workforce Initiative in Cleveland, and how "employer voice" has been injected at all levels of workforce policy and practice. Jessica Laufer and Sian Winship, in chapter 9, report on focus groups held with employers in three regions that suggest employer skepticism toward low-skilled workers and many of the workforce organizations that advocate for them. They offer strategies to deal with this "branding" challenge. Roberta Iversen, in chapter 10, draws from her ethnographic study of working families to discuss how families experience the opportunities and challenges of career advancement, and the roles that WIs and other support organizations can play. Laura Leete, Chris Benner, Manuel Pastor, and Sarah Zimmerman, in chapter 11, report on a new survey of workers in Milwaukee and San Jose regarding their experience with different types of intermediary organizations.

The New Directions Section contains three chapters that sketch in broad and specific ways a number of policies that can be developed to support WIs and their role in promoting career advancement for low-skilled workers/jobseekers. In chapter 12, Jerry Rubin, Marlene Seltzer, and Jack Mills offer concrete suggestions for how to finance the expansion and capacity building of WIs, as well as career advancement using local, state, federal, private sector, and philanthropic resources. In chapter 13, William Ryan draws on interviews with workforce providers to argue that capacity building for WIs should focus on key administrative functions and most importantly "adaptive capacity," the ability to learn and change. He offers several scenarios about how to build such support for WIs. Chris Walker and John Foster-Bey, in chapter 14, draw lessons from the community development field over 30 years that are helpful for building the field of WIs.

In the concluding chapter 15, I present a more specific agenda for enhancing the capacity of WIs to play their unique, brokering implementation role promoting career advancement for low-skilled workers/jobseekers. This chapter draws upon recommendations made in the other chapters, but most importantly reports on The American Assembly dialogue about WIs in February 2003 and the recommendations that Assembly members endorsed. A copy of The American Assembly report, "Achieving Business Success: Advancing Careers, Regions, and Growing Economies," is included in this volume.

Substantial opportunity exists today and in the coming years to increase access to economic opportunities, pathways to careers and family self-sufficiency, and business development. Taking advantage of these opportunities will serve low-skilled workers/jobseekers, business, and our society at large.

A growing number of workforce intermediaries provide needed connections between low-skilled workers and these economic opportunities. They come in many shapes and sizes, but they always deeply engage employers, connect with communities, and assemble a wide array of support and educational institutions. This chapter, and the chapters to come, demonstrates significant accomplishments by workforce intermediaries and the partnerships, social entrepreneurs, and strategic visions that guide their efforts.

> The key strengths of these programs are their flexibility and their intimate knowledge of the industries they serve. Because of their expertise, people who run these programs often go beyond providing training to become active advocates and supporters of the industries they serve. And they seek out ways to improve the productivity and position of the industry while better meeting the potential of the low-skill workers they seek to train. (Aspen Institute, 2002)

NOTE

Acknowledgments: The author gratefully acknowledges comments and suggestions from Elizabeth Biemann, Lisa Gordon, Ed Hatcher, Richard McGahey, Brandon Roberts, and the participants of The 102nd American Assembly.

REFERENCES

Annie E. Casey Foundation. 2000. *Stronger Links: New Ways to Connect Low-Skilled Workers to Better Jobs.* Baltimore: Annie E. Casey Foundation.

Aspen Institute. 2001. *Measuring Up and Weighing In: Industry-Based Workforce Development Training Results in Strong Employment Outcomes*. Washington, DC: The Aspen Institute.

Aspen Institute. 2002. *Grow Faster Together Or Grow Slowly Apart: How Will America Work in the 21st* Century. Washington, D.C.: Aspen Institute, Domestic Strategy Group.

Bartik, Timothy. 2002. "Poverty, Jobs, and Subsidized Employment." *Challenge*, 45(3). (May/June).

Berry, Daniel. 1998. "The Jobs and Workforce Initiative: Building New Roads to Success in Northeast Ohio." *Economic Development Quarterly*, 12.

Campbell, Brett. 1994. "Investing in People: The Story of Project Quest." San Antonio, TX: Communities Organized for Public Service and Metro Alliance.

Carnevale, Anthony, and Kathleen Reich. 2000. *A Piece of the Puzzle: How States Can Use Education to Make Work Pay for Welfare Recipients*. Princeton, N.J.: Education Training Services.

Center for Workforce Preparation. 2001. *Keeping Competitive: A Report from a Survey of 1,800 Employers*. Washington, DC.: Center for Workforce Preparation. (September).

Ellwood, David. 2002. "Worksheet for Labor." *Washington Post*, A23. (September 2).

Fitzgerald, Joan. 2000. *Community Colleges as Labor Market Intermediaries: Building Career Ladders For Low Wage Workers*. Boston: Center for Urban and Regional Policy, Northeastern University.

Fleischer, Wendy. 2001. *Extending Ladders: Findings from the Annie E. Casey Foundation's Jobs Initiative*. Baltimore: Annie E. Casey Foundation.

Giloth, Robert, and William Phillips. 2000. *Getting to Outcomes*. Baltimore: Annie E. Casey Foundation.

Golanka, Susan, and Lisa Matus-Grossman. 2001. *Opening Doors: Expanding Educational Opportunities for Low-Income Workers*. New York: Manpower Demonstration Research Corporation.

Greater Cleveland Growth Association. 2002. *Jobs and Workforce Initiative Outcomes: A Five Year Retrospective, 1997–2002*. Cleveland: Greater Cleveland Growth Association.

Grogan, Paul, and Tony Proscio. 2001. *Comeback Cities: A Blueprint for Urban Neighborhood Revitalization*. New York: Basic Books.

Grubb, W. Norton. *Learning to Work: The Case for Reintegrating Job Training and Education*. New York: Russell Sage Foundation.

Harrison, Bennett, and Marcus Weiss. 1998. *Workforce Development Networks: Community-Based Organizations and Regional Alliances*. Thousand Oaks, CA: Sage Publications.

Howard, Craig, Jennifer Miller, and Frieda Molina. 2002. *Work Support Centers: New Vehicles to Reach Low-Wage Workers*. New York: Manpower Demonstration Research Corporation. (November).

Hughes, Mark Alan. 1996. *The Administrative Geography of Devolving Social Welfare Programs*. Washington, DC: Brookings Institution, Center on Urban and Metropolitan Policy.

Jenkins, Davis. 1999. *Beyond Welfare-to-Work: Bridging the Low-Wage Livable-Wage Employment Gap*. Chicago: University of Illinois at Chicago, Great Cities Institute

Kanter, Rosabeth Moss. 1995. *World Class: Thriving Locally in the Global Economy*. New York: Simon and Schuster.

Kato, Linda. 1999. "Diffusing Responsive Social Programs by Learning Organizations: The Case of the Center for Employment Training (CET) National Replication Project." Unpublished Doctoral Dissertation, Massachusetts Institute of Technology.

Lautsch, Brenda A., and Paul Osterman. 1998. "Changing the Constraints: A Successful Employment and Training Strategy." In Robert Giloth, ed. *Jobs and Economic Development: Strategies and Practices*. Thousand Oaks, CA: Sage Publications.

Lafer, Gordon. 2002. *Job Training Charade*. Ithaca, NY: Cornell University Press.

Melendez, Edwin. 1996. *Working for Jobs: The Center for Employment Training*. Boston: University of Massachusetts, Mauricio Gaston Institute.

National Leadership Institute for Workforce Excellence. 2002. *The National Association of State Workforce Board Chairs. Second National WIB Survey Report*. Washington, DC.: National Leadership Institute for Workforce Excellence (January).

New Deal Task Force. 1999. *Bridges to Work: New Directions for Intermediaries*. London: New Deal Task Force.

Orr, Larry, H.S. Bloom, and S.H. Bell. 1995. *Does Training for the Disadvantaged Work? Evidence from the National JTPA Study*. Washington, DC: Urban Institute Press.

O'Shea, Daniel, and Christopher King. 2001. *The Workforce Investment Act of 1998: Restructuring Workforce Development Initiatives in States and Localities*. Albany, NY: The Nelson A. Rockefeller Institute of Government (April).

Osterman, Paul. 1999. *Securing Prosperity*. New York: Century Foundation.

Parker, Eric. 2000. "Wisconsin Regional Training Partnership: Hooking Community Residents up to Jobs." *Neighborhood Funders Group Reports*, 2(7). (Summer).

Pearce, D., and J. Brooks. 1999. *The Self Sufficiency Standard for Pennsylvania*. Harrisburg, PA: Women's Association for Women's Alternatives.

Project Quest. 2000. *Project Quest, Inc.: Quality Employment Through Skills Training. An Update*. San Antonio: Project Quest (May).

Regional Workforce Partnership. 2002. *Workforce and Economic Development: An Agenda for Pennsylvania's Next Governor*. Philadelphia, PA: The Reinvestment Fund.

Riedl, Brian, and Robert Rector. 2002. *Myths and Facts: Why Successful Welfare Reform Must Strengthen Work Requirements*. The Heritage Foundation Backgrounder, No. 1568 (July 12).

Smith, Steven Rathgeb, and Susan Davis. 2004. "The Seattle Jobs Initiative." In Robert Giloth, ed. *Workforce Development Politics: Civic Capacity and Performance*. Philadelphia, PA: Temple University Press.

Smith, Whitney, Jenny Wittner, Robin Spence, and Andy Van Kleunen. 2002. *Skills Training Works: Examining the Evidence*. Washington, DC: The Workforce Alliance.

Stone, Clarence N. 1998. "Urban Education in Political Context." In Clarence N. Stone, ed. *Changing Urban Education*. Lawrence, KS: University of Kansas Press.

Stone, Clarence, and Donn Worgs. 2003. "Poverty and the Workforce Challenge." In Robert Giloth, ed. *Workforce Development: Civic Capacity and Performance*. Philadelphia, PA: Temple University Press.

Strawn, Julie, and Karin Martinson. 2000. *Steady Work and Better Jobs: How to Help Low-Income Parents Sustain Employment and Advance in the Workforce*. New York: Manpower Demonstration Research Corporation.

Wilson, W.J. 1998. *When Work Disappears*. New York: Basic Books.

Workforce Strategy Center. 2002. *Building A Career Pathways System: Promising Practices in Community College-Centered Workforce Development*. New York: Workforce Strategy Center.

2

Whose Job Is It?
Creating Opportunities for Advancement

NAN POPPE, JULIE STRAWN,
AND KARIN MARTINSON

OVER THE PAST DECADE FEDERALLY FUNDED WORKFORCE DEVELOPment programs have shifted their focus from developing skills to helping individuals find entry-level jobs quickly. There is a well-developed service infrastructure and research base for such rapid job placement services. By contrast, there has been little programmatic focus or research on services to help low-wage workers advance to better jobs. Policy makers have increasingly recognized this gap and are seeking ways to fill it, in part because the welfare reform experience has illustrated both the strengths and limits of the "Work First" approach: many recipients found jobs, but a lack of skills and limited access to employers left most stuck in low-paid work. Workforce intermediaries are of interest primarily because they are viewed as part of the solution to the job advancement problem for low-wage workers.

Workforce intermediaries are defined elsewhere in this volume as having several essential characteristics, including addressing the needs of both employers and low-wage workers and helping to integrate funding streams, public and private sector services and programs, and information sources. The most successful workforce intermediaries have gone beyond job matching to offer a comprehensive set of services to individuals, such as education and training, career and family counseling, and supportive services, and to employers, such as customized job training, job coaching, and supervisor training.

If workforce intermediaries are one means of promoting job advancement, a key question still remains: what are the most effective ways to help low-wage workers advance? To shed light on this question, we first examine research on the experiences of low-wage workers in the labor market and on the types of employment and training strategies that have been effective for advancement. We then move from this research to describing key elements drawn from practitioner experience that policy makers and workforce intermediaries should consider including in a job advancement strategy. We highlight, in particular, "career pathways" as one model for developing training and job placement efforts that bring together the long-term needs and goals of workers and employers.

We conclude with a brief review of the challenges that policy makers and workforce intermediaries face in implementing job advancement strategies and suggest some federal policy changes that could promote success. One fundamental issue is a void of leadership and stable funding, especially at the national level. Currently no federal agency or program views job advancement for low-income adults as its core mission. Consequently, our nation lacks sustained leadership and investment in building the infrastructure of services low-wage workers and jobseekers need to advance.

WHAT MATTERS FOR JOB ADVANCEMENT?
LESSONS FROM THE LABOR MARKET

Many American workers have low earnings at some point in their lives; a smaller, but still substantial, share has persistently low earnings. Low earnings are typically due to a combination of low wages and less than full-time, year-round employment. As a practical matter, policy makers are most concerned about workers stuck in low-wage jobs. A recent study following prime-age (25–54 years old) workers over three years in the early to mid-1990s (Holzer et al., 2002) found that nearly a fifth of the workforce (18 percent) had persistently low earnings over three years. These same workers were tracked again through a second three-year period in the late 1990s, and almost half of those with earnings persistently below $12,000 in the earlier period had moved up. Their earnings remained quite low, though, with only 6 percent of them earning consistently above $15,000 in the latter period. Studies of former welfare recipients have found similar patterns of modest earnings growth on average and persistently low earnings over time (Cancian and Meyer, 2000; Cancian et al., 2002; Johnson and Corcoran, 2002). Further, a recent study tracking young recipients for a decade after leaving welfare found they make the most economic progress in the initial years after leaving welfare, with much less improvement in their earnings and poverty rates five to ten years after exit (Meyer and Cancian, 2001).

What Factors Are Linked to Moving Up to Better Jobs over Time?

While low earnings are common and persist for a substantial share of workers, the fact that some low-income workers do escape to better paying, more stable employment raises the question of what factors matter most for job advancement. Researchers have looked at low-wage workers over time and used statistical techniques to try to isolate the importance of various personal and job factors for labor market success. This type of research cannot control for unobservable factors such as individual motivation, workplace culture, and discrimination; nevertheless, it can help policy makers and workforce intermediaries to at least focus their job advancement strategies on the observable factors most strongly linked to moving up to better jobs. These studies suggest the following factors matter most for advancement, independently of each other.

- *Staying with the same job pays off only modestly over the long term for those with little education, for those who have low earnings initially, and for those in jobs requiring few cognitive skills. Staying at part-time work yields little to no wage growth. Steady work at large firms pays off more.*

A national study of workers generally between 1986 and 1993 found that how much staying with a job pays off depends on the worker's educational attainment. For example, among women who stay with the same employer, those without a high school diploma see annual wage increases of less than 1 percent (0.7 percent); those with a high school diploma about twice that (1.4 percent); while the wages of those with a college degree grow five times as fast (3.6 percent) (Connolly and Gottschalk, 2001). Similarly, a study of current and former welfare recipients in Michigan from 1997 to 2000 found wages grew about 2 percent (1.8 percent) for full-time work experience and not at all for part-time, after controlling for recipients' skills and other characteristics. Even for the 19 percent of women who had worked in *every* month of those three years, only about 42 percent were employed in "good" jobs—defined as full-time, hourly wages of at least $7 with health benefits, or $8.50 without—at the end of the period. In addition, three out of five of the women who worked part time did so involuntarily (Johnson and Corcoran, 2002). Similarly, the Holzer et al. study finds that for those who had persistently low earnings initially and stayed with their jobs over the long run, their earnings increased by about 2 percent a year.[1] Those who subsequently escaped to higher earnings were more likely to be with larger firms.

- *Switching jobs strategically can be a path to higher wages later on, due to wage increases at job changes and to higher wage growth in the new jobs. Increases in wages at job changes are higher for those with more education.*

In the Holzer et al. study, those who had persistently low earnings initially and switched jobs saw their wages increase by 30 percent within two years. Job changes that were also a change in industry especially paid off; three-fourths of those who completely escaped low earnings did so through a job change, and nearly half of escapers changed industry as well as job. Interestingly, once a low earner has changed from his or her initial job to a new one, staying with that new job over time pays off considerably more than staying with the old one did. This appears to be due to the new job more fully rewarding personal characteristics, such as skills, and to the new worker obtaining more access to the benefits of a higher quality firm than existing workers. For example, within firms that paid above market wages to individuals, someone who changed jobs was more likely to get access to those wages than someone who stayed with a job in those firms.

The benefits of job changes vary, however, for different groups of workers. Job changes pay off less for women (Holzer et al., 2002) and for the less educated. For example, the study of workers between 1987 and 1993 found that women with just a high school diploma saw their wages increase by 2.9 percent when they switched jobs while those with some college obtained a wage increase of 4.5 percent with job changes (Connolly and Gottschalk, 2001). Importantly, less educated workers are also much more likely to transition from a job to unemployment than they are to move from a job to another job. Job changes that are involuntary and/or interrupted by a spell of unemployment are generally linked to wage declines (Holzer et al., 2002; Johnson, 2002; Connolly and Gottschalk, 2001; Gladden and Taber, 2000).

- *Access to higher quality employers is an important determinant of how much either job tenure or job changes pay off; intermediaries may improve access to these employers.*

Among workers with persistently low earnings initially, the Holzer et al. study finds that black and Hispanic males have lower subsequent wages than white males, due in large part to lesser access to higher quality employers. In the study these quality characteristics included firms with lower turnover, firms paying above market wages for a worker, and larger firms. As noted later, educational attainment and cognitive skills help determine who obtains higher quality jobs, but this research indicates that there are other, less observable barriers as well that workforce intermediaries can possibly help workers to overcome. For example, Holzer et al. find that initially low earners who start with temp agencies earn considerably less than comparable workers while with the agency but earn more at their subsequent jobs. This suggests that notwithstanding their low pay, temp agencies may improve access to higher quality jobs for some workers, especially through placements in manufacturing. Changing to a job that is union from a nonunionized one increases wages, though staying with a unionized job typically means flatter wage growth (probably due to union seniority rules).

- *Jobs that require reading and writing provide greater opportunity for wage growth, in part because they provide more formal and informal opportunities for learning on the job.*

A recent study of current and former welfare recipients in Michigan finds that those who change to jobs that require daily reading and writing from jobs that do not require such skills see an immediate increase in their wages, and their wages grow more over time with experience, regardless of the characteristics of the worker. The researchers conclude this is because these new jobs provided more opportunities for on-the-job training. Further, jobs requiring more use of reading and writing skills show less turnover, suggesting that workers are less inclined to quit when given a chance to learn on the job. When these workers do change jobs, they are more likely to do so voluntarily and more likely to transition from "bad" jobs to "good" than other workers who have not used reading and writing in a recent job (Johnson, 2002). This underscores the importance of cognitive skills for job advancement, not simply because it improves access to jobs that pay more initially but because jobs requiring these skills have more potential for wage growth over time.

- *Starting out in certain industries or occupations is linked to higher earnings later on.*

The Holzer et al. study found that both job changers and job stayers who escaped low earnings were more likely to be in the construction, manufacturing (with the exception of apparel/textile), transportation/communications/utilities (TCU), and wholesale trade industries and less likely to be in retail or services. Within the services, where women are more likely to work, health and, to a lesser extent, educational services were good sectors for escaping low earnings. A recent study on prospects for job advancement just within the service sector found that three industries held the most promise: banking, hospitals, and education, though it also found education largely requires four-year degrees for the better jobs (Mitnik et al., 2001). The two studies also identify industries with little room for advancement, chiefly eating/drinking establishments, hotels, childcare, and retail trade.

Occupations also vary in their potential for advancement. One study that followed former welfare recipients in the labor market for five years found that, compared with those who began working in sales, women who started out in clerical positions earned 22 percent more per hour five years later, those in production and manufacturing or building cleaning and maintenance earned 17 percent more per hour, and those in private care (which includes healthcare and formal childcare) earned 15 percent more per hour. Different initial occupations were also associated with differing poverty rates in the fifth year (Cancian and Meyer, 1997). Generally, the occupations offering workers without any college education the greatest wage potential tend to be held by men, such as machinist, equipment repairer, and truck driver. While sales and administrative/clerical jobs can be better paying for those who work their way up to supervisory positions, only a small portion of these jobs are supervisory—so few can expect to attain such positions (Nightingale, 1999 and 2002).

- *Higher cognitive skills and post secondary education or training are linked to higher initial wages and higher wage growth.*

Research generally finds that both higher cognitive skills and schooling beyond the high school level each are linked to higher starting wages and higher wage growth, controlling for other personal and job characteristics. Interestingly, whether someone has a high school diploma or not appears to matter little for wage growth after controlling for other factors (Cancian and Meyer, 1997; Johnson, 2002; Loeb and Corcoran, 2001; Tyler et al., 2000). As noted earlier, this higher wage growth may reflect that both job tenure and job changes pay off more for those with more education. A recent study of events that trigger exits from poverty finds that increases in educational attainment are nearly as important as employment changes in triggering exit from poverty, especially if the individual obtained an associate degree or higher (McKernan and Ratcliffe, 2002). Similarly welfare recipients with higher educational attainment are less likely to return to the welfare roles than less educated ones (Loprest, 2002).

Employers demand skills, and particularly credentials, for better paying jobs. The study of Michigan welfare recipients found that "good" jobs— those that were full time and paid $7 an hour with health benefits, or $8.50 without—required far more education than welfare recipients typically had.

Further, employers hired even higher skilled individuals than they said the jobs required. For example, 82 percent of those hired into "bad jobs" had a high school diploma or GED even though employers said just 55.7 percent of those jobs required it. Few "good" jobs—just about 9 percent—required no credentials, compared to a third of "bad" jobs. Job task requirements, such as daily reading and writing or computer skills, were also higher in "good" jobs (Johnson and Corcoran, 2002).

Implications for Policy and Practice

Knowing what personal and job factors matter for job advancement can help policy makers and workforce intermediaries to focus a job advancement strategy in ways that increase its effectiveness. In particular, the quality of the employer and the quality of the job stand out as key factors that have received too little attention in policy and practice. This has important implications for publicly funded workforce development programs where the dominant view in recent years has been that any job can enable an individual to work out of poverty.

Policy makers and workforce intermediaries should be selective, to the extent possible, about employer and job quality in job placement and skill upgrading efforts. The research summarized here suggests that workforce intermediaries should focus their efforts on particular industries that offer the most potential for advancement and avoid those that offer few opportunities. Intermediaries should also target higher wage sectors, firms with low turnover, larger firms with internal career ladders, and jobs that offer opportunities to learn on the job, whether formal or informal. While the research described here can offer some general guidelines, it is also critical that intermediaries take a close look at the patterns in their own local labor market.

Helping workers attain post secondary occupational credentials and improve their basic skills, especially reading and writing, should be a central focus of skill upgrading efforts. Training and skill certifications may be especially important for gaining access to better jobs. Basic skills and educational attainment matter directly in that they help determine a worker's starting wage and wage increases both within jobs and at job changes. These factors also matter indirectly as a means by which workers obtain jobs that then in themselves promote greater wage growth through more opportunities for formal and informal on-the-job training. Policy makers and workforce intermediaries should pay careful attention to research lessons for program design and quality described in the next section, however, as skill upgrading efforts have not been consistently effective.

Other mechanisms, beyond skill upgrading, are also needed to help workers access better jobs. In the Holzer et al. study, women and nonwhite workers had substantially less access to higher quality jobs and employers, regardless of their other characteristics. The authors speculate that this may reflect a variety of factors: spatial mismatch, racial discrimination, weak employment networks, and weak early work experience. Whatever the reasons, the example of temp agencies and manufacturing suggests that workforce intermediaries can play an important role in helping to change who obtains access to which types of employers and jobs. Other means, such as publicly funded internships or "try out" jobs with private employers, on-the-job training subsidies, or marketing of public supports (case management, childcare subsidies, etc.) to employers as retention services may also help open doors to better jobs.

Finally, it is worth noting that the study of welfare recipients in Michigan found that physical and mental health problems, domestic violence, and learning disabilities all significantly diminished the women's chances of transitioning to "good" jobs over time (Johnson and Corcoran, 2002). While more research is needed as few studies have looked at the relationship between these factors and job advancement, these early findings highlight that any successful job advancement strategy must be comprehensive and take into account the full range of challenges that low-wage workers face.

WHAT WORKS FOR JOB ADVANCEMENT? LESSONS FROM PROGRAM EVALUATION AND PRACTICE

Understanding which factors are important for labor market success is a critical first step toward choosing strategies that enable low-income workers to move up to better jobs.[2] But knowing that a factor is important is not the same as knowing how to change it. The remainder of this chapter discusses research findings and promising practices for a comprehensive advancement strategy that includes helping workers get access to better jobs directly and helping workers to upgrade their skills before and after starting employment. Clearly other antipoverty policies are also quite important, such as policies that directly improve the quality of entry-level jobs (e.g., incentives for employers to improve wages and benefits, minimum wage laws) and policies that help workers stay employed despite low wages (e.g., childcare and healthcare subsidies, Earned Income Tax Credit). These policies are outside the scope of this chapter, however.

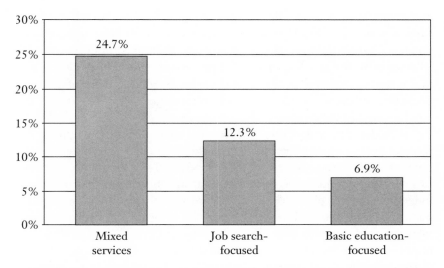

FIGURE 2.1   Average Increase in Earnings Over Five Years of Different Welfare-to-Work Strategies

Source: Hamilton et al. (2001). Available at www.mdrc.org.

The clearest finding from rigorous[3] program research is that the most effective programs focus on employment goals and provide a range of services—including job search, basic education, and job training—that are individualized to each participant's circumstances. Such "mixed services" programs perform far better than programs more narrowly focused on job search or basic education activities (Figure 2.1). In addition, programs that have helped adults obtain better paying jobs have typically set job advancement as a central goal and made substantial use of job training and other post secondary education. Further, nonexperimental research from a number of small-scale workforce development programs suggests that focusing job advancement efforts on particular sectors of the economy may make them more effective (Fleischer, 2001; Rademacher, 2002).

Connecting to Better Jobs Directly

The labor market research described above suggests that different workers have varying levels of access to higher quality jobs, regardless of their skills and work experience. Program evaluation research suggests it is possible for workforce intermediaries to play an important role in increasing access to higher quality jobs, especially for those workers who have solid basic skills, work experience, and a high school diploma or GED. Because a person's initial position in the labor market appears to affect future opportunities for advancement, helping low-income people connect to better jobs initially may bring future as well as immediate benefits. Further, it is one of the most cost-effective strategies that states and communities can pursue for helping low-income people advance in the workforce.

Workforce intermediaries that serve the unemployed can use initial job placement as an opportunity to begin working with people on career development issues, goal setting, resolution of personal and logistical challenges to sustaining employment, and placement in a better job that fits into a longer term career plan. For those who are already working, post employment services at the worksite or at a convenient location in the community near the workplace can provide similar opportunities. Many of the tasks required to help low-income working adults advance are the same as for the unemployed; however, service delivery is complicated by competing work demands—and, often, parenting demands as well.

What the Research Says. The most recent rigorous evaluation research in this area comes from the National Evaluation of Welfare to Work Strategies (NEWWS), which studied 11 different welfare-to-work programs in the 1990s. The most successful site studied, Portland, Oregon, shows it is possible to connect some low-income people to better jobs directly, without upgrading their skills beforehand. After two years of follow up, Portland helped those who entered the program with high school diplomas or GEDs to increase their hourly wages and to gain greater access to full-time jobs with health benefits. For those with recent work experience, the wage increase was even higher. Portland also helped parents find more stable employment, and this impact persisted over the long term (Freedman et al., 2000; Freedman, 2000; Hamilton et al., 2001).

Portland achieved this result by encouraging participants to be selective about jobs and to seek ones that were full time, paid well above the minimum wage, and included benefits and potential for advancement. High school graduates or GED holders in Portland's program who had work experience typically first entered a job club, which used job developers to help people find better jobs. Everyone who entered the program was assessed for job readiness, including basic skills, substance abuse, mental health, and domestic violence issues. Case managers also took work history and personal goals into account when making assignments to activities or job placement, tailoring services to individual needs (Scrivener et al., 1998).

Lessons for Policy and Practice. If policy makers want workforce development programs to help low-income people find better jobs than they would find on their own, the state or locality has to communicate in concrete ways the importance of this goal through performance measures, funding incentives, assistance in understanding local labor markets, and other means. For example, state-set performance standards may have been a key factor in Portland's success in placing welfare recipients in better jobs. The standards included a wage-at-placement target that was well above the minimum wage (Scrivener et al., 1998).

In addition, programs themselves have to create strong, ongoing relationships with employers, gather good formal and informal labor market information, have internal performance incentives focused on advancement, give in-depth training to staff, provide a comprehensive set of work supports, and define the program's advancement goals clearly. Services should include career counseling, soft skills training, job development, and job clubs aimed at connecting people to better jobs. Finally, subsidies such as on-the-job training and publicly funded, paid internships with private employers can help open doors to employers that would not otherwise hire some low-income adults (Strawn, 1998). Promising practices for strategic job development efforts are described further in the next section.

Upgrading Skills while Unemployed

While better job matching and an emphasis on job quality can help some low-income people enter better jobs directly, many will need to upgrade their skills in order to compete effectively for better jobs. Recent research on long-term outcomes of welfare-to-work programs provides new evidence that the most successful welfare-to-work programs made substantial use of education and training in support of clear employment goals; that programs that helped people obtain higher paying, longer lasting jobs increased access to job training or other post secondary education; and, that among those with lower skills initially, the biggest benefits are to those who go on to job training. This discussion is restricted largely to results from experimental program evaluations as researchers have the most confidence in those findings; however, nonexperimental research also finds that job training can help low-income workers increase their earnings and obtain access to better jobs (Smith et al., 2002; Mathur et al., 2002; Fleischer, 2001; Rademacher, 2002).

Because low-income adults have the most time to focus on improving their skills during periods of unemployment, a key goal of pre-employment services should be to help people improve skills enough to gain access to jobs that will then support further skill upgrading. Indeed, while post employment job advancement services are a critical piece of a comprehensive strategy, research to date suggests that a fairly small percentage of low-income workers at any point in time avail themselves of these services, which is not surprising given competing work and family demands (Hill et al., 2001; Paulsell and Stieglitz, 2001).

What the Research Says. The most recent evidence in this area is again from the NEWWS evaluation where Portland was the most effective site overall, and especially effective in promoting job advancement and employment stability. Two community colleges were the lead contractors for the program and emphasized placement into better jobs and work focused skill upgrading. Over five years of follow up, the program resulted in a 21 percent increase in employment, a 25 percent increase in earnings, and a 22 percent reduction in the time spent on welfare, all as compared to similar recipients who were part of a control group (Hamilton et al., 2001). These impacts far surpassed the other NEWWS sites—which typically focused on job search or on basic education—as well as results from other evaluations.

The Portland program also resulted in the largest improvements in job quality after two years of follow up—increasing hourly wages and access to employer provided health insurance—and employment stability (Freedman, 2000; Hamilton et al., 2001). Beyond these immediate benefits, while job search programs have short-term effects that fade over the years, the initial investments in work focused education and training made in Portland appeared to pay off over time, as individuals found higher paying jobs and stayed employed. Past evaluations have shown a similar result, with mixed service programs producing longer lasting impacts than those that provided mostly job search assistance (Hotz et al., 2000; Friedlander and Burtless, 1995).

Education and training likely played a key role in achieving these results. The Portland program substantially increased participation in education and training programs—particularly job training and other post secondary education—and placed a strong emphasis on job quality while maintaining a clear employment focus. Among skill upgrading activities, for those with a high school diploma the program primarily increased self-initiated participation in job training and other post secondary education after their initial job placement. Over half of this group attended a community, two-year, or four-year college at some point in the five years after entering the program—a 66 percent increase as compared to a control group. For those without a high school diploma, the program increased use of basic education and post secondary education or training. It should be noted that while education and training were common activities, job search was also used extensively (Hamilton et al., 2001).

Whether provided before or after employment, what type of skill upgrading is provided and how it is provided are important determinants of how much it will pay off in the labor market. In particular, programs that provided primarily basic education, without strong links to job training and employment, have not had better results than job search focused programs. Instead, a growing body of evidence from the welfare reform arena points to the importance of job training and other post secondary education in producing wage gains and improving job quality.

- *Job training and other post secondary education can produce substantial employment and earnings gains, even for those with lower skills, if basic education and training are closely linked.*

Portland increased the proportion of participants who obtained a high school diploma or GED *and* a second education or training credential (usually a trade license or certificate)—a result no other evaluated program has achieved. While the other education focused sites in NEWWS did increase receipt of GEDs or high school diplomas, none had an impact on receiving a trade license or certificate. None of the employment focused programs had impacts on the receipt of any credential (Hamilton et al., 2001). In addition, the three NEWWS sites that most increased hourly pay for nongraduates after two years of follow up—Portland as well as Columbus and Detroit—also boosted participation in post secondary education or training for this group (Freedman et al., 2000).

The NEWWS evaluation also showed significant economic returns to job training and other post secondary education in a study of outcomes in three other sites for those without a high school diploma. This nonexperimental research found that those who participated in basic education had substantially larger increases in longer term earnings and self-sufficiency if they subsequently participated in skills training or college—an additional $1,542 (or 47 percent increase) in earnings in the third year of follow up compared to those who participated only in basic education (Bos et al., 2001). (See Figure 2.2.) Other studies have shown the benefits of job training when integrated with basic education, such as the evaluations of the Center for Employment Training, which allowed people to enter job training immediately, regardless of their educational attainment, and integrated remedial education directly into this training for a specific job (Zambrowski and Gordon, 1993; Cave et al., 1993).

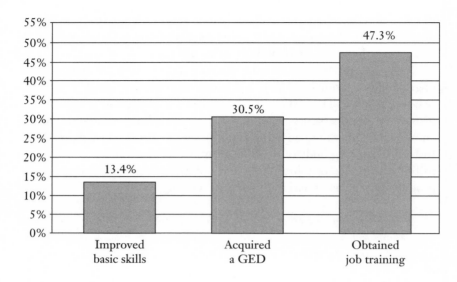

FIGURE 2.2 Increase in Earnings for Adult Education Participants in Welfare-to-Work Programs, by Educational Outcome

Source: Bos et al. (2001). Available at www.mdrc.org.

While job training and other post secondary education can pay off for those with lower skills, an ongoing issue has been that few individuals without high school diplomas gain access to these activities. For example, in the three NEWWS evaluation sites that produced the large earnings gains from job training and other post secondary education (this substudy did not include Portland), only 15 percent of those who participated in basic education went on to training (Bos et al., 2001). Low levels of participation appear due to several factors including weak linkages between basic education and training, training programs that bar high school dropouts or people with very low literacy levels, including many welfare recipients, and Work First programs that discourage extended participation in education and training.

- *Job training and other post secondary education can also pay off for high school graduates.*

Welfare-to-work evaluations indicate that job training and other post secondary education are also an important path to higher wages for high school graduates. As discussed above, the Portland program produced the largest earnings impacts of all the NEWWS sites for this subgroup and substantially increased use of job training and other post secondary education by high school graduates. Although the Portland program did not have any effect on the proportion getting college degrees, over the long term it did have a positive effect on the receipt of trade licenses or certificates for this group (Hamilton et al., 2001). Further, the basic education focused program with the largest earnings impacts for high school graduates in the NEWWS evaluation, Atlanta, produced a substantial increase in participation in job training and receipt of trade certificates for these recipients (Hamilton et al., 2001). Finally, the Alameda County, California, Greater Avenues for Independence (GAIN) program, which operated in the 1980s and increased the level of training received by high school graduates, also helped high school graduates find higher paying employment (Riccio et al., 1994).

- *Helping people increase their basic skills and/or obtain a GED also pays off in the labor market but more modestly than job training and other post secondary education.*

A nonexperimental analysis from the NEWWS evaluation in three sites showed that program participants also increased their earnings if they obtained a GED or increased their basic skill levels (Portland was not one of the sites studied). Receipt of a GED increased annual earnings by $771 in the third year after starting the program. The analysis showed the increase in earnings was due to having the credential itself, rather than any increase in basic skills that occurred in the process. Increased reading skills resulted in a smaller annual earnings gain of $354. While these gains are significant, they are considerably smaller than the $1,542 increase in annual earnings that resulted when individuals participated in job training and other post secondary education after basic education (Bos et al., 2001).

- *For those with lower skills, it can take a substantial amount of time to participate in both basic education and training, yet that combination pays off much more than basic education alone.*

The Portland program, which produced large impacts on receipt of educational and occupational credentials for those without a high school diploma, used relatively short stays in basic education and encouraged individuals to go on to training, typically in community college certificate

programs. The total length of time needed to participate in both basic education and training at the college was about a year.[4] Similarly, in the three
NEWWS evaluation sites that showed the large financial gains for those
who participated in basic education and then went on to post secondary
skills training, the average length of time spent in these programs was 12.7
months. This is likely an underestimate of how long it typically took as
almost 30 percent were still enrolled in post secondary programs at the end
of the two-year follow up period (Bos et al., 2001).

Lessons for Policy and Practice. While skill upgrading can help low-income
adults advance to better jobs, policy makers and workforce intermediaries
should pay close attention to program design and outcomes over time.
Among the most important steps policy makers and workforce intermediaries can take to increase the effectiveness of skill upgrading are involving employers in the design and delivery of services, making occupational
training accessible to those with low skills and to those who are working,
and connecting shorter term training with opportunities to earn post secondary degrees. Promising practices for designing effective skill upgrading
approaches are discussed in detail in the next two sections, but some key
steps that policy makers and intermediaries can take to increase the effectiveness of skill upgrading programs are:

- Target local employers who can offer jobs with higher-than-average
  wages, benefits, and potential for advancement.
- Give participants an opportunity to learn about different career
  options before choosing a training program.
- Assess student strengths and goals, as well as supportive service
  needs, to ensure a good fit between individuals and training and to
  arrange for necessary supports.
- Use a curriculum developed in partnership with employers that is
  based on mastering specific job competencies, as well as teaching
  broader skills.
- Train on job content ("hard skills"), general workplace skills ("soft
  skills"), life skills, and basic education skills (including English language proficiency).
- Provide training in employer facilities or in a job-like setting, using
  a mix of instructional methods.
- Make training intensive, with a substantial number of hours of
  instruction each week, and closely monitor participant attendance
  and progress.

- Develop links to community partners—such as substance abuse, mental health, and vocational rehabilitation agencies—for other services that enable individuals to succeed in training and employment.
- Offer college credit for training and link shorter term training with opportunities for further skill upgrading.
- Integrate basic education and English as a Second Language (ESL) into occupational training, or at least provide it concurrently and in the context of real work and life tasks.
- Create fast-track GED courses to enable those with moderately low skills (roughly 7–8th grade) to obtain a GED quickly, and move on to occupational training.
- Create short-term "bridge" training to open up training opportunities, either with employers or service providers, to low-skilled individuals who might not otherwise gain entry to them.
- Compress existing long-term occupational certificate and degree programs into short, intensive ones so that low-income people can enter training year-round and complete it quickly
- Divide training into "chunks" or modules that can be completed at different points in time.
- Create supportive work placements for the lowest skilled (roughly 0–3rd grade) that incorporate close supervision and opportunities for learning basic skills, soft skills, and marketable job skills.

Other features of high-quality education and training programs include developing a well-defined mission; providing classes in cohorts so that students can support each other's learning, having skilled, experienced teachers; emphasizing staff development; communicating regularly with staff of other relevant agencies; and promoting a high degree of teacher-student and student-student interaction (Bos et al., 2001).

Upgrading Skills while Working

Three main approaches have been tried to help low-income workers upgrade their skills: 1) creating public-private partnerships with employers to do training at the worksite; 2) redesigning existing employment and training services to make them more accessible to workers; and 3) providing financial support for low-income workers to upgrade skills on their own. Little rigorous research has been conducted so far on any of these approaches, though there is now a national evaluation underway of services for current and former welfare recipients. That evaluation and several state pilots of post employment services have focused on the latter two approaches to skill development, which largely depend on low-income workers being willing to pursue skill upgrading in the evenings or weekends, in addition to their hours on the job. Participation to date in such services by low-income workers has been very low (Bloom et al., 2002; Hill et al., 2001; Paulsell and Stieglitz, 2001).

What the Research Says. Rigorous research on post employment skill upgrading services for low-income workers is not yet available. Nonexperimental research and the experiences of practitioners suggest that services provided at the worksite achieve the best participation by workers and that state funded, employer focused training for existing workers can raise earnings and retention. A study of California's Employment Training Panel—the state's customized training agency—found that participants had higher earnings and job security than nonparticipants (Moore et al., 1995). Nonexperimental research on customized training in New Jersey also found higher wages, more promotions, and greater job retention among training participants than among similar workers not in the training (Regional Technology Strategies, 1999). The scale of this approach is limited, however, by the extent to which employers can be persuaded to do it. And until recently, these types of programs have rarely included low-income, low-skilled workers.

Partnering with existing state customized training agencies could speed efforts to open up such training to low-income people. These agencies are experienced in creating the public-private partnerships central to customized training. States that are already using customized training agencies to help low-income workers advance in the labor market include California, Iowa, Minnesota, New Jersey, and North Carolina. Two of these agencies, Minnesota's Job Skills Partnership and California's Employment Training Panel, have large efforts to deliver customized training to welfare recipients or other low-wage workers (Strawn and Martinson, 2000).

Lessons for Policy and Practice. Because there is so little rigorous research in this area, these tentative lessons are based on the experiences of practitioners. The most promising strategy for helping people to upgrade skills while working is to create public sector/employer partnerships, with training provided at or near the work site, during work hours. Both the Minnesota Pathways and California Career Ladder programs, run by the states' customized training agencies, take this approach. A study of state customized training programs by the National Governors' Association found that certain elements were important for the success of such initiatives (Simon, 1997):

- Fund training with grants or contracts, not tax credits or wage subsidies, as this ensures that the public funds go directly to offset the employer's costs of training.
- Require release time for training so that it can be conducted during work hours.
- Customize training curriculum but only for skills transferable to jobs with other employers.
- Include training on soft skills, specific job skills, and basic and English language skills.
- Offer upgrade training for the existing workforce beyond the target population.

Because the scale of customized training programs tends to be small, workforce intermediaries are likely to find it necessary to also adapt existing job placement, career counseling, adult education, and job training services outside the workplace to make them more accessible and responsive to the needs of working parents. These services have to be provided when workers are off work, chiefly in the evenings and on weekends. Practitioners who have run such programs suggest that they should include these features:

- Offer incentives to participate such as cash bonuses, gift certificates for children's clothing, movie tickets, haircuts, etc.
- Help stabilize the family. Workers cannot participate successfully unless their family situation is secure and stable.
- Build on job success. Workers are typically not ready to begin working on job advancement until they are settled in their current job and feel successful in it.
- Provide activities for kids and childcare. Working parents are more likely to come if they can bring their children and feel positive about what their children are gaining from being there, too.
- Provide meals for the workers and their families. Especially on weekday evenings, it is often difficult for workers who are parents to participate if they have to go home and feed their families before attending class.

Finally, for the smaller number of low-income workers who can navigate all the logistics on their own, policy makers should consider providing financial aid and support services for low-income workers to upgrade their skills on their own through existing post secondary services in the community. Several states, such as Michigan, Ohio, Utah, and Washington, do this for at least some low-income workers. Policy makers can increase the likelihood that workers can use such aid by also investing in community college and other post secondary institution efforts to meet the needs of low-income workers, through modularizing curriculum, expanding evening and weekend classes, providing on-site childcare and by providing career counseling, bridge training, and other needed services.

In sum, recent research on workforce development services for low-income workers, which comes principally from evaluations of welfare-to-work programs, shows that both better job matching services and pre-employment skill upgrading combined with job search can be effective in increasing wages and job stability over time. There is little research on post employment services, but employer based efforts are likely to be the most successful in engaging workers to participate in a sustained way. Policy makers and workforce intermediaries should, therefore, create a continuum of pre- and post employment services that provide a comprehensive array of activities and use job matching and skill upgrading to help people move up to better jobs. In particular, career pathways are a promising means of helping service providers and participants think long-term about the mix of pre- and post employment services that can help people get on a career path and move up to better jobs.

CREATING AND IMPLEMENTING A JOB ADVANCEMENT STRATEGY

Workforce development policy has traditionally focused on job placement as its end goal. This focus has been successful in moving many welfare recipients and other low-income individuals into entry-level jobs. However, it is clear that in and of themselves, these initial job placements rarely lead to long-term economic independence. To ensure that individuals and families cross above the poverty threshold, attention must be given to job advancement. Creating and implementing a successful job advancement strategy is a formidable challenge and requires coordination among a range of intermediaries in the workforce development and social services system, as well as the engagement of employers.

A successful job advancement strategy has two parts. The first part is the initial preparation or package of services provided by intermediaries before an individual begins employment (pre-employment). The second part (post employment) is the services that allow individuals to continue their learning and skill development after they have gone to work. It is absolutely essential that there be connections between pre- and post employment services. Better integration would allow individuals to pursue longer term career and educational goals as each education or training class builds on the previous ones. It would also enable localities to pay more attention to the appropriate balance of investment between pre- and post employment services. All too often, in our fragmented workforce development system, those connections are missing because the different workforce intermediaries are not coordinating their services with each other or with employers.

In the end, individual outcomes for job advancement are difficult to predict because they are influenced by a wide variety of personal, social, job, and labor market factors. For example, a single parent with a child who develops a chronic health condition may never have time to pursue the additional education needed for career advancement. How far individuals ultimately advance is dependent upon their motivation and personal and family situations. However, a successful strategy allows low-income individuals multiple opportunities for accessing a holistic set of services that support participation.

Key Elements of Pre-Employment Services

Pre-employment services form the foundation or "jumping off" point for post placement advancement services. In other words, planning for job advancement should begin the first day a participant begins a pre-employment program. This critical notion often gets lost when workforce intermediaries charged with providing pre-employment services are focused solely on the "quantity" of job placements rather than the "quality" of those placements or use only performance measures that reflect job placements rather than continuing education and long-term retention and advancement measures. The goal of all pre-employment programs should be to use the allotted time and resources to leverage the participant into the best possible initial job placement and build a foundation for future advancement.

SHIFTING THE FOCUS FROM JOB PLACEMENT TO PLANNING AND BUILDING CAREER PATHWAYS

If job advancement over time is the goal, then staff should work with participants to shift their focus from "getting a job" to "planning for a career." This is not an easy proposition. Individuals need to be able, in very concrete terms, to see how they can move from an initial entry-level job along a pathway that eventually leads to a high-wage job. This notion of building career pathways is a model that allows individuals to visualize their career developing over a long period of time. It also provides a framework for workforce development intermediaries to align their education and support services to focus on moving low-income individuals along a career pathway. Holding a vision of career pathways—beyond the job placement end game—requires workforce intermediaries to sustain momentum for culture change across their organizations.

It is important in mapping career pathways that all intermediaries in the workforce development system share a common understanding and model of career progression. The model should include a solid foundation of basic skills, entry-level occupational training, and opportunities for further skill training and education upgrades. A career pathway, in essence, is a road map that shows how an individual progresses from an entry-level job to a high-wage job in a particular career field. It identifies multiple entrance and exit points that are tied to specific jobs in the labor market. In turn, the education, training, and work experience required for each job are delineated as well. In a broad sense, individuals should always be able to see where they are in the "pathway," what the next level of job opportunities is, and what they need to acquire in terms of additional education or work experience to achieve the next step. Intermediary staff need to build their capacity to influence an individual's world view beyond the immediate goal of getting a job to the value of commitment to a career. Staff and participants must also understand that to be successful in this new economy it will be necessary to continually blend work with education.

Helping Individuals Choose the Right Career Pathway

Workforce intermediaries who are providing pre-employment services should identify the eight to ten high-demand growth occupations in their region and work with employers and industry representatives to chart out potential career pathways. A clear understanding of what employers and employees need at each point in the pathway allows for better articulation with the education and training system.

Participants in workforce development programs should select potential career fields after they have had the opportunity to assess their interests and aptitudes and align those with the realities of their regional labor market. Individuals should be directed into high-demand growth occupations that have good job mobility and progression opportunities. Intermediaries should pay special attention to those industries and occupations that require a relatively low level of skills and formal education at entry, but allow workers to progress to a moderate wage with on-the-job experience and further training.

Intermediaries should help individuals to acquire a clear understanding of the occupational area and the typical job classifications, and also grasp exactly what is going to be required to advance within a given occupation. In addition to advancement opportunities, the staff can help individuals to be realistic about what kinds of occupations best fit the realities of their life and home responsibilities. For a single mom with three young children and limited childcare options, an occupation where rotating shifts and irregular work hours are the norm probably is not the best fit, even if it offers rapid job advancement.

In order to help individuals make informed career decisions, it is imperative that workforce intermediaries hire the appropriate staff. Staff should be able to identify barriers and assess skills and interests. They also need to understand career development principles and provide guidance in mapping out an advancement plan. Success in mapping paths for advancement requires a high level of knowledge about the overall labor market as well as about specific local industries and employers.

Designing Pre-Employment Services that Maximize Post Employment Outcomes

Successful workforce preparation programs focus on job readiness and retention skills as well as basic education, English proficiency, and technical training. A vital aspect of job readiness services is to help individuals resolve personal and social barriers, such as substance abuse or mental health issues, that can prevent successful full-time employment. Ensuring that support services, such as childcare and transportation, are available for the transition to work is also critical. Integrating the soft skills training with the basic education and/or occupational training increases an individual's job "fit" and ability to adapt to workplace culture.

Beyond job readiness training, any job advancement strategy must have access to post secondary education and training as its core guiding principle. To advance to a high-wage job, individuals must acquire the necessary education and skills. The latest Census data (2000) confirm that women with an associate degree earn more than twice as much as those without a high school diploma (about $24,000 compared to about $11,000). Degrees, certificates, and credentials recognized by employers are key and for many will determine how far they can progress in their career pathway.

With this in mind, it is clear that post secondary educational institutions should be a key partner in the provision of both pre- and post employment services. Recent literature including Fitzgerald (2002), Grubb (2001), and Alssid (2002) has focused on the community college as the most logical institution to perform this role. Given its national infrastructure of over 1,100 institutions and its wide range of credit and noncredit offerings, community colleges are poised in many areas to serve as the foundation for a comprehensive job advancement strategy.

The goal of any pre-employment services plan should be ensuring that the resulting initial job placement is the best possible one for the participant's individual circumstances and long-term career goal. It is important that whatever time and resources are allotted for pre-employment services are well spent. Throughout the process (both pre- and post employment services) the individual's time and training dollars will always be in short supply. Therefore, it is critical that every service supports the long-term goal of a high-wage job.

Workforce intermediaries often make two critical mistakes. The first is encouraging people to take "any job" quickly, rather than think strategically about how a particular job placement can help individuals move along a career path. The second common mistake is providing technical training that does not carry credit or articulate toward a degree or certificate. In the current workforce development environment very few individuals are going to get all the training they need for a high-wage job before their initial placement into a job. This is because most pre-employment programs work with individuals for three months or less and have limited training dollars to spend on each person. Even when policy mandates and/or program resources are more generous, most people simply cannot afford to be unemployed for a long time. Therefore, it is important that what they begin during pre-employment services can be continued after placement and that it all build toward a recognized credential, such as a degree or certificate. All too often individuals will complete a noncredit, short-term training program, get a job, and then discover that when they are ready for more education, their previous training does not count toward a degree. Again, because time and resources are so constrained, it is important to help individuals access credit or alternative credentialing programs as quickly as possible.

The purpose of basic education and occupational training in a career pathway approach is to provide the foundation for continued skill upgrading and educational attainment after someone goes to work. One of the most significant impediments to low-wage workers accessing the education and training they need to qualify for high-wage jobs is that they are not academically prepared for college-level work. They cannot score high enough on the placement tests or meet the prerequisites to get into the training and educational programs that provide the credentials they need to advance their career. Therefore, the workforce intermediary who is providing pre-employment services should focus on enhancing each individual's basic skills as well as providing occupational training. Basic skills include reading, writing, math, and computer literacy, in addition to language acquisition for nonnative speakers.

Strategic Job Placement Efforts

The final element in pre-employment services is a strong job development and placement component. The goal should be placement into the best job possible at the time with the understanding that this job will be the first step on a career pathway. With this in mind it is important to look for employers who are committed to advancement and lifelong learning and to sectors that have strong advancement potential. Not all employers are created equal when it comes to career advancement opportunities for their employees. Some quality employer indicators to consider include:

- Willingness to partner with educational institutions to provide pre- and post employment training.
- Train front-line staff on career development strategies and tools, so that they can craft individual paths to obtaining better jobs.
- Help parents develop short- and long-term career goals.
- Develop assessment tools to help staff match the skills needed in particular jobs with the skills of training participants.
- Maintain close and continuous contact with local employers.
- Create mechanisms for identifying up front any potential logistical, personal, or family challenges to employment.
- Supportive supervision at the worksite that encourages creativity and learning.
- Clearly defined jobs with skills standards.
- Management support for career advancement.
- Work release time for training.
  - Tuition reimbursement for all levels of employees, not just mid- or high-level ones.
  - On-the-job training programs.
- Overall quality of the workplace.
  - Maintain a culture of respect.
  - Value continuous learning.
  - Offer a range of employee benefits.

Key Elements of Post Employment Services

The second part of a successful job advancement strategy is the services provided to individuals after their initial job placements. These services should be available to all low-wage workers in a community. Services should be targeted at both job retention and job advancement.

Retention services are those that allow an individual to keep his or her job, such as childcare, emergency transportation services, and short-term or one-time cash aid. Initially, it is critical to have a structure in place that ensures that individuals are knowledgeable of and receiving all the transitional benefits or work supports, such as the Earned Income Tax Credit, that are available to them. In addition, the ability to quickly connect people who need support services with community resources can help prevent job loss. Ultimately, job advancement strategies will not work until stability is achieved on the job and in an individual's personal life.

In terms of advancement, the goal should be moving individuals along their career pathways. The individual should have a detailed plan about his or her next job goal and what it will take to get there. It is important for the individual to look at what resources or opportunities are available at his or her place of employment. In-house training programs, tuition reimbursement, or work release time for education need to be explored. It is important for the workforce intermediary to work closely with employers, unions, and trade associations. Often college classes can be offered at the workplace or college credit can be earned by completing an employer training program.

Continued access to education and training leading to a recognized credential are critical. For a person working 40 hours a week with family responsibilities, time and money are going to be the biggest obstacles to upgrading skills. Individuals need help in putting together a schedule that will fit with the reality of their lives. It may be taking one class a term; it may be a distance education class; it may be a class at their worksite; or it may be a weekend college accelerated program. The key to sustaining motivation is a clear understanding of the pathway and the economic payoff for completing each step along the way.

In addition to retention services, access to further education and training, and ongoing support for career development, the final piece of a post employment strategy is ongoing job placement assistance as described earlier. As people gain more skills and work experience, job placement assistance to help them get to the "next job" is crucial. A workforce intermediary's knowledge and connections can greatly enhance movement along the career pathway.

In providing the above post employment services the following proven strategies should be utilized:

- Most job loss occurs within the first three months. Intermediary staff should have frequent contact during this time to help participants make a successful transition to work.
- When appropriate, intermediary staff should let employers know that they are available to help with workplace or personal issues that arise.
- Providing small work related payments to low-income parents can help overcome unexpected financial crises that could result in job loss.
- Intermediary staff providing post employment services should have a practical problem-solving orientation and be comfortable and experienced in working closely with the private sector.
- Intermediary staff and services need to be available during evenings and weekends.
- Intermediary staff should provide opportunities for individuals to maintain the peer and staff relationships they developed during pre-employment services.

Implications for Workforce Intermediaries

If the goal is job advancement, not just job placement, it has implications for workforce intermediaries—who they are and what kinds of capacity are required.

- No one organization is going to be able to meet all the needs of individuals and employers. To be successful, it takes a group of workforce intermediaries and partners working seamlessly together.
- Employers should be engaged throughout the process as key partners in both pre- and post employment strategies.
- The services of the workforce intermediaries, both pre- and post employment, should be coordinated.
- Post secondary institutions should be key players in continually providing access to education and training that will help individuals move up a career pathway.
- Intermediaries must have the capacity to analyze the regional labor market, map out career pathways, and provide career development services.

- Community based intermediaries need to have the infrastructure to provide support services and connections to vital community resources over the long term.
- Intermediary staff should be trained in-depth in the provision of services to individuals as well as to employers.

Creating Career Pathways

As the primary provider of occupational or technical training in many localities, community colleges across the country are trying to repackage their curriculum into smaller sets of courses that can be taken in one or two terms and that prepare students for discrete jobs. This bundling of educational experiences into smaller "chunks" than a typical one- or two-year degree is the framework upon which career pathways can be constructed. This makes it much easier to truly connect pre- and post employment services. Ideally, during the pre-employment phase participants can bring their academic skills up to college level and complete the first "chunk" of an occupational program that leads to an entry- or mid-level job. Then after they get stabilized on the job, they can continue on to the next "chunk" of the occupational program until eventually they earn a credential.

A fully developed career pathway system includes the following features:

- "Bridge programs" that prepare academically underserved populations or nonnative English speakers to enter credit based occupational programs.
- "Chunked" or modular curriculum where certificate and degree programs are broken into smaller job sets of courses that can be taken independently and ultimately linked toward a credential.
- Access to support services such as tutoring, career counseling, childcare and transportation resources, and emergency student loans.
- Opportunity for internships or cooperative work experiences related to the content of the training.
- Job placement services that help students quickly obtain jobs in their career area.
- Pathways or "road maps" that graphically depict the alternative courses or curriculum chunks a student can take to achieve their specific educational and employment goals.
- Staff and faculty who work closely with business and industry to determine which sets of courses prepare students for which jobs.

- A research and development operation that conducts research with business and industry to crosswalk skill sets needed for specific jobs with the college curricula, identifies effective and accessible instructional delivery methods, develops employer partnerships, and provides ongoing feedback to improve the system.
- Advocacy by the leadership of workforce intermediaries for state sanctioned credentialing of modularized curriculum, such as Oregon's new Employment Skills Training Certificates.

One of the benefits of a career pathway system is that it can utilize both new and existing community college curricula. This allows for pre-employment training to be offered on a tuition basis for college credit. Using the existing community college curricula allows for programs and pathways to be sustainable over the long term because they are a part of the regular infrastructure of the college. Too often government agencies spend thousands of dollars setting up training programs that are not connected to existing certificates and degrees and disappear when the pilot or demonstration is over and the funding goes away. Using existing college curricula also allows a wide range of individuals to benefit regardless of eligibility for specific federal or state programs.

Another advantage of the career pathway system is the development of "road maps" that graphically show the various routes a student can take to achieve employment outcomes. This has been lacking in the past. With thousands of courses to choose from in a given community college catalog, it has often been unclear even to "insiders" which collection of courses, short of a one- or two-year certificate or degree, lead to which jobs in the local labor market. Without a clear road map or structure, too many students bounce from course to course, without achieving a meaningful credential. Finally, another unique feature of pathway programs is the creation of "learning communities" where students can progress through a block of courses as a group or cohort. Cohort activities increase student success and job readiness and tutoring components can be easily added.

Portland Community College (PCC) in Oregon has put together a number of career pathway programs that allow students to complete an initial term of courses that will qualify them for a job in their career field, and get them on a pathway to a degree (Figure 2.3A). These pathway programs have some unique features. All courses are existing PCC classes. However, the delivery of the courses is often restructured to allow students to complete more coursework in a term than would normally be possible. For example, if course "X" were a prerequisite for course "Y" normally a student

Business Administration (BA) Pathway (14 credits)

Over a ten-week term students attend classes 20 hours per week and complete 4 credit classes and one non-credit class. Upon completion, they can exit with entry-level jobs ($9–10 per hour) in the Accounting/Bookkeeping field or continue on to a second term, which includes four more classes of the 1-year Accounting Certificate plus an internship.

> *Accounting/Bookkeeping*
> BA 95—Introduction to Accounting
> BA 101—Introduction to Business
> BA 131—Computers in Business
> BA 228—Accounting Applications
> Job Readiness Class (non-credit)

Criminal Justice Administration (CJA) Pathway (12 credits)

Over a ten-week term students attend classes 15 hours per week and complete 4 credit classes. Upon completion they exit with entry-level jobs ($9–10 per hour) in the Criminal Justice field.

> CJA 100—Introduction to Professions in Criminal Justice
> CJA 113—Introduction to Criminal Justice System
> CJA 260—Corrections/Introduction to Penology
> CJA 263—Introduction to Corrections Casework

Machine Technology (MCH) Pathway (20 credits)

Over a ten-week term students attend classes/labs for 35 hours per week and complete 20 credits. Upon completion they exit with jobs as Computer Numerical Control (CNC) Operators ($9–10 per hour).

> MCH 269/270—Computer Numerical Control—Levels 1 and 2
> MCH 280—3.0 Credit Internship
> MCH 199a—Job Readiness for CNC Operators

For students who are not ready for college-level work, workforce intermediaries should develop "bridge" programs customized to occupational sectors.

Healthcare Bridge Program

Training is 19 weeks long, Monday through Friday, 8:00 am to 4:00 pm. The focus is on entry-level jobs within health care.

Classroom Training	*Internship Training*
Computers	Pharmacy Packaging
Workplace Communication	Sterile Processing
Safety Procedures	Lab Assistant
Hospital Culture	Medical Records
Medical Vocabulary	General Clerical
Job Readiness	Physical Therapy Aide

Like most bridge programs, this one combines basic skills and "hands on learning" to leverage students into entry-level jobs in area hospitals.

FIGURE 2.3a   Examples of Portland Community College Career Pathway and Bridge Programs would take course "X" (30 hours) in the first ten-week term and course "Y" (30 hours) in the second ten-week term. Under the pathway programs, the college often divides the term into two parts. During the first five weeks the student would take course "X" (30 hours), and then in the second five weeks he or she would take course "Y." Typically, students in these programs attend classes 20–25 hours per week versus the 12–15 hours per week a traditional student would be in class. It is important to note that not all curricula lend themselves to this type of acceleration.

Figure 2.3b shows a particular pathway, in microelectronics, in its entirety. The first box in this figure illustrates the "bridge" component that was designed specifically for limited English proficiency students. From there students can proceed through various "chunks" of PCC's two-year degree program. Each set of courses they complete qualifies them for a better paying job. This pathway was developed in conjunction with a consortium of high tech employers in the area.

KEY CHALLENGES AND POLICY RECOMMENDATIONS

The experience of workforce intermediaries that have pursued one or more of these job advancement strategies suggests that significant challenges lie ahead. These include the following.

Building Leadership and a Stable Resource Base for Job Advancement Strategies. In recent years, public policy toward workforce development and welfare reform has moved in the opposite direction, de-emphasizing advancement and focusing on rapid placement in entry-level jobs. In addition, overall federal funding for job training outside of welfare reform has shrunk dramatically. For substantial federal funds to be devoted to advancement, Congress would have to broaden the focus of workforce development and welfare reform efforts to include supporting work and job advancement. At the state and local level, for the workforce development and welfare systems to take on a new job advancement mission, there would need to be concrete leadership, staff development, and specific rewards to localities, service providers, and front-line workers for making this shift. In states that have launched job advancement efforts without an accompanying shift in incentives, the result has been a low rate of referrals to job advancement services. Another issue is how to share resources and credit across all the partners needed to make a job advancement strategy successful. This can be especially complicated in light of often-conflicting missions and rules of principal federal and state funding streams.

Students enter different trainings based on their skill level. Once students complete a training component they can move to the next training, or they can obtain employment and pursue the next level of training later, or they can combine work and training.

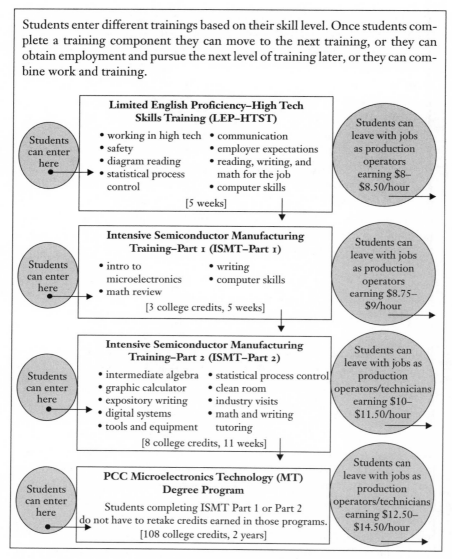

FIGURE 2.3b   Career Pathway to High Tech Training and Jobs

Employers in Job Advancement Efforts. Employer involvement is critical to the success of any workforce development effort. It is especially important for post employment job advancement services, however. The logistical obstacles to combining work and learning are most easily overcome when skill upgrading can take place at or near the worksite and during work hours.

Employers typically have been willing to partner in this way on skill upgrading when the training related to specific workplace needs and involved mid- or upper-level employees. It has been less clear that employers were willing to invest in training for entry-level employees, especially when training did not directly relate to carrying out jobs (such as GED preparation or other basic skills). Most states have customized training agencies, however, that with leadership by the governor or the legislature could become the building blocks of employer partnerships with workforce intermediaries around career ladders for low-wage workers.

Engaging Low-Income Workers in Job Advancement Services. Combining work and learning can be a daunting proposition for many people, especially single parents who frequently lack good transportation and childcare options. In addition, there can be real short-term financial tradeoffs between working additional hours or leaving time for school, even though skill upgrading may increase wages in the long term. Finally, many low-income people have had poor experiences with the education system in the past, do not see themselves as successful learners, and may not be able to envision a different career and educational path for themselves in the future. These issues may all contribute to the low participation that a number of providers have experienced when they offered evening and weekend job advancement services to low-income workers.

Increasing Access by Low-Income Workers to Mainstream Post Secondary Education and Training. To date, job advancement services typically have been provided as "add-on," contract funded services outside of the certificate and degree granting programs of community colleges and other post secondary institutions. This allows states and localities to get services up and running quickly; yet over the long term, there are important reasons for trying to improve access to mainstream post secondary programs. First, when a community based organization or community college provides short-term training but without college credit, the worker cannot apply this toward a longer term educational goal, such as an associate or bachelors degree. Second, current funding for job advancement services—primarily the federal welfare block grant—may not be a stable source over the long term; already these services are being cut back as welfare caseloads rise in many states during the current recession. Third, financing job advancement with welfare funds raises equity arguments as to why certain low-income workers—namely, single parents—should gain access to job advancement services while others are denied them. However, low-income workers seeking access to post secondary education face a number of financial, logistical, and educational barriers. These arise from a complex array of policies in individual colleges, states, accreditation bodies, and federal student aid programs. Resolving these issues will be a long-term task—but one that is necessary to creating a permanent infrastructure of job advancement services for low-income workers.

Federal Policy Recommendations

Workforce intermediaries could be helped to meet a number of the challenges described above if there were leadership from national policy makers and from employers to address the issue of job advancement and better align federal policies, incentives, and program funding with this goal. For example, Congress could revise existing programs—at minimum the Workforce Investment Act (WIA), the Temporary Assistance to Needy Families (TANF) block grant, and the Higher Education Act (HEA)—to better support the efforts of low-income adults to advance in the workforce. These programs have moved away from skill upgrading in recent years to emphasize rapid placement in entry-level jobs. For example, both participation in and spending on education and training programs have declined substantially under TANF. Less than 1 percent of federal TANF funds were spent on education and training in 2000, and only 5 percent of TANF recipients participated in these activities in the same year (Center for Law and Social Policy). Similarly, the number of adults receiving job training nationally appears to have declined by about two-thirds since implementation of the Workforce Investment Act (Savner et al., 2002). This curtailment in the use of education and training, prompted in part by disincentives in these laws to invest in skill upgrading, is not supported by the research, which unequivocally shows the benefits of a more balanced approach.

The Higher Education Act sets policy and provides funding for federal student aid programs and for improving post secondary institutions. The aid programs were largely written with traditional students in mind, yet a majority of undergraduates now have nontraditional characteristics, such as being financially independent from their parents, working full time, being older, or having dependents. Given the importance of for-credit skill upgrading in helping workers obtain portable occupational credentials and build toward degrees over time, it is imperative that student aid programs be updated to better reflect the needs of the new undergraduate, including low-income, working adults.

There are a number of possible federal policy changes that would increase the ability of workforce intermediaries to help low-income workers advance. In WIA, Congress should increase funding to reflect new responsibilities associated with One Stop Centers and Individual Training Accounts. It should also set aside a portion of WIA funds for training to ensure that at least as many adults can receive training as did prior to WIA. The sequential eligibility process should be changed so that training is no longer viewed as the service of last resort. Eligibility and reporting requirements for training providers and the system as a whole should be simplified and provide Congress with better core information on what is happening in the program. Outcome measures and funding cycles for WIA and those for TANF should be made as consistent as possible with each other.

For TANF, Congress should consider giving states additional room to count education and training toward work requirements; allowing adults more than a year in full-time training so that they can complete both basic education and training to earn an occupational certificate; and keeping the overall hours of work required reasonable so that parents can balance work, family, and school. In addition, Congress could provide leadership to states on job advancement by offering incentives to states to provide support services and work-study positions to low-income parents who are students; by encouraging states to provide post employment services focused on retention and advancement; and by providing demonstration grants and technical assistance that build the capacity to create career ladders in partnership with employers.

For the Higher Education Act, Congress should revisit the needs analysis and other aspects of Pell Grants to ensure that low-income adults, whether unemployed or working, with or without a high school diploma or GED, can obtain aid to upgrade their skills. It should also make it easier for adults to combine aid from Pell Grants, TANF, WIA, and other sources to meet the educational and living expenses associated with college, especially for those who have children. Education tax credits should be restructured so that low- and moderate-income families can benefit from them. In addition, Congress should consider using various HEA grant programs to help institutions build their capacity to serve low-income adults, especially through creation of career ladder programs.

Finally, federal "seed money" should be available to help expand the capacity of workforce intermediaries and to help them replicate best practices. For example, the TANF reauthorization bill passed in 2002 by the Senate Finance Committee included funding for Business Linkages grants that would help state or local consortia of employers, training, and social service providers to create job advancement services for low-income workers, especially those least likely to get such training on their own because of low skills or limited English proficiency.

NOTES

1. Unlike the other studies discussed here, this study did not have data on hourly wages or on workers' basic skills and educational attainment, though it tries to control indirectly for the latter.

2. This section is drawn from Strawn and Martinson (2000) and Martinson and Strawn (2003).

3. By "rigorous" or "experimental" we mean evaluations that use random assignment methodology, such as is used in medical trial, to isolate the effects of the program.

4. Interview with Nan Poppe, former director of the Portland's JOBS program, known as Steps to Success, May 2002. No formal data are available from the NEWWS evaluation on length of participation in Portland by type of activity.

REFERENCES

Alssid, Julian I., D. Gruber, D. Jenkins, C. Mazzeo, B. Roberts, R. Stanbuck-Stroud. 2002. *Building a Career Pathways System: Promising Practices in Community College-Centered Workforce Development.* New York: Workforce Strategy Center.

Bos, J., S. Scrivener, J. Snipes, G. Hamilton. 2001. *Improving Basic Skills: The Effects of Adult Education in Welfare-to-Work Programs.* Washington, DC: U.S. Department of Health and Human Services, Administration for Children and Families and Office of the Assistant Secretary for Planning and Evaluation; and U.S. Department of Education.

Bloom, D. 1997. *After AFDC.* New York: Manpower Demonstration Research Corporation.

Bloom, D., J. Anderson, M. Wavelet, K. Gardiner, and M. Fishman. 2002. *New Strategies to Promote Stable Employment and Career Progression: An Introduction to the Employment Retention and Advancement Project.* Washington, DC: Administration for Children and Families, U.S. Department of Health and Human Services.

Cancian, Maria, and D.R. Meyer. 1997. "Work After Welfare: Work Effort, Occupation, and Economic Well-Being." Paper prepared for the Annual Meeting of the Association for Public Policy Analysis and Management, Washington, DC.

———. 2000. "Work After Welfare: Women's Work Effort, Occupation, and Economic Well-Being." *Social Work Research,* 24(2).

Cancian, Maria, R. Haveman, D. Meyer, and B. Wolfe. 2002. *Before and After TANF: The Economic Well-Being of Women Leaving Welfare.* Madison, WI: Institute for Research on Poverty.

Carnevale, Anthony, and S. Rose. 2000. "Who Are the Low Wage Workers in the New Economy? Who Employs Them?" In R. Kazis and M. Miller, eds. *Low-Wage Workers in the New Economy.* Washington, DC: Urban Institute Press.

Cave, G., H. Bos, F. Doolittle, and C. Toussaint. 1993. *JOBSTART: Final Report on a Program for School Dropouts*. New York: Manpower Demonstration Research Corporation.

Center for Law and Social Policy analysis of TANF participation and expenditure data from the U.S. Department of Health and Human Services. Data available at http://www.acf.dhhs.gov/programs/ofa/annualreport5/index.htm

Connolly, H., and P. Gottschalk. 2001. "Returns to Education and Experience Revisited: Do Less Educated Workers Gain Less From Work Experience?" Working Paper. Chestnut Hill, MA: Boston College.

Fitzgerald, Joan. 2000. *Community Colleges as Labor Market Intermediaries: Building Career Ladders for Low Wage Workers*. Boston, MA: Center for Urban and Regional Policy. Northeastern University.

Fleischer, Wendy. 2001. *Extending Ladders: Findings from the Annie E. Casey's Jobs Initiative*. Baltimore: Annie E. Casey Foundation.

Freedman, S. 2000. *National Evaluation of Welfare to Work Strategies: Four Year Impacts of Ten Programs on Employment Stability and Earnings Growth*. Washington, DC: U.S. Department of Health and Human Services, Administration for Children and Families and Office of the Assistant Secretary for Planning and Evaluation; and U.S. Department of Education

Freedman, S., D. Friedlander, G. Hamilton, J. Rock, M. Mitchell, J. Nudelman, A. Schweder, and L. Storto. 2000. *Evaluating Alternative Welfare-to-Work Approaches: Two-Year Impacts for Eleven Programs*. Washington, DC: U.S. Department of Health and Human Services, Administration for Children and Families and Office of the Assistant Secretary for Planning and Evaluation; and U.S. Department of Education.

Friedlander, D., and G. Burtless. 1995. *Five Years After: The Long-Term Effects of Welfare-to-Work Programs*. New York: Russell Sage Foundation.

Gladden, T., and C. Taber. 2000. "Wage Progression Among Less Skilled Workers." In David Card and Rebecca M. Blank, eds. *Finding Jobs: Work and Welfare Reform*. New York: Russell Sage Foundation.

Greenberg, M. 2001. *How Are TANF Funds Being Used? The Story in FY 2000*. Washington, DC: Center for Law and Social Policy.

Grubb, W. Norton. 2001. *Second Chances in Changing Times: The Role of Community Colleges in Advancing Low Skilled Workers*. Berkeley, CA: University of California.

Hamilton, G., S. Freedman, L. Gennetian, C. Michalopoulos, J. Walter, D. Adams-Ciardullo, A. Gassman-Pines, S. McGroder, M. Zaslow, S. Ahluwalia, J. Brooks, E. Small, and B. Richetti. 2001. *How Effective Are Different Welfare-to-Work Approaches? Five Year Adult and Child Impacts for Eleven Programs*. Washington, DC: U.S. Department of Health and Human Services, Administration for Children and Families and Office of the Assistant Secretary for Planning and Evaluation; and U.S. Department of Education.

Hill, H., G. Kirby, and T. Fraker. 2001. *Delivering Employment Retention and Advancement Services: A Process Study of Iowa's Post-employment Pilot*. Washington, DC: Mathematica Policy Research.

Holzer, H., J. Lane, and F. Andersson. 2002. *The Interactions of Workers and Firms in the Low Wage Labor Market.* Washington, DC: U.S. Census Bureau.

Hotz, V. J., G. Imbens, and J. Klerman. 2000. "The Long-Term Gains from GAIN: A Re-Analysis of the Impacts of the California Gain Program." Working Paper 8007. Cambridge, MA: National Bureau of Economic Research.

Johnson, R.C. 2002. *Wage and Job Dynamics of Welfare Recipients Post-PRWORA: The Importance of Job Skills.* Ann Arbor: University of Michigan.

Johnson, R.C., and M. Corcoran. 2002. *Welfare Recipients Road to Economic Self-Sufficiency: Job Quality and Job Transition Patterns Post-PRWORA.* Ann Arbor: University of Michigan.

Loeb, S., and M. Corcoran. 2001. "Welfare, Work Experience and Economic Self-Sufficiency." *Journal of Policy Analysis and Management.*

Loprest, P. 2002. *Who Returns to Welfare?* Washington, DC: The Urban Institute.

Martinson, Karin, and Julie Strawn. 2003. *Built to Last: Why Skills Matter for Long-Run Success in Welfare Reform.* Washington, DC: The Center for Law and Social Policy and the National Institute for Literacy.

Mathur, A., with C. Wisely, J. Reichle, and Julie Strawn. 2002. *Credentials Count: How California's Community Colleges Help Parents Move From Welfare to Self-Sufficiency.* Washington, DC: Center for Law and Social Policy.

McKernan, S., and C. Ratcliffe. 2002. *Transition Events in the Dynamics of Poverty.* Washington, DC: The Urban Institute.

Meyer, D., and Maria Cancian. 2000. "Ten years later: Economic well-being among those who left welfare." *The Journal of Applied Social Sciences*, Vol. 25, No. 1.

Miller, C. 2002. *Leavers, Stayers, and Cyclers: An Analysis of the Welfare Caseload.* New York: Manpower Demonstration Research Corporation. (November).

Mitnik, P., M. Zeidenberg, L. Dresser. 2001. *Can Career Ladders Really Be a Way Out of Dead-End Jobs?* Milwaukee, WI: Center on Wisconsin Strategies.

Moore, R. W., D.R. Blake, and G.M. Phillips. 1995. *Accounting for Training: An Analysis of the Outcomes of California Employment Training Panel Programs.* Northridge, CA: California State University, Northridge School of Business Administration and Economics.

Nightingale, D. 1999. "Low-Wage and Low-Skill Occupations: Identifying the Best Options for Welfare Recipients." Unpublished discussion paper. Washington, DC: The Urban Institute. Available at www.urban.org

————. 2002. "Work Opportunities for People Leaving Welfare." In A. Weil and K. Finegold, eds. *Welfare Reform: The Next Act.* Washington, DC: The Urban Institute.

Paulsell, D., and A. Stieglitz. 2001. *Implementing Employment Retention Services in Pennsylvania: Lessons from Community Solutions.* Princeton, NJ: Mathematica Policy Research.

Rademacher, Ida. 2002. *Working with Value: industry-specific approaches to workforce development.* Washington, DC: The Aspen Institute. (February).

Regional Technology Strategies, Inc. 1999. *A Comprehensive Look at State-Funded, Employer-Focused Job Training Programs.* Washington, DC: National Governors' Association.

Savner, S., A. Frank, M. Greenberg, N. Patel, and Julie Strawn. 2002. *Comments on WIA Reauthorization and Linkages with TANF.* Washington, DC: Center for Law and Social Policy.

Scrivener, S., G. Hamilton, M. Farrell, S. Freedman, D. Friedlander, M. Mitchell, J. Nudelman, and C. Schwartz. 1998. *The National Evaluation of Welfare-to-Work Strategies: Implementation, Participation Patterns, Costs, and Two-Year Impacts of the Portland (Oregon) Welfare-to-Work Program.* Washington, DC: U.S. Department of Health and Human Services and U.S. Department of Education.

Simon, M. 1997. *Investing Public Resources to Support Incumbent Worker Training.* Washington, DC: National Governors' Association.

Smith, W., J. Wittner, R. Spence, and A. Kleunen. 2002. *Skills Training Works: Examining the Evidence.* Washington, DC: The Workforce Alliance.

Strawn, Julie. 1998. *Beyond Job Search or Basic Education: Rethinking the Role of Skills in Welfare Reform.* Washington, DC: Center for Law and Social Policy.

Strawn, Julie, and Karin Martinson. 2000. *Steady Work and Better Jobs: How to Help Low Income Parents Sustain Employment and Advance in the Workforce.* New York: Manpower Demonstration Research Corporation.

Tyler, J. H., M.Murnane, and J.B. Willett. 2000. *Cognitive Skills Matter in the U.S. Labor Market, Even for School Dropouts, Report #15.* Cambridge, MA: National Center for the Study of Adult Learning and Literacy.

Zambrowski, Amy, and Ann Gordon. 1993. *Evaluation of the Minority Female Single Parent Demonstration: Fifth Year Impacts at CET.* Princeton, NJ: Mathematica Policy Research.

II

WHO ARE WORKFORCE INTERMEDIARIES AND WHAT DO THEY DO?

3

What Do Workforce Intermediaries Do?

RICHARD KAZIS

S AN FRANCISCO WORKS, A NONPROFIT ORGANIZATION CREATED TO increase business engagement in the city's welfare-to-work efforts, launched an automotive services program in 1999. Targeted to entry-level automotive technician jobs, the program consisted of a one-week life skills course followed by a five-week introductory course to the automobile and its systems delivered at City College of San Francisco. Graduates were placed in jobs at local service shops. SFWorks and its partnering agencies provided employers and employees with support to help reduce turnover in the first few months of employment. To date, SFWorks has coordinated two cycles of the program.

At Pennzoil Ten Minute Oil Change, one of the employer partners, program graduates started at wages of $8/hour (plus commissions averaging $1 to $2) with the potential to advance to $14/hour with higher commissions over several years. One graduate of the first cycle is now a manager, making $65,000 a year. Although Pennzoil's owner was primarily motivated by the desire to help welfare recipients succeed, he believes that working with the SFWorks program provided him with workers who stayed longer, were motivated, and were less costly to recruit.

Here is what San Francisco Works did to get the program off the ground.

First, as a result of its regular assessment of labor market trends conducted through frequent contact with employers, public agencies, and training providers, SFWorks decided that automotive service was a high-demand job that paid reasonably well at entry level and could be a steppingstone to better-paid employment. It then convened an employer breakfast to ascertain industry interest in a new training program. At the meeting, employers complained bitterly of the dearth of qualified entry-level workers. They

73

agreed to work together to identify the technical and other skills they needed in their employees. SFWorks managed the process and began to create specifications for a training program.

At that point, SFWorks brought the community college to the table. Existing automotive service programs did not really suit employer needs: they took too long, the curricula were too abstract, and programs were not well linked to existing job opportunities. Responding to employer guidance, college administrators and faculty designed the introductory five-week training course.

SFWorks then turned to the next challenge: recruiting participants who were motivated and well suited to automotive employment. The organization contracted with a local community based service provider it knew well and trusted—the Northern California Service League, which works primarily with ex-offenders and former substance abusers—to recruit participants, deliver the life skills class, and provide case management.

A few other pieces still needed to be put into place. SFWorks secured public and philanthropic funding for the program. It made sure that employers who were likely to hire from the program came to the classes, made presentations, and interviewed prospective employees. It set up a system to collect and track data about program graduates. According to SFWorks Executive Director Terri Feeley, "This may sound silly, but it is important: we also made sure that lunch came every day to the people in that training program."

NEW WORKFORCE INTERMEDIARIES: AN INITIAL DEFINITION

San Francisco Works is one of a growing number of organizations around the country that believe the best way they can help low-income workers advance to better income and career opportunities is by becoming a trusted, valued partner serving the needs of both employers and less-skilled individuals. These organizations—called workforce intermediaries throughout this volume—share several important characteristics, even though their institutional origins, programmatic priorities, and long-term ambitions vary. They:

- *Pursue a "dual customer" approach:* Workforce intermediaries are committed to promoting advancement by serving two customers at the same time: employers in need of qualified workers and lower skilled workers or jobseekers. They believe that only by addressing the needs of both groups can they succeed in helping low-income individuals prepare for and secure better paying jobs and careers.

- *Organize multiple partners and funding streams toward common goals:* Workforce intermediaries play a critical organizing and planning function within their local labor market. Like SFWorks, they bring together employers, educational institutions, social service agencies, and other providers to design and implement programs and policies to improve labor market outcomes. The current funding environment is characterized by fragmented, categorical funding streams managed by multiple governmental agencies. Intermediaries must frequently organize not just the partners but also the resources needed to turn a program idea into a reality.

- *Provide and/or broker labor market services to individuals and employers that include, but go beyond, job matching:* Workforce intermediaries address identifiable labor market problems, by either providing necessary services directly or arranging for their provision by others. They often target specific industry or occupational sectors. These organizations see better job matching as an important service, but one with limited impact on advancement unless accompanied by strategies that assure both the job readiness and skills of low-income jobseekers and the quality of jobs and advancement opportunities offered by employers.

- *Project a vision that motivates and guides its partnerships and activities:* Workforce intermediaries are mission driven organizations guided by strongly held views on what both firms and their workers need to prosper in today's economic and policy environment. An important part of their work is to mobilize other institutions in the community to join efforts to create a more efficient and equitable regional labor market with varied advancement paths for low-skill workers.

Richard Kazis (1998) and Benner et al. (2001) have identified a broad range of organizations that function as intermediaries. These include: community based nonprofit organizations, Chambers of Commerce or other employer associations, labor-management partnerships, community colleges, and governmental agencies, including some Workforce Investment Boards (WIBs).

THE ECONOMIC CONTEXT SHAPING WORKFORCE INTERMEDIARIES

The intermediaries described in this chapter are a subset of a broader phenomenon: the growth of third-party institutions operating between employers and workers in response to sweeping changes in the rules and structures of the U.S. labor market. As described in detail elsewhere in this volume (see chapter 6), global competition, new technologies, and intensifying pressure from capital markets have worked their way through the labor market, with powerful results. The system of advancement through internal labor markets, which once dominated U.S. employment relations, has all but collapsed. Job tenure is shortening. Advancement paths are increasingly "externalized," i.e., moved outside the firm. At the same time, employers' expectations about workforce skill levels have risen steadily and significantly. Employers are increasingly interested in general skills and flexibility rather than narrow, job-specific competencies. Labor unions—the institutions that often mediated for workers in the employment relationship under the old system—have lost members and influence, a trend that is both a factor in and a symptom of that system's decline.

In this environment, the need for new labor market institutions to address career mobility is evident across all income and skill levels. Temporary help firms, Internet job sites, independent contractor associations, and industry consortia focused on high-skill technical workers are a few of the institutions trying to help U.S. workers navigate a more volatile and dynamic labor market.

The problem is particularly acute, however, for low-skill, low-wage workers. Labor market trends have dramatically widened the income gap between the haves and have-nots. According to Edwin Melendez and Luis Falcon (1999) and Bennett Harrison and Marcus Weiss (1998), advancement out of low-wage work has become more difficult, posing a serious obstacle to entry-level workers moving up to jobs that pay family-supporting wages.

Workforce intermediaries that are the focus of this volume have consciously taken on the challenge of improving labor market outcomes for low-income individuals and their employers. In so doing, they address not just an economic trend but also a public policy objective—income adequacy and opportunities to advance for those who work. The work of these intermediaries is therefore critical to broader efforts to improve the ability of the public workforce development system to move its intended beneficiaries into the mainstream of our economy and society.

HOW PAST POLICIES AFFECT
INTERMEDIARY PRIORITIES

Workforce intermediaries have evolved as much in response to the disappointing results of past workforce development policies as to powerful global economic changes. This is particularly true in four important areas of intermediary activity: employer engagement, job matching, training, and securing funding for workforce activities. Workforce intermediaries set goals and pursue partnerships that emphasize employer engagement, job quality, advancement opportunities, and the better integration of services.

In the past decade, the public workforce system has begun to change in ways that parallel and sometimes promote the priorities of workforce intermediaries. Evidence of this interplay can be seen in the evolving relationship between workforce and welfare systems, the design of Workforce Investment Boards and One Stop Career Centers under the Workforce Investment Act (WIA), federally funded demonstration programs such as Regional Skills Alliances and the H1-B visa grant program, and state incumbent worker training programs.

Federal welfare and workforce reform legislation enacted in the mid-1990s has been particularly significant. Welfare reform pushed hundreds of thousands of low-skilled women into the labor market in a short period of time, spurring new demand across the nation for intermediary services and providing significant new funding for some of the services intermediaries provide. Responding to the poor outcomes of past federal policy, WIA has given legitimacy (if not much funding) to many of the strategies that are at the heart of new workforce intermediary efforts: dual customer approaches that engage employers and meet their needs; greater attention to retention and advancement, as demonstrated in a broadening of performance measures beyond placement outcomes; and the integration of multiple programs and funding streams through consolidation and greater coordination among agencies.

A Workforce Investment Board created under WIA can assume the roles of a workforce intermediary, bundling Temporary Assistance to Needy Families (TANF), WIA, and other funding sources and organizing employers and other stakeholders to provide quality advancement services for low-wage workers. For reasons of history, culture, staffing, and their role as a public institution, most WIBs will decide not to expand their functions and become a workforce intermediary. It is not impossible, though: the Boston Private Industry Council has decided to do so.

Reauthorizations of TANF and WIA may bring federal law into even closer alignment with intermediary goals and priorities. In the meantime, workforce intermediaries pursue strategies whose impetus can often be traced back to the limits and failings of past and present policies.

Engaging Multiple Employers with Similar Needs. The traditional publicly funded workforce system tends to address the needs of one worker or one employer at a time. In a more volatile labor market and competitive environment, where new technologies can change employer skill demands overnight across whole industries, this retail strategy is too slow, laborious, and inflexible. Moreover, it misses opportunities to link workforce investments with economic development approaches designed to strengthen a cluster of firms in an industry or occupational sector of importance to regional economic growth.

In response, workforce intermediaries organize groups of employers with common needs. They build working partnerships within the industry to identify and address employers' common needs. They aggregate employer demand for services or training, typically within the same or related industries, so employers can have greater influence in the marketplace.

Job Matching. Historically, the government has funded job matching through the Employment Service (ES), created during the New Deal and jointly administered by the federal government and the states. Traditionally, the publicly funded workforce system's primary focus has been job placement: the ES has served as a passive posting service for employers of low-skill workers. The theory was: get someone into the labor market and they will advance over time as they accrue seniority and gain skills. The theory may have made sense during the heyday of the postwar labor market, but today this approach is clearly inadequate. The ES primarily serves low-wage workers, and, as researchers note, it does not do a particularly good job of that. According to Paul Osterman (1999), new registrants with the ES get their jobs from the service, and many of the jobs listed with the ES are temporary, low-skill jobs at the very bottom of the labor market.

In reaction to the public sector's poor record, today's workforce intermediaries pursue more active job matching strategies. They seek out better quality jobs that require low to moderate levels of skill. They try to find for their clients jobs that are a step on a clearly defined pathway to advancement.

Publicly Funded Training. The publicly funded workforce system has been involved in training for low-skill workers since the early 1960s. Overall, the results have been disappointing. Conceived primarily as a social rather than economic program, publicly funded training was only loosely connected to employer demand or to growth industries. With limited funding, programs trying to serve hard-to-employ individuals were typically of short duration and limited intensity. Not surprisingly, they resulted in at best modest gains in employment and income, according to Norton Grubb (1996). Funding was earmarked primarily for pre-employment training, delivered by service providers with little connection to mainstream educational institutions and their credentialing programs.

Workforce intermediaries are not content with the traditional model of publicly funded training: they build close working relationships with employers and look for ways to balance investments in pre-employment training with work based learning, on-the-job training, and post employment supports. Partnering with community colleges, many are trying to link training to educational credentials valued in the labor market.

Connection to Other Public Systems. Until quite recently, the public workforce system stood on its own, with few if any connections to economic development efforts at the national or state level or to mainstream educational institutions, social service systems, or the welfare system. This began to change in the 1990s, as welfare reform forced the two systems together. The Workforce Investment Act, with its One Stop Career Centers, has encouraged greater co-location and integration of referrals to services within and outside the workforce system. The workforce and education systems are also moving closer, as evidenced by the growing importance of community colleges in public workforce and economic development strategies nationwide. However, old traditions die slowly, and varying rules, regulations, eligibility requirements, and funding cycles make it difficult to overcome the fragmented, multiple-silo structure of public systems.

Workforce intermediaries recognize the need for greater integration and bundling of funds and services. They see the opportunity to act as integrators for their dual customers, working across different public systems to simplify and make more transparent services that are available to individuals and employers.

WORKFORCE INTERMEDIARIES TODAY: WHAT DO THE INNOVATORS ACTUALLY DO?

The roles that workforce intermediaries play in improving and reconstructing regional labor markets fall into two overarching categories: 1) organizing and planning roles, in which the intermediary mobilizes stakeholders—employers, individual workers, education, training, and other service providers, and government officials—to work together to improve labor market outcomes for employers and low-income workers; and 2) service provision and/or brokering roles that involve the organization in the delivery of job matching, training, support, and other services to both low-income jobseekers and the employers who hire them.

To be successful, workforce intermediaries combine planning and organizing roles with targeted labor market services. Credibility and effectiveness derive from being able to do both. Success in one arena makes it easier to make progress in the other. According to Fred Dedrick of The Reinvestment Fund in Philadelphia, "Successful intermediaries won't all do the same thing. However, they all need to do more than one thing. We found that being a credible data source and providing workforce development services make our policy work more influential. On its own, the policy work would not have enough traction." Eric Parker, executive director of the Wisconsin Regional Training Partnership, makes a similar argument: "Our value comes from two sources. First, we bring jobs to the table through our work with employers and unions. Second, we orchestrate the process of helping the partners get services they want."

At the same time, each workforce intermediary concentrates on some activities more than others. "Most workforce intermediaries start with a narrow agenda, trying to solve one specific problem facing a group of employers they work with," notes John Lederer of Shoreline Community College in Washington State. "Over time, as they build capacity and trust, they expand their horizons."

The origins and institutional bases of intermediaries often determine their priorities and relative strengths. A labor-management partnership, for example, is well positioned to address internal workplace practices and to serve the needs of an industry's employers and incumbent workers. A community college that serves as an intermediary for one or more industry sectors is likely to focus on training and alignment of educational programs with employer needs. Community based organizations bring a different set of relationships, interests, and strengths to the work. According to Benner et al. (2001), an ongoing research project on labor market intermediaries in Silicon Valley and Milwaukee (see chapter 12) is taking a systematic look at some of these institutional variations and how they affect efforts to improve placement and advancement for low-income workers.

Another factor affecting the mix of priorities and activities is the ambition of the intermediary organization. MIT human resources professor Paul Osterman (1999) distinguishes between two kinds of intermediaries. One works closely to meet employer and low-wage worker needs, serving customers on both sides of the labor market. It does so, however, without changing the "terms of trade" in the labor market. A more ambitious kind of intermediary, of which there are few, goes further. These organizations use their credibility and support in the community and in workplaces to prod employers to change firm behavior in ways that improve job quality and opportunities for advancement.

Providing or Brokering Labor Market Services That Promote Advancement

The provision or brokering of labor market services to particular employers and jobseekers is often the most visible and easiest intermediary activity to describe and assess. These activities tend to be specific and quantifiable. This is what we typically think of when we envision workforce development activities: outreach to individual employers and jobseekers; assessment of individuals' skills and/or employer hiring needs; technical, basic skills, and/or "soft skill" training; placement, either without training or following it; provision or referral to important support services, such as childcare, transportation, and social services; and, less frequently, on-the-job support, career counseling, and training that help workers adjust to a new job, stay employed, and advance.

WIRE-Net, a workforce intermediary targeting manufacturers on Cleveland's West Side, created its Hire Locally program in 1989 to help match local unemployed workers with manufacturing jobs that could pay relatively decent starting wages. WIRE-Net has balanced its mission of helping local residents advance with the imperative of delivering consistent quality service to employers seeking qualified workers. The program, upgraded in 2002 and now called WorkSource, offers a job referral service, three orientation workshops, assessment of job readiness in math and reading, and referrals to childcare and other services. Only upon successfully completing all aspects of the orientation does the candidate qualify for job matching and placement assistance, and some post placement support. In addition to WorkSource, WIRE-Net offers intensive skilled training through its Precision Machining Program, which links training providers with employers and with training candidates recruited and screened by WIRE-Net. Other employer partnerships include a nationally recognized pre-apprenticeship machining program for NASA's Glenn research center and a number of incumbent worker training programs in areas such as supervisory training, workplace safety, and employee retention.

In Charlotte, North Carolina, the local Chamber of Commerce partnered with Central Piedmont Community College to create a short-term welfare-to-work program that features academic, social, and job-specific training. The program links the college with the state Department of Social Services, community businesses, and other local organizations. According to the U.S. General Accounting Office (2001), students prepare for jobs in one of five occupational areas determined by a study of local needs, including medical office administration and customer service representative. Employers assist program graduates in finding a job at their worksite or elsewhere.

Project QUEST in San Antonio provides post placement assistance for individuals making the transition to employment. This assistance includes: paying for licensing or certification tests; continuing childcare and transportation subsidies for a minimum of 30 days after placement; re-employment assistance for those who need it; and six months of follow up assistance and monitoring of employment and wage progress.

Innovative and well-designed matching, training, and post employment support efforts like these can be provided by organizations other than workforce intermediaries. However, for most intermediaries, provision of such services is a primary focus of their effort, encompassing both traditional pre-employment services and the less common and more difficult to fund post placement supports and training for employed workers.

Some workforce intermediaries also work with employers around changing internal human resources practices to promote employee advancement and opportunity. The Wisconsin Regional Training Partnership (WRTP) has worked with several employers to change more than 100 temporary jobs into permanent positions with benefits and better integration into the firm. WRTP demonstrated a negative impact of so large a temporary staff on quality and productivity and convinced the firm that the change would be cost-effective. In California, the state Economic Development Department (EDD) funded the California Association of Health Facilities to change the structure of jobs as well as develop worker skills. According to EDD Director Mike Bernick, the association, made up of long-term healthcare facilities, convinced employers to create a position between Certified Nurse Assistant (CNA) and Licensed Vocational Nurse and provided training to make it possible for CNAs to move up.

Intermediaries debate the extent to which they should directly control the provision of labor market services. San Francisco Works' Terri Feeley argues for remaining a neutral broker: "We are able to assess providers' abilities, priorities, and mind-sets and match them with employers' needs and cultures. We don't provide services ourselves and we don't have loyalty to a specific provider." Eric Parker of WRTP says: "We decided it was important to become a prime contractor for services, so that we could bring resources to the table." In reality, the lines are not so starkly drawn. WRTP has partnered with the YWCA of Greater Milwaukee for case management services for WRTP participants. WRTP also contracts for training services. SFWorks has at times provided case management directly to clients when service providers have failed to meet the organization's quality standards. The "make-buy" choice is a business decision driven by capacity and quality considerations, not a core definitional question for workforce intermediaries.

Organizing and Planning Roles

Job matching and career advancement services are discrete, visible, and measurable. However, they are often the end products of an equally critical but less visible role that workforce intermediaries play. This is the role of organizing stakeholders in the regional labor market, often around industry or occupational lines, to create workforce development programs and strategies that lead to improved outcomes.

This organizational function is critical. Without the consensus building, strategic planning, and mobilizing work that is so much of what a good workforce intermediary does, it would be very difficult to overcome the funding constraints, institutional misalignments, and poor implementation that have long plagued the workforce field.

The following are among the most important organizing and planning roles of workforce intermediaries.

Aggregate Employer Demand. Employers frequently have common workforce development interests but lack effective mechanisms for exercising collective voice. Workforce intermediaries help identify opportunities for collective action to meet workforce needs and work with employers to develop strategies to meet those needs. "We act as a consolidator for employers. We simplify their task by linking them with others who have a similar need," says John Fitzpatrick, executive director of the Capital Area Training Foundation in Austin, Texas. What individual employers have neither the time, capacity, nor desire to do alone—find upgrade training for a small number of employees, for example—they might be very willing to participate in if a third party lowers the transaction costs. Daniel Berry of the Greater Cleveland Growth Association puts it this way: "Our strategy is to aggregate demand for services among employers in particular high-growth occupations. If we have a committed group of employers ready to go, that gives us both access and influence with education and training providers."

Organize Key Stakeholders. The coordination and organizing role that intermediaries play among institutions in their local labor market "is the least glamorous, most time consuming, and most necessary work we do," according to SFWorks' Terri Feeley. As one intermediary staffer puts it, "The more you slog through it together, the more you commit to staying at the table, the more opportunities you'll have to make things happen." The ongoing and labor-intensive relationship building and the establishment of a regular venue for discussing needs and opportunities enables intermediaries to understand needs and package resources, partners, and ideas. Getting the governance issues right is critical, according to Eric Parker. For WRTP, that means restricting membership in the partnership to employers and unions and ensuring that other stakeholders who come to the table—service providers, community colleges, and other organizations—do not determine WRTP's direction and priorities. It also meant starting with manufacturing, expanding into other industries only after WRTP had cemented deep relationships among key manufacturing partners.

Collect and Use Good Local Labor Market Information. Workforce intermediaries collect and use up-to-date, fine-grained, industry-specific information on local labor markets. Good data help improve program design and implementation. Greater Cleveland Growth Association (GCGA) produces a biannual Information Technology "Barometer" based on a survey of local firms. This ear-to-the-ground information helps GCGA mobilize employers and negotiate with service providers for more responsive training programs. GCGA has also created a novel feedback mechanism on a website that inventories training options in northeast Ohio: employers can provide feedback from their own experience on providers' quality and responsiveness. Good labor market information can help partners design new career ladder programs by identifying both the steps up the ladder from the lower rungs and the skills employers want to see in those looking to advance. Good labor market data also help politically. Documenting skill shortages can promote employer involvement and influence policy makers. Well-timed neutral reports on labor market trends, such as those conducted by the Greater Cleveland Growth Association, Philadelphia's Reinvestment Fund, and WRTP, increase credibility and become the basis for advocacy of policies and funding priorities.

Organize and Negotiate with Providers. Having built close working relationships with both employers and service providers, intermediaries can mobilize providers to respond to employer demand in ways that the public sector traditionally cannot. A few years ago, a major bank in Cleveland had to fill 50 jobs in three or four predominantly entry-level job categories. The bank called GCGA on Wednesday. By Thursday, the association had communicated with its network of service providers and identified a few to take the lead in a hiring fair. By the end of the following Tuesday, the providers had recruited enough people to apply and have first and second interviews with bank personnel at the job fair that 32 qualified candidates were identified. Twenty were hired by the end of the week. Project QUEST learned that the local community college was planning to cut a 12-month Licensed Practical Nurse course by one month, reducing geriatric training. Knowing that nursing homes were having trouble finding people with skills working with geriatric patients, QUEST staff advocated for going back to the 12-month program. The college reversed its plans.

Conduct Research and Development. Intermediaries frequently experiment with the design of new programs they believe might be effective and replicable. The Boston Private Industry Council (PIC) sees part of its role as testing models and then trying to have the state take over some of the best ones. "Having a concrete project to work on forces you to get into the mindset of the partners and to understand their interests and constraints," says the PIC's Rebekah Lashman.

Advocate for Public Policies. Many strategies for promoting advancement of low-skill workers require changes in public policy—securing funding for activities underfunded through traditional public sources and removing obstacles to innovation in current policies. Many workforce intermediaries engage with policy makers regularly and with determination—and such efforts can have a significant payoff. "Neither employers nor service providers have the time to focus on policy and identify opportunities to promote advancement strategies that serve both constituencies," notes Terri Feeley of San Francisco Works. "We simplify the process, identify opportunities, and help connect spokespeople with the legislature and the media."

WRTP's policy advocacy strategies align with the state's two-year budget cycle. A few years ago, WRTP helped convince state legislators to set aside $20 million of surplus TANF funds for a Workforce Attachment and Advancement Fund that supports incumbent worker training for low-wage workers. While the fund did not prove as easy to tap for incumbent worker training as WRTP had hoped, it has already been renewed once by the legislature. In Boston, the Private Industry Council went to the state legislature when customer service in the local One Stop Career Centers became too driven by TANF rules and regulations rather than the centers' customers. According to the PIC's Rebekah Lashman, because of the advocacy campaign, "The state created a budget line item that enables the centers to manage a more flexible set of core services—to manage the system as they think can best serve their customers."

Policy advocacy does not always mean securing more funding for advancement. It can also involve efforts to change rules or revise performance standards. In order to drive advancement more effectively, Project QUEST and the city of San Antonio negotiated a contract that requires the intermediary to place graduates in jobs that pay at least $10/hour and that specify some wage progression for those who are placed.

WHAT DISTINGUISHES
A WORKFORCE INTERMEDIARY?

The power of workforce intermediaries derives in part from the range and combination of roles they play in local labor markets. Yet some organizations are better able to achieve ambitious goals than others. *How* these organizations do their work is often as important to their ability to grow and have impact as the activities themselves.

What does it take to function well as a workforce intermediary? Intermediaries rise and fall on their ability to win trust—trust of employers, first and foremost, but also of other stakeholders, including organized labor where it has a presence, workforce service providers, educational institutions, and local and state officials. That trust must be built up over time. It is fueled by personal relationships, deepened by proof of commitment, and cemented by visible outcomes.

High-performing intermediaries tend to share several other characteristics. They are *entrepreneurial organizations*, flexible in their agenda setting and able to seize opportunities that present themselves. They are *politically savvy*: they understand that their ability to achieve their goals frequently requires support and intervention from private and public sector leaders. In addition, these organizations are *committed to achieving outcomes* that matter for their dual customers. They are driven to perform in ways that yield better labor market results for low-income individuals and their employers than did traditional workforce development programs and systems.

To win employer trust, workforce intermediaries develop and maintain an intimate knowledge of the industry or industries with which they work. They try to stay abreast of industry trends in real time and at a level of detail that can be acted upon. An Aspen Institute (2002) study on industry-specific approaches to workforce development emphasizes that "programs cannot afford to settle for a bird's eye view of the industry and the occupations they target." They must find varied ways to connect with industry and develop relationships that enable them to understand the practical functioning of the industry.

Some intermediaries undertake regular surveys of employer needs. Most hire staff with private sector experience. Ultimately, it is personal relationships and the regular contacts with employers that enable intermediaries to design new and better services. To this end, some union and community based intermediaries also enlist the input of people who have been trained and placed in the industry.

Being "bilingual" is critical to building trust, according to Margaret Berger Bradley of The Reinvestment Fund: "Public systems speak their own languages. But we speak the employers' language as well as the language of the public workforce system."

Intermediaries also build trust by demonstrating long-term commitment to an industry and its well being. District 1199C's Training and Upgrading Fund has worked for over 30 years to improve training for low-wage workers in Philadelphia's healthcare industry. Employers have gradually moved from hostility to skepticism to recognition of the union as a dependable partner in the quest for productivity and employee skill development. The Boston Private Industry Council attributes its current success in developing healthcare career ladder programs to relationships initiated more than a decade ago when the organization launched a major school-to-work effort.

Successful intermediaries are entrepreneurial to their core. In a fluid regional economic and political environment, the preconditions for successful workforce initiatives come and go quickly. Organizations must be ready to move quickly—and to change direction with industry needs. "You rarely know the design of your next initiative ahead of time. It's like a puzzle that you put together as you find the pieces," explains Rebekah Lashman of the Boston PIC. "And you can only find the pieces by being in a lot of places over time, talking to people, and listening to their needs."

Speed, responsiveness, and flexibility distinguish workforce intermediaries from the more constrained institutions of the public system. In 1997 the Eaton Corporation in central city Milwaukee wanted to fill 100 new electronics assembly jobs paying $12.50 an hour. The local public system simply could not move fast enough. Once the jobs were given to the public system to fill, the technical college had to submit a proposal to the local Private Industry Council for funding for a training course; the application for funds had to be reviewed and approved; and trainees had to be recruited, trained, and placed. "It was just too slow," according to Eric Parker of WRTP. "In the end, it took a year for the public system to train 12 people. That led us to try to streamline recruitment, training, and placement." WRTP moved from being a broker between the WIB and the technical college to being the financial intermediary for manufacturing training. With the technical college, WRTP developed a standardized entry-level training program, making it easier to launch new training classes. WRTP has also taken advantage of WIA's individual vouchers to speed up what had been an inefficient sequential process of individual eligibility determination, program design and approval, and course scheduling.

Workforce intermediaries tend to look for staff who can function effectively in a less bureaucratic and more employer-responsive environment. Mary Pena of Project QUEST says that she tries to hire industry liaison staff who have no prior experience in the public welfare or workforce systems because they tend not to be sufficiently entrepreneurial and flexible. "Staff the organization well," advises Eric Parker of WRTP, "because performance is the key to developing trust and clout."

In the end, the commitment to helping low-income individuals succeed in the labor market is more important than any particular set of services or activities. This is what motivates workforce intermediaries—and they tend to set standards for their performance higher than those that currently guide the publicly funded system. SFWorks looks for partnerships that result in full-time, benefited positions. According to Terri Feeley, the organization will not get involved in projects where wages are under $9/hour: "We talk with our employers about job quality and career pathways. If jobs are temporary, pay no benefits, or are low wage, we discuss ways to improve job quality. If the employer isn't interested, we may refer them to another organization for help." In one instance, SFWorks convinced an employer to change the probationary period for benefits from 150 days to 30 days.

Workforce intermediaries try to fill gaps they see in the services and opportunities available to low-income individuals through traditional workforce, education, and training programs. Cheryl Feldman of the District 1199C Training and Upgrading Fund puts it well: "We are trying all kinds of strategies to bulk up the system."

ISSUES FOR FURTHER RESEARCH AND ANALYSIS

Workforce intermediaries as defined in this volume are distinct in their mission driven approach, their commitment to serving dual customers, and their approach to improving labor market outcomes by changing both the quality of the labor supply and the quality of employment opportunities available to low-skill jobseekers. This chapter has tried to define the distinctiveness of these organizations and provide a rich picture of how leading intermediaries conceive of and do their work.

Several important definitional issues remain, issues particularly relevant to policy proposals that could promote intermediary expansion.

Intermediaries and Their Relationship to the
Institutions of the Evolving Publicly Funded System

The relationship between the publicly funded workforce system and workforce intermediaries is complex and in flux. The nation cannot afford duplicative or parallel systems. For this reason, clearer distinctions are needed among the roles of intermediaries vis á vis those of Workforce Investment Boards and One Stops. In some communities, intermediaries complement rather than conflict with WIBs and One Stops. Intermediaries' targeted, industry-specific focus, their emphasis on relationships and on-the-ground interaction with employers and other partners, their commitment to advancement strategies that are difficult to finance under current workforce legislation, and their pursuit of outcomes that are more ambitious than those of the public system—these are some important distinctions.

WIBs might best be seen as the regional labor market institution that sets goals, allocates resources based on needs, and monitors system performance. Intermediaries' planning and organizing roles tend to be more industry specific, targeted, and relationship rich. One Stop Career Centers as currently constituted and financed cannot undertake the kind of intensive services and roles that are at the heart of what many workforce intermediaries do. Nevertheless, the One Stops' mandate to improve coordination across public agencies and other stakeholders is in line with the approach intermediaries take to achieving their labor market goals. As these institutions grow and mature, their respective roles and highest added value will become clearer. More work is needed, though, in practice and policy to ensure that scarce public resources are used efficiently and do not yield a duplicative infrastructure.

Intermediaries as Part of an Infrastructure for Career Mobility

It is important not to put the cart before the horse when defining and characterizing intermediaries. The importance of workforce intermediaries is their ability to promote advancement for low-wage workers in unique and powerful ways that meet both workers' and employers' needs. If the intermediary is effective, it functions as a hub in a broader network of relationships, partnerships, and institutional arrangements among employers, providers, public agencies, and, where relevant, unions. This network of relationships is the key to building and sustaining diverse pathways to advancement in the local labor market.

There is a foreground-background tension, then, in conceptions of workforce intermediaries as stand-alone organizations that undertake the many roles highlighted above. The organization both creates and depends upon the network of collaborating institutions, yet it must have its own identity and capacity if it is to drive that network forward. It will be important to define more clearly the kinds of leadership, management, communications, and other skills needed for workforce intermediaries to be successful in advancing individual projects and a collaborative network that involves public and private institutions. Further research is needed on how best to move this agenda when any given intermediary has limited direct authority over its partners through governance, financing, or accountability mechanisms.

From a financing and policy perspective, the distinction between the workforce intermediary organization and the network of relationships within which it operates is important. Obtaining financing for intermediaries themselves must be only one part of a policy agenda to improve career mobility for low-income individuals. Funding that addresses service gaps will also be needed, not just funding to spur the development and expansion of workforce intermediaries. (See chapter 13 for a discussion of financing issues.) In addition, as current practice indicates, creating a few strong intermediaries is not sufficient. According to Bernhardt et al. (2000), without a broader infrastructure for career mobility that includes but extends beyond intermediaries, local efforts will remain too fragmented, partial, and difficult to navigate for many individuals and institutions.

Universal versus Targeted Strategies

There is a longstanding debate in this country about whether social policy investments should target those most in need or be more universal so that the political base for their perpetuation is broader. This debate is relevant to strategies to grow and strengthen workforce intermediaries. Even if "low income" is defined in terms of family self-sufficiency rather than federal poverty guidelines, low-income workers are not the only people in need of greater assistance in this volatile labor market. Perhaps a less targeted, more universal system would be more politically attractive. Employers may also be more interested in getting help from organizations that address not only entry-level workforce needs but also workforce needs at higher levels. The definition of intermediaries presented here takes a strong position in favor of targeting low-wage workers. The strategic implications of this definition of workforce intermediaries should be assessed carefully.

Performance and Power

This chapter has described activities, roles, and characteristics of an emerging group of labor market institutions. In the end, though, the particular mix of activities is less important than the *performance* of these organizations—the outcomes they deliver in the labor market. As intermediaries grow—and particularly if policy makers invest in their expansion and development—there will be a need for performance measures that both drive toward retention and advancement outcomes and also support innovative organizing, planning, and network building roles.

Performance is the key to credibility and clout, notes Eric Parker of WRTP. An intermediary is only as good as the results it achieves for both its customers. Sometimes, intermediaries need to use the clout they earn in order to achieve desired outcomes. Not all employers are alike; some jobs are better than others. Workforce intermediaries that are committed to an advancement strategy must promote and meet high standards in terms of wages, benefits, retention on the job, and career progression over time. If they let labor market trends alone dictate their efforts, they are likely to end up reinforcing negative outcomes and moving people into jobs and occupations with little mobility. For this reason, promoting advancement sometimes requires more than skill in developing trust. Sometimes it takes the will and the power to negotiate with individual employers, industry associations, service providers, and public agencies for performance standards—and changes in both policy and practice—that put career advancement first.

REFERENCES

The Aspen Institute. 2002. *Working with Value: Industry-Specific Approaches to Workforce Development. A Synthesis of Findings.* Washington, DC: The Aspen Institute.

Benner, C., B. Brownstein, L. Dresser, and L. Leete. 2001. "Staircases and Treadmills: The Role of Labor Market Intermediaries in Placing Workers and Fostering Upward Mobility." Paper presented at the Industrial Relations Research Association Annual Meeting.

Bernhardt, A., M. Pastor, E. Hatton, and S. Zimmerman. 2000. "Moving the Demand Side: Intermediaries in a Changing Labor Market." Unpublished paper. Madison, WI: Center on Wisconsin Strategy.

Grubb, W. Norton. 1996. *Learning to Work: The Case for Reintegrating Job Training and Education.* New York: Russell Sage Foundation.

Harrison, Bennett, and Marcus Weiss. 1998. *Workforce Development Networks: Community-Based Organizations and Regional Alliances.* Thousand Oaks, CA: Sage Publications.

Kazis, Richard. 1998. "New Labor Market Intermediaries: What's Driving Them? Where Are They Headed?" Task Force Working Paper #WPO3. Cambridge, MA: MIT Sloan School of Management.

Ma, P., and T. Proscio. "WIRE-Net and the Hire Locally Program." In C. Evans and Richard Kazis, eds. *Improving the Employment Prospects of Low Income Job Seekers. Case Studies: The Role of Labour Market Intermediaries. Case Studies.* London and New York: New Deal Task Force and the Rockefeller Foundation.

Melendez, Edwin, and L.M. Falcon. 1999. "Closing the Social Mismatch: Lessons from the Latino Experience." In S. Perez, ed. *Moving Up the Economic Ladder: Latino Workers and the Nation's Future Prosperity.* Washington, DC: National Council of La Raza.

Osterman, Paul. 1999. *Securing Prosperity. The American Labor Market: How It Has Changed and What to Do About It.* Princeton: Princeton University Press.

United States General Accounting Office. 2001. *Small Business Workforce Development Consortia Provide Needed Services.* GAO-02-80. Washington, DC: U.S. GAO.

4

The Workforce Intermediary: Profiling the Field of Practice and Its Challenges

CINDY MARANO AND KIM TARR

WORKFORCE DEVELOPMENT ORGANIZATIONS ACROSS THE UNITED States number in the thousands. They include Workforce Investment Boards, community colleges, One Stop Career Centers, vocational and adult schools, literacy providers, welfare-to-work programs, community based organizations providing workforce services, employer associations, and the Employment Service. Yet many of these organizations provide limited services to those who need assistance and are having limited success. Longitudinal data on the success of the full spectrum of workforce services have not proven impressive—either in terms of earnings gains for clients or in terms of meeting the nation's workforce shortages. This chapter explores the experience of a subset of this larger universe that appears to be achieving more promising outcomes. We have named these high-performing workforce developers "workforce intermediaries."

The chapter explores:

- What types of organizations that work with low-wage workers and the unemployed significantly improve their wages and career opportunities?
- How many of these organizations make a significant and simultaneous investment in responsively meeting employers' workforce needs?
- What are these organizations like? What types of services do they offer?
- How are they financed?
- What are the challenges they face in doing their work?

- How can the United States build on the experience of these groups to improve the outcomes of the larger, more diffuse workforce system now in place?

The intermediaries profiled in this chapter are not easy to characterize. They do not all have the same structure, tax status, or "branding." They exist in different kinds of communities and are funded in a wide variety of ways. The majority of states have several of these organizations, but even these may look quite different from one another. In fact, what is challenging in the quest to multiply the intermediaries described here is that there are as many organizations in the same general categories—Workforce Boards, community based organizations, or community colleges, for example—that are producing poor outcomes or are operating without connection to the employers in their communities. This chapter describes the intermediaries from their own perspectives—documenting their strategies, outcomes, and financing mechanisms and sharing what they see as their challenges. It is also the goal of the chapter to consider what might make it possible to expand the number of successful workforce intermediaries and to make it possible for those that currently exist to flourish and build their services to scale.

METHODOLOGY

The information provided in this chapter is based upon results of an August/September 2002 survey of workforce organizations conducted by the National Network of Sector Partners (NNSP). NNSP is the national support center for industry-specific workforce development initiatives across the United States. A project of the National Economic Development and Law Center, NNSP was founded in 1999 to expand the use of the sector strategy, to expand resources for this type of strategy, and to improve the state of practice. Sector initiatives are one segment of the workforce intermediary universe, sharing many elements in common with the intermediaries profiled here. They target specific industries (or sectors), however, and work to achieve better outcomes and systemic change for workers and employers in those industries.

This chapter describes a larger universe of organizations that are implementing high-performance strategies. Four criteria were used to identify groups for this survey. The organizations selected:

1. Operate programs with a focus on *two primary customers*—those whose skills are being built and the employers/industries in which the workers do or will work.

2. Expressly work with *low-income individuals and low-wage workers* to benefit their position in the labor market. While low-income individuals may not be their only service population, the organization is focused on investing in this population and has designed its efforts to address the needs of this group.

3. Provide a *menu of services, not just job placement* and create and manage a *mix of funding streams* to support this menu.

4. Provide an investment in the longer term *career advancement* of those it serves, extending services past the placement of an individual into a job.

Survey respondents described in this chapter identified themselves as meeting all four of these criteria. While the National Network of Sector Partners did extensive outreach to identify these programs and then to gather surveys from those that appeared to meet the criteria, it is clear that there may be other organizations that meet the criteria that were not a part of our study. A list of the organizations that contributed to the study is appended to this chapter, organized by state.

NNSP collected mailing lists and contact names from a wide variety of groups to do the initial identification of those who met the criteria. Initial research identified nearly 1,400 groups to survey, and survey instruments were sent to these organizations. NNSP staff then prioritized a group of 486 whose work most appeared to match the criteria. This group was contacted via e-mail and telephone calls and was provided an incentive bonus if they responded to the survey. Two hundred seventy-two surveys were returned (nearly a 20 percent response rate, although organizations were not encouraged to return the survey if they did not meet the criteria). The surveys that were returned were then categorized and analyzed. Of this number, 29 did not meet the criteria. There were three categories of groups that were excluded—groups that operate in the workforce development field as advocates and monitors at the local and state level but do not provide or broker services to individuals, those that have no or little focus on serving low-income people or low-wage workers, and those that showed no evidence of program elements related to career advancement or post placement services. Those that remained met all four criteria. Research results were tabulated by an external research firm and then analyzed by NNSP staff. This chapter presents the findings that emerged from this work.

The chapter is based entirely upon self-reporting by those who completed the survey and is not based on external verification of the information reported.

The survey instrument used was designed by NNSP, with input from two colleague organizations, Jobs for the Future and the Aspen Institute. The Working for America Institute of the AFL-CIO helped NNSP reach labor management workforce intermediaries. Comparisons used in this chapter are based on the following sources: an NNSP comparable 2000 survey, information collected in several learning forums conducted by NNSP in 2001 and 2002, and research findings collected by a variety of other organizations, each noted as used. Information about these sources is provided in the reference list.

KEY FINDINGS

While this chapter explores many findings in depth, it produced nine major findings:

- *Number.* NNSP identified 243 organizations that met the workforce intermediary criteria used here. We estimate that this is about 10 percent of the workforce development field.
- *Location.* The 243 intermediaries identified were located in 39 states. Over half of the programs are located in urban areas (51 percent) and serve the city in which they are located and surrounding counties. Twenty percent define themselves as regional organizations, serving a multicounty or statewide area. Only 18 percent define themselves as located in rural areas. Intermediaries are located in most major metropolitan regions.
- *Institutional Type.* Though the types of institutions in which these programs are housed are quite diverse, 73 percent are housed in nonprofit organizations versus government or for-profit institutions. This includes Workforce Investment Boards, many of which have established nonprofit structures.
- *Age.* The workforce initiatives carried out by these groups varied widely in age. More than half were less than 10 years old. Of the sector initiatives, 78 percent are five years old or younger. This implies that the high-performance segment of workforce institutions is growing.
- *Industry Focus.* Fifty-six percent of the intermediaries reported that they are conducting industry-specific workforce development initiatives, or "sector initiatives."
- *Scale.* Nearly 66 percent of those surveyed serve more than 500 persons each year, more than half of whom are low-income individuals

or low-wage workers. They provide services to multiple employers, with 82 percent serving more than 11 employers every year.

- *Outcomes.* The intermediaries outperform the general workforce development universe, with 55 percent gaining wages at placement that exceed $9.50 per hour, and with 29 percent reporting wage at placements over $11.00 an hour. Only 9 percent report wages at placement that match the more common workforce outcomes of $5.15 to $7.50 per hour. Of those responding, 66 percent report job retention rates for clients of above 50 percent six months after services. Few track their outcomes for employers, but among those who do, greater retention in jobs, improved promotion prospects, and lowered training costs are the primary gains.

- *Financing.* The financing of these workforce intermediaries is a patchwork process. Fifty-three different types of funding sources were used to support the programs surveyed. Most support their work by packaging together a wide variety of sources. Their budgets vary significantly in size. Although nearly 40 percent have workforce development program budgets exceeding $2 million, another 55 percent have budgets of less than $750,000 per year. Financing their organizations and attracting the funding they need is the greatest challenge across all of the organization types. The sources used to support different types of intermediaries vary significantly.

  Most workforce intermediaries struggle year to year to mesh together multiple funding sources. Most report that the funds they do receive are not designed to cover all of the key activities they carry out to meet their goals. Many are unable to finance adequate management information systems and staff for follow up that would enable them to report their longer term outcomes and the outcomes of their employer partners. Many others alternate between growth and reduction in staff depending upon funding sources. This creates a destabilized environment for the nation's best performing workforce institutions. Given the current climate of budget cutting across most of the sources that these programs utilize, there is risk of even further destabilization.

- *Challenges.* Attracting funding was the challenge of greatest concern to the survey respondents. Other challenges varied dependent upon the workforce intermediary's institutional base. Most see themselves as benefiting from external help in growing and sustaining their organization.

This chapter explores these and other findings and when possible compares and contrasts the findings to what is known about the larger universe of workforce development organizations.

HOW MANY ARE THERE?

As reported above, the NNSP survey found 243 workforce intermediaries that met the criteria of workforce intermediary used here. Twenty-nine intermediaries who completed the survey either did not consider themselves intermediaries, did not meet one of the criteria, or were pure advocacy or research organizations working on workforce issues without either providing or brokering services to employers or low-income people.

As shown in Figure 4.1, the West and Midwest are home to the most workforce intermediaries. Workforce intermediaries were found in 39 states, with nine states having ten or more programs meeting the high-performance criteria. These are California (38 intermediaries), Massachusetts (20), Illinois and Texas (15 each), Washington (11), Pennsylvania (11), Michigan (10), and Minnesota (10). Intermediaries are located in each of the major metropolitan regions, including Los Angeles, San Francisco, Houston, Detroit, Chicago, Atlanta, District of Columbia, Boston, and New York. In 11 states, NNSP did not identify any workforce intermediaries who meet the criteria used in this chapter. They are Alabama, Alaska, Delaware, Hawaii, Kansas, Montana, North Dakota, South Dakota, Utah, Vermont, and Wyoming. This is not to say that there are no workforce intermediaries in these states but to say that we were unable to identify those meeting the criteria for this chapter in these states.

According to this survey, there is a dearth of intermediaries in the area of the country that extends from the plains states across the Rocky Mountains.

WHAT IS THE PROFILE
OF WORKFORCE INTERMEDIARIES?

As indicated in Figure 4.2, the types of organizations in which the intermediaries can be found vary widely. Though the types of institutions in which these intermediaries are housed are quite diverse, 73 percent are housed in nonprofit organizations versus government or for-profit institutions. This includes Workforce Investment Boards, many of which have established nonprofit structures.

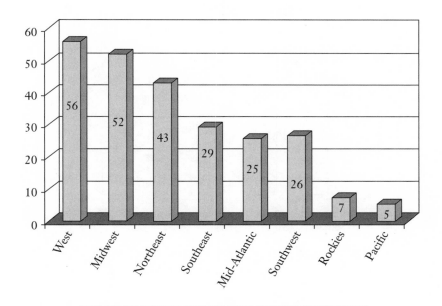

Region	States
West	AL, CA, HI, OR, WA
Midwest	IL, IN, MI, MN, OH, WI
Northeast	CT, MA, ME, NJ, NH, NY, RI, VT
Southeast	AL, AR, FL, GA, KY, LA, MS, NC, SC, TN
Mid-Atlantic	DC, DE, MD, PA, VA, WV
Southwest	AZ, NM, NV, OK, TX, UT
Plains	IA, KS, MO, ND, NE, SD
Rockies	CO, ID, MN, WY

FIGURE 4.1   Quantity of Workforce Intermediaries, by Region and State

Over 70 percent of the workforce intermediaries are housed within institutions that have been in operation for 15 years or longer. The age of workforce intermediaries, however, is fairly disparate: 50 percent are under 10 years of age, while the other half have been operating for over 10 years.

Staff size varies considerably in the intermediaries surveyed. While 40 percent of survey respondents report staffs of over 21 individuals, 29 percent have five individuals or less. Business associations dedicated to workforce development tend to have the smallest staffs.

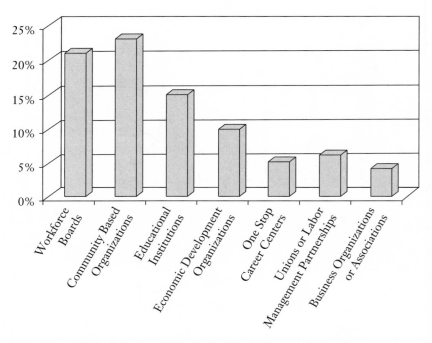

FIGURE 4.2   Workforce Intermediaries, by Institutional Profile

WHAT DO THEY DO?

The majority of survey respondents report workforce development as the "central" or "one of the primary" functions of their institution (81 percent). Though most of the intermediaries are housed within larger institutions that offer a number of services, 21 percent report that workforce development is the sole activity of their institution. Of the community based organizations identified as workforce intermediaries, only 8 percent report that workforce development is the "central work" of the institution.

Workforce intermediaries offer a wide variety of services to their employer and low-income clients, as illustrated in Figure 4.3. Identifying employer needs was the most commonly reported strategy that intermediaries utilize (82 percent). Preparing individuals for the workforce by offering job readiness services (81 percent), occupational skills training (80 percent), and career counseling/career management (80 percent) were widely implemented strategies. Not surprisingly, 79 percent report that they place individuals into jobs. Services and strategies that differentiate intermediaries from traditional programs do more than simply prepare

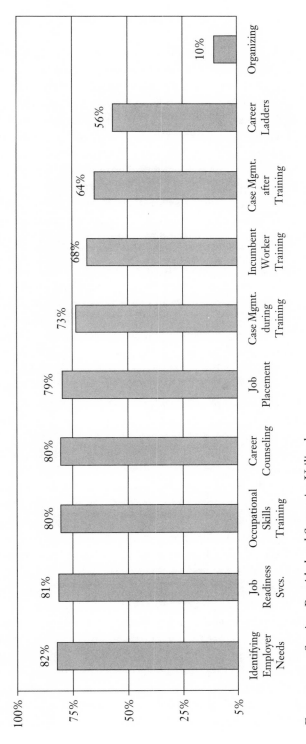

FIGURE 4.3 Services Provided and Strategies Utilized

individuals for and place them into jobs. Intermediaries, by definition, offer some post placement and career advancement services. Many of the respondents report utilizing one or more of these strategies. Nearly 70 percent of the intermediaries profiled offer incumbent worker training. Fifty-six percent of respondents are working to create career ladders for entry-level staff to advance within an industry. While 73 percent offer case management during training, 64 percent offer case management *after* placement. The findings reveal that some strategies are more widely used than others. Organizing workers was the least commonly reported strategy, with only 10 percent of respondents using this strategy. Sometimes organizing was part of a labor management partnership, sometimes a strategy used in a community based organization to build understanding of the needs of workers.

Many intermediaries are unable to provide all of the necessary services to their clients "in-house" and therefore serve as a broker, referring clients to other organizations for training and other services. Seventeen percent of respondents identified their organization as a "broker of training and other services." A number of labor management partnerships play this broker role, negotiating the needs of workers and their unionized employers and building bridges to both training facilities or community support systems.

The most common employer service intermediaries provide is documenting the needs of employers, as noted above, at 82 percent. Seventy-six percent of respondents report that they provide services directly to employers, with 66 percent noting that they offer employer technical assistance. Serving the employer client with supervisor training and human resource services is currently being provided by less than half of all intermediaries (42 and 43 percent, respectively). Sixty-six percent of all respondents report that they conduct industry and labor market research and analysis, and 57 percent have staff members participate in industry associations.

Over half of the intermediaries self-identified that they are targeting specific industries for their work (56 percent). These industry-specific workforce development initiatives, or sector initiatives, are currently underway in 136 of the 243 intermediaries. Figure 4.4 compares the top four industries currently targeted to the leading industries targeted in 2000. Of the survey respondents that are currently operating an industry targeted program, healthcare (61 programs), information technology (53 programs), manufacturing (47 programs), and construction (35 programs) are the most commonly targeted industries. These four most targeted industries have remained the same since NNSP's 2000 survey of industry-specific workforce development programs. Their ranking has changed, however.

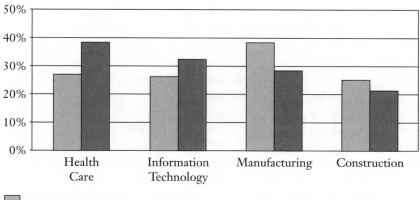

FIGURE 4.4   Industry Prevalence

In 2000, the leading industries were: manufacturing (37 programs), health-care (26 programs), information technology (25 programs), and construction (24 programs). Manufacturing saw a decline over the two years, while the number of healthcare initiatives grew dramatically (26 initiatives in 2000; 61 in 2002). Though the information technology industry has experienced volatility since 2000, the number of workforce programs has grown sharply.

The most noteworthy survey findings regarding industry-specific workforce development are:

- *Rise in total number of programs.* Of the sector initiatives, 78 percent are five years old or younger.
- *Growing number of new industries targeted.* Since 2000, industry-specific workforce development programs have developed. Industries targeted include: office services (27 programs), biotechnology (12 programs), tourism (6 programs), retail sales (5 programs), cleaning (4 programs), and financial services (3 programs).

These are all sectors of the economy in which sector initiatives had not begun in 2000. These industries now account for a total number of 47 programs. The number of programs in the food service industry jumped from 5 to 18 in the two years. Transportation, another growing industry, had an increase in programing from 2 to 22.

WHAT DO WORKFORCE INTERMEDIARIES CALL THEMSELVES?

Aside from the fact that they can be housed in a variety of institutions, the branding of the intermediaries is made more complex by the fact that the groups that conduct such programs do not agree on how they should be labeled. Twenty-three percent of workforce intermediaries describe themselves as "workforce developers," while 16 percent use the description "business-community partnership." Other descriptions include workforce broker (12 percent) and "training partnership" (12 percent). There has not been a commonly used term to distinguish this group.

WHO DO THEY SERVE?

Across all the intermediaries surveyed, 66 percent served more than 500 individuals in 2002. Twenty-four percent served between 100–500 clients, while only 11 percent served less than 100 clients annually.

Because workforce intermediaries, by our definition, work to serve low-income and less-skilled individuals, virtually all projects work with low-income persons. Intermediaries also target specific disadvantaged groups including Temporary Assistance to Needy Families (TANF)/welfare recipients (78 percent), low-wage workers (86 percent), and displaced workers (77 percent), as shown in Table 4.1. Intermediaries are also serving adults with limited literacy (72 percent) and adults with limited English proficiency (69 percent).

Table 4.1   Client Populations Served

Low-income adults	87%
Low-wage workers	86%
TANF/welfare recipients	78%
Displaced workers	77%
Adults with limited literacy	72%
Incumbent workers	71%
Adults with limited English proficiency	69%
Ex-offenders	65%
Out-of-school youth	62%
Persons with disabilities	62%
Homeless adults	61%
Public housing residents	61%
In-school youth	56%
Immigrants/Refugees	51%

Serving the Employer Partners

Employers are very involved in the function of the intermediaries surveyed. Eighty-six percent of intermediaries surveyed worked with more than 11 employers in the last year. Employers serve as members of the governance structure in 75 percent of the intermediaries. Employer partners give in-kind support, such as curriculum, instructors, or equipment, to nearly half of the intermediaries surveyed. Once individuals are placed in jobs, intermediaries continue working with the employer to ensure that workers stay on the job. Just over half of the intermediaries engage employers in promotion and retention efforts (51 percent), 64 percent offer case management *after* placement, and 50 percent provide case management to clients in *employer settings*.

WHERE DO WORKFORCE INTERMEDIARIES GET THEIR FUNDING?

The workforce intermediaries surveyed in the NNSP study are struggling to patch together their budgets from a wide variety of sources. Annual budgets for their workforce development programs vary widely. While 37 percent have workforce development budgets that exceed $2 million, it is also the case that 55 percent have budgets less than $750,000 a year, and among these, 13 percent have budgets less than $200,000 a year.

Size of budgets varies with organizational type conducting the workforce development services. For example, while 64 percent of the Workforce Investment Boards who meet the criteria have budgets for their work that exceed $2 million, 10 percent have budgets less than $500,000. Similarly, while 44 percent of high-performing community based organizations have budgets of less than $500,000 for their workforce development work, 25 percent also have workforce development budgets over $2 million. Fifty-five percent of business associations working as workforce intermediaries have budgets less than $500,000; 11 percent have budgets exceeding $2 million.

The 243 workforce intermediaries are receiving 53 different funding sources. Most patch these funds together each year (see Figure 4.5). But a deeper look reveals that the predominant sources vary considerably by organizational type. Figure 4.6 illustrates this story, documenting the five greatest funding sources for each type of institution.

The majority of workforce intermediaries find it especially hard to finance some of their program elements that they carry out. These include:

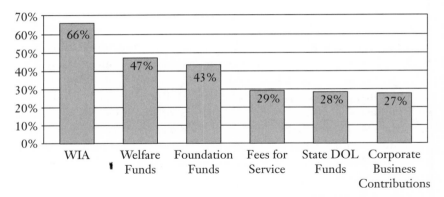

FIGURE 4.5   Predominant Funding Sources for Workforce Intermediaries

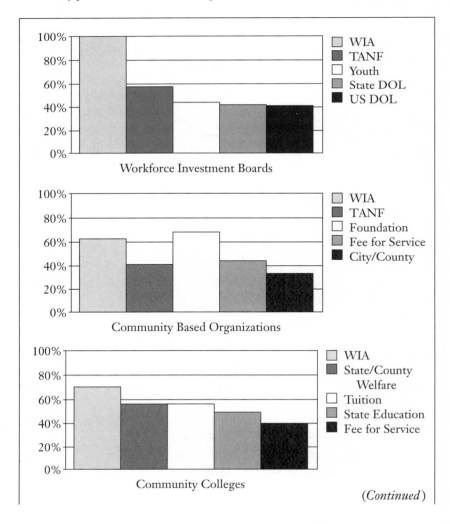

(*Continued*)

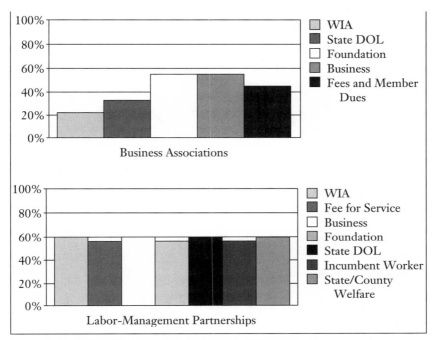

Figure 4.6   Top Five Funding Sources, by Institutional Base

- Supportive services needed by their clients.
- Incumbent worker training.
- Industry labor market analysis.
- Literacy and ESL services.

WHAT ARE THEIR OUTCOMES?

The workforce intermediaries profiled here report a range of positive outcomes that distinguish them in the larger workforce development universe. The outcomes can be categorized in two ways—outcomes for the participants they serve and for the employers with whom they work.

Outcomes for Participants

For the participants served, the following are some of the key outcomes that emerged in the survey.

Table 4.2   Wage at Placement

$5.15 and $7.49	9%
$7.50 and $9.49	36%
$9.50 and $10.99	26%
$11.00 and $14.99	24%
$15.00 or more	5%

Wage at Placement. Survey respondents reported average wage at placement rates for the individuals they serve as shown in Table 4.2.

More than half report wages above $9.50 per hour. Of course, the wage rates achieved are somewhat dependent upon the jobs and occupations in which individuals were placed and the typical wages in those jobs. A home healthcare aide, for example, might receive an average hourly wage in a particular community of $6.25 but be placed at $7.25 by the workforce intermediary.

The national Joint Training Partnership Act (JTPA) study cited in *Evaluating Job Training Programs in the United States* found average wage at placement of $8.27 per participant (Grubb, 1995). *Earnings and Well-Being after Welfare: What do we know?* published by the Institute for Research on Poverty in 1999 found average wages among welfare leavers of $7.52 per hour (Cancian et al., 1999). Recent studies conducted by the Aspen Institute of sectoral programs found average hourly wages at $9.67 (Rademacher, 2001). In the 2000 NNSP survey, the majority of sectoral programs reported average hourly wages in the $7.50 to $9.49 range (Kellner, 2000). While there is no real capacity to compare the wages responded in the survey to these deeper studies, the findings reported by respondents seem promising.

Benefits. Forty-one percent of intermediaries report that more than half of those they served gained health benefits in the jobs in which they became employed. Thirty-three percent of those who responded do not track this information. Among the sectoral programs in the survey, more than 70 percent reported that more than half of their clients received these benefits.

While many national workforce development studies also have not captured this data, there are several studies to review contextually. A Greater Avenues for Independence (GAIN) study, which reviewed welfare leaver outcomes, reported that 28 percent of those who were employed had access to healthcare benefits. An Urban Institute study conducted in 2001 found that 42 percent of all low-wage workers in the U.S. receive these benefits (Riccio, 1994). Among the sector programs studied by the Aspen Institute, 75 percent of the jobs into which clients were placed offered health benefits (Rademacher, 2001).

Information on additional types of employment benefits was not captured in the NNSP survey and is rarely captured by other evaluations of education and employment training. Information is available in the Aspen Institute study, referred to previously, documenting the impact of sector programs on paid vacation, sick leave, and life insurance—all benefits that assist low-income workers to balance work and family responsibilities and build assets. While these benefits are a significant factor in job quality, very few workforce intermediaries have the resources or management information systems that make tracking these benefits possible (Rademacher, 2001).

Job Retention and Career Advancement. More workforce intermediaries keep data on their clients' job retention rates than their acquisition of benefits. Only 22 percent do not keep this data. Sixty-six percent of workforce intermediaries reported that more than half of their clients retained their jobs six months after placement. Longer term retention data were not available.

With regard to career advancement, while all of the 243 profiled here provide services after placement and a variety of career advancement services, 70 percent do not collect outcome data on these services. Among those who do keep the data, 19 programs reported that they could document career advancement promotions for between 10 and 25 percent of their clients one to three years after placement. Another 16 programs reported that they could document career advancement for between 25 and 50 percent of their clients over a three-year period, and 18 programs reported career advancement data for between 50 and 75 percent of their clients in the first three years after placement. Nine programs reported that more than 75 percent of their clients achieved career advancement in the first three years following placement.

Strategies Used. How does this group of intermediaries achieve the outcomes described here? Among the group there is a range of strategies that includes: targeting higher waged jobs and worksites with benefits at the start, investment in post secondary and credentialed training that has a higher earnings payoff, longer range services to individuals allowing them to achieve career and earnings gains over time, building joint union and management plans for workforce improvement into bargaining agreements, and career ladder programs in employer settings that help move lower wage employees to higher wages and benefits on the job. The partnership with the employer community engages the employer in the process of achieving these gains and creating a more stable workforce.

Outcomes for Employers

While 68 percent of the workforce intermediaries surveyed lack a formal process for documenting the employer benefits of their programs, the most frequently collected data were for improving worker retention. Forty-two percent of those who collect this data reported that their programs had been able to increase worker retention for their participating employers. Other information on employer benefits included:

- 34 percent of those who collect employer data reported that their programs had resulted in reduced worker recruitment costs for employers.
- 32 percent reported lowered training costs for employers.
- 22 percent reported increasing the promotion capacity of the workers of their employer partners.

In addition to these areas, survey respondents also provided a number of ways in which employers have expressed receiving benefits from their programs:

- Growing requests from employers for workers from the program.
- Appreciation for the more appropriate skill levels of workers from the program.
- High ratings on employer customer satisfaction surveys.

WHAT ARE THE CHALLENGES WORKFORCE INTERMEDIARIES FACE?

The most significant challenge for all survey respondents was attracting and sustaining funding. This was of deepest concern to business associations and community based organizations, but it was the primary concern of all of the groups.

After their concern about funding, challenges varied depending upon the institutional base of the intermediary. For community based organizations, the next greatest concern was the lack of key supportive services available to meet client need (such as childcare and transportation), collecting the data they need, and addressing the intensive needs of their clients. For

Workforce Investment Boards, the next issues of greatest concern were engaging the employer community and meeting their performance standards. For community colleges, the deepest concerns were responding to industry change, engaging the employer community, and managing the mix of funding sources. For labor management partnerships, the greatest challenges were responding to industry change, managing the mix of funding sources, and meeting performance standards. For economic development groups, the greatest challenges were engaging the employer community and responding to industry change. And for business associations, the greatest challenges were conducting labor market analyses, responding to industry change, and working with the employment and training system.

DO INTERMEDIARIES NEED HELP?

Sixty-one percent of survey respondents believe that their organization would benefit from technical assistance. There are six areas in which respondents felt that technical assistance would be beneficial. Topping the list was the area of fundraising, which is seen by virtually all of the respondents as an area where they could use assistance.

Strengthening organizational capacity/organizational development was cited as the second most important challenge in which technical assistance would be helpful, as noted in Figure 4.7. The challenge of maintaining and leading an institution in a destabilized funding environment is critical. Leader burnout, leadership transitions, and the complexity of managing multiple strategies are all organizational development challenges. Survey respondents also felt the need to learn more about best practices in other workforce development settings. Other top concerns (in ranked order) include strategic planning, research and development, and building relationships with employers.

Intermediaries were interested in receiving assistance in a variety of ways. The majority of the intermediaries surveyed would prefer to receive technical assistance at workshops and conferences. On-site, individualized consultation was the second most preferred method. In terms of technical assistance providers, experienced workforce program staff was the top choice among respondents (42 percent). Specialized, independent consultants were respondents' second choice (26 percent).

Perhaps more critical than the help needed by the surveyed respondents are the needs of the 90 percent of workforce organizations that are not reaching the performance outcomes of those described here. Providing technical assistance to the larger universe of workforce organizations to create more

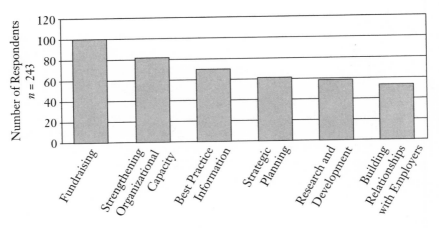

FIGURE 4.7   Technical Assistance Needs

effective institutions capable of serving both the low-income and employer audiences is an even greater imperative.

Yet few resources are available to support these types of help. Investment in technical assistance services matching the needs of both current workforce intermediaries and those who need help to achieve better outcomes is a high need in the workforce development arena.

WHAT COULD BE DONE TO GROW AND STRENGTHEN THE FIELD?

From an analysis of the surveys and other learning forums in which NNSP has held dialogues with workforce intermediaries, NNSP has identified five goals that could be met by a variety of policy, philanthropic, and programmatic players nationally, at the state level, and locally.

Goal One: Redesign federal workforce policy to support a strategic menu of workforce activities shaped at the local level that improve outcomes for employers, jobseekers, and workers. Workforce development policies at the federal level—like the Workforce Investment Act, Perkins Vocational Education Act, and Temporary Assistance for Needy Families—should be more flexibly directed to the local level to support a broader menu of services designed to be accessible to jobseekers and those who are working in low-wage, entry-level jobs with limited skills. The menu might include:

- Research and analysis related to employer workforce needs and industry standards.
- Career counseling, career case management, and career advancement services.
- Job readiness and job placement services.
- Basic skills enhancement and services for those with limited English skills.
- Occupational skills training, including post secondary education.
- Supportive services needed by clients to succeed in training, on the job, and to balance work and family responsibilities.
- Incumbent worker and career ladder training.
- Technical assistance services to improve employer human resources and more productive workplaces.
- Follow up and operation of management information systems to track outcomes for individual program participants and employers.
- The development and maintenance of community/business partnerships that coordinate and broker the set of services outlined above.

Public policies designed to support workforce development need to include a menu like this or a similar range of services/activities that are eligible for receipt of workforce development dollars across federal programs. This range of services could be included in each policy or be consolidated in a single policy in which monies could flow to the local level to support local workforce institutions to conduct these services.

Federal policies should not dictate which sequence of services should be developed in each community (as dictated in the design of One Stop Centers or as limited or prohibited in current TANF policy) or which entities should provide the services. These sequences, menus, and delivery systems should be tailored at the local level to the employment opportunities available and the needs of the local workforce and employers.

Goal Two: Design a more strategic, better performing system and invest in building capacity and continuous improvement at the state and local levels without creating/financing new institutions. Federal policy across the workforce systems might direct resources to the states to provide technical assistance monies to strengthen performance and achieve continuous improvement of workforce systems and intermediaries as well as tackle key workforce crises (i.e., risk of loss of key industries, statewide skill shortages, improvement of vocational literacy and ESL programs, management information and performance accountability systems, or changing technologies). Finally, federal workforce development policy might mandate similar or complementary outcomes, performance standards, and management information systems across work-force legislative areas so that program operators on the ground and federal administrators and policy makers can consistently view how the systems are working to achieve increased earnings, reduced poverty, greater job placements, improved retention on the job, acquisition of worker benefits, and career advancement as well as measures of both client and employer satisfaction.

State policy makers—whether governors, legislators, state boards, or state administrators—could then plan and direct workforce investments in their states that consolidate resources from a variety of federal and state sources to analyze their economies, provide additional focused training dol-lars for both new entrant and incumbent workers in key industries, and build skills that can make their economies more competitive across firms. They can also collect performance data from across the legislative areas and set continuous improvement goals for local areas and institutions to reduce poverty, increase earnings, gain greater placement rates, improve retention in employment, acquire employment benefits, and gain career advance-ment. And state workforce policy makers can invest in technical assistance for the underperforming local systems in need of quality improvement.

Goal Three: Corporate and business leaders—too often disconnected from the workforce development system—need to be fully re-engaged in the system. As research has shown, business leaders are often disconnected from and dis-affected by the current workforce development system. Yet the workforce intermediaries surveyed by NNSP have had success engaging business part-ners—and indeed some of these efforts are led by business partners. From the federal policy level to the local service delivery system, new roles that illustrate a clear employer benefit need better articulation and delivery. Simple numbers and requirements for employer participation are neither successful nor sufficient. Ensuring and measuring employer benefit as a part of the performance system is one way to address this concern. Another is to be sure that workforce dollars are available to address the needs articu-lated by business, from ensuring that new entrants like those transitioning from welfare have both the skills and supportive services they need to be successful workers, to providing public support to career development sup-port for incumbent workers, to connecting workforce and economic devel-opment activities so that key jobs are retained in communities and new jobs are created. Such activities as these now occur only in the most high-performing areas. When they do, employers stay at the table.

Once more successfully engaged, business leaders have key roles to play. They can assist in the improvement of the current system by working with others in business, government, and the community to improve the skills development, social supports, and career development of their own workers and potential new entrants. They can participate actively in partnerships designed to address these issues and help to design measures that capture how these partnerships benefit their businesses. Businesses can also examine innovative human resource strategies that can make entry-level jobs better for low-wage workers, build appropriate career ladders in their firms where possible, explore how to assist low-wage workers gain appropriate work supports, and contribute to the costs of training in public-private partnerships.

Corporate leaders at the national level—and employer associations—can help lead the charge for a more responsive, more investment oriented system. Participating actively in the policy debate to achieve a better performing system—as they currently do on tax and regulatory issues—would be a great step forward. Tying corporate giving nationally and at the local level to the development of more responsive intermediaries would also be a great contribution.

Goal Four: Stimulate greater philanthropic investments at the national, regional, and local levels that are focused on supporting redesign of the workforce system and promising practice. Foundations and charities—including the United Way—might direct their community and economic development resources to assist in building a better workforce system. Their monies could be targeted, not to service delivery, but to the building of strategic community partnerships, financing systems to track clients and mesh public funds, engaging industry involvement over time, supporting leadership and staff development, financing pilots of new strategies, as well as other capacity development needed by existing workforce intermediaries and those working to build continually improved quality of service and outcomes. Understanding that any one of a variety of institutions—community organizations, workforce boards, labor management partnerships, business associations, educational institutions, or community development corporations—can take the lead in system redesign should guide the giving practices of those who are making funding decisions. Assisting these groups to finance bringing their voices and their involvement in systems and redesign and policy change in the workforce system can also be a critical contribution.

Foundations and charities have in many cases reduced their giving in the area of workforce development, sometimes discouraged by the outcomes achieved. In a period of public budget constraints and high opportunity, investments by the philanthropic world in workforce development redesign would make it more possible for that redesign to take place in an effective manner.

Goal Five: Ensure a role for successful workforce intermediaries in systems redesign efforts so that their work becomes more the norm than the exception and set in place incentives, technical assistance, and accountability measures to move less performing players forward toward success. Current workforce intermediaries are a treasure chest of solutions for improving the workforce development system as a whole. These institutions need to be seen as a vital resource to the system and to become actively involved in strategies to grow their numbers and expand the efficacy of the system as a whole. Listening to the voices of those who have been successful and ensuring that new policy does not erect new barriers to their success is one need. Another is the mining of lessons learned in these institutions for technical assistance materials and technical assistance activities that might help less successful parts of the system improve performance. Financing the time of the successful performers to participate in these policy and technical assistance efforts will be important so that diverting their energy does not put their own successful efforts at risk.

For the broader spectrum of workforce organizations, incentives and accountability measures are needed to bring about continuous performance improvement. The policy changes outlined above will be needed to stimulate change. Investment in technical assistance for those who need it will also be an important step.

CONCLUSION

The National Network of Sector Partners is committed to documenting the needs and experiences of organizations like those described in this chapter and to ensuring that the voices of groups like this inform policy development at all levels. NNSP works to promote the expansion of programs like these— most particularly those that have taken an industry-specific approach. NNSP is impressed with the promise represented by the organizations that have developed high-performing strategies and the promising results that are being achieved for both low-income workers and their employers.

Many more U.S. stakeholders will be needed to call for policies and other approaches that utilize what has been learned by the organizations described here. Reshaping of current federal policy, financial investment in change, delivery of effective workforce solutions to industry, investment in quality improvement activities for workforce organizations that are not succeeding, and respect and reward for innovation created at the local level are all needed but appear low on the nation's priority list.

The workforce intermediaries whose experiences are described here live day to day, producing impressive results in an atmosphere that is often hostile at a time when their work is desperately needed to revitalize the economy. They point the way to solutions that can be a win-win for all.

APPENDIX: WORKFORCE INTERMEDIARIES PARTICIPATING IN NNSP SURVEY

Arkansas

Good Faith Fund	Pine Bluff
NW Arkansas CDC	Fayetteville

Arizona

City of Phoenix Workforce Investment Board	Phoenix
Cochise County Workforce Development	Sierra Vista
Navajo Nation Local Workforce Investment Board	Window Rock
Primavera Services/ Primavera Works	Tucson
Southern Arizona Institute of Advanced Technology	Tucson
Southwest Center for Economic Integrity	Tucson

California

Asian Neighborhood Design	San Francisco
Bay Area Construction Sector Intervention Collaborative (BACSIC)	Oakland
Bay Area Industry Education Council	Fremont
Bay Area Video Coalition	San Francisco
Cabrillo College	Aptos
Community Development Technologies Center	Los Angeles
County of Ventura	Ventura
Employers' Training Resource, County of Kern	Bakersfield
Farmworker Institute for Education & Leadership Development	Keene
Florence Crittenton Services	San Francisco
Foothill Employment and Training Consortium	Pasadena
Greater Golden Hill CDC	San Diego
Jewish Vocational Service	San Francisco
Lao Family Community Development	Oakland
Local Economic Assistance Program	Oakland
Los Angeles County Department of Social Services	Los Angeles
Marin Jobs and Career Services	San Rafael
Mayfair Improvement Initiative	San Jose
Napa Valley Economic Development Corporation	Napa
North Bay Employment Connection	Napa
Riverside County Economic Development Agency	Riverside
Rubicon Program, Inc. Richmond Sacramento Employment & Training Agency	Sacramento
San Diego Workforce Partnership	San Diego
San Francisco Center for Applied Competitive Technologies	San Francisco
San Francisco Works	San Francisco
San Mateo County Central Labor Council	Foster City
Santa Ana WIB	Santa Ana
Santa Barbara County Dept. of Social Services	Santa Maria
Solano County Workforce Investment Board	Fairfield

Sonoma County Human
Services—WIB   Santa Rosa

South Bay Workforce
Investment Board   Hawthorne

Verdugo Workforce
Investment Board/City
of Glendale   Torrance

Women at Work   Pasadena

Workplace Hollywood   Hollywood

Youth Employment
Partnership, Inc.   Oakland

Colorado

Employment Services
of Weld County   Greeley

Larimer County
Workforce Center   Fort Collins

Mayor's Office of
Workforce Development   Denver

Mi Casa Resource Center
for Women   Denver

Project Self-Sufficiency
of Loveland—Fort Collins   Loveland

Connecticut

NE WIB   Chaplin

The Workplace, Inc.   Bridgeport

Washington DC

Howard University   DC

Jubilee Jobs   DC

Florida

Broward Workforce
Development Board   Lauderhill

Florida Crown
Workforce Board   Lake City

Polk County Workforce
Development Board   Bartow

Resource Center for
Women Largo Workforce
Central Florida   Winter Park

Georgia

Atlanta Regional Commission
—Workforce Development
Division   Atlanta

Atlanta Workforce
Development Board   Atlanta

Northwest Georgia
Workforce Investment
Area Region 1   Rome

Kirkwood Community
College, Job Training
Partnership Activities   Cedar Rapids

Idaho

East Central Idaho Planning
and Development
Association   Rexburg

North Idaho WIB   Hayden

Illinois

CAEL   Chicago

Center for Labor and
Community Research   Chicago

Chicago Commons
Association   Chicago

COMPTIA   Oakbrook Terrace

Greater North-Pulaski
Development Corporation   Chicago

IAM CARES   Chicago

Illinois Manufacturing
Foundation   Chicago

Institute for Latino
Progress   Chicago

Jane Addams
Resource Corp.   Chicago

Lincoln Land
Community College   Springfield

North Lawndale
Employment Network   Chicago

Transition Center/Olney
Central College   Olney

West Central Workforce
Development Council,
Inc.   Carlinville

Indiana

East Central
Opportunities, Inc.   Muncie

Indiana State AFL-CIO
Labor Institute for
Training (LIFT)   Indianapolis

Shawnee Trace Workforce
Investment Board   Vincennes

Southern Seven Workforce
Investment Board Inc.   New Albany

United Way of Central
Indiana, Inc.   Indianapolis

Workforce Investment Board
of Southwest Indiana   Evansville

Career Resources, Inc.   Louisville

Louisiana

Delgado Community
College   New Orleans

Lafayette Consolidated
Government Workforce
Development Program   Lafayette

Ouachita Parish Police
Jury, Employment &
Training Office   Monroe

Work Initiative Network,
WIN for St. Tammany   Covington

Massachusetts

Acre Family Day Care
Corporation   Lowell

Berkshire Plastics Network   Pittsfield

Boston Private Industry
Council   Boston

Boston Workforce
Development Coalition   Boston

City Skills, Inc.   Boston

Commonwealth Corporation   Boston

Educational Development
Group/Greater Boston
Hotel Employees Local 26   Boston

Jamaica Plain Neighborhood
Development
Corporation   Jamaica Plain

Job Training & Employment
Corporation   Hyannis

Massachusetts Worker
Education Roundtable   Boston

Metro South/West Regional
Employment Board   Norwood

North Central
Mass. WIB   Leominster

Regional Employment
Board   Springfield

Twin Cities Community
Development Corp.   Fitchburg

Valley Works Career
Center   Lawrence

Western Massachusetts
Precision Institute   W. Springfield

Women in the Building
Trades   Dorchester

Women's Educational
and Industrial Union   Boston

Maryland

Baltimore Workforce
Investment Board/Mayor's
Office of Employment
Development   Baltimore

Frederick Community
College   Frederick

Occupational Training
Center   Cantonsville

St. Louis Regional
Jobs Institute   St. Louis

Susquehanna Workforce
Network, Inc.   Havre de Grace

Western Maryland
Consortium   Hagerstown

Maine

Aroostook/Washington
County Workforce
Investment Board   Caribou

Center for Workplace
Learning   Gorham

Central/Western Maine Workforce Investment Board — Lewiston

Coastal Enterprises, Inc. — Wiscasset

Maine Centers for Women, Work and Community — Augusta

Women Unlimited — Augusta

Michigan

Career Alliance Inc. — Flint

Community Action Agency — Adrian

Flint Area STRIVE — Flint

Flint Genesee Economic Growth Alliance Commerce Center — Flint

Flint Genesee Job Corps Center — Flint

Flint West Village CDC — Flint

Focus:HOPE — Detroit

Goodwill Industries of Greater Grand Rapids — Grandville

Macomb/St. Clair Workforce Development Board — Clinton Township

Thumb Area Michigan Works! — Marlette

Minnesota

Community Employment Partnership — St. Paul

Heartland Community Action Agency, Inc. — Willmar

Meta 5—Displaced Homemaker Program — Brainerd

Ramsey Action Programs, Inc. — St. Paul

Southwest Minnesota WIB — Marshall

Stearns Benton Employment & Training Council — St. Cloud

Twin Cities Rise! — Minneapolis

Women Venture — St. Paul

Workforce Development Inc. — Rochester

Workforce Solutions Ramsey County — N. St. Paul

Missouri

Northeast Missouri Workforce Investment Board, Inc. — Paris

South Central Region/ Ozark Action Inc. — West Plains

Mississippi

Department of Training and Development — Lawrence

IAM CARES — Pascagoula

Tri-County Workforce Alliance — Clarksdale

North Carolina

Capital Area Workforce Development Board — Raleigh

Lumber River Workforce Development Board — Lumberton

Region L Job Training Consortium — Rocky Mount

Southeastern Community College — Whiteville

Sustainable Jobs Development Corporation — Durham

Nebraska

Greater Omaha Workforce Development — Omaha

YWCA Omaha — Omaha

New Hampshire

Strafford County CAC — Farmington

New Jersey

Atlantic Cape Community College — Atlantic City

Essex County College Training Inc. — Newark

Women Rising, Inc. — Jersey City

New Mexico

New Mexico Department
of Labor Job Training
Division — Santa Fe

Northern Area Local
Workforce Development
Board — Santa Fe

Nevada

Nevada Partners/Culinary
Training Academy — Las Vegas

New York

Artisan Baking
Center — Long Island City

Center for Employment
Opportunities — New York

Consortium for Worker
Education — Long Island

Garment Industry
Development Corporation — New York

Cooperative Home Care
Associates — Bronx

La Guardia Community
College — Long Island

Women's Housing and
Economic Development
Corporation — Bronx

Workplace Project — Hempstead

Ohio

CAMP Ohio — Cleveland

Center for Employment
Training — Cleveland

Columbus State Community
College, Community
Education & Workforce
Development — Columbus

Cuyahoga Workforce
Development — Cleveland

Greater Cleveland
Growth Assoc. — Cleveland

Sinclair Community
College — Dayton

Upper Valley JUS Adult
Division — Piqua

WIRE-Net — Cleveland

WSOS Community
Action Commission, Inc. — Fremont

Oklahoma

Office of Workforce
Development — Oklahoma City

Tulsa Workforce
Investment Board — Tulsa

Oregon

Chemeketa Community
College — Salem

Clackamas Community
College — Oregon City

Mt. Hood Community
College — Portland

Region 12 Workforce
Investment Board &
Work-Links — Pendleton

Umpqua Community
College — Roseburg

Worksystems, Inc. — Portland

Pennsylvania

Campus Boulevard
Corporation — Philadelphia

District 1199C Training
& Upgrading Fund — Philadelphia

Home Care Associates — Philadelphia

Lancaster County WIB — Lancaster

Mantec, Inc. — York

Manufacturers
Association of
MidEastern — Pottsville

New Century Careers — Pittsburgh

New Choices/
New Options — Lewistown

North Central WIB — Ridgeway

The Reinvestment
Fund — Philadelphia

Women's Association
for Women's
Alternatives   Swarthmore

Rhode Island
Manufacturing Jewelers
& Suppliers of America   Providence
Providence/Cranston
Workforce Development
Office   Providence
Workforce Partnership
of Greater Rhode
Island   E. Providence

South Carolina
Low County Council
of Governments   Yemassee
Pendleton District
Workforce Investment
Board   Pendleton
Trident Workforce
Investment Board   Charleston

Tennessee
Upper Cumberland
Human Resource Agency   Cookeville
Workforce Investment
Network/City of Memphis   Memphis

Texas
Alamo Community
College District   San Antonio
Brazos Valley Council
of Governments   Bryan
Community Service
Program, AFLCIO   Baytown
Concho Valley Workforce
Development Board   San Angelo
East Texas Council of
Government   Kilgore
Houston Community
College   Houston
North Central Texas
Workforce   Arlington
Project QUEST, Inc.   San Antonio

Texas Engineering
Extension Service   College Station
WorkSource—Gulf Coast
Workforce Board   Houston
Upper Rio Grande
Workforce Development
Board   El Paso
West Central Workforce
Development Board   Abilene
Work Advantage   Fort Worth
WorkSource—Austin
Workforce Development
Board   Austin
WorkSource for Dallas
County   Dallas

Virginia
Laborers—AGC Education
& Training Fund   Alexandria
Norfolk State University   Portsmouth
Opportunity, Inc.   Norfolk
Region 2000 Regional
Commission   Lynchburg

Washington
Clover Park Technical
College   Lakewood
Columbia Basin College   Pasco
Lake Washington
Technical College   Kirkland
Life Skills/Women's
Programs   Spokane
North Seattle
Community College   Seattle
Office of Port JOBS   Seattle
Pioneer Human Services   Seattle
Seattle Jobs Initiative   Seattle
Seattle Youth
Employment Program   Seattle
Shoreline Community
College   Shoreline
Walla Walla Community
College   Walla Walla

| YWCA Seattle King County | Seattle | Wisconsin Regional Training Partnership | Milwaukee |

Wisconsin
Bay Area Workforce Development Board, Inc. — Green Bay
Milwaukee Graphic Arts Institute — Milwaukee
Voces de la Frontera — Milwaukee

West Virginia
USWA/Institute for Career Development — Merrillville
Workforce Investment Board of Kanawha County, Inc. — Charleston

NOTE

1. Workforce development organizations may operate targeted programs in more than one industry. Therefore, the percentages listed here reflect the number of respondents indicating that their organizations currently operate a program in a specific sector, and do not total 100 percent.

REFERENCES

Cancian, Maria, et al. 1999. "The Wisconsin Welfare Leavers' Study, Work, Earnings, and Well-Being After Welfare: What Do We Know?" Chicago: Northwestern University/University of Chicago, Joint Center for Poverty Research.

Conway, Maureen, and Lily Zandniapour. 2000. *Sectoral Employment Development Learning Project Report No. 3: Gaining Ground: The Labor Market Progress of Sectoral Employment Development Programs.* Washington, DC: The Aspen Institute.

Grubb, W. Norton. 1995. "Evaluating Job Training Programs in the United States: Evidence and Explanations." *Training Policy Study No. 17.* Geneva: International Labor Organization.

Kellner, Stephanie. 2000. "Scanning the Field: A Profile of Sector Practitioners Nationwide." Oakland, CA: National Network of Sector Partners/National Economic Development and Law Center.

Rademacher, Ida. 2001. "Measure for Measure: Assessing Traditional and Sectoral Strategies for Workforce Development." Washington, DC: The Aspen Institute.

Riccio J., D. Friedlander, and S. Freedman. 1994. "GAIN: Benefits, Costs, and Three-Year Impacts of a Welfare-to-Work Program." New York: Manpower Demonstration Research Corporation.

5

Workforce Intermediaries: Recent Experience and Implications for Workforce Development

RICHARD McGAHEY

IN THE PAST SEVERAL YEARS, POLICY EXPERTS AND ANALYSTS WHO concentrate on employment and training issues have paid increasing attention to the role of institutions and organizations that provide a variety of brokering activities to connect employers and workers. Although there are a wide variety of activities and institutions involved, these organizations have come to be known as "intermediaries" because they provide services to make markets work more effectively on both the supply and demand sides.[1]

Although it is not necessitated by the concept, "intermediaries" in the context of labor market institutions have become identified with providing assistance to low-wage, low-skilled workers, and linking them to employers. This is the concept of "dual customers"—employers and workers—that underpins much intermediary activity, analysis, and advocacy.[2]

National policy makers are now paying more attention to intermediaries as an increasingly important part of workforce development policy. Fueled in part by the disappointing results and evaluations of mainstream employment and training policies, in part by some noteworthy and well-publicized successful cases, and by a decade of investment from private foundations in program operations and evaluations, workforce intermediaries may be in a position to be a vital element in national employment and training policy. As major legislation that affects employment and training comes before Congress for reauthorization, how to support and foster intermediaries will likely be an important question for lawmakers to consider.

Yet, as with many public policy innovations, the information base of intermediary activity and the knowledge we possess from program evaluation is somewhat fragmented and not fully linked to major employment and training legislation and systems. This chapter reviews the growth of interest in intermediaries during the 1990s, assesses what we know about their effectiveness, and offers suggestions about issues for further program experimentation and analysis.

Existing evaluations of workforce intermediaries suggest real success in improving the economic status of low-skilled workers, and the programs report that the "dual customer" focus has been a critical factor in that success. But the variety of program models and evaluation approaches, while providing rich detail on specific programs, makes it hard to generalize these findings. The next wave of workforce intermediary programs needs to build on the successes and lessons to date in a more systematic fashion, while not losing the innovation and attention to local, specific conditions that are central components of successful workforce intermediaries.

The driving factor for employment and training policy throughout the 1990s was, and remains, the widening earnings gaps across levels of education. These earnings differences are closely associated with levels of education, although industrial change, the decline of labor union membership, weakening of long-term employment relationships, and other factors also have contributed to the stagnation for lower earning cohorts and increasing overall inequality (Ellwood, 2002).

There are a variety of explanations of this problem, and a variety of solutions offered to address it, but providing more effective education and job training has been a core element in many policy proposals.

However, policy proposals in the 1990s concentrated on issues of system governance, credentials, and federalism, not on the specific practices of workforce intermediaries.[3] This focus was combined with ongoing proposals to amend or replace the Job Training Partnership Act (JTPA), which had been criticized for several years as ineffective for workers and unresponsive to private employers. Although the role of Private Industry Councils (PICs) was strengthened under JTPA, the program drew increasing criticism on several grounds, including that of nonresponsiveness to employers.

Program evaluations of JTPA showed partially positive results for some cohorts, and relatively low, although still positive, cost-effectiveness data. But other cohorts, especially male youth, showed no measurable positive impacts, leading to overly sweeping criticisms that "nothing works" in employment and training policy. The overall disappointing results from the JTPA evaluations helped to fuel congressional interest in replacing the program (Heckman, Roselius, and Smith, 1993). JTPA also was criticized on the same dimensions as CETA, being characterized as having a cumbersome bureaucratic structure dominated by elected officials and nonprofit groups and a lack of employer input and engagement.

One of the principal factors driving the current interest in workforce intermediaries comes directly from the issue of effective connections with employers. Exemplary intermediary organizations are seen to effectively serve "dual customers"—both disadvantaged jobseekers and private employers—in ways that other training programs do not. Program evaluations (reviewed below) emphasize the focus on and success with private employers for several workforce intermediary programs.

The emphasis on "dual customers" is now a feature of most discussions of intermediaries. But this articulation emerged from a variety of other concerns and issues. It was fostered during the 1990s by several major program and evaluation efforts funded by national foundations. Reviewing those efforts, and the knowledge they have generated about intermediaries in workforce development, illustrates both the state of current knowledge and the challenges facing the next wave of policy and program development.

WORKFORCE DEVELOPMENT INTERMEDIARIES IN THE 1990S

One of the striking things about the developing interest in workforce intermediaries is how the growing interest was fostered not primarily by federal policies, but by local efforts that were funded and encouraged by private foundations. By and large, these efforts were identified and supported by foundations that had the economic improvement of the disadvantaged as their primary goal. At both a practical level and, increasingly, at a conceptual level, this work grappled with the question of why programs seemed unable to connect disadvantaged workers to good private sector jobs. Each concentration on intermediaries took a different starting place in addressing the problem, but it is striking how much convergence occurred as these efforts went forward, fueled in part by foundation investments in evaluation, assessment, and communication. This section reviews several major efforts during the 1990s that all feed into the current interest in workforce intermediaries. After reviewing the nature and development of these efforts, the following section then reviews what we know from evaluation and research on these programs.

Strengthening Community Development Corporations—Building Bridges

One important early effort that helped fuel the interest in workforce development intermediaries grew out of a Ford Foundation supported project that was rooted in ongoing interest in Community Development Corporations (CDCs). In 1991–92, the foundation supported a team of researchers, led by Bennett Harrison and Marcus Weiss (1995), to "examine the extent and significance of employment training activity within the community economic development movement."

Although many CDCs had been involved with employment and training during the 1970s, their level of participation and interest had flagged during the 1980s, due to a combination of reduced funding, other organizational imperatives, a frustration with the public systems that administered the programs, and a skepticism about the utility of working with for-profit employers. As a result, according to the report published by the foundation, "By the 1990s, most CDCs had little or no experience in this area."

The research team developed detailed case studies on 10 programs around the country, including organizations focused on economic development for specific communities and industries, housing, racial justice, and linkages with public agencies like port authorities. Much of the report sounds familiar themes that reflect the immediate problems facing these organizations, especially a lack of public funding and an unresponsive public bureaucracy that inhibits effective programs by having too many rigid rules and procedures. Given the report's primary focus on CDCs, there also was a major theme about how and when locally based and geographically defined organizations can or should work outside of their own boundaries—in other words, should community based organizations have a major focus on finding jobs for residents outside of their immediate communities, and if so, what is the most effective way to do so?

This concern led the research team to focus on the development of "networks" by successful programs, seeing CDCs as potential hubs or participants in organizing the broad range of services and supports needed to find good jobs for disadvantaged jobseekers, especially when those jobs were located outside of the community or organizational capacity of the CDC. The "network" concept was deepened and articulated in a book by Harrison and Weiss (1998), which presented their original case studies in more depth, added other examples, and addressed a wider range of issues.

By this time, the discussion over workforce intermediaries had progressed a good deal, fueled in part by a set of foundation funded projects that concentrated on community initiatives and on particular sectors of the economy as a means to improve the economic outcomes of disadvantaged workers. There also were two highly influential programs that showed promising results and were important in countering the broad skepticism about the effectiveness of employment and training programs.

Project QUEST and the Center for Employment Training

The case studies by Harrison and Weiss included two programs that showed success in improving the economic well being of low-skilled workers—Project QUEST and the Center for Employment Training (CET). These programs were extensively studied and evaluated, with positive results, encouraging advocates of employment and training programs. But most importantly for the growing discussion of intermediaries, these programs seemed to have developed new and innovative approaches to many problems facing employment and training programs, especially in establishing sustained connections with employers.

Project QUEST in San Antonio, Texas, grew from work done by two Industrial Area Foundation (IAF) projects—Communities Organized for Public Service (COPS) and Metro Alliance. The project, designed in response to continuing difficulties in the San Antonio economy, had goals that included economic improvement for individual workers, but also sought to have an impact on the policy environment in the city and to help revitalize the local economy.[4]

The project had a number of elements that strengthened its effectiveness in the community, including deep involvement with community organizations and continuing ties to political and policy decision makers. But one critical element that stood out was the emphasis on working directly with employers. As Osterman and Lautsch (1996) noted: "What is distinctive about Project QUEST is that it works with employers in identifying likely future needs. When this works well QUEST is functioning as an extension of the firm's human resources department. . . ."

Given the perennial problem of ties with private employers in many employment and training programs, QUEST's combination of strong community ties and meeting employer needs, and the documentation of these ties by independent analysts, drew a good deal of attention from analysts and policy makers. Rather than a training program that was cut off from the needs of private employers, or a community advocacy group that could not work effectively with for-profit employers, QUEST seemed to have "squared the circle," finding a way to serve the workers in their community while meeting employer needs.[5]

The other program that drew attention, for similar reasons, was the Center for Employment Training in San Jose, California. CET was given substantial support by the Rockefeller Foundation. In its various forms, CET had been evaluated by a variety of analysts over two decades and found to have sustained impacts on the employment and earnings of the low-wage workers that worked with the program.

Like QUEST, CET had strong community credibility and ties and many other features that could be found in other strong community organizations. But like QUEST, CET seemed relatively unique in its successful ties to employers, which it achieved through continuous communication with business clients and having business-like activities in its own programs. Edwin Melendez's (1996) case study cited an "institutionalization of the 'employer mentality'" at CET, while also emphasizing its strong community ties and "embededness" in Hispanic politics and culture.

Like QUEST, CET had undergone high-quality evaluation, calling attention to a successful program at a time when skepticism about these programs was the dominant theme in national debates. The Office of the Chief Economist at the U.S. Department of Labor (1995) gave CET a prominent role in the report *What's Working (and What's Not)*, particularly noting the positive impact that CET had on annual earnings for out-of-school youth, a group where most other program evaluations, most notably JTPA, had failed to find any consistent positive impacts.[6]

The evaluations of QUEST and CET gave more shape to the emerging outline of organizations that now are classified as intermediaries. Both programs had strong community ties. They organized a variety of services for their participants, rather than providing a single set of training activities. And, most importantly, they made working with employers a central, conscious part of their mission, going beyond traditional job development and placement services to engage employers on a continuing basis. Finally, they both had aspirations not only to place low-income workers in jobs but also to influence their respective labor markets, hoping to go beyond individual placements and affect public policy and the private labor market.

Sectoral Employment Strategies

Another major stream that feeds into the current interest in intermediaries comes from efforts during the 1990s focusing on industry- and sector-specific programs to assist low-income workers. Supported initially by the

Charles Stewart Mott and Ford Foundations, with additional support from
the Annie E. Casey Foundation, there have been two main demonstration
and research efforts: the Aspen Institute's Sectoral Employment Development Project (SEDLP) and the Sectoral Employment Initiative (SEI), analyzed by Public/Private Ventures.

The logic of sectoral approaches resonates with economic development
policy, arguing that focusing on specific industry concentrations allows targeting of potential employers, gathering of industry and occupation-specific
knowledge, customizing of education and training efforts, and the potential
for career development. Sectoral approaches also make it easier to aggregate
and focus demand, with the possibility that aggregations of both employers
and training institutions could have positive effects on the workforce development system. Like QUEST and CET, sectoral programs have ambitions
that go beyond individual job placements to having an impact on policy and
the operations of the private labor market.

Sectoral approaches for low-waged workers to some extent mimic
processes and institutions in the larger labor market that have been successful. Building and construction trade unions have for many years had
programs that provided training, access to employment, and aggregation of
demand across many small employers.[7] Occupation-specific skill training is
a feature of many private training efforts, with particular growth during the
1990s of information technology related training. Both construction union
and private IT training programs claim good success in providing industry
relevant skills, a system of providing recognized skills for employers

There also are some risks to industry and sectoral targeting. Obviously,
if a targeted industry suffers disproportionate economic losses during cyclical downturns, or structural economic shifts, then workers trained in such
efforts will be at a disadvantage. Leading sectoral programs attempt to antic-
ipate this problem through having access to, or developing, deep knowledge
of the industry, including likely growth trajectories and potential risks.

The Aspen Institute's SEDLP project began with participation from
six organizations in major cities around the country. The programs had
developed in their own local markets and were not predesigned to fit a specific model or intervention. All were programs that came to the attention
of Aspen Institute researchers as they looked in more depth at programs
that held some promise for improving the economic circumstances of low-
wage workers. The six programs concentrated on working with specific
industries, ranging from home healthcare to manufacturing, including the
garment industry and precision metalworking (Clark and Dawson, 1995).[8]

SEDLP was designed from the start as a "learning project," one that
had ongoing research, assessment, and communication as a core goal. The

project published an ongoing series of reports, including research method-ologies and summaries, and case studies of the six projects. The program's strategy was to conduct both qualitative and quantitative evaluation throughout the life of the project, providing feedback from the findings so the participating projects could make use of them. SEDLP found that the projects, taken as a whole, improved labor market outcomes for partici-pants, although many were still facing significant challenges in becoming self-sufficient (Rademacher, 2002).

Although SEDLP began with, and maintained throughout, a primary focus on improving the economic prospects of low-skilled workers, it was more self-conscious about interactions with private sector employers than the work in *Building Bridges*. Employers were primarily considered in their industry or sectoral roles; rather than a generic discussion of "employers," SEDLP's analysis stressed the specificity of employers in particular sectors.

In 1998 the Mott Foundation launched a second round of sectorally focused efforts. The Sectoral Employment Initiative involves 10 organiza-tions around the country, with two approaches to improving labor market outcomes for low-skilled workers: working on particular sectors through improved training and close work with employers and trying to improve the quality of low-wage jobs.

SEI has involved several organizations that have been active in workforce development and community development, but that have not had a specific sectoral focus in their prior work. This outreach is part of a conscious strat-egy to build on the lessons from the SEDLP, and to see if the lessons learned from that project can be adapted to other organizations. As with the SEDLP, the SEI has built into it an assessment, evaluation, and reporting strategy, car-ried out in this case by Public/Private Ventures (Elliott et al., 2001).

The theme of job quality has become increasingly more important as the discussion of workforce intermediaries has unfolded. Many of the jobs available to low-skilled workers are low paying, often without healthcare, retirement, or other benefits, and may offer relatively little prospect for advancement. As the objective of the foundation supported efforts dis-cussed here ultimately is to improve the economic condition of low-income workers and their families, the issue of job quality has taken on a more important dimension.[9]

Approaches to improving job quality include better training, working with employers to reduce turnover, providing improved childcare and other supports to workers, and participating in policy debates at the local and state levels. The conscious engagement with policy debates also reflects another goal that has become more articulated in the intermediary discussion—having an impact on the training system, both by providing examples of promising or best practices, and by engaging more directly to identify laws, regulations, and institutional practices that create barriers to increasing the well being of low-income workers.

This goal may seem like a large burden to place upon programs that already are struggling with carrying out their day-to-day mission, and that face the many problems that confront nonprofit organizations in effective daily operation. But it often is a goal of the programs themselves, who see legal, policy, and practice barriers as making their mission more difficult to achieve. This focus also is of significant interest to the foundations that have invested in workforce development; in their view, without system change, programs and low-income people will continue to face unnecessary barriers that can block their economic advancement, even when they work with exemplary programs.

Community Focus and System Change

In 1995, as the sectoral initiatives described above were being launched, the Annie E. Casey Foundation embarked on an ambitious eight-year $30 million effort in six cities to assist low-income residents of urban areas. The Jobs Initiative seeks to find ways for these low-income residents to get jobs that can sustain them and their families above poverty. In order to achieve this goal, the foundation sought to develop and implement "strategies that cut across welfare, job training, education, human services, and economic development systems," that would "necessitate changes in the way employers recruit and supervise workers," and that would result in "modifications in the way work is structured and compensated" (Fleischer, 2001).

These ambitious goals derived from an analysis that saw persistent poverty rooted in the regular structure, operation, and policies of urban labor markets. The goal is not only to improve labor market outcomes for individuals and their families, but, by developing effective strategies for that goal, to provide the basis for changes in public policy and employer practices that will help improve conditions for all low-income workers in a city, not just for the program participants.

As with the sectoral strategies, monitoring and reporting on progress, data analysis, and evaluation were built into the project from the start. Findings from the analyses are provided to the sites, so they can improve their practice. As with the sectoral projects, the findings from the Jobs Initiative are communicated in a series of reports that go to researchers, policy makers, foundations, employers, community organizations, unions, and others with an interest in economic advancement for low-income workers.[10]

Like the sectoral programs, QUEST, and CET, the Jobs Initiative views working effectively with private employers as a core element. A recent report from the Casey Foundation states this as one "core principle" of the initiative: "Employers and disadvantaged jobseekers are equal participants" (Fleischer, 2001). Like the sectoral efforts, Jobs Initiative sites developed knowledge about specific industry needs and economic conditions, in order to work more effectively with their local employers.

As with many of the other programs reviewed here, many of the employers that the Initiative works with are small or medium sized. The competitive pressures in their industries, and their size, mean that they are necessarily somewhat reactive in their human resource policies and training and education (Abt Associates Inc. and the New School for Social Research, 1999).

Unlike the sectoral initiatives, the Jobs Initiative did not identify sectors in advance, and did not always turn to existing organizations to implement the program. Qualifying for the program required a strong and sustainable commitment to the ambitious goals of the initiative, and the cities and organizations that ultimately were selected represented a combination of existing organizations and new ones.

There is a good deal of variation among the six sites, which was a deliberate design feature of the initiative. By picking diverse cities with varying economic conditions and industry composition, and by stressing the necessity of community involvement in the definition of problems and the identification of solutions, this type of variation was ensured. Keeping core operating principles in view while encouraging local responsiveness and variation creates challenges for analysis and reporting, and the foundation simultaneously invested in a comprehensive evaluation, with a series of reports on different topics of importance.

The Jobs Initiative, like sectoral programs, and like CET and Project QUEST, has several distinctive features, especially the focus on employers as core participants and as critical customers of workforce development efforts. This theme continued to emerge with more and more clarity during the 1990s. The focus was driven in part by the repeated failures of earlier workforce development programs to engage private sector firms on a sustained basis, but also from the practical experiences of the successful organizations that seemed to differ qualitatively from earlier employment and training programs.

Employer Organizations as Intermediaries

The growing focus on the importance of private sector firms and organizations for the success of workforce development efforts is underscored in the Workforce Innovation Networks (WINs) project. A partnership among the workforce centers of two major private sector employer organizations, the U.S. Chamber of Commerce (USCOC) and the National Association of Manufacturers (NAM), and Jobs for the Future, WINs started in 1998 with funding from the Ford Foundation and now receives additional support from the Casey and MacArthur Foundations.

WINs shares many of the same goals and principles as other intermediary projects—improving the economic position of low-skilled workers, seeing employers and workers as "dual customers," and an interest in policy and system change. But it is distinguished by the central role of national employer associations, in partnership with a national nonprofit organization. Of the various intermediary projects discussed here, WINs goes most directly to issues of private sector employer needs.

However, it did not immediately go to employers in specific local markets, but rather started with national organizations of employers, who have thousands of affiliates around the country. During the 1990s, as the nation experienced the tightest labor markets in several decades, finding and retaining productive employees became a major concern for private sector firms. The pressure was especially acute for smaller firms, as labor force participation rose to historic highs while unemployment fell to the lowest sustained level since the 1960s.

In large part, the establishment of workforce development centers at NAM and the USCOC derives from their nature as membership organizations. These employer associations depend on dues from members for their operation and existence, and if their services are not responsive to member demands, they will not be sustained. As employers increasingly stressed their problems in the labor market, both business organizations developed increasingly sophisticated workforce development centers.[11]

The other unique aspect of the WINs partnership is the pairing of the business organizations with Jobs for the Future (JFF), a nonprofit whose mission is to improve the job and economic prospects of low-income workers. This combination of access to employer organizations with a partner whose focus is on low-income workers was important in attracting Ford Foundation funding and later support from the Casey and MacArthur Foundations.

WINs is necessarily a long-run proposition. The business organizations cannot command their local affiliates; because of their nature as membership organizations, they need to respond to member needs. The early phases of WINs required some experimentation and rethinking of the different roles for the partners. Again, like the sectoral programs and the Jobs Initiative, the foundation funding and goals for WINs included evaluation and research to produce lessons beyond the immediate program.

The WINs partners developed a complex, multilayered strategy that includes "deepening," "broadening," and "research and development (R&D)" activities. "Deepening" involves working with a small number of sites around the country on specific activities aimed at improving labor market operations for employers and labor market outcomes for low-income workers. "Broadening" includes using communication and other methods to encourage improvement in workforce development for the larger group of affiliates that do not receive "deepening" services. And the "R&D" work involves producing materials that are meant to be useful to employers and others seeking to carry out effective "dual customer" strategies.

Like the other efforts discussed here, WINs has a goal of not only improving the economic position of low-income workers and of private sector firms, but seeks to have an impact on the workforce development system and on employer human resource practices. This focus on system issues and the desire to influence changes parallels the concern in the sectoral and community efforts that views system and policy issues as barriers to more effective and sustained achievement of the project's economic goals.

The emergence of a vigorous set of programs and an emerging consensus on principles is somewhat remarkable, especially considering that the intermediaries movement has received almost no support from the federal government. Instead, the emergence and current definition of workforce intermediaries was supported in the main by private foundations, which invested substantial time and resources in the development and evaluation of these programs.

Given the growing policy interest, it is useful to step back and consider what the state of knowledge actually is about workforce intermediaries, as the knowledge base is drawn from a very diverse group of projects and from a relatively small number of case studies. The next section reviews what we know about intermediary effectiveness and what remains unanswered. Following that discussion, the chapter concludes by identifying questions and concerns for the next wave of policy development and research on these issues.

What Do We Know about Intermediary Effectiveness?

The foundation supported work that provides the basis for the current interest in workforce intermediaries also has supported research, analysis, and evaluation. In several cases, as noted above, positive evaluations helped attract the interest of other funders and policy makers. There is a rich literature of case studies of different intermediary organizations and projects, and sometimes different case studies and analyses of the same organization at different points in time, or for different aspects of their programs.[12]

The intermediary projects also sought to assess the impact of the programs on the economic and labor market outcomes for program participants. A central goal of all the initiatives discussed above is improving the economic well being of low-income people and their families. Helping the labor market to work more efficiently and effectively for employers is, for these projects, an important means, but not the end goal.

The outcome data for participants, reviewed below, are generally positive. But the varying nature of the programs, their location in different cities, and the differing economic conditions in which they operate all make it necessary to approach the data with caution. And the qualitative work from the projects is very rich, with well thought out case studies, research reports, ethnographies, and other approaches to analyzing, documenting, and capturing program issues. But, perhaps even more so than with the qualitative work, the very diversity and richness of the information makes it difficult to generalize about results. Both the quantitative and qualitative results are reviewed below.

Impacts on Program Participants

The Aspen Institute's SEDLP conducted a three-year longitudinal survey of participants in the sectoral program, which collected data at four points in time: a baseline at entry into training, 90 days after the end of training, one year after the end, and two years after the end. Like all of the analyses reviewed here, the study did not employ an experimental design or a full comparison group analysis.[13] Rather, the study used a quasi-experimental approach, which they label "reflexive control," using program participants' baseline characteristics as the basis of comparison for program effects.[14] The sample was designed to have the sample cohort reflect the overall characteristics of the program participants. As with many longitudinal studies, the sample deteriorated over time, to 74 percent of the baseline after one year and 51 percent of the baseline after two years (Zandniapour, 2000).

The findings showed significant gains for participants. One year after training, reported average annual earnings increased by $7,203, and hourly wages were up by 20 percent over the baseline period. Ninety-four percent worked at some point during the year, and 55 percent worked for the entire year, a gain of 32 points from the baseline. Increases were noted in job benefits as well, including access to healthcare (from 50 to 78 percent) and paid vacation (from 44 to 73 percent).

The findings for the sample at two years after training completion also were positive. Median earnings were up 24 percent over the first post program year, with average hourly earnings increasing by 31 percent over the entire two-year period. Because the time period studied was during a major economic expansion with record low unemployment, the researchers compared wage growth for the sample to wage growth for the 30th percentile or below for hourly wages, which grew for all workers by 7.9 percent during the same period (Zandniapour and Conway, 2002).

The second wave of sectoral projects, the SEI, has not finished at the time of this writing. But a September 2001 report by Public/Private Ventures presents initial findings on various aspects of employment, although the researchers note that the programs had very differential rates of start up and recruitment, so that aggregating the data has to be taken cautiously (Elliott et al., 2001).

Seven of the ten SEI sites provided training as the centerpiece of their programs. In the first two years, the seven sites had enrolled 788 participants. Across the seven programs, 43 percent graduated, and 10 percent were still in the program at the time of the analysis. Graduation rates among the programs ranged from 12 percent to 93 percent, underscoring the variation in start up and operations and very possibly differences in the background of participants at different sites. For those graduating, job placement rates were very high, from a low of 64 percent to a high of 97 percent, with an average of 84 percent. Prior to program entry, more than half of the participants were unemployed for at least six months of the previous two years, and 36 percent of them had been unemployed for one year or more.

Wages for program graduates showed a positive gain as well. The median starting wage for graduates was $8.50 per hour, compared to a median wage of $7.00 per hour at the last job held prior to program entry. Median wages for graduates, however, were quite dispersed across the programs, ranging from $5.75 to $11.50 per hour, reflecting the particular sectors they worked in, along with regional economic differences. Workers trained in information technology and manufacturing tended to earn the highest wages.

The 1996 evaluation of Project QUEST found similar positive outcomes. The researchers attempted to contact all 825 people who had participated in the program up to the time of the survey, and completed interviews with 66 percent. Some apparent selection bias appeared, with the final sample being somewhat skewed toward current program participants, with more positive terminations and higher levels of people with some college. As the researchers note, this sample composition "probably leads to a somewhat more positive picture" of post program outcomes, although they also note that "the differences are not great." And the baseline data are drawn from a census of all 825 participants, allowing a clear picture of the initial characteristics of the QUEST participants (Osterman and Lautsch, 1996).

QUEST participants increased their employment substantially after the program, going from slightly less than half working prior to the program to 71 percent working afterwards, with another 10.6 percent in school or training. Wages were harder to compute, due to the composition of the sample and the program database, but wages were computed in several different ways to account for this problem. These estimates ranged from an increase in hourly wages between $1.36 and $2.42 an hour. Combined with a higher probability of employment, the analysis estimated that annual earnings increased for participants between $4,923 and $7,457. The impact on hourly wages is especially noteworthy; as the authors note, "other job training programs often achieve their gains [in earnings] by increasing hours worked but not wages."

Data from the Jobs Initiative, as with the other intermediary programs reviewed here, show positive results. Overall, for those placed in jobs through the initiative, the average placement wage was $9.13 per hour. The initiative aims to put people into jobs with the possibility of advancement, and the "retention wage" for those working across the different sites was $9.66. The wages of participants continued to increase after their first job, on average to around $2.00 an hour more than they earned prior to the program, with an estimated annual gain of about $4,000 for full-time workers (Abt Associates Inc. and New School University, 2000).

Over 83 percent of participants had access to health insurance after they were placed, compared to 32 percent prior to the program, although the health coverage only included the family slightly less than half of the time. Job retention rates for participants as a whole were 64 percent at six months and 54 percent at one year after placement. However, as with other initiatives reviewed here, these averages cover a wide range of particular experiences, with several projects in different cities showing one-year retention rates ranging from 65 to 83 percent.

The initiative consciously involves a number of different employment strategies, again making it a rich source of information, but with the consequence that average numbers can obscure diverse approaches and outcomes. For example, in four cases of different employment strategies, ranging from rapid attachment to long-term job training, wage increases ranged from 6.9 percent to 40.2 percent, and one-year retention rates ranged from 34 percent to 78 percent (Fleischer, 2001).

The research on the initiative also has examined the goal of getting low-income families out of poverty. "Living wage" standards were estimated for the different sites, and wages for the participants were compared to them.[15] (The data do not have information on other earners in the household, so it may be that households were making more progress against this benchmark than individual wages alone might indicate.) The data indicate that "single adults receiving the average . . . retention wage in their city would be earning close to or above the living wage standard. . . ." Figures for larger households, assuming only one earner, would tend to fall short of that standard.

This brief summary does not cover many of the more detailed issues analyzed for each program and initiative. But it is clear that, even with the limitations on the data, the variations introduced by differences in economic sectors, regional economies, and program models, there have been encouraging economic results for individual participants in these different programs.

However, as the research reports note, many of these analyses and programs were conducted during the very tight labor markets that persisted into 2000, and the recession and economic slowdown in the American economy since that time could well have eroded these gains. But while understanding the constraints on interpretation of the data, and the possibility of negative impacts from the business cycle, the evidence does suggest that the Jobs Initiative, like the other programs reviewed here, has shown positive gains in employment and earnings for low-income, low-skilled program participants.

The employment and earnings gains documented in these programs—the sectoral initiatives, Project QUEST, CET, and the Jobs Initiative—are one of the principal reasons that policy makers, analysts, and others have become interested in workforce intermediaries.[16] In a climate that is very skeptical about the utility of training programs, these varied efforts seem to have developed the ability to assist low-income workers in making significant improvements in their economic situations.

However, the programs themselves, and the assessments of them, do not attribute these gains only to increased human capital among participants. Central to all of the programs above, and to the "dual customer" perspective, is another goal—building ongoing, meaningful connections with private employers, with the hopes that such work will provide the basis for changes in public policy and labor market operations. For the programs all theorize that, in the absence of those goals, low-income workers will continue to struggle, and individual programs will operate against a backdrop of negative forces that undermine their mission.

Connections with Private Sector Employers

All of the efforts reviewed here stress the importance of ongoing, effective connections with private sector employers. And all would attribute a good deal of their success for participants to these connections. The term "dual customer" is now common parlance among these and similar programs, underscoring that private employers and low-income workers are equally important "customers," if for no other reason than job placement and retention and economic advancement strategies must take place largely in the private sector. The phrase "employer driven" also is common, meaning ". . . valuing employers as an integral part of program design and operation," although the programs also look to employers to recognize and reward skill development and to make jobs easier to obtain and hold, and more rewarding, for these workers (Giloth, 2000).

In itself, a rhetorical stress on the need for private sector involvement is nothing new. All employment and training programs invoke this goal. The first Private Industry Councils were begun under CETA, not JTPA. Their role was strengthened in JTPA, and the private sector role in system governance was further increased under WIA. The *America's Choice* report looked to the private sector to guide development of skill standards, direct (and perhaps operate) local labor market boards, lead school-to-work programs, and the like.

However, all of these efforts to engage the private sector generally are seen to have failed.[17] And the emerging intermediaries movement addresses the private sector question differently. Rather than stressing issues of system governance—who is on the PIC (or its successor, the Workforce Investment Board, or WIB), what are its powers, should business leaders engage at the local or state level, what is the role of industry certifications— the programs described here concentrate on firms and specific industries as customers of the training, seeking a detailed understanding of employer needs and building ongoing relationships to facilitate successful placement, retention, and advancement of low-income workers. Of course, governance issues are very important, but the emerging intermediaries have built up from specific employer needs and experiences, rather than stressing a top-down, governance driven approach that has yielded limited results.

In addition to the quantitative outcomes documented for program participants, most of the analyses of the sectoral, community, and employer intermediary projects look at the impact on employers of the different programs. However, virtually all of this analysis is qualitative, based on case studies. In general, specific quantitative outcome measures of impact for employers have not been gathered, and the qualitative data have not been combined or integrated with the quantitative outcome data.

The case studies provide a rich amount of detail, which strengthens the case that these intermediary programs treat employers as true "dual customers" and that participant success is tied in part to the programs' adoption of this perspective. For example, the SEDLP analyses include specific case studies on all six of the participating programs. Those studies analyze each specific program in turn and also are used to consider crosscutting issues for the initiative.

Given the SEDLP's focus on changing employment dynamics in industry sectors, and in regional labor markets, it is perhaps not surprising that relatively little discussion is presented on specific employer interactions. Each of the case studies shows that the programs have worked effectively with various employers in their target sector, but the details of those interactions are not discussed in a great deal of detail. Specific examples from case studies are used to support conclusions about the impact of the programs on changing "how the targeted labor market trains, recruits, hires, compensates, or promotes low-income individuals" (Rademacher, 2002).

These goals, which are similar to those set by the other programs under discussion, are quite ambitious, and the progress of the programs in achieving them is presented by describing highly specific activities and promising practices. But there is relatively little presented in the way of measuring or validating the progress toward system goals, as distinguished from individual examples of success. Although the researchers carried out a variety of interviews with employers, the material presented in the final case studies is relatively sparse and relies fairly heavily on the program's own accounts of their work with employers.[18] The positive outcome data for participants, and the researchers' documentation of program operations and focus on employer issues, help to buttress their conclusions about the value to employers, but detailed discussion of employer issues is not a central focus of the reports.

Similarly, the Osterman and Lauch evaluation of Project QUEST spends relatively little time on specific employer issues, discussing them primarily in a chapter on "Institutional Change," where employer issues are analyzed along with community college issues. Of course, QUEST had a central focus on making training providers more responsive to both their participants' needs, and to employers, so this focus reflects the project's own goals. Like much of the case study work on other projects, this analysis uses qualitative interviews with employers to validate interviews with program staff and participants, to provide a context for the outcome studies, and to provide some assessment of the program's reaching its stated goal of working effectively with employers, and changing the labor market.

The most detailed analysis of employer issues was carried out as part of the ongoing evaluation of the Jobs Initiative. A report by Abt Associates Inc. and the New School for Social Research (1999) examined the database that Jobs Initiative sites keep on employers where they made program placements. MIS limitations in some of the programs means that the data are somewhat underreported, and also does not incorporate the role of employers who worked with sites in an advisory or planning capacity but had not yet employed any participants.

The database provides a more detailed understanding of the employers who hired Jobs Initiative participants as of March 1999. Not surprisingly, given the design of the initiative and the concentration on community based employment, most of them were small—54 percent had 50 or fewer employees, spread across a variety of sectors that reflect regional labor markets and the specific strategies chosen by each site. Given the size of the firms, it is not surprising that 90 percent of the firms hired from one to three participants

Perhaps more than other intermediary projects, the Jobs Initiative sought to involve employers in a variety of ongoing roles. Most of the sites had private employers on their governing boards or established advisory committees to work with the sites. Employer involvement carried over to project design and operation, although in varying intensity among the different sites. As with other intermediary projects, employer input was particularly sought in the development of training programs and curricula, partly in hopes that the employers would help provide leverage with training providers like community colleges, who were not always seen as responsive to the needs of either low-wage workers or small employers. Similar input was sought, but obtained with less consistency, on providing support services necessary to employment, like childcare, transportation, counseling and support, and the like.

Finally, like other projects, the Jobs Initiative has a goal of systems change, and employer involvement is seen as critical to that goal, both to legitimate the suggested system changes and to provide political support for them. The most tangible impact to date has been with training providers, as it has been with other projects.

The most distinctive part of the Jobs Initiative report on employers is the section on employer satisfaction. Again, the basis for this analysis is qualitative interviews, linked to specific theories of how the programs would seek to meet employer needs. Not surprisingly, employers were especially interested in having a larger pool of qualified job candidates with both "hard" (occupation or industry-specific) and "soft" (teamwork, attitudinal, and communication) skills.[19] Small firms, like those who hire most

Jobs Initiatives participants, and like many firms where low-wage workers seek and find jobs, do not have elaborate human resource (or often any specific) departments and rely mostly on informal word-of-mouth or other recruiting mechanisms.

"Qualified" applicants did not just mean occupation-specific skills. Employers were very concerned about finding drug-free candidates, especially for jobs that involved power tools or equipment, access to cash or valuables, or other similar factors. This concern mapped very closely to concerns about crime and criminal records. As a result, many of the sites built a drug screening and drug education component into their programs. Finally, the Jobs Initiative sites in several cases conducted candidate screening and organizing of support service, functions that often were beyond the abilities of any single small firm.

Employers generally reported satisfaction from their involvement with the Jobs Initiative, although the small number of participants hired at any one site and the somewhat self-selected nature of the employers (who had hired participants) caution against overgeneralization of these results. Of course, firms who hire several participants, and especially those who return to the sites to hire multiple times, are very good market indicators of customer satisfaction.

The sites, like others projects, have emphasized not only hiring but also retention. Given the difficulties that these employers cite in finding and retaining good employees, sites have found it surprising "how much businesses spend on hiring and how little they think about retention, especially for entry-level workers" (Fleischer, 2001). But the reports from the Jobs Initiative document in detail that the sites are "highly oriented to businesses as both critical customers and powerful allies" (Abt Associates Inc. and the New School for Social Research, 1999) and that they see this attention to business needs as vital to any sustained success that they may achieve.

The most explicit intermediary project oriented to the private sector, WINs, has a different strategy for reaching this goal. Two of the three WINs partners are the workforce development affiliates of major national employer organizations. Working with Jobs for the Future, these employer partners first spent time in developing a strategy and working out their respective roles and then seeking to work with their own affiliates. The partners have a four-part strategy: "deepening" (working with specific sites to develop and provide more effective programs), "broadening" (spreading the message about workforce development through their affiliates), research and development (developing materials that can be useful to employers and others), and public policy (highlighting issues at the local, state, and national level with suggestions for change and reform).

Two unique aspects of WINs are the involvement of the national employer associations and the active partnership with a nonprofit focused on low-income workers. It was felt that the involvement of the national associations would increase the project's credibility and also would facilitate the recruiting of private employers. Also, by putting private sector employer associations at the center of the project, WINs attempts to deal with the oft-leveled criticism that employment and training programs are not responsive to employer needs.

The project was initially slower to get started than anticipated, in large part because of the need to build trust and understanding among the partners. Although all three organizations shared broad common goals, they had not anticipated the time and energy involved in moving to an operational level that reflected a deep understanding of the others' needs.[20] The approach adopted by WINs was to first build trust and working relationships with employer groups in specific sites, and move from there to outreach, training, and placement of low-skilled workers. In this way, the project inverted the development sequence of the sectoral and Jobs Initiatives projects, which began with community based groups who targeted specific employment sectors.

The assessment of WINs' first phase showed considerable progress in winning the trust of employers and providing useful services. WINs local sites used a business oriented vocabulary and presented the program as an outgrowth of activities, or another service, that the national business organizations wanted to provide to their members. The national business organizations have consistently stressed that they must service their local affiliates for the project to succeed as they are membership driven organizations that cannot impose programs or models on local affiliates. And at the national level, workforce development (especially for low-skilled workers) can only at best be one of a variety of activities and interests of large, multi-issue organizations like the National Association of Manufacturers or the U.S. Chamber of Commerce.

By and large, the first phase of WINs succeeded in clarifying the working relationship among the national partners and in building relationships and providing services to local affiliates. But the first phase had little direct concrete results to show in terms of outcomes for low-wage workers. This was consistent with the project's design, and the succeeding phases of WINs are working towards that goal, along with an emphasis on public policy and R&D issues. The challenge, as noted in the first evaluation report, "remains in meeting the dual goals of WINs: more effective services to private sector employers, along with improved labor market outcomes for low-wage workers" (McGahey et al., 2001).

THE NEXT WAVE OF INTERMEDIARY
PROJECTS AND RESEARCH

To date, the projects that have come to be clustered under the heading of "workforce intermediaries" have shown a good deal of promise in addressing the employment needs of low-skilled workers. Outcome measures, where they have been gathered, are positive, especially when benchmarked against the impacts of other programs with similar populations. The engagement of private sector employers, a perennial problem for public employment and training programs, is a central design feature of these projects, and they have all shown the ability and commitment to work effectively, on a sustained basis, with private sector firms.

But there are limits to this promising picture, limits that should be addressed in the next wave of projects, in order to refine the approach more clearly and build lessons for broader, more effective programs and public policy. This chapter concludes with outlining several issues that are important in order to leverage the promising experience to date with these innovative labor market programs.

Going to Scale

All of the programs reviewed here operate on a relatively small scale. That is appropriate for their nature as demonstration and knowledge building projects, but there is a long history in the employment and training field of individual innovative programs that never reached scale on their own or had a major influence on public policy and the larger world of labor market programs.[21] Getting to scale may threaten the very innovation that characterizes these programs and also would be very costly. Most of these programs are more expensive on a per-participant basis than other public employment and training programs. Public funds will likely be necessary in order to achieve scale, along with more aggressive exploration of how private firms themselves might pay for services.

Defining the Approach

The first wave of intermediary projects learned a good deal about what makes the programs successful. Jobs for the Future (2001) has provided a good summary of five core activities:

- Convening and supporting employers.
- Brokering and providing services.

- Improving the delivery of education training and supportive services.
- Conducting research and development.
- Improving the workforce development system.

But, as this chapter has documented, these five broad activities encompass a wide range of specific activities. For public funding to be involved on a large and continuing scale, more specific definitions of activities are likely to be necessary for program accountability, analysis, and guidance to practitioners. Getting this specificity without stifling the entrepreneurial and innovative spirit of these programs will be a challenge.

Research on Linking Outcomes to Practice

Expanded public funding, and more systemic guidance to practitioners, also will call for research and assessment that more clearly examines the linkage between specific program activities and labor market outcomes for employers and low-skilled workers. The foundations that have fostered these innovative efforts also have invested in evaluation, assessment, and communication, and any expansion of scale needs to continue with similar investments. Given the variety of labor market needs, local economic conditions, and different populations and communities, establishing a single program model that could be the subject of a classic experimental evaluation is unlikely, at least in the next several years.[22] But more rigorous attempts to link quantitative outcome measures with more systemic analysis of qualitative data, and feeding the lessons from those analyses back to practitioners and policy makers, will be needed. Local sites and programs also must do a better job of keeping good data, both for their own management purposes and for assessment that is properly grounded.

Changing the Labor Market as a Central Goal

All of the projects reviewed here want not only to assist low-skilled workers, but to do so by better meeting employer needs. They also all, in one form or another, have the goal of changing labor markets themselves: "Changing how labor markets function rather than individual jobs projects alone promises the scale, sustainability, and structural changes needed to create and access good jobs and career ladders for low-income jobseekers" (Giloth, 2000). This is a hard premise to argue with, but a daunting goal for these or similar projects. Labor market operations in this discourse cover not only labor market information, training, hiring, retention, and advancement, but also the internal structure of firms and their reward systems. In many projects, this goal overlaps onto a desire to change the way that various public systems, including educational institutions, labor market agencies, and others, operate by affecting laws, regulations, and daily operational practice and culture. To fully realize the vision of many of these projects, these changes ultimately are necessary but quite daunting. And expanding to scale, especially with public funds, may create some tension around these larger system change goals. Aligning other more specific goals for workforce intermediaries within this broad, encompassing framework is likely to be necessary for building practice and for working with public sector funding or for leveraging private sector dollars.

Retaining the Focus on Low-Skilled Workers

Another challenge is to some extent the inverse of the previous one. All of the intermediary projects have as a core goal the sustained improvement of the economic position of low-skilled workers and their families. Holding this goal as a central objective, while still meeting the immediate needs of private sector employers for a well trained, reliable, and tractable labor force, may present major challenges. It is no criticism of private sector employers to state that, in the main, they seek the most reliable and productive labor force at the least cost to the enterprise. Most of the organizations in the first wave of programs have a deep commitment to the goal of aiding low-income workers, and the foundations that funded these projects saw this as the central reason for their involvement. As labor market intermediary programs move to a larger scale, holding on to this commitment with a wider range of projects and programs will be in a creative tension with the objective of meeting private sector needs.

What Institutions Serve as Intermediaries?

The projects discussed here concentrate on nonprofit organizations and employer associations as workforce intermediaries. These projects have been at the center of the emerging discussion over these policies, and also have the largest investment in evaluation and communication. However, intermediaries are defined not *a priori* by their institutional character, but by the range of activities they undertake, and there are several other types of institutions that can play this role. For example, community colleges, which are central in providing training for many of the projects discussed here, also can take on a wider range of functions and act as an intermediary. As mentioned above, labor unions, especially in the building trades, have a long history of providing training, aggregating demand, and brokering jobs with employers; unions in recent years have expanded these approaches to other industries, especially in hospitality and healthcare. Perhaps more controversially, the establishment of One Stop Centers, either directly operated by government or contracted by them, has been viewed by some as an expansion of the intermediary role. And finally, for-profit temporary services firms make their living by brokering employees to employers, staying in touch with employer demand, and providing training and other services to workers. As the next wave of intermediary experimentation proceeds, considering these and other institutions will need to be part of the discussion.

Sustainability over the Business Cycle

Finally, as the beginning years of this decade have underscored, sustaining these (or other) innovative labor market programs over the business cycle will be a challenge. It is no accident that these programs developed during some of the tightest labor markets experienced in decades, and many programs report more difficulty in making job placements, much less sustaining the retention and advancement of program participants. The long-term demographics of the U.S. labor force provide a structural basis for the need for innovative labor market programs; the native-born workforce grew 44 percent in the last 20 years, but is projected not to grow at all in the next 20 (Ellwood, 2001). But businesses, government, and programs in the U.S. are very sensitive to the economic cycle, and it will be hard to develop and sustain innovative programs over that cycle, especially when the per-participant costs are higher than other programs.

The development of these innovative programs for low-skilled workers, fostered by foundation investments and carried out by community and business innovators around the country, has created a good deal of interest among policy analysts and public officials seeking to provide more effective labor market services and outcomes for businesses and low-income workers. The next wave of experimentation and innovation is likely to be just as challenging.

NOTES

Acknowledgments: Dr. McGahey thanks Scott Hebert and Robert Giloth for helpful comments and Richard Giragosian for research assistance.

1. The term "intermediaries" has been in common use in financial markets and analyses of those markets for some time. Financial intermediaries are organizations that flesh out a chain of activities that link supply and demand, working to

overcome barriers to smooth and efficient operation of markets. See McGahey et al. (1990).

2. For example, for-profit temporary employment agencies, whose core business is linking workers and employers, have grown significantly during the 1990s. But they usually are not discussed in the debate over workforce intermediaries. Following the definitions in this volume, "workforce intermediaries" is used in this chapter as dual customer, high-performing partnerships with a focus on low-skilled workers.

3. One highly influential report, *America's Choice: High Skills or Low Wages*, focused on improving formal linkages between school and work, creating more transparent and employer relevant skill standards and credentials, proposals to finance expanded training through "pay or play" tax policy, empowering customer choice in the selection of job training programs, and governance issues for the existing public system (National Center on Education and the Economy, 1990). There was attention to improving responsiveness to private sector needs, principally through governance changes at the state and local level and improved labor market information, not through the practices that have been developed by workforce intermediaries.

4. There are several pieces on Project QUEST; an important document that called attention to the project is Osterman and Lautsch (1996). For later developments in Project QUEST, see Rademacher, Bear, and Conway (2001).

5. The late Jim Lund, director of Project Quest, once told the author in the early 1990s that QUEST success was due to "political support in the community and a focus on employers as customers." Although pairing these issues is now more common in workforce development discussions, at the time it represented a striking change from many earlier perspectives on private sector firms and community economic development.

6. The title of this report underscores the defensive posture that advocates of employment and training programs were in throughout the 1990s.

7. In the view of critics, some union programs also have restricted access to employment.

8. The variety of programs studied in this and other work discussed in this chapter both illustrates the creativity and variation in this field and underscores the challenge in drawing systematic conclusions.

9. Job quality issues also have been a major concern in the debate over the effects of welfare reform.

10. The sustained focus by the foundations on evaluation, reporting, and communication that characterizes these projects has been a critical factor in the rapid development of the discussion on workforce intermediaries.

11. The rise of such centers was not automatic; in complex, multipurpose organizations like NAM and the USCOC, there are constant demands for resources and attention on a very wide range of issues, ranging from tax policy to international trade to environmental regulation. The creation and growth of these centers in this institutional context is one of the most interesting developments in the WINs initiative. See McGahey et al. (2001).

12. This is especially true for CET, which has been evaluated at different points in its lifetime, and with Project QUEST, which has undergone several independent evaluations at different times and appears as a participant or a case study in more than one intermediary project or analysis.

13. The varying nature of the interventions—geographically, sectorally, and conceptually—and the deliberate feedback of research findings to change program activities, along with costs, would militate against experimental designs for these analyses.

14. The methodology is often called "reflexive comparison." It can produce sometimes confounding effects when used over an extensive time period to assess program impacts, as the normal course of development or other time based factors may account for any observed variation. The researchers did have repeated measurement, rather than one single data point, and the method is often used for detecting either large, "gross" effects, or the lack thereof, rather than specific refined estimates.

15. These standards estimated costs for housing, childcare, food, transportation, healthcare, and other expenses, and then computed the after-tax wage levels required to meet these needs.

16. At this writing, WINs does not have measured outcomes for program participants, and they did not expect to at this point in their development.

17. Policy debates paint with a broad brush, and the disappointment about private sector involvement in employment and training downplays successful efforts like the Boston Compact, welfare-to-work partnerships with private sector firms, and union-industry partnerships in healthcare, hospitality, and other industries.

18. For example, the case study of Project QUEST devotes four of its 80 pages to a specific focus on employer issues. See Rademacher, Bear, and Conway (2001).

19. Evidence of "repeat customers" as signaling positive outcomes for employers also was noted in the Project QUEST and CET evaluations.

20. Slower than anticipated startup is reported for virtually all new intermediary projects.

21. Attempts to reproduce the CET model outside of its original San Jose site met with disappointing results, to some extent because the particular nature of the model in its original location proved very hard to duplicate elsewhere.

22. Emerging "theory of change" approaches hold some promise, as they are explicitly designed for situations where models vary, deliberately, and where results are fed back to programs in order to encourage program changes and improvement. See, among others, Weiss (1995); for one attempt to develop and apply this framework to the analysis of workforce intermediaries, see McGahey et al. (2001).

REFERENCES

Abt Associates Inc., and the New School for Social Research. 1999. *Private Interests, Shared Concerns: The Relationship Between Employers and the AECF Jobs Initiative.* Cambridge, MA: Abt Associates Inc.

Abt Associates Inc., and New School University. 2000. *AECF Jobs Initiative Evaluation Report on the Capacity Building Phase.* Cambridge, MA: Abt Associates Inc.

Clark, Peggy, and Steven L. Dawson. 1995. *Jobs and the Urban Poor: Privately Initiated Sectoral Strategies.* Washington, DC: The Aspen Institute.

Elliott, Mark, et al. 2001. *Gearing Up: An Interim Report on the Sectoral Employment Initiative.* Philadelphia: Public/Private Ventures.

Ellwood, David. 2002. "How We Got Here," in *Grow Faster Together. Or Grow Slowly Apart: How Will America Work in the 21st Century.* Washington, DC: The Aspen Institute.

Fleischer, Wendy. 2001. *Extending Ladders: Findings from the Annie E. Casey Foundation's Jobs Initiative.* Baltimore: Annie E. Casey Foundation.

Giloth, Robert P. 2000. "Learning From the Field: Economic Growth and Workforce Development in the 1990s." *Economic Development Quarterly.* (summer).

Harrison, Bennett, with Marcus Weiss, and Jon Gant. 1995. *Building Bridges: Community Development Corporations and the World of Employment Training.* New York: The Ford Foundation. (January).

Harrison, Bennett, and Marcus Weiss. 1998. *Workforce Development Networks: Community-Based Organizations and Regional Alliances.* Thousand Oaks, CA: Sage Publications.

Heckman, James, Rebecca L. Roselius, and Jeffrey A. Smith. 1993. "U.S. Education and Training Policy: A Re-evaluation of the Underlying Assumptions Behind the 'New Consensus.'" Working Paper CSPE94-1, Center for Social Program Evaluation, University of Chicago. (December).

Holzer, Harry. 1996. *What Employers Want: Job Prospects for Less-Educated Workers.* New York: Russell Sage Foundation.

Jobs for the Future. 2001. *Everybody WINs: Effectively Involving Business in Workforce Development.* Boston: Jobs for the Future.

McGahey, Richard et al. 1990. *Financial Services, Financial Centers: The Competition for Markets and Jobs.* Boulder, CO: Westview Press.

————. 2001. *Evaluating the Workforce Innovation Networks (WINs): A Report to the Ford Foundation.* Bethesda, MD: Abt Associates Inc.

Melendez, Edwin. 1996. *Working on Jobs: The Center for Employment Training.* Boston: The Gaston Institute, University of Massachusetts at Boston.

Moss, Philip, and Chris Tilly. 1995. "'Soft' Skills and Race: An Investigation of Black Men's Employment Problems." New York: Russell Sage Foundation.

National Center on Education and the Economy. 1990. *America's Choice: High Skills or Low Wages.* Washington, DC: National Center on Education and the Economy.

Osterman, Paul, and Brenda A. Lautsch. 1996. *Project QUEST: A Report to the Ford Foundation.* Cambridge, MA: M.I.T. Sloan School of Management.

Rademacher, Ida, Marshall Bear, and Maureen Conway. 2001. *Project QUEST: A Case Study of a Sectoral Employment Development Approach.* Washington, DC: The Aspen Institute.

Rademacher, Ida, ed. 2002. *Working With Value: Industry-Specific Approaches to Workforce Development.* Washington, DC: The Aspen Institute.

U.S. Department of Labor, Office of the Chief Economist. 1995. *What's Working (and What's Not): A Summary of the Research on the Economic Impacts of Employment and Training Programs.* Washington, DC: U.S. Government Printing Office.

Weiss, Carol H. 1995. "Nothing So Practical As Good Theory: Exploring Theory-Based Evaluations for Comprehensive Community Initiatives for Children and Families." In James P. Connell et al., eds. *New Approaches to Evaluating Community Initiatives.* Washington, DC: The Aspen Institute.

Zandniapour, Lily. 2000. *Methodology and Findings from the Baseline Survey of Participants.* Washington, DC: The Aspen Institute, SEDLP Research Series, Report No. 1.

Zandniapour, Lily, and Maureen Conway. 2002. *Gaining Ground: The Labor Market Progress of Participants of Sectoral Employment Development Programs.* Washington, DC: The Aspen Institute.

III

ECONOMIC AND POLICY RATIONALES FOR WORKFORCE INTERMEDIARIES

6

Labor Market Intermediaries in the Modern Labor Market

PAUL OSTERMAN

IN THE MIDST OF THE POSTWAR EXPANSION, *THE ORGANIZATION MAN*, by William H. Whyte, described a world in which managers spent their lives within the same organization, striving to climb the ladder and never thinking about moving to another firm. During this same period automobile workers, unlike managers, faced layoffs during cyclical downturns, but these layoffs were typically followed by recalls. They too could look forward to spending their careers with the same employer.

Hard numbers confirm this story. Job tenure data—which measure the years an employee spends at the same firm—showed that the typical American worker averaged the same number of years at their employer as did the average Japanese employee, who lived under a system that was dubbed "lifetime employment" (Hall, 1982).

The Organization Man and the world of the secure blue-collar employee characterized the working careers of many Americans during the long period of prosperity. Of course, not everyone shared in this security. Many, particularly poor people and racial minorities, were confined to insecure jobs in what researchers called the "secondary labor market." Many women were also denied access to the stable secure jobs at the core of the economy. And so, what emerged during this period was a two-tier labor market. In the top tier, people hired on for the long term rarely changed jobs and had little need for assistance in making transitions. In the remainder of the job market turnover was much higher, but it led nowhere. There was constant recycling through a series of low-wage, no-future jobs.

One consequence of this postwar system was that in much of the job market there was relatively little need for labor market intermediaries. In a few specialized niches intermediaries played a role (head hunting firms at the top and the Employment Service at the bottom), but by and large they were not relevant. Furthermore, in the case of the Employment Service the outcomes were poor (Balducci, Johnson, and Gritz, 1995).

Another consequence of the postwar arrangement was that the public employment and training system, which included intermediaries, was not seen by core firms in the private sector as an important part of their operation. These firms hired people and kept them, and they also provided most of the skills training required by their labor force. As a consequence, the public system was viewed either as a form of charity or else as an extension of the welfare system. This in turn reduced its ability to deliver high-quality jobs to its clients (since the public system was not effectively connected to the source of good jobs), and a negative feedback loop ensued in which weak performance increased the isolation of the system from the core of the economy.

In recent years circumstances have changed, and a real opportunity has emerged to fashion a positive and respected role for public intermediaries. One reason that the situation is more hopeful is that, through careful evaluation and consideration of best practice, we have learned a good deal about what designs for public programs work best. As a consequence it is possible to create public intermediaries whose services are higher quality and that are attractive to firms. The other reason why intermediaries enjoy new opportunities is that the underlying employment model in the core of the job market is changing. The world of the Organization Man and of layoffs followed by recall is fading, and instead employment has had higher turnover and has become more volatile, not just at the bottom of the labor market but also for many other employees. There is thus a greater need for intermediary services than in the past. To some extent the private sector has responded to these signals, and we have witnessed the emergence of temporary help firms, Internet based job search services, and other intermediaries. However, there is also a need and an opportunity for an expanded public role.

WHAT LED TO CHANGE

The old system was blown apart by several forces. The willingness and ability of firms to maintain stable employment and to share profits via rising wages was based upon secure product markets and a surplus of profits. However, competition toughened a great deal in the final two decades of the last century. In part this was due to pressures of international competition, but at least as important was the wave of deregulation—in airlines, banking, insurance, telecommunications, and trucking—that transformed the competitive landscape.

A second factor was the spread of new technologies that enabled companies to organize work in new ways. Some of these technologies were physical, notably information technology, which permitted both the dispersion of production and more powerful managerial control. Equally important were organizational innovations—just-in-time inventory, teams, quality programs, outsourcing—that led to increased productivity with leaner staffing.

A set of important political and institutional changes also undermined the old model. The increased concentration of stock holding among institutional investors and the rise of new forms of finance, such as junk bonds, enabled stockholders to pressure managers to focus more single-mindedly on maximizing profits and to avoid sharing profits with employees beyond the strict demands of the market.

A final key shift was the changing nature of skill and of skill provision. Economists typically distinguish between specific skills, which are useful only in the firm in which a person is employed, and general skills, which have broad applicability. When skills are specific, firms have an incentive to provide training, and people see little gain from mobility. However, when skills are general, firms will be reluctant to train because people can pick up their skills and utilize them elsewhere. In the presence of specific skills, firms' turnover will be lower and careers will be built inside of one firm.

The diffusion of information technology has arguably led to skills becoming more general and hence transferable (Gould, 2002). Linked to this has been the growth of a very substantial vocational training infrastructure (community colleges and proprietary schools) that also removes some of the incentives for employers and employees to build longlasting relationships.

These changes also led to a new management idea: that firms should focus on their core competencies. This implies extensive outsourcing of "non-core" business functions, and it also means that the firm is constantly considering which activities should remain within its boundaries and which should be removed. Thus the pressure on employment stability, and hence on turnover, is continual.

The pressures described above led firms to substantially reconsider their employment systems. Taken together, the changes that ensued created a higher turnover and a less secure, more volatile labor market. Ironically, the demand for skill and commitment also rose, for reasons described below. Firms thus increasingly face the dilemma of how to achieve the flexibility they desire while at the same time acquiring a labor force whose characteristics match what they need.

THE VOLATILE LABOR MARKET

There is good reason to believe that job security has been undermined for all groups of employees. For example, firms are more willing to lay off employees for reasons other than declining sales. Osterman (1999) classified the reasons for layoffs in 1972 and 1994 as either due to poor sales or to restructuring. The fraction due to restructuring rose substantially. In a study of stock market reaction to layoffs researchers found that layoffs in the 1990s were seen by Wall Street in a positive light whereas stock prices previously had been punished by layoff announcements (Farber and Hallock, 1999).

The nature of layoffs has also changed: they are not followed by recall as they were in the past. Seventy percent of those who are unemployed due to layoffs experienced permanent (versus temporary followed by recall) layoffs, and, related to this, the fraction of those unemployed who are experiencing long-term spells has also grown.[1]

There are other indications that job security has weakened. Every two years since 1984 the monthly survey of the labor force collects data on employee dislocation, defined as permanent layoffs due to business decisions of firms (e.g., plant closings or end of a shift, as opposed to poor individual performance). It is possible, therefore, to track how worker dislocation correlates with overall business conditions. Analysis of these data suggests that although there is a strong cyclical component to dislocation, during the 1990s there was more dislocation than would be expected given the tight labor market of that period (Farber, 2001).

The same data suggest that the costs of dislocation are substantial.[2] On average about 35 percent of those dislocated are not re-employed at the time of the survey. Of those who do find jobs, about 10 percent of those who previously held full-time jobs work part time after dislocation. The average earning loss experienced by those who do find work is about 12 percent. Although the probability of being re-employed does increase with time since dislocation, the earnings penalties are not reduced, and hence there is a substantial long-term cost associated with dislocation. Finally, in the 1990s expansion of the costs of dislocation were reduced, but by no means eliminated.

Additional evidence that there is more turnover in the labor market (and hence greater need for intermediaries) comes from the fact that firms that engaged in layoffs and restructuring in the 1990s also hired new employees at the same time. In an American Management Association survey conducted in 1996, 31 percent of the firms surveyed said that they were hiring and laying off at the same time, and the average firm that engaged in layoffs was in fact growing by 6 percent (Cappelli, 2001).

One of the notable characteristics of the past decade has been the growing threat to previously secure white-collar and management jobs. Whereas in the past the burden of layoffs and volatility has fallen upon service and blue-collar workers, now people in the upper reaches of the job market are also at risk. An American Management Association survey showed that while salaried jobs accounted for 40 percent of employment, they constituted 60 percent of job cuts (Capelli, 1999). In the dislocated worker surveys a gap remains in the fortunes of white- and blue-collar workers, but that difference has notably narrowed over time.

Yet another indicator of greater volatility is the spread of temporary employment. The increased utilization of staffing firms has been dramatic. Between 1979 and 1995 staffing firms grew 11 percent annually, five times faster than the average for nonagricultural employment. (Autor, 2000a). Between 1990 and 2000 temporary help firms were responsible for 10 percent of net job growth (Autor, 2000b). Clearly temporary work, by loosening the ties between employers and employees, is another aspect of how work and careers are changing in the direction of a higher turnover labor market.[3]

Given all of this, one would expect that were summary data available on job security, it would show a sharp decline. But this is where the picture gets murky. The best available data along these lines are the job tenure information collected every two years as part of a supplement to the Current Population Survey. These data measure the number of years that the respondent has worked for the same employer.

Table 6.1 provides these data for the entire labor force and for men and women, both with and without age distinctions. The basic story is clear. There is a downward trend in the proportion of men holding long-tenure jobs, and the trend is especially pronounced for middle age men whom one would normally expect to be well ensconced in their organizations. However, the trend is quite different for women who, by contrast, have experienced a long-term increase in the fraction holding high-tenure jobs. The net effect is a mild decline in long-term tenure.

It is easy to see, from looking at the tenure data for men, why observers may feel that stable careers are crumbling. Although even in 2000 over half of men age 50–54 held long-tenure jobs, the decline has been sharp, and the trend, if extrapolated forward, certainly is not promising. However, if we ask about the stock of long-tenure jobs in the economy then the experience of women offsets much of what has happened to men. There is clearly a story to be told about why the fortunes of men and women diverge so sharply, but for the purposes of understanding employment systems, the first approximation is that stable careers seem to be in mild retreat, but nothing as dramatic as some commentators in the popular press would have it.

Table 6.1   Percent of Employees with 10 or More Years
of Tenure with Current Employer

	1983	1991	1996	2000
Both sexes over 25	31.9%	32.2%	30.5%	31.7%
Both Sexes Age 40–44	38.1	39.3	36.1	35.9
Both Sexes Age 50–54	53.5	51.4	50.4	48.6
Men over 25	37.7	35.9	33.1	33.6
Men Age 40–44	51.1	46.3	41.7	40.4
Men Age 50–54	62.3	58.5	54.9	51.6
Women over 25	24.9	28.2	27.6	29.5
Women Age 40–44	23.4	32.0	30.4	31.4
Women Age 50–54	42.5	43.4	45.8	45.6

Source: Bureau of Labor Statistics.

Additional evidence in the direction of moderation is found in the Bureau of Labor Statistics' survey of contingent work. As part of yet another supplement to the Current Population Survey, respondents are asked every two years about whether they hold contingent jobs. There are three alternative definitions of what is meant by contingent work, and the most expansive is simply employees who do not expect their jobs to last indefinitely (for reasons other than personal). Among people between the ages of 25 and 64, in February 2001, 3.2 percent reported that they held contingent jobs. This compares with 3.9 percent in 1995, 3.5 percent in 1997, and 3.3 percent in 1999. There is thus no upward trend in the fraction of the workforce holding precarious jobs.

When all of the foregoing is taken into account, the picture that emerges is of a job market in which security has frayed substantially, although for many people the older patterns remain in place. However, even people who have managed to keep their jobs find themselves in a potentially more insecure position than in the past. In addition, for employers a new set of practices has emerged that implies that they can no longer count on a secure supply of labor emerging from an internal job ladder. Firms must rely more heavily than in the past on the external labor market to supply labor, and this also has important consequences for the role of labor market intermediaries.

PRESSURES FOR COMMITMENT AND SKILL

Increased turnover and reduced commitment would not necessarily be a problem if work were being dumbed down. If this were the case then there would be much less to worry about regarding the capacities of the labor force, and companies would not face any costs from the loss of job security and the increase in mobility. However, what is happening is just the opposite of dumbing down. The skill needs of firms are increasing. According to many commentators, the increased demand for skill lies behind the sharp rise in the educational wage premium. Whereas in 1973 people with only a high school degree earned 68 percent of those with a college degree, by 1999 this had fallen to 57 percent (Mishel, 2001). The fortunes of high school dropouts took an even worse turn.

There are at least two reasons why the demand for skill has increased. One is the diffusion of new technologies, notably information technology, which places increased demands on employees. Although there is controversy over the role computers play in explaining wage inequality[4] there is broad agreement that the expanded use of computers has increased the demand for skill. While there are cases of computers substituting for high-level jobs (for example, telephone repair people now can simply replace circuit boards instead of engaging in complicated rewiring), on balance computers require more, not less, skill. For example, those industries that invested most heavily in computers were also the ones that tended to increase their proportion of college relative to high school graduates.

Skill demands have also increased because firms have adopted ways of organizing work that require more judgment from employees and that place a premium on people working together to solve problems. These new work systems, termed "high-performance work organizations" emerged in the 1980s and early 1990s as a response to competitive challenges. They have been implemented in both manufacturing and in service sector firms.

At the core of the new systems are changes in how employees do their job. Perhaps the most typical innovation is the introduction of work teams. The idea of teams is that the employees take responsibility for a group of tasks, that there is a sense of responsibility for the team's product, that the workers are broadly skilled, and that there is an element of job rotation.

In many "transformed" firms employees are involved in aspects other than direct work activities. The most common example is problem-solving groups in which cross-sections of employees come together, to some extent obviating traditional managerial/nonmanagerial distinctions. These groups address problems such as production techniques, quality issues, and health and safety.

To understand the spread of these systems I conducted two surveys, one in 1992 and the other in 1997, that asked a representative sample of private sector establishments with 50 or more employees about their work organization practices (Osterman, 2000). I asked about self-managed teams, quality circles, job rotation, and total quality management. An establishment was recorded as utilizing a given practice if half or more of its "core" employees were involved. In 1992, 14 percent of the establishments had three or more practices in place and 26 percent had two. By 1997, these figures had increased to 39 percent and 70 percent. Both the substantial rate of diffusion and the increase since 1992 point to the power of these ideas as well as their surprising ability to flourish even in an era of downsizing and employment insecurity.

As firms transform their work systems, it seems likely that the skills they need from their labor force will also change, both in terms of level and content. In the 1992 establishment survey there was a very clear relationship between work organization and training: the level of training in those establishments that had two or more of the practices in place was 35 percent higher than in establishments that had not modernized their work practices. This finding remains even after controlling for an extensive set of characteristics of the firm and the employees (Osterman, 1995).

The emergence of these new work systems, when thought of in the context of increased turnover and reduced job security, point to an important paradox in the job market. The new work systems require higher levels of skill and of commitment, as employees are asked to share their ideas with the firm and to make the extra effort to produce quality. However, changes in job attachment point to reduced commitment. Thus far, this paradox has been managed by firms, largely because employees are concerned enough about their future that they are willing to play ball. Whether this delicate balance can be maintained in the future is an important, unresolved question.

THE EMERGENCE OF PRIVATE SECTOR INTERMEDIARIES

If the foregoing trends in the labor market are truly significant, then it is reasonable to expect that the private sector would react by creating or expanding labor market intermediaries to meet the emerging needs. In fact, this is just what has happened. Between 1987 and 1997 revenue for the largest executive search firms grew from $45.2 million to $157.2 million (Cappelli, 1999). However, the growth of intermediaries has been much broader than in this relatively narrow niche. Perhaps the most dramatic example is the spread of temporary help or staffing agencies.

Temporary and Contract Work

I discussed earlier the extent of temporary work in the context of looser attachments between firms and workers, however it is also important to understand important shifts in the role staffing firms play in the labor market. Although many companies still use temporary help agencies to meet peak loads and fill temporary vacancies, what is striking about these firms is the new roles they are playing. They have penetrated into a wide range of occupations, and they are an important element in many firms' recruiting and training strategies.

Based on their survey of establishments, Abraham and Taylor (1996) concluded that one motivation of contracting out is to obtain greater flexibility in the wage structure. Although this is often taken to mean paying lower wages (and avoiding benefits) other case studies show that staffing firms can sometimes enable firms to pay certain categories of workers higher wages without being forced by the wage structure of the firm to increase the compensation of all employees.[5]

It is also increasingly clear that temporary help firms are performing intermediary functions. The movement from "temp to perm" is quite common, and firms increasingly use the temporary phase as a new version (with fewer legal complications) of probationary employment. In a survey I conducted, 24 percent of temporaries were eventually hired by a firm to which they were assigned. Census data report that 57 percent of workers in a temporary job were in a permanent job the next year (Cappelli, 1999). In a morphing together of two strata in the job market, Manpower Inc. has created an alliance with the search firm Drake Beam Morin.

Temporary help firms also train their employees. Manpower invests 2 percent of payroll on just R&D for training, a figure that is about the training budgets of most firms. It has 150 self-paced modular courses (Cappelli, 1999). In a 1994 government survey of temporary help firms, 68 percent provided some form of computer training (Autor, 2000b).

The Internet

The need for better intermediary services in the new environment has combined with the spread of new technology and led to what appears to be an explosion in job matching via the Internet. According to one estimate, there are currently 7 million unique resumes posted and 25 million (not necessarily unique) jobs advertised on-line. In August 2000 one of the leading sites, Monster.com, had 3.9 million resumes and 430,000 jobs (Autor, 2001). There are also sites, such as guru.com, that will work with firms to staff particular projects.

On its face this development promises a much more fluid labor market and much better intermediary services. It clearly has some advantages. For example, the cost of Internet job postings is much less than are newspaper help-wanted ads. Hence to some extent these new jobs sites are simply a competitive effort to substitute a lower cost bulletin board (the Internet) for a high-cost one (newspapers). However, it seems reasonable to think that they are also a response to increased demand for intermediation. Nevertheless, there are a variety of reasons to think that the Internet is a complement to, not a substitute for, intermediary services provided in a more hands-on manner.

When people are hired for any but the simplest jobs, firms are concerned about personal traits such as ambition, honesty, conscientiousness, etc., which cannot be detected on resumes. In fact, the Internet is likely to cause special problems in this regard because people with traits that are unattractive will find it easy to post their resumes in the hopes that there will be little detailed follow up. Phone calls and letters from past employers are a partial solution, but these are often rose-colored. For these reasons there will continue to be a strong need for institutions to vouch for potential hires. These intermediary institutions have a deeper knowledge of the traits of candidates and also have their own reputation and relationships with employers that they will want to protect. Therefore, there is no reason to believe that the Internet spells the death of institutional intermediaries and, in fact, may very well stimulate demand for them.

Employer and Union Centered Networks

In the past decade there have been a growing number of examples of clusters of firms, and sometimes unions, coming together to help organize the labor market and provide intermediary services. At their best these efforts bring together the parties to discuss common technical, marketing, and employment problems. They work to find resources to address these issues, they engage the participants in designing common training programs for their labor force, and they create a mechanism to enable people to move easily from one firm to another.

In some instances these networks are business driven, such as the programs run by local chapters of Chambers of Commerce, the National Association of Manufacturing, and business associations such as the National Tooling and Machining Association. Similar networks have been created under union auspices, for example the Garment Industry Development Corporation in New York that is affiliated with the apparel union, UNITE. Another well-developed example of how networks can operate is the Wisconsin Regional Training Partnership. The partnership consists of a consortium formed by manufacturers, unions, and public sector partners in the Milwaukee metropolitan area.

OPPORTUNITIES FOR PUBLIC POLICY

Public labor market policy throughout the postwar period was based on the assumption that for most employees, jobs were full time, long term, and relatively stable. Frequent job changing was thought to be characteristic only of young workers searching for their niche, and after a relatively short period of time, even they were expected to settle down and develop careers within their "permanent" places of employment.

Linked to this assumption was a corollary point about where people worked. With the exception of special cases like the construction trades and parts of the entertainment industry, the traditional assumptions envisioned the typical workplace as a large, often industrial, firm. In reality, workers have always been distributed across large and small employers, and large enterprises were perceived to be on the vanguard of technology and work practices. Thus what they did in these areas was seen as progressive, "leading edge," and thus worthy of emulation—even if it did not appear to fit other, smaller firms.

Recent changes in the world of work have undermined these assumptions. In so doing, they have eroded the foundations of our current labor market institutions. The forms that work takes have become more varied. Many people no longer expect to play out the major portion of their work lives attached to a single employer. Companies have indeed become much more willing to layoff workers, not only as they always did in response to business downturns but even in periods of prosperity as shifts in technology and markets change the mix of labor requirements or in response to pressures from financial markets to increase returns on capital. Workers in turn increasingly see the need to move across enterprises to expand their skill base and maintain information networks in the course of their careers. Alternative forms of work and employment relationships have developed through temporary help agencies and independent contracting.

In a variety of ways, public policy has been undermined by these developments. We lack strong institutions for linking together a series of short-term work opportunities into a continuous stream of employment and income, now that this function is no longer performed within large enterprises to which workers are permanently attached. We lack institutional guidance for workers negotiating their careers through a sequence of skills developed by moving across the borders of different firms. Smaller entrepreneurial firms, which have been the source of much of the dynamism in the U.S. economy, are poorly served by the current system.

When firms increasingly hire from the outside into positions that were once part of closed job ladders, they will need assistance in identifying, screening, and training potential recruits. In the old world, firms had ample opportunities to observe and assess people as they climbed internal ladders. These ladders also were the vehicle through which much training occurred. Now this pattern is less viable, and new institutions—intermediaries of various stripes—have the chance to fill the void. The private sector has responded and created new institutions to fill these needs. However, there also remains a need, and an opportunity, for creative public policy.

The case for public policy is given additional impetus by demographic trends. Without intervention it will be increasingly difficult for firms to obtain the kind of labor force they need. Whereas the labor force grew by 38.7 percent between 1980 and 2000, it is projected to grow by only 19.4 percent between 2000 and 2020. Furthermore, the labor force will increasingly consist of groups who traditionally face significant challenges. Whereas native-born whites accounted for 78.9 percent of the labor force in 1980, they will account for only 63.1 percent in 2020. Projected levels of educational attainment also imply a substantial slowing relative to the 1980 to 2000 experience (Ellwood, 2001).

Training is one important example of the importance of public policy. Firms view training as an investment, and in a high turnover environment the investment is less likely to pay off. Consistent with this expectation, survey evidence shows that employers with higher levels of turnover invest less than firms with lower levels. In addition, the flattening of organizations and the elimination of rungs in the job ladder reduce opportunities for people to learn new skills in small increments as they move up in the organization. Hence the new ways of organizing work are likely to decrease companies' investments in training just at the time that the demand for skill is growing due to technology and work systems such as teams and quality programs.

The case for more aggressive public policy with respect to training is threefold. First, there are important social benefits to increased training, and because these benefits are broadly shared, no firm is likely to consider them in making its own training decisions. Second, there are serious collective action problems. That is, any firm that makes a substantial investment has to worry that other firms will simply hire away its employees after the investment has been made. Third, there are distributional issues. People at the bottom of the job market are often ignored because the costs and risks of training them are perceived to be high. Yet these are the very people who are of concern from the viewpoint of equity and social justice.

In addition to training, public intermediaries can play an important role in helping firms access a labor force that they might otherwise ignore. People experiencing labor market difficulty often lack the networks, which connect them with good jobs, and they also do not have people or institutions to vouch for their skills and reliability. An effective intermediary can help people get jobs and also assist them in remaining employed after they are hired.

The public employment and training system has long been seen as isolated from the core of the job market. However, the labor market developments outlined in this chapter may offer new opportunities for public intermediaries to overcome this stigma. Because firms now need these services more than ever, they may well be more responsive to public intermediaries that offer quality assistance. Whereas in the past the employment and training system was viewed as essentially an extension of the welfare or charity systems, and hence not taken seriously, today well-designed programs may be able to sell their services to a wider range of employers. If we are able to take advantage of this opportunity then the benefits will flow to people who had previously been confined to a stigmatizing system. The challenge will be to assure that programs are indeed effective and hence can take advantage of the opening that the newer, more volatile job market offers.

NOTES

1. These data refer to 2001 and are from Employment and Earnings, January 2002.

2. The data in this paragraph are taken from Farber (2001). Similar findings are reported in Osterman (1999).

3. If one looks at the level of temporary employment instead of growth rates the figures are a bit more moderate. In 2001 the Census's Current Population Survey found that 3 percent of employees classified themselves as on-call workers, employees of staffing firms, or contract workers. However, this figure is a bit misleading because the high turnover of temporary workers implies that more people flow through these jobs in a given year than appear in them at any point in time. A reasonable estimate is that between seven and eight times as many people hold the jobs over the course of a year than at any point in time. A fair conclusion is that the spread of temporary work is one more indicator of the volatile insecure labor market, but in and of itself this employment form is far from the norm.

4. There is a correlation in data on individuals between computer usage and wage levels. Furthermore, those industries that have computerized the fastest seem to have the highest levels of wage inequality. On the other hand, computer usage may simply be a proxy for a person's place in the occupational hierarchy, and any other proxy (e.g., use of pencils) would also produce the same effect. Furthermore, the diffusion of computers in the economy does not track very well the timing of the explosion of wage inequality. For a summary of this literature and a skeptical view about the relationship of computers to inequality see Card and DiNardo (2002).

5. Abraham and Taylor (1996) find evidence of this high-wage pattern in their data on contracting out, and Houseman, Kalleberg, and Erickeck (2003) also found examples of exactly this rationale in their case studies of temporary workers in healthcare.

REFERENCES

Abraham, Katherine, and Susan Taylor. 1996. "Firms' Use of Outside Contractors: Theory and Evidence." *Journal of Labor Economics*, Vol. 14, No. 3.

Autor, David. 2001. "Wiring the Labor Market." *Journal of Economic Perspectives*, Vol. 15, No. 1. (Winter).

———. 2000a. "Outsourcing At Will: Unjust Dismissal Doctrine and the Growth of Temporary Help Employment." Working Paper 7557, National Bureau of Economic Research. (February).

———. 2000b. "Why Do Temporary Help Firms Provide Free General Skill Training?" Working Paper 7637, National Bureau of Economic Research. (April).

Balducci, David, Terry Johnson, and R. Mark Gritz. 1995. "The Role of the Employment Service." In Christopher J. O'Leary and Stephen A. Wadner, eds. *Unemployment Insurance in the United States, an Analysis of the Policy Issues*. Kalmazoo, MI: Upjohn Institute.

Cappelli, Peter. 2001. "Assessing the Decline of Internal Labor Markets." In Ivar Berg and Arne Kalleberg, eds. *Sourcebook of Labor Markets: Evolving Structures and Processes*. New York: Kluwer.

———. 1999. *The New Deal at Work*. Boston: Harvard Business School Press.

Card, David, and John DiNardo. 2002. "Skill Biased Technological Change and Rising Wage Inequality; Some Problems and Puzzles." Working Paper #876, National Bureau of Economic Research. (February).

Ellwood, David. 2001. "The Sputtering Labor Force of the Twenty First Century." In Alan Krueger and Robert Solow, eds. *The Roaring Nineties: Can Full Employment be Sustained?* New York: Russell Sage Foundation.

Farber, Henry S. 2001. "Job Loss in the United States, 1981–1999." Working Paper #453, Industrial Relations Section, Princeton University. (June).

Farber, Henry S., and Kevin F. Hallock. 1999. "Changing Stock Market Response to Announcements of Job Loss: Evidence From 1970–97." IRRA 51st Annual Papers and Proceedings.

Gould, Eric. 2002. "Rising Wage Inequality, Comparative Advantage, and the Growing Importance of General Skills in the United States." *Journal of Labor Economics*, Vol. 20, No. 1. (January).

Hall, Robert. 1982. "The Importance of Lifetime Jobs in the U.S. Economy." *American Economic Review*. (September).

Houseman, Susan N., Arne L. Kalleberg, and George Erickcek. 2003. "The Role of Temporary Agency Employment in Tight Labor Markets." *Industrial and Labor Relations Review* (October).

Mishel, Lawrence, Jared Bernstein, and John Schmitt. 2001. *The State of Working America, 2000/2001.* Ithaca, NY: ILR Press.

Osterman, Paul. 1994. "How Common is Workplace Transformation and How Can We Explain Who Does It?" *Industrial and Labor Relations Review.* (January).

———. 1995. "Skill Training, and Work Organization in American Establishments." *Industrial Relations*, Vol. 34.

———. 1999. *Securing Prosperity: How the American Labor Market Has Changed and What To Do About It.* Princeton, NJ: Princeton University Press.

———. 2000. "Work Reorganization In An Era of Restructuring; Trends in Diffusion and Effects on Employee Welfare." *Industrial and Labor Relations Review.* (January).

7

The Political Economy of Labor Market Mediation in the United States

ANTHONY P. CARNEVALE
AND DONNA M. DESROCHERS

BROADLY CONCEIVED, LABOR MARKET INTERMEDIARIES ARE THE SET of informal conventions, public and private institutions, as well as public laws and regulations, that link individuals and communities with market economies. In concept, the scope of labor market intermediation includes a broad array of functions such as human capital development, supportive social services, employment services, income security, housing, and healthcare as well as a voice in economic and social decision making. While the dialogue among the European nations on the public role in labor market intermediation has been expansive, the American dialogue on workforce intermediaries has been narrowly focused on facilitating "Work First" policies that encourage permanent transitions from public dependency to private employment.

The public dialogue on the structure of labor market intermediaries in the United States is consistent with a unique cultural emphasis on economic individualism, a political preference for limited government, and an economic strategy that emphasizes deregulation and flexibility as a core competitive asset. As a result, the evolution of labor market intermediaries has been characterized by a privatized, market based, and fragmented provision of skill development, job search and hiring, as well as similar trends in access to childcare, healthcare, and pensions.

But as the United States moves farther into the post industrial era, the dialogue on the scale and scope of public intermediaries may become re-energized. Systemic changes in both economic and employment relationships suggest a growing need for public intermediation to encourage efficiencies and mitigate inequalities in the labor market. Competition in the global marketplace and the pace of change have intensified, and finding skilled workers has become more important to employers as they try to maintain an edge in product and service markets. Declining job security increases workers' needs for intermediary services to find new jobs and maintain benefits coverage. And with the retirement of the baby boom population on the horizon, labor markets will tighten and labor shortages will likely reach unprecedented levels, especially among skilled workers. Efficient allocation of human resources will be critical if we are to maintain our economic competitiveness.

At the same time, unskilled workers are increasingly competing against low-wage production workers abroad, or are employed in low-paying service jobs with minimal, if any, benefits that offer few internal career ladders or learned skills that allow their next job to be a better job. Economic inequality has persisted between the nation's most and least fortunate throughout the 1990s, fueling skepticism on the efficacy of "a rising tide lifting all boats" since inequality has narrowed only slightly, and well after the longest economic expansion in postwar history was solidly underway. Changes in the employment structure have given rise to "poverty traps" that, for many, are not easily escaped simply by going to work.

The case for expanding the scale and scope of labor market intermediaries in the United States is compelling. Nevertheless, support for the development of a more pervasive intermediary system waxes and wanes with the economic tides. To a large extent, the education system has already become the primary, or "first chance," institutional intermediary for distributing economic opportunity and subsequent access to further learning and private benefits. The United States has struggled to develop workforce intermediaries as part of a "second chance" system for those who are excluded or dislocated from mainstream education institutions, but the "second chance" system has never achieved a scale sufficient to serve a majority of those eligible or to change aggregate income patterns.

Expansion in labor market mediation faces intellectual as well as financial barriers. While the U.S. market based system of intermediaries is criticized for its regressive distributional impact, it is generally applauded for its flexibility in response to economic change—especially in comparison with the European welfare states. Advocates of the American system claim that American flexibility improves economic adaptability, promotes job creation, minimizes credentialing barriers to individual opportunity, and reduces public dependency. The flexibility and fragmentation of the American system also are deemed by many as especially appropriate for twenty-first century labor markets that are, themselves, fragmenting and changing rapidly.

Advocates for an expansion in the scope and scale of publicly funded workforce intermediaries dispute these claims. First, proponents argue that increased public intermediation in labor markets would improve rather than discourage labor market flexibility. They argue that the empirical evidence of a demonstrable connection between economic rigidity and expanding access to intermediary services such as job search and retention services, childcare, education and training, and healthcare is weak or nonexistent—even in the European case. They make the intuitively compelling argument that an expansion in the scale and scope of workforce intermediaries would increase, not decrease, flexibility. In addition, workforce intermediaries targeted toward the least 15 percent of the labor force would benefit those served but would have little impact on the overall flexibility of the labor market. Their minimal impact would result from their relatively small size and the fact that they are focused on people who are at the fringes, rather than the core, of the labor force.

Second, advocates for expanding the skill development functions of workforce intermediaries argue that education and training are necessary intermediary functions for overcoming rising skill barriers to sustained employment in jobs that pay enough or provide enough income mobility for real social inclusion.

Third, there is convincing evidence that social changes in the structure of families justify new intermediary functions. Women have increased their labor market participation, profoundly changing the economics of family life. In a society whose youth and adult labor force is fully mobilized, support for new capabilities that mediate between work requirements and family needs becomes crucial. In addition, the traditional system of intermediaries may have become outmoded with the growing diversity of household structures that has accompanied the aging of the workforce and the decline in the prevalence of the traditional paternalism of the heterosexual male–headed household.

Fourth, many argue that increased public commitments to workforce intermediaries are necessary to compensate for declining private commitments between employers and workers that have led to reduced trust and a loss of individual economic autonomy critical to a democratic society. In this view, the pursuit of market flexibility has shifted too much risk to workers and too much power to employers. Many analysts argue that this decline in labor power, in conjunction with increasing skill requirements, has been especially detrimental to low-wage families. They argue that it has resulted in a declining real value of the minimum wage as well as new policy barriers to an equitable distribution of education, training, affordable housing, healthcare, and legal services. These changes, along with declining union membership, are portrayed as the dominant cause of the dramatic decline in the relative wages of workers with high school or less as well as the growing dispersion in family incomes.

Fifth, advocates for increased public intermediation point toward fundamental demographic changes that will necessitate more aggressive public interventions in labor markets to ensure growth and prosperity. Baby boom retirements, along with a dramatic falloff in college-level attainment, will result in equally dramatic worker shortages, especially among skilled workers. The combined effects of flat labor force participation rates, baby boom retirements, and a slowdown in educational attainment could result in an overall shortage of more than 20 million workers by 2020, including a shortage of 14 million highly skilled workers with at least some education or training beyond high school. These demographic, economic, and educational trends will ultimately shape labor market intermediaries in the United States in the next few decades.

THE FLEXIBILITY DEBATE

Support for intermediaries, even "workforce intermediaries" narrowly targeted toward the disadvantaged, has been frustrated by a broader bias against public intervention in labor markets. Many believe that public interventions of any kind will create barriers to flexible adaptation to economic change both among companies and individual workers. Moreover, flexibility is aggressively protected because it is widely regarded as America's unique and key economic asset in global competition and in minimizing public dependence among individuals.

Because of its allegiance to market based flexibility, the American labor market is qualitatively different from that in other nations. It tends to cluster with Britain, Australia, New Zealand, Canada, and other more market oriented systems. By way of comparison, workforce intermediaries in the market oriented systems have less scale and scope than the Nordic, German, and southern European systems, which are based on highly structured and aligned social partnerships among education institutions, unions, and employers at both the policy and operational levels.

Both the European and American systems have costs and benefits. Many European nations use their dense, nationwide institutional networks to provide strong social supports and economic security by linking employment, education, and training with other intermediary services (Shavit and Muller, 1998). Critics of the European model find its dense institutional networks a barrier to flexible, fast responses to economic and technological

changes, as well as the source of incentives that distort resource allocation, impair efficiency, and encourage dependency (Esping-Andersen,
1996; Heckman, 2002).

The American model is decidedly different. In contrast to the European
systems, the American model relies less on state provided welfare benefits
and more on labor markets and wage flexibility to allocate earnings (Esping-
Andersen, 1996). This flexibility is largely credited with incubating the
"employment miracle" of the 1990s, allowing companies to create new jobs
as well as enabling them to respond with agility to changing economic
conditions via wage adjustments and hiring and firing workers. While this
strategy is beneficial for companies and the highest skilled workers, the
immediate cost of such a market based employment strategy has been greater
economic uncertainty and inequality for low-skilled or redundant workers.

But forced choice between the welfare regimes of Europe and the market based American model presents a false set of alternatives. Choices
between efficiency and equity, flexibility and security, and private and public provision are not a zero-sum game. Implementing social protection programs may not impede labor market flexibility if countries with extensive
social protection systems find other ways to adjust. The effect of intermediaries on economic flexibility also depends on the balance between the
provision of equal and economic protections and services that promote
adjustment such as education, training, job search, and benefits portability.
Or perhaps in markets already distorted by taxes, regulation, and transfer
programs, social programs can serve to offset some of these distortions with
little impact on the flexibility of mainstream institutions (Blank, 1994).
Moreover, in the market based systems, workforce intermediaries can benefit recipients outside the mainstream but have little effect on the mainstream institutional bias in favor of market based flexibility.

THE CHANGING STRUCTURE OF
EMPLOYMENT, EDUCATION, AND EARNINGS

Early in this country's history and, in fact, pretty much through our first
200 years, a job was easy to find—especially an entry-level, low-skilled job.
Throughout our history, the American dream and the American reality
have been that people could start at the bottom and, without much formal
education, work their way to the top. But in the last 40 years, globalization
in product and capital markets, coupled with a technological revolution,
prompted profound changes in the American economy making education,
more than work effort, the lever of opportunity.

The concentration of jobs in the United States today is radically different than it was in 1959 (Carnevale, 1999; Carnevale and Rose, 1998). In the new economy, the number of high-paying, blue-collar jobs available to workers with high school diplomas is shrinking, largely as a result of productivity improvements. The shares of factory and natural resource jobs, such as farming and mining, have each declined by at least one-half—factory jobs declined from 32 to 17 percent of all jobs between 1959 and 2000, and natural resource jobs declined from 5 to 1.5 percent over the same period. And farm and factory jobs have not only lost employment shares but have suffered actual job losses. The share of jobs in low-skilled services has remained relatively stable at roughly 20 percent.

New job creation has been concentrated in "knowledge jobs" rather than production jobs or natural resource jobs. Tracking the share of total employment shows that jobs in hospitals and classrooms have grown substantially, to 15 percent of all jobs, but white-collar office employment has grown the most—accounting for almost 40 percent of all jobs in 2000. The overall number and share of technology jobs also has grown, but they still do not represent a large share of all jobs (7 percent).

The recent increase in educational requirements on the job is also remarkable. In 1973 nearly one-third of prime-age workers (age 30 to 59) were high school dropouts, and another 40 percent had graduated from high school but did not attend a post secondary institution. In 2000 fewer than one in ten workers were high school dropouts, while about one-third terminated their education with a high school diploma.

In general, educational upgrading has occurred across all occupational groups. While the fastest growing occupations—those in offices, classrooms, healthcare, and technology—were always high skilled, they now employ significantly larger shares of educated workers. Generally, at least three-quarters of workers in these fast growing occupations have completed some post secondary education. At the same time, workers in service, factory, and natural resource jobs also have become relatively more skilled, although a majority of workers still only have a high school diploma or less.

Coincident with the shift from a high-wage, low-education goods producing economy to a high-skilled, high-wage service economy is an increase in earnings inequality. Beginning in the late 1970s and continuing through the 1980s, the earnings of the highest paid 30 percent of workers increased, while the earnings of the bottom 70 percent either held stable or declined. Inequality persisted (but did not grow) throughout the early 1990s. Only in 1995 did the increases in inequality begin to narrow slightly, prompted by decreasing inequality in the bottom half of the earnings distributions. The top half of the distribution continued to experience a widening in wage inequality (Mishel, Bernstein, and Schmitt, 1999).

Much of the increase in earnings inequality is reflected in education. Those workers with the most education have experienced the greatest earnings gains, while among the least educated, women have experienced less robust gains, and their male counterparts have suffered actual declines in their inflation-adjusted earnings. As a result, the earnings disadvantage associated with low-skilled jobs had been rising until the mid-1990s when less-educated workers did experience a real gain in earnings. The college wage premium—the earnings advantage of college educated workers over high school graduates—in 1979 was 36 percent for men and 34 percent for women. By 1999 however, the premium rose to 76 and 72 percent for men and women, respectively (Mishel, Bernstein, and Schmitt, 2000). The college wage premium rose even though the supply of college educated workers increased by 60 percent over the period. Even after controlling for other factors that affect wages, the college/high school wage premium for men more than doubled between 1979 and 1999 from 20 to 42 percent, while the premium for women increased from 27 to 48 percent (Mishel, Bernstein, and Schmitt, 2000).

Because earnings are strongly associated with occupation and education, better job matching and investments in education and training are powerful strategies for assisting workers. But using only these mechanisms to assist workers may be a myopic solution that excludes other potential avenues for redress.

INSTITUTIONS AND ECONOMIC CHANGE

Changes in institutions and policies brought about by globalization and changing economic relationships, while beneficial for the economy, business, and skilled workers, have left the least advantaged in an increasingly precarious position. Significant reversals in these changes or policies are unlikely, and perhaps appropriately so, to the extent they foster economic growth and more flexible and efficient resource allocation. But those workers left behind need social and economic supports, including workforce intermediaries, greater than ever before.

Skill based technological change has often been the favored explanation for the increase in earnings inequality that began in the late 1970s (Cappelli, 1993 and 1996; Katz and Murphy, 1992; Levy and Murnane, 1992; Murphy and Welch, 1993). Technology and earnings are inextricably linked. For example, workers who use computers on the job earn 15 to 25 percent more than workers who do not (Freeman, 2002; Krueger, 1993; Mishel and Bernstein, 1995). In addition, the effects of technology changes have favored high-wage workers. Their principal effect has been to increase the earnings of the managers and service professionals who deploy and use them, not the technical workers who make and repair them (Carnevale and Rose, 2000). But at the same time, a substantial share of earnings differences between high school and college educated workers appears to result from declining labor power and public policy, including the decline in the value of the minimum wage and public income transfers, deindustrialization, and the falloff in union membership (Card and DiNardo, 2002; Mishel, Bernstein, and Schmitt, 2000).

The growing economic inequality that occurred in the 1980s was accompanied by a profound decrease in the inflation adjusted value of the minimum wage. Legislated increases in the early 1990s still did not bring it up to earlier levels. The decline in the real value of the minimum wage hurt the lowest paid workers, particularly women, and explains a majority of the wage dispersion at the lower end of the earnings distribution (Card and DiNardo, 2002; Lee, 1999).

Although the devaluation of the minimum wage may have contributed to the increase in inequality, it is not clear that simply raising the minimum wage will provide the lowest paid workers with a substantial increase in their standard of living. Estimates suggest that even a raise of $1.90 an hour would propel fewer than one in seven one-parent families out of poverty and have little impact on those low-income families above 200 percent of the poverty level (Acs, Phillips, and McKenzie, 2001). Using workforce intermediaries to help these workers obtain jobs that allow them to work more hours may prove a more effective strategy in propelling these workers out of poverty (Acs, Phillips, and McKenzie, 2001).

Many low-wage workers in today's economy are impacted by the increased globalization of markets because globalization results in trade that eliminates low-skilled, highly paid jobs and creates global competition among low-wage workers. Jobs lost to trade tend to be low-wage, low-skilled jobs. Jobs gained from trade tend to be more highly skilled and highly paid, both in manufacturing and in the economy on the whole. Some estimates suggest that trade accounts for as much as 30 percent of the increase in wage disparities since the 1970s (Mishel, Bernstein, and Schmitt, 2000). Ultimately, trade affects wages more than the number of jobs. For instance, there were 20 million fewer factory jobs in 2000 than would have existed had the 1959 share of employment continued. Nevertheless, probably only about 3 million of those jobs were actually lost to trade; the other 17 million were lost to productivity improvements that substituted fewer highly skilled workers for many low-skilled workers. Trade tends to increase the relative earnings of skilled workers in manufacturing and in the economy on the whole but, at the same time, drives down the earnings of low-skilled labor. So while trade can have positive effects on economic growth by promoting a more efficient use of human and capital resources, not all workers benefit. The least advantaged workers are those most likely to suffer the downside of trade.

Wage stagnation and job declines in manufacturing have been exacerbated by an accompanying decline in unionization. Throughout the 1980s, union density declined by 1 percentage point a year, from 25 percent in 1978 to 16 percent in 1989 (Freeman, 1993). In addition to the direct wage effects from declining union membership, deunionization introduces a ripple effect because nonunion employers face less pressure to raise wages. As a result, about 15 to 20 percent of the increase in male earnings inequality is attributed to the decline in unionization and its associated effects (Card, 1998; DiNardo, Fortin, and Lemieux, 1996; Freeman, 1993). However, de-unionization has little effect on the rising earnings inequality among women, primarily because the share of women belonging to unions has remained relatively constant.

CHANGING EMPLOYMENT RELATIONSHIPS

The profound economic changes that have occurred in recent years have been accompanied by distinct changes in employment relationships that have created a vacuum between workers and employers that needs to be filled by more effective workforce intermediation. In many respects, employment has become more tenuous. Temporary help and contingent work are more prevalent and allow the labor market to operate more efficiently, but they also create a need for institutions that mediate between workers and employers. At the same time, there has been a decline in job attachment, with workers having less job stability and job security creating a need for re-employment services (see chapter 6).

Today's shift away from internal labor markets and toward more market oriented systems is not a new relationship between employers and workers. In fact, throughout the nineteenth and early twentieth centuries, employers routinely relied on contingent workers. Like the writing, editing, payroll, and web design services contracted out in many companies today, in the eighteenth century, employers routinely used off-site contract workers to manufacture and handcraft products like shoes and clothing.

While this increased flexibility and reduced plant and equipment costs, problems with quality control and reliability prompted many companies to bring the contractors on-site by the late 1800s. As companies learned how to set up and manage the functions of the inside contractors, they eventually replaced them by hiring their own, less costly, employees. But it wasn't until the introduction of the assembly line, specialized training for line jobs, and associated management practices that internal labor markets were fully formed (Blair and Kochan, 2000; Cappelli, 2000).

After more than a half-century of corporatist employment policies, by the 1980s employers again began contracting out whole functions as well as individual jobs. Globalization, flexible information technology, and financial streamlining all prompted employers to revert to a more market based system. Looking back, we may see the period of "roughly the 1930s through the 1980s as a temporary departure from the more robust forms of market-mediated relationships" (Cappelli, 2000).

In some respects, the new sense of job insecurity stems from a change in expectations. In the 1950s, relatively few workers looked forward to lifetime employment with health and retirement benefits. At the same time, most workers thought that lifetime security was expanding from union and government workers to eventually include a larger share of the workforce. Moreover, workers associated higher skills with job security. Since the 1970s, expectations of expanding lifetime employment have virtually disappeared in spite of the fact that education levels have risen (Kochan, 2000; Reich, 2001).

ECONOMIC MOBILITY

Declining job tenure is troubling when it results in declining incomes, but changing jobs can be a happy experience when the next job pays more. Job instability and income inequality become less critical if workers can still count on economic mobility to eventually propel themselves upward into the middle class and beyond. In other words, "If income mobility were very high, the degree of inequality in any given year would be unimportant. . . ." (Krugman, 1992).

Because of our reliance on upward mobility, principally through a meritocratic education system, we have higher tolerances for disparities in economic outcomes. Americans support equality of individual opportunity, not equal outcomes. Income differences are tolerated because of a widespread belief that there is substantial income mobility, especially through education and subsequent work effort.

The evidence suggests that most workers do experience significant economic mobility. Studies of changes in relative mobility show that over the long term, roughly 60 percent of low-wage workers and their families moved into a higher income quintile. But there exists a minority of low-earning workers and families who do not move up the income distribution, and many of those who do move up do not make it very far. Of those workers in the bottom quintile, between one-fifth to one-third were upwardly mobile in one year, and 40 to 47 percent moved out of the lowest quintile within about a decade (Burkhauser, Holtz-Eakin, and Rhody, 1997; Gottschalk, 1997; Gittleman and Joyce, 1995; Mishel, Bernstein, and Schmitt, 2000; Sawhill and McMurrer, 1996). Of the nearly 60 percent who moved up over 25 years, one-quarter moved into the second income quintile, 16 percent moved into the middle quintile, 12 percent moved into the second highest quintile, while only about 6 percent reached the highest quintile (Mishel, Bernstein, and Schmitt, 2000).

Significant year-to-year fluctuations are apparent in income measures. Averaging income over three years to smooth out the income spikes shows somewhat lower mobility. Across both ten- and twenty-year periods, only about 40 percent of families moved out of the bottom quintile. Among those who did move up, about one-quarter moved into the second lowest earnings quintile, roughly 9 percent moved into the middle quintile, but only about 6 percent moved into the top two quintiles combined (Mishel, Bernstein, and Schmitt, 2000).

Low-earning workers are also more likely to leave the labor force than are other workers. Roughly 15 percent of low earners leave the labor force within five years, compared with fewer than 10 percent of higher earning workers (Carnevale and Rose, 2001b). Of those low-wage workers employed full time, four in ten were either working part time or not at all five years later (OECD, 1997). Low-paid women were much more likely than low-paid men to leave the labor force or reduce their hours. And among those workers who remained in the labor force, men were much more likely to move up than women—while nearly one-half of male workers transitioned out of the lowest earnings group within one year, only 28 percent of women moved up. Disparities in the economic mobility of men and women persist over time; even after 10- and 15-year intervals only one-half of women advanced into a better economic position, while three-quarters of men advanced (Carnevale and Rose, 2001b).

The balance of the literature suggests that income mobility has remained relatively stable over time. And while the United States promotes its economic flexibility and mobility as providing opportunity, income mobility appears to be similar across countries (Aaberge et al.,

2000; Burkhauser, Holtz-Eakin, and Rhody, 1997; Sawhill and McMurrer, 1996).

THE DEMOGRAPHIC TWIST

Although future economic realities favor higher levels of education and a broader array of skills, a reversal in longstanding demographic trends may make it difficult to fulfill these needs without increasing investments in labor market intermediation. The most powerful of these trends is the retirement of the baby boom. These boomers are working today, but they will age beyond 55 years from here on out, prompting a rapid depletion of workers from the American labor force over the next 20 years. The depletion of workers is expected to be especially strong among the most experienced and highly educated workers because it is those baby boomers who have the greatest access to retirement income that supplements social security. By 2020 there will be about 46 million baby boomers with at least some college who will be over 55 years of age (Carnevale and Fry, 2001).

While successive generations have acquired more schooling, educational attainment has plateaued among American youth over the last several years in spite of a doubling in the college/high school wage premium since the early 1980s. Between 1980 and 2000, the share of workers with at least some college increased by 20 percentage points. If current rates of college going persist, the share of Americans with at least some post secondary education or training will only increase by 4 percentage points between 2000 and 2020 (Aspen Institute, 2002). Moreover, the recent collapse of public budgets at a time when 4 million additional 18- to 24-year-olds are moving into their critical college going years suggests that rates of post secondary educational attainment will remain flat or decline.

Baby boom retirements and flat educational attainment rates are especially troublesome in the context of broader demographic and employment trends. The U.S. workforce, whose size has increased by almost 50 percent over the past 20 years, or roughly 39 million workers, will slow its growth to only 16 percent over the next several decades (Ellwood, 2001). Assuming even moderate employment growth rates of 15 percent and a continuing increase in skill requirements on the job, the combined effects of these trends should result in significant labor shortages of at least 20 million workers, especially in jobs that require the most skill and provide the greatest economic value added. Two-thirds of the expected shortage in 2020 will likely arise in the most skilled jobs, resulting in a net deficit of workers with at least some college of about 14 million workers.

In the face of sharply reduced labor force growth rates and possible skill shortages, education and training policies will have to play the lead role. In addition, family supports will be necessary to maintain or increase labor market participation, especially among women. Higher minimum wages, more flexible benefits, and an expanded Earned Income Tax Credit (EITC) also may be necessary to encourage labor force participation. We know that a plethora of policies underlying the social safety net has effects on individuals' decisions to work. While lowering the social safety net even further might increase the size of the labor force, only expensive and politically difficult policy changes are likely to increase the available numbers of highly skilled workers (Ellwood, 2001).

Increasing retirement ages, for instance, will sustain labor force participation most among those most dependent on social security payments for retirement. These tend to be the lowest paid and least skilled workers. Further increases in the labor force participation of married women by expanding childcare assistance to the middle class may be the best bet for bringing more skilled workers, but would be extremely expensive (Ellwood, 2001). Large-scale, skill based immigration policies would be effective but politically sensitive.

SIZE OF THE PROBLEM

Make no mistake, expanding a labor market mediation system to reach a labor force of 140 million people will be a costly and complex undertaking. Even reaching out only to low-wage workers will require a sizable increase in investments. While welfare reforms in the mid-1990s were aimed at about 4.5 million adults, the size of the low-wage population earning less than $15,000 is more than 10 times as large at 46.2 million, or about one-third of the labor force. The core of the low-wage labor force is somewhat smaller with fewer than one-half of those workers (20.2 million) residing in low-income families earning less than $25,000 a year. Fewer yet are the 15.6 million workers—or one-third of all low earners—who are significant contributors to total family income (Carnevale and Rose, 2001a). But still, this workforce is nearly three and one-half times larger than the adult welfare population when the rolls were bulging.

In addition to the sheer size of just the low-wage population, there are inherent barriers that compound the problem. While alleviating macroeconomic and institutional barriers and increasing job matching and attachment assistance may help workers access better jobs, many workers still have formidable skill barriers that prevent them from moving up the earnings ladder. Unlike creating innovative childcare, transportation, or housing solutions, skill problems are not always quickly resolved. About 15 percent of the labor force (22 million) are only minimally adept at performing everyday work and life related skills and cannot, for instance, calculate postage costs or interpret instructions from an appliance warranty (Carnevale and Desrochers, 2002).

Education and training programs already in place and targeted to assist these lowest skilled workers serve only a fraction of the roughly 20 million low-wage or minimally adept workers. For example, the former Job Training Partnership Act (JTPA) programs titles I, II, and III only served about 550,000 people a year, while Adult Education Programs serve about 4 million people a year.

Expanding education and training programs to improve the skills of all low-wage workers will be costly. For many of these workers, the investment will be well spent, and providing access to the "first chance" education system is likely to have the greatest long lasting effects. But for those who need years of basic education or training to meet the minimum expected skill levels in better than low-wage jobs, the costs may exceed the public's willingness to pay. Better access to "second chance" social and income supports may be a more cost-effective and politically acceptable alternative.

FLEXIBILITY AND SCALE ARE NOT ENOUGH TO GUARANTEE OUR COMPETITIVE POSITION

In the future, our ability to produce high levels of skill will be critical to the overall performance of the American economy in global competition. Currently, as in the past, our global competitiveness relies less on the quality of our human capital and more on the size of our labor force and the flexible ways we use our human capital. In the future, the general scarcity of labor in America, especially skilled labor, may force us to change our global strategy. Moreover, many of our competitors already have a superior quality of human capital, and their advantages may be increasing. For instance, already Great Britain and three other European nations have higher college graduation rates than the United States (OECD, 2001). In addition, our competitors are rapidly learning to compensate for the U.S. advantages in flexibility and scale by reducing rigidity in their systems of labor market mediation and by creating multinational trading blocs such as the European Communities and the Asia Pacific Economic Cooperation.

Our historical reliance on flexibility and scale, more than human capital development in global competition, is evident in the apparent disconnect between our global economic and educational rankings. For instance, our scores on international tests are consistently sub-par. When compared to other developed nations, the United States ranks in the middle on international measures of skill. Although the United States tends to have a larger share of high-skilled workers than most other countries, it also harbors a larger share of low-skilled workers (OECD, 2000). And while American educational performance is improving at home, among youth aged 25 to 34 who have a high school diploma, we have quietly dropped to sixth in the world behind Norway, Japan, Korea, Czech Republic, and Switzerland (OECD, 2001).

How can we reconcile our mediocre skill assessment and educational attainment standings in the world and our economic success in the high tech global economy? The answer is that we may not have, on average, the world's best stock of skills, but we are pretty good and, because of our size, we have more top workers. For instance, our population is roughly four times the size of that of France, Italy, and the United Kingdom, and more than three times the size of Germany. So while the United States and Germany have similar shares of high-skilled workers, the sheer size of the U.S. labor force translates into roughly 38 million highly skilled U.S. workers, as compared to 11 million German workers.

More is not always better. But oftentimes, four pretty good engineers tackling a business problem are better than one very good engineer working alone addressing the same issue. Similarly, four companies in the software business competing directly against each other are likely to produce better software than a single company.

A second advantage that allows us to be the number one economy with a mediocre educational performance is our flexibility (Bertola, Blau, and Kahn, 2001). Flexible U.S. labor markets allow employers enormous agility in hiring, paying, and allocating workers. America's agility gives us an edge in the global race because it allows us to make better use of our talent.

In Europe and Japan, by comparison, access to jobs and pay is highly regulated by skill certification and seniority, which contributes to job security and income security as well as structural rigidity. European and Japanese education and labor market systems have a tough time redesigning jobs or shifting human and machine capital investments in response to economic and technological change. In recent years, the equitable but inflexible European and Japanese models have driven up costs, suppressing job creation and driving up unemployment. In contrast, the agile American model has boosted job creation and income inequality.

America's characteristic flexibility also means that employers don't need to rely on the nation's homegrown talent. Immigration is a major source of talent among math and science professionals. For instance, a majority of America's civil engineers are foreign born, and more than a third of all engineers are foreign born (National Science Foundation, 2002). In addition, American companies are free to produce offshore if they cannot find the talent at home at the right prices.

The problem is that our advantages won't last. We cannot remain a first-rate economic power with mediocre human capital. All forms of advantages are temporary in global economies. The European and Japanese versions of highly planned economies surged in the 1970s but lost out to American flexibility in the 1980s. Eventually, our competitors will narrow our economic lead as they learn how to create their own versions of agility and scale. At that point, the competition will really come down to who has the best human capital especially in a world where people are no longer nation bound and technology and financial capital ignore national boundaries as they hop across borders from one entrepreneurial opportunity to the next.

At some point soon, if we are to retain the lead in the global economic race, we will have to rely on our homegrown human capital and a more cohesive system of labor market mediation for our competitive edge. Eventually, we will have to close the education gap between our competition and ourselves.

CONCLUSION

Shortages of both skilled and unskilled labor, as well as increases in earnings dispersion, should increase support for workforce intermediaries both in scale and in the scope of services they provide. Whether or not these forces will provide sufficient pressure to break down the current dualism in the structure of mediating institutions and labor markets remains to be seen.

A scarcity of labor, resulting from the combined effects of baby boom retirements and a flattening of labor force participation and educational attainment, is likely to generate a variety of responses. Scarcity should increase labor power, unionization, and the political viability of proposals to "make work pay" in order to encourage labor force participation and to promote flexibility. The need to sustain female participation should increase political leverage for family support services such as childcare and after school programs. Shortages in skilled labor also will increase support for education and training both in the "first chance" and "second chance" systems. Scarcity should create support for using workforce intermediaries to access these and other services such as healthcare. Of course, cost will be a barrier to expansion, and public budget austerity will increase pressures for accountability throughout intermediary institutions.

Alternate proposals such as increased immigration, including an increase in skill based immigration, will be supported by employers, but will run afoul of populist political responses. Increased imports and offshore production to satisfy domestic consumer demand have similar political liabilities because offshore strategies increase trade deficits and export wealth and jobs. Global strategies could be especially sensitive if labor scarcities result in the exportation of high-wage, high-skilled jobs.

Encouraging policies that stall retirements will only affect the lowest paid, lowest skilled workers and provide little relief for shortages in skilled occupations. Economic incentives to keep baby boomers on the job will be expensive because skilled workers over 55 years of age have high expectations for earnings, public and private benefits, and flexible work schemes.

In the short term, the American system of mediation among individuals, communities, and labor markets is likely to remain market based, privatized, and divided into "first chance" and "second chance" tracks. First of all, the market based and privatized system, already in place, benefits the most advantaged who are not likely to be willing to dilute its benefits—the national healthcare debate is a case in point. To some extent, emerging labor shortages will encourage "cherry picking," and the most skilled among the disadvantaged population should be able to transition from the "second chance" to the "first chance" system. At the same time, austerity in public budgets will discourage more extensive investments in the least skilled, leaving "Work First" combined with strategies to "make low-skilled work pay" as the likely path of policy development.

In the long term, the core strategy for developing skilled workers and reducing our runaway income inequality is through inclusion in the "first chance" mainstream educational system. In the meantime, expanding social and economic inclusion beyond access to working poverty and dead-end jobs requires that we dramatically increase the scale and scope of the income and social supports in the "second chance" system. At a minimum, mediating services that support working families need to include expanded access to include healthcare, daycare, and after school programs. In order to "make work pay," substantial increases in the minimum wage need to be accompanied by an expansion in the EITC. In order to encourage economic mobility, education and training should be generally available and supported by family services and stipends that assist people who are in school and out of work.

REFERENCES

Aaberge, Rolf, Anders Bjorklund, Markus Jantti, Marten Palme, Peder J. Pedersen, Nina Smith, and Tom Wennemo. 2002. "Income Inequality and Income Mobility in the Scandinavian Countries Compared to the United States." Retrieved November 18, 2002 at http://www.swopec.hhs.se/hastef/papers/hastefoo98.pdf

Acs, Gregory, Katherin Ross Phillips, and Daniel McKenzie. 2001. "Playing by the Rules, but Losing the Game: Americans in Low-Income Working Families." In Richard Kazis and Marc Miller, eds. *Low-Wage Workers in the New Economy.* Washington, DC: The Urban Institute Press.

Aspen Institute, Domestic Strategy Group. 2002. *Grow Faster Together. Or Grow Slowly Apart. How Will America Work in the 21st Century?* Washington, DC: The Aspen Institute.

Bertola, Guiseppe, Francine D. Blau, and Lawrence M. Kahn. 2001. "Comparative Analysis of Labor Market Outcomes: Lessons for the United States from International Long-run Evidence." In Alan B. Krueger and Robert Solow, eds. *The Roaring Nineties: Can Full Employment Be Sustained?* New York: The Russell Sage Foundation and The Century Foundation.

Blair, Margaret M., and Thomas A. Kochan, eds. 2000. *The New Relationship: Human Capital in the American Corporation.* Washington, DC: The Brookings Institution.

Blank, Rebecca M., ed. 1994. *Social Protection versus Economic Flexibility: Is There a Trade-off?* Chicago: The University of Chicago Press.

Burkhauser, Richard V., Douglas Holtz-Eakin, and Stephen E. Rhody. 1997. "Labor Earnings Mobility in the United States and Germany During the Growth Years of the 1980s." *International Economic Review,* Vol. 38, No. 4. (November).

Cappelli, Peter. 1993. "Are Skill Requirements Rising? Evidence from Production and Clerical Jobs." *Industrial and Labor Relations Review,* Vol. 46, No. 3. (April).

———. 1996. "Technology and Skill Requirements: Implications for Establishment Wage Structures." *New England Economic Review,* (May/June).

———. 2000. "Market-Mediated Employment: The Historical Context." In Margaret M. Blair and Thomas A. Kochan, eds. *The New Relationship: Human Capital in the American Corporation.* Washington, DC: The Brookings Institution.

———. 1998. "Falling Union Membership and Rising Wage Inequality: What's the Connection?" NBER Working Paper 6520. Cambridge, MA: National Bureau of Economic Research.

Card, David, and John E. DiNardo. 2002. "Skill Biased Technological Change and Rising Wage Inequality: Some Problems and Puzzles." NBER Working Paper 8769. Cambridge, MA: National Bureau of Economic Research.

Carnevale, Anthony P. 1999. *Education=Success: Empowering Hispanic Youth and Adults.* Princeton, NJ: Educational Testing Service.

Carnevale, Anthony P., and Donna M. Desrochers. 2002. "The Missing Middle: Aligning Education and the Knowledge Economy." Paper commissioned by the U.S. Department of Education, Office of Vocational and Adult Education.

Carnevale, Anthony P., and Richard A. Fry. 2001. "The Economic and Demographic Roots of Education and Training." In Center for Workforce Success *What's Working Newsletter,* November/December 2001, No. 11. Washington, DC: The Manufacturing Institute, National Association of Manufacturers. www.nam.org/workforce

Carnevale, Anthony P., and Stephen J. Rose. 1998. *Education for What? The New Office Economy.* Princeton, NJ: Educational Testing Service.

———. 2000. "Inequality and the New High-Skilled Service Economy." In Jeff Madrick, ed. *Unconventional Wisdom: Alternative Perspectives on the New Economy.* New York: The Century Foundation Press.

———. 2001a. "Low Earners: Who Are They? Do They Have a Way Out?" In Richard Kazis and Marc S. Miller, eds. *Low-Wage Workers in the New Economy.* Washington, DC: The Urban Institute Press.

———. 2001b. "Career Paths: How Education Prepares Young Workers for Labor Market Success." Princeton, NJ: Educational Testing Service. Unpublished Mimeo.

DiNardo, John E., Nicole Fortin, and Thomas Lemieux. 1996. "Labor Market Institutions and the Distribution of Wages, 1973–1992: A Semi-Parametric Approach." *Econometrica.* (September).

Ellwood, David T. 2001. "The Sputtering Labor Force of the 21st Century: Can Social Policy Help?" In Alan B. Krueger and Robert Solow, eds. *The Roaring Nineties: Can Full Employment Be Sustained?* New York: The Russell Sage Foundation and The Century Foundation.

Esping-Andersen, Gosta. 1996. "After the Golden Age? Welfare State Dilemmas in a Global Economy." In Gosta Esping-Andersen, ed. *Welfare States in Transition: National Adaptations in Global Economies.* London: Sage Publications Ltd.

Freeman, Richard B. 1993. "How Much Has De-Unionization Contributed to the Rise in Male Earnings Inequality?" In Sheldon Danziger and Peter Gottschalk, eds. *Uneven Tides: Rising Inequality in America.* New York: Russell Sage Foundation.

———. 2002. "The Labour Market in the New Information Economy." NBER Working Paper 9254. Cambridge, MA: National Bureau of Economic Research.

Gittleman, Maury, and Mary Joyce. 1995. "Earnings Mobility in the United States, 1967–91." *Monthly Labor Review,* Vol. 118, No. 9. (September).

Gottschalk, Peter. 1997. "Inequality, Income Growth, and Mobility: The Basic Facts." *The Journal of Economic Perspectives,* Vol. 11, No. 2. (Spring).

Heckman, James J. 2002. "Flexibility and Job Creation: Lessons for Germany." NBER Working Paper 9194. Cambridge, MA: National Bureau of Economic Research.

Katz, Lawrence, and Kevin Murphy. 1992. "Changes in Relative Wages, 1963–1987: Supply and Demand Factors." *Quarterly Journal of Economics*, Vol. 107, No. 1. (February).

Kochan, Thomas A. 2000. "Reconstructing the Social Contract in Employment Relations." In Ray Marshall, ed. *Back to Shared Prosperity: The Growing Inequality of Wealth and Income in America*. Armonk, NY: M. E. Sharpe, Inc.

Krueger, Alan. 1993. "How Computers Have Changed the Wage Structure: Evidence from Microdata, 1984–89." *Quarterly Journal of Economics*. (February).

Krugman, Paul. 1992. "The Right, the Rich, and the Facts: Deconstructing the Income Distribution Debate." *The American Prospect*. (Fall).

Lee, David S. 1999. "Wage Inequality in the United States during the 1980s: Rising Dispersion or Falling Minimum Wage?" *The Quarterly Journal of Economics*, CXIV, No. 3. (August).

Levy, Frank, and Richard J. Murnane. 1992. "U.S. Earnings Levels and Earnings Inequality: A Review of Recent Trends and Proposed Explanations." *Journal of Economic Literature*, XXX. (September).

Mishel, Lawrence, and Jared Bernstein. 1995. *The State of Working America, 1994–95*. Armonk, NY: M. E. Sharpe, Inc.

Mishel, Lawrence, Jared Bernstein, and John Schmitt. 1999. *The State of Working America, 1998–99*. Ithaca, NY: Cornell University Press.

———. 2000. *The State of Working America, 2000–01*. Ithaca, NY: Cornell University Press.

Murphy, Kevin M., and Finis Welch. 1993. "Occupation Change and the Demand for Skill, 1940–1990." *AEA Papers and Proceedings*, Vol. 83, No. 2. (May).

National Science Foundation. 2002. "Characteristics of Doctoral Scientists and Engineers" (Table 5). Retrieved January 31, 2002 at http://www.nsf.gov/sbe/srs/srs01406/start.htm.

Organization for Economic Cooperation and Development (OECD). 1997. *Employment Outlook*. www.oecd.org

———. 2000. *Literacy in the Information Age: Final Report of the International Adult Literacy Survey*. Paris, France: OECD Publications.

———. Centre for Educational Research and Innovation. 2001. *Education at a Glance: OECD Indicators 2001*. www.oecd.org.

Reich, Robert B. 2001. *The Future of Success*. New York: Alfred A. Knopf, Inc.

Sawhill, Isabel V., and Daniel P. McMurrer. 1996. "Economic Mobility in the United States. A Companion Piece to 'How Much Do American Move Up and Down the Economic Ladder?'" Retrieved June 26, 2002 at http://www.urban.org/oppor/opp_031.htm.

Shavit, Yossi, and Walter Muller. 1998. *From School to Work: A Comparative Study of Educational Qualifications and Occupational Destinations*. Oxford, UK: Clarendon Press.

IV
CUSTOMER VOICES

8

Creating and Sustaining a Coherent Voice for Employers in Workforce Development: The Cleveland Experience

DANIEL E. BERRY

ORGANIZING A VOICE TO ARTICULATE HOW WORKFORCE DEVELOP-ment systems could better respond to the needs of employers was the focus of Cleveland's Jobs and Workforce Initiative. This ongoing initiative is but one example of the national growth of intermediary interventions in workforce development systems that are aimed at serving both the needs of businesses and jobseekers. As the employer voice created in Cleveland grew louder and more coherent, it stimulated a broad agenda of change efforts. These included advocacy with public agencies and others for fundamental systems reform and brokering the creation of new training programs through innovative partnerships. Examining how this voice was articulated and sustained, and the degree to which it was heard, provides both theoretical and practical lessons about the effectiveness and limitations of intermediary functions in producing workforce system change.

Cleveland is not unique in its desire to involve employers in local workforce development systems. Policy makers and practitioners throughout the U.S. have struggled for years to design systems that effectively engage employers. Writing about American workforce policy nearly two decades ago, MIT's Paul Osterman (1993) observed that there had been "a tenuous relationship of the employment and training system to the private market. . . . the Bureau of National Affairs found that only nine percent of firms surveyed concerning training programs had any involvement with the Job Training Partnership Act."

Although the federal government intended that the 1998 Workforce Investment Act (WIA) should give employers a position as major partners in local workforce development systems, progress toward achieving this goal has been uneven in many communities. In a recent national survey of more than 160 local workforce system professionals, 43 percent indicated that their single most important challenge was engaging employers in their programs, and 66 percent said employers did not use their services because they do not meet employer needs (Jobs for the Future, 2002).

ABOUT THE JOBS AND WORKFORCE INITIATIVE

Cleveland's response to the challenge of engaging employers more actively in workforce development began in 1996 when the Greater Cleveland Growth Association, one of the nation's largest metropolitan Chambers of Commerce, undertook the Jobs and Workforce Initiative (JWFI). This was an ambitious and comprehensive initiative based on the assumption that major system reform was required to strengthen the region's capacity to educate and train the workforce and better connect residents with jobs and careers. This meant altering resource allocations to leverage changes that would achieve larger scale results along with changes in policies and procedures that would contribute to significant improvement of system operations in ways that would engage employers.

Working with several leading community organizations, the Growth Association formed a potent partnership to undertake the JWFI. It included two of the area's leading foundations, The Cleveland Foundation and The George Gund Foundation, as funders and Cleveland Tomorrow, the economic development arm of the chief executives from the region's largest companies, as founding partners. Operating partners were the Cleveland Advanced Manufacturing Program (CAMP), the Greater Cleveland Roundtable, and the Greater Cleveland Hospital Association. In conjunction with these partners, the Growth Association recruited more than 100 senior company executives to participate in a year-long planning process (Berry, 1998).

Early on, the JWFI employers agreed on three principles that would guide their recommendations. Workforce development efforts should be: 1) employer driven, 2) regional in scope, and 3) partnership based. Guided by these principles, the JWFI employers devoted a year's work to reviewing national best practices, site visits to other communities, focus groups, surveys, and analysis of employment forecasts. In January 1997 the JWFI offered specific recommendations to:

1. Respond to immediate occupational shortages.
2. Link workforce development to economic development.
3. Upgrade basic and technological skills of current, future, and transitional workers.
4. Create customer oriented workforce development services.
5. Build employer driven systems.

To help implement the recommendations, the JWFI garnered nearly $4 million in support to invest in specific initiatives. Contributions from area companies and The Cleveland Foundation and The George Gund Foundation comprised the bulk of this support. But national funders like the Annie E. Casey Foundation and the Joyce Foundation, intrigued with the systems reform implications of the JWFI, also provided significant support. The Growth Association formed a new workforce preparation department with dedicated staff to oversee efforts to advance the recommendations (Berry, 1998). An advisory committee comprised of business leaders who were involved in the JWFI planning process remained in place to oversee and monitor implementation.

An Ever-Changing Environment

Before reviewing the JWFI outcomes, it may be useful to step back for a moment to review the environment as the effort began. At the time, the Cleveland region was confronting what the Hudson Institute has described as a worker dearth, both in the quantity and quality of its workforce (Judy and D'Amico, 1997). The strong economy had increased the demand for workers and reduced the unemployment rate in northeast Ohio to levels not seen since the 1960s. Early JWFI surveys of employers indicated that more than 50 percent of companies were having difficulties in finding workers. Paradoxically, good jobs were going unfilled.

From a perspective of labor market inefficiencies, the region was faced with skills mismatches (weak basic skills, a shortage of technical skills, and relatively low educational attainment levels) and spatial mismatches in that the geographic distribution of jobs did not coincide with where many prospective workers lived. Information asymmetry (lack of information or misinformation) further complicated the situation. Residents did not know about career opportunities that existed in the region, and companies did not know about the resources that were available to help address their workforce needs.

At the same time, the region's demographics were ominous. The workforce's average age was older than the national average, and large numbers of skilled workers were approaching retirement with few replacements in sight. Projections indicated that northeast Ohio would have a smaller cohort of new entrants into the labor force than in the past and that the region was not growing through immigration. Thus, in an essentially no-growth region, increasing attention to training and education of the current residents was an absolute need. Almost by definition, this meant that large numbers of the region's disadvantaged, unemployed, and low-wage working population had to be brought into more productive roles in the labor force in order for the region to remain economically competitive.

But the workforce environment is not static. Over the five-year course of the JWFI, major changes in the workforce policy environment occurred that required significant shifts in direction or diverted energy away from implementation. For example, the federal government implemented national welfare reform, focusing enormous attention and resources in the state and region on immediately finding jobs for welfare participants. Additionally, the federal government enacted the Workforce Investment Act. While the WIA embodied many principles similar to those advocated by the JWFI, the challenges of implementing the legislation created considerable confusion and diverted energy away from pursuing the recommendations to compliance with new regulations.

Parallel with WIA implementation, the state of Ohio began a process of reforming its workforce development systems, initially by merging the departments of Human Services and Employment Services into a new agency, the Ohio Department of Jobs and Family Services. The difficulties with implementing this merger have further complicated achievement of proposed reforms at the local level.

More benign developments also affected the JWFI directions. For example, the Growth Association and others completed a major research project in the region to identify industry clusters that were important to the region's economic future. The partners in this project subsequently organized groups of companies drawn from the clusters to articulate what they needed to survive and grow. Workforce issues quickly emerged as a major priority, and the JWFI responded with several cluster-specific workforce initiatives.

In another positive development, the state enacted legislation under which the mayor of Cleveland assumed responsibility for administration of the Cleveland school system. As a result, the mayor appointed a new school board and chief executive officer for the Cleveland Municipal School District. This new leadership has focused on significantly improving the quality of inner city education and has supported several of the JWFI initiatives to engage business as partners in the education system.

Most significantly, the economy has slowed down substantially since the inception of the JWFI. The tight labor market that had motivated many employers to work with the JWFI no longer exists. The most prominent workforce challenge for the community now is to find jobs for thousands of dislocated workers. Even so, the fundamental demographics of the region remain unchanged, and the problems that motivated formation of the JWFI will re-emerge as the economy recovers.

WHAT HAPPENED AS A RESULT OF THE JWFI?

When the JWFI employers presented their report to the community, it attracted considerable attention in the local media, including headline and lead editorial coverage in the region's largest newspaper and strong editorial support from the area's major business publication. In the early years of implementation, the media routinely covered the progress of specific initiatives in a number of follow up stories.

The JWFI also received national attention and acclaim. In 1998 the National Alliance of Business recognized it as a national best practice for building regional business coalitions to address workforce challenges. As recently as 2002, the U.S. Chamber of Commerce highlighted the JWFI's efforts to address workplace literacy as a best practice in a national web-cast and included a case study of this work in its *Chamber Guide to Improving Workplace Literacy*, (Center for Workforce Preparation, 2002).

While media recognition and national awards are important, the value of the JWFI must be measured by its outcomes. As shown is this chapter, the JWFI has made significant progress. While many unforeseen obstacles and new challenges slowed or stymied implementation of some recommendations, the following sections summarize the progress achieved within each of the five original JWFI objectives.

Objective One: Responding to Immediate Occupational Shortages

As an organizing practice, the JWFI convened companies with similar worker needs and brokered a response from the appropriate training provider. The assumption was that more cost-effective and larger scale training would be possible by aggregating demand for workers among companies. The JWFI supported several new training programs based on this assumption.

1. *Corporate Bound.* As its first training initiative, the JWFI partnered with Cuyahoga Community College to develop a customer service training program. It convened 19 companies from various industries that needed these skills to help design curricula, provide guidance and oversight, and hire graduates of the program. With additional support from SBC Ameritech, this program continues and has been modified to focus on call center training. As of June 2001, 227 individuals had completed training in 11 classes, resulting in 114 new placements. The average wage was $9.47 per hour for first-time jobholders and $11.50 per hour for jobholders with prior work experience.

2. *Center for Employment Training (CET) Cleveland.* In partnership with the Urban League, Vocational Guidance Services, and the Cleveland Advanced Manufacturing Program, the JWFI invested resources to replicate the San Jose based Center for Employment Training, widely recognized as a national best practice. CET Cleveland now offers training in four skill tracks: machining, welding, printing/graphics, and shipping/receiving. Financed through various public sector resources, CET has trained 774 workers, of whom 434 are currently employed in their field of training. The six-month retention rate is 85 percent, and the average wage is $8.65 per hour, plus benefits.

3. *Cable Installer Training.* A local cable television company provided the JWFI with $50,000 to design a training program for cable installers. Two other cable companies subsequently joined in to sponsor the program at Polaris Career Center that trained 32 workers, 85 percent of whom were retained for more than 90 days. Although problems within the cable industry have slowed demand for workers, the center will be able to offer the program again when market conditions improve.

4. *Spirit of Hospitality.* The Convention and Visitors Bureau initiated this program, again in partnership with Cuyahoga Community College, which provided technical training in hospitality occupations, and with the Urban League, which provided soft skills training. Some 12 hotels, motels, and restaurants agreed to offer work based learning as part of the training and to consider hiring program graduates. The JWFI participated in planning the program and assisted with start up expenses. A total of 80 individuals participated in the training. After two years, the program was modified and refocused as a school-to-career program.

These training initiatives established early successes for the JWFI that enhanced credibility and added momentum to the implementation efforts.

Objective Two: Link Workforce Development to Economic Development Priorities

To link workforce development to economic development priorities, the JWFI has supported training initiatives that address the needs of industry clusters. The clusters include polymers, metalworking, automotive manufacturing, insurance, biomedical, information technology, and electronic instruments and controls. Similar to its approach to addressing immediate occupational shortages, the JWFI has supported several initiatives that respond to the common workforce needs of cluster companies.

1. *WIRE-Net Machinists Training Initiative.* Along with other national and local funders, the JWFI invested in a partnership led by WIRE-Net, a business led community based organization on Cleveland's west side, along with the federal research facility NASA Glenn and Cuyahoga Community College. Its purpose was to increase numbers of entry-level machinists in northeast Ohio. This program has received recognition from the National Association of Sectoral Practitioners as a national best practice. Since the program's inception, of the 213 trainees who have been enrolled, 140 have graduated. Of these, 115 have been placed in jobs at 80 companies.

2. *Northeast Ohio Manufacturing Awareness Consortium (NEOMAC).* In another partnership with WIRE-Net, the association has supported NEOMAC, a collaborative effort aimed at promoting and strengthening metalworking education and career awareness. Three metalworking trade associations are partners. The consortium has worked with training and education groups to integrate National Institute of Metalworking Standards (NIMS) skills standards into their curricula. To date, five education and training organizations have adopted NIMS.

3. *Region of Manufacturing Excellence (ROME).* Both WIRE-Net and NEOMAC are involved with this multipartner initiative to develop ways of increasing the quantity and improving the quality of the workforce pool for manufacturing. It includes efforts to attract people to careers in manufacturing through career marketing, programs to increase the quality of training and education through adoption of skill standards, and an initiative to develop a new technology and advanced manufacturing high school in inner city Cleveland. The school district has committed resources to the effort, and requests for funding to support ROME are pending with the state of Ohio and the federal government.

4. *Health Care Coalition.* On behalf of the Cuyahoga County Workforce Investment Board, the JWFI secured and managed a sectoral grant from the U.S. Department of Labor to develop a strategic plan for addressing workforce needs of Northeast Ohio's healthcare industry. All the major hospitals and several large nursing care facilities were involved with the effort. The Cleveland Center for Health Affairs will oversee implementation of the recommendations and will submit proposals to area Workforce Investment Boards and local foundations to support the effort.

5. The JWFI also worked with several organizations in northeast Ohio to form a *Regional Skills Training Alliance* focused on information technology (IT) careers. Support from the Ford Foundation enabled the alliance to craft a plan for meeting IT skills needs of companies while providing more opportunities for disadvantaged residents to pursue IT careers. The partners included several community colleges, the Northeast Ohio Software Association (NEOSA), the Greater Akron Chamber, and Northeast Ohio Technology Council. Subsequent to the plan, NEOSA assumed leadership responsibility for advancing the goals of the alliance. The JWFI continues to finance the administration of the *IT Barometer,* a biannual workforce assessment of the demand for information technology occupations and skills in the region. Area colleges and universities have used this information to develop new certificate and degree programs.

Interaction with cluster companies has taken the JWFI in the direction of working more closely with higher education institutions to insure that they are offering a right mix of degree programs that produces graduates in the disciplines needed by industry. Some progress in stimulating new academic offerings at area universities, particularly in technology related degrees, has been achieved, and colleges routinely consult the JWFI to seek input from cluster companies in their degree and curriculum planning.

Another outgrowth of the focus on industry clusters is a new JWFI emphasis on retaining college graduates in the region by expanding the use of cooperative education and internships, partly as a recruitment tool for companies. These efforts increase student awareness of career opportunities in the region with a special focus on promoting internships with cluster companies. The expectation is that a large portion of the interns ultimately will remain in Cleveland when they are ready to seek permanent employment. The flagship initiative is the Graduates Council, created to use internships to retain high-achieving high school graduates who are attending college in Ohio and at out-of-state schools. A business led leadership board oversees the council. The Cleveland Scholarship Programs operates it with financial support from the JWFI. Currently, over 500 student members and 70 companies are participating in the council with the goal of increasing engagement to at least 600 students and 100 companies within a year.

Two other tools developed with assistance from the JWFI are complementary to the goals of the Graduates Council. The first is Cleveland-intern.net, a web site created by a consortium of six colleges and universities in the Cleveland area known as the Northcoast Consortium for Career Advancement. It provides a system on which employers can post internships and co-op opportunities. Students from colleges and universities across the region can gain access to these postings. The consortium will make the system available to the other 16 higher education institutions in the region once it has been debugged.

The second tool is an Internship Guidebook, created and produced to provide employers with "how to" information for establishing internships. The guidebook provides supervisors and human resource personnel with suggestions that can be used for hiring interns and maximizing the experience for both students and employers. The association is distributing 1,500 guidebooks and will conduct employer workshops on structuring internship programs.

Significantly, the JWFI influenced two system changes through the combination of these efforts. First, the Fenn Educational Fund of The Cleveland Foundation (the primary funder of co-op education and internship programs at Cleveland-area colleges) has developed new guidelines. They require that all proposals address how the colleges will connect their internship and cooperative education programing to the needs of industry cluster companies. Second, an initiative of the governor, the state of Ohio has created a statewide program to fund college graduate retention programs, modeled extensively on the experience of the Graduates Council. This new program has directed some resources to support the Graduates Council and similar retention efforts across Ohio.

Objective Three: Upgrade Basic and Technological Skills of Incumbent, Future, and Transitional Workers

The JWFI used an organizing framework that segmented the workforce into incumbent, future, and transition elements to guide recommendations to address high-priority skills development needs.

Incumbent Workers. Early on, the JWFI leaders agreed that continuous learning was essential in the modern workplace. In their view, increasing company competitiveness in the global economy and improving residents' access to jobs with career advancement potential both required continuous skills upgrading. Accordingly, the JWFI supported efforts to promote more attention to the need for skills upgrading of incumbent workers with a major emphasis on basic literacy.

1. *Worker Investment in Skills Enhancement (WISE).* The JWFI invested resources in a pilot computer assisted skills upgrading program administered by the Old Stone Education Foundation and the Adult and Continuing Education Division of Cleveland Municipal Schools. Participating companies in and near downtown Cleveland provided released time during the workday to employees with growth potential but who needed basic skills upgrading. The program has completed four training cycles involving 80 workers. The latest class includes dislocated steelworkers along with several of their spouses who are being forced to enter the workforce to supplement family incomes.

2. *Work in Northeast Ohio Council-Northcoast Education Services Initiative.* In partnership with The Cleveland Foundation, the JWFI supported a demonstration program to improve basic skills of current workers through direct training interventions in companies and to document the outcomes of the intervention. It provided on-site basic skills assessments and tailored skills upgrading to companies. Eight companies participated in the demonstration, resulting in training of 208 workers, with reported gains in productivity, safety, attendance, and employee morale.

These efforts subsequently contributed to one of the JWFI's major achievements in leveraging broad system reform in 1998. Drawing on pilot and demonstration program experiences, along with the results of a national best practices study, the Growth Association took the lead in advocacy that convinced the state of Ohio to enact a marginal tax credit to companies to support up to 50 percent of the costs of skills upgrading for incumbent workers. After a disappointing first year that led to program modifications, in 2000 the state approved credits for the full allocation of $20 million, thereby leveraging another $20 million in training investment from the participating companies. In 2001 the state issued $11.1 million in credits to 165 companies before putting the program on hold because of its fiscal problems, proving that success can be fleeting. However, the state has indicated that applications will be accepted again during 2003 for credits it will issue in 2004.

Future Workers. Several JWFI recommendations were aimed at ensuring that young people leaving area high schools, particularly those from the inner city, have a better understanding of the skill requirements of the modern workplace and awareness of career opportunities.

1. *Business and Education Network (BEN).* This is an attempt to substantially increase the level of business participation in public education by engaging companies to provide career education and works based learning for students and teachers. In 2000 the JWFI developed a partnership with Youth Opportunities Unlimited (Y.O.U.) to operate BEN as a centralized recruitment and matching system to provide easy and useful access for businesses. To support BEN's employer recruitment efforts, the JWFI collaborated with the Cleveland Society for Human Resource Management to produce and distribute 3,000 employer guidebooks on effective works based learning for high school students. Some 296 companies are involved and have provided 11,079 works based learning experiences to area high school students through 2002.

2. *Priority Hiring Status (PHS).* At the request of Cleveland's mayor, the JWFI took the lead in negotiating an arrangement on behalf of the business community whereby companies would provide jobs to the graduates of the Cleveland Municipal Schools. Originally proposed by the mayor as a "jobs guarantee," the JWFI redefined this initiative as a commitment to offer Priority Hiring Status to the young people. Its purpose is to provide high school graduates who meet a rigorous set of job readiness criteria and are not attending college with first access to appropriate job openings at participating companies. Begun in 2001, this is now a collaborative effort among the city of Cleveland, the Growth Association, and the Cleveland Municipal School District (CMSD). In the first year, 96 of 150 eligible students at six inner city high schools participated, resulting in 51 job placements with PHS employers.

To support systems reform, the JWFI has worked closely with the Cleveland Municipal School District to incorporate the JWFI job readiness standards identified as important to employers into its academic areas. In addition, the CMSD also has established an office of School to Careers to further the implementation of work based learning, skill standards, and technical education academies.

Transitional Workforce. Several JWFI efforts in addressing the transitional workforce have been focused on building community capacity to address the welfare-to-work challenges confronting Cleveland. For example, the JWFI provided financial support and collaborated with the county, the Regional Transit Authority, and the Solon Chamber of Commerce to develop a reverse commute program that linked inner city jobseekers with employment opportunities in the suburbs. As a result, the transit authority ultimately developed a new "flyer" bus line to ease the commute from the central city to the eastern suburbs.

Through an investment of its resources, the JWFI also was instrumental in encouraging Cuyahoga County to replicate national best practices in work readiness training for welfare-to-work participants. The JWFI brought Community Link (a STRIVE adaptation) from St. Louis to provide technical assistance to community organizations. As a result, two African American Baptist churches in inner city Cleveland have adopted the Community Link model and have graduated a total of 267 individuals and placed 200 in jobs thus far.

Because of the JWFI, the Growth Association was one of seven employer organizations in the U.S. asked to participate in the Workforce Innovation Network (WIN), a demonstration program operated by Jobs for the Future and funded by the Ford Foundation. WIN's purpose was to develop services and tools that would help companies address ways of building career ladders within and across companies that provide advancement opportunities for entry-level workers. The focus of this ongoing effort is to develop career paths for low-wage workers through skills credentialing within nursing care facilities that can transfer across to hospitals.

Although not a direct JWFI initiative, the Growth Association has played a significant advocacy role in urging the city and county to support Cuyahoga Community College's Training Academies. These academies provide low-wage workers with access to short-term skills training in skilled trades, health careers, information technology, and customer service. Certification and academic training can help these individuals advance in their employment and gain better and higher paying jobs. By the end of June 2002, 2,445 adults and 219 youth had enrolled in the academies. Of these individuals, 2,419 were pursuing advanced education under formal Education Development Plans. Initially funded through Temporary Assistance to Needy Families (TANF), continuation of the academies is now threatened by funding reductions. Because this effort has achieved significant scale in such a short time, the Growth Association is urging the city and county to devise funding solutions to sustain the program.

Objective Four: Create Customer Oriented Workforce Development Services

A call for a One Stop workforce development system in Cuyahoga County that would effectively engage and serve both employers and residents was the major recommendation of the JWFI. Because this recommendation was so important, support for efforts to advance the One Stop system comprised the single largest category of JWFI expenditures. Resources were used to benchmark other One Stop systems around the country, pay for consultants to assist in planning and design of the Cleveland-Cuyahoga County one stop system, and assist with developing the technology plan for the local system.

In 1997 these efforts resulted in a $650,000 grant to Cuyahoga County from the state of Ohio to implement the Cleveland-Cuyahoga One Stop Workforce Development System, awarded under the U.S. Department of Labor's One Stop demonstration program. Along with the Growth Association, the other partners in submitting this proposal were Cuyahoga County, the city of Cleveland, the Ohio Bureau of Employment Services, the Cleveland Municipal School District (Adult Education), and Cuyahoga Community College. Through this grant, a job matching technology system was developed and the state ultimately certified two One Stop Centers.

However, uneven commitments among the partners to developing a partnership based One Stop system, extensive staff turnover in various agencies throughout the planning process, and the major distractions resulting from passage of welfare reform legislation and the Workforce Investment Act all hampered the One Stop development effort. Under enormous pressure to place large numbers of welfare-to-work clients in jobs, the county pursued its own system of neighborhood service centers focused on serving the welfare-to-work population. The city of Cleveland adopted its own One Stop model and developed two career centers targeted at serving the traditional JTPA clientele. The state of Ohio simply renamed its employment service offices as "One Stop Workforce Development Centers." In the meantime, the community college, apparently frustrated by the public sector's lack of focus, developed its own One Stop Career Centers primarily to serve its students on each of its three campuses.

In practice, this collection of independent One Stop initiatives has fallen short of providing high-quality services to either a universal population of jobseekers or to businesses. This influenced the JWFI's decision to try an alternative approach to engage employers, in the hope that organized employer demand would, in turn, help shape a more useful system for jobseekers. In 1999 the Growth Association agreed to incubate Employment

Central (EC) on behalf of the One Stop partners for a period of 12–18 months. The expectation was that EC would be incorporated into the new One Stop system mandated under the Workforce Investment Act once it was created.

EC was intended to serve as a single point of contact through which employers could gain easy access to a range of workforce developments services in the area—including, and most importantly, employee recruitment and screening. A primary market target was small to medium sized companies that do not have a great deal of internal capacity in their human resources departments to manage employee recruitment. It also was intended to serve larger companies, especially those looking for large numbers of workers in a short time frame.

Employers' access was provided through a web site and a toll-free telephone number supported by a staff of company account representatives to assist the companies. Initially, the One Stop partner agencies delegated a total of 12 part-time staff (five full-time equivalents) to work with EC in the Growth Association's offices as account representatives responsible for administering a coordinated job development and placement system.

Ultimately, the loaned staffing model did not work. The employees of the various partner agencies were routinely called back to their home offices to perform tasks deemed by their supervisors to be of higher priority. Only the Growth Association and one remaining partner, the Adult and Continuing Education Division of the Cleveland Municipal Schools, ultimately ended up providing staff to EC. Consequently, EC's redefined mission has become much narrower than originally conceived, serving primarily as a connection between companies and nontraditional sources of workers. Job orders received from companies are distributed to a network of 65 community based training organizations that screen their clients' skills against the position requirements. At present, 314 companies are engaged, with more than 150 current job postings, and 20–25 new orders are placed each week. There are currently 3,600 jobseeker listings in EC's jobseeker bank.

Although useful to some employers, the current arrangement falls short of realizing the vision of the JWFI and the partnership that guided the early One Stop planning. It is missing the essential commitment from the partners to use EC as their primary job development and placement mechanism. For these reasons, the association is winding down its involvement with EC and incorporating some of its functions into member services, while continuing its advocacy for a true One Stop system. Encouragingly, the United Way Services Vision Council has joined in as an important new ally in advocating for a better One Stop approach in the community, adding the voice of the human services community.

Objective Five: Build Employer Driven Systems

Part of the reason that the Cleveland area does not yet have an effective One Stop workforce development system is because it does not have a governance structure that demands such a system and is responsible for overseeing it. Although the JWFI leaders were optimistic that the new Workforce Investment Boards required under WIA would lead the charge for an employer driven system, these hopes have not been realized. Despite the urging of the JWFI, the city of Cleveland and Cuyahoga County have opted to create their own separate workforce systems. This has diluted business engagement and limited the coordination of resources to achieve better focus and larger scale of impact.

The JWFI is fortunate that several of its business executives were appointed by the governor to serve on the State Workforce Policy Board. It also was successful in placing several of the JWFI employers in leadership positions on both the city and county Workforce Investment Boards. The JWFI continues to provide these individuals with support to help them provide leadership on these bodies. While the city and county have not pursued an integrated system, they have begun to collaborate more on service delivery and now are considering a joint strategic planning process, at the urging of business leaders.

Beyond its involvement with the WIBs, the JWFI has communicated the message to the broader community that workforce development systems should be employer driven by sponsoring regional forums on workforce development. Convened by business organizations throughout the region, the purposes of the forums were to develop a common understanding of the workforce challenges confronting the region and commitments from the various stakeholders to take individual or collective actions to address the challenges. They served as an important vehicle for elevating workforce development to a high priority in the region. For example, a major *Plain Dealer* series on educational attainment in the region drew heavily on information presented and issues discussed at the 1999 forum. Encouragingly, the Cuyahoga County Workforce Investment Board has indicated an interest in convening a similar forum in 2003.

Within the employer community, the JWFI supported efforts to help improve employer access to the region's workforce development services by educating them about available resources. With support from the U.S. Chamber of Commerce, the JWFI and the Council of Smaller Enterprises (COSE), the Growth Association's small business division, sponsored a Workforce Academy for small businesses to help identify recruitment and retention resources. Two training sessions were held in which a total of

70 companies participated. The academy curriculum has been placed on COSE's web site as a resource for member companies.

THE INTERMEDIARY FUNCTIONS OF THE JWFI

Mechanisms like the regional forums and the workforce academies have been helpful in engaging some businesses, but they are isolated events and too labor intensive to reach and engage large numbers. Articulating what *all* employers want from a workforce development system in places like Cleveland is not a simple proposition. From the perspective of some employers, improving the quality of public education so that entry-level workers can read and write is the workforce solution. Other employers want a system that will deliver entry-level employees with a strong work ethic, while others want help in attracting highly skilled scientists and engineers to live and work in Cleveland. In still other cases, employers want assistance with training current workers.

These different perspectives show up clearly in the results of a survey of Cleveland employers conducted jointly by the U.S. Chamber of Commerce and the Growth Association's small business division, the Council of Smaller Enterprises. That survey found that 24 percent believed job applicants had the wrong skills; 12.7 percent said applicants had no skills; and 23.3 percent said they had poor skills (Center for Workforce Preparation, 2001).

There is no single intervention that can respond to such a wide range of concerns and opinions. Forging a single voice out of this cacophony is complicated. The challenge is more one of melding a choir from these different voices. Almost as difficult is sustaining that voice. As one JWFI business leader noted, "Employers are fickle. They will jump ship if their needs aren't quickly met, and it's difficult to keep them engaged beyond the point when their needs are met."

Two metaphors from the business world help explain the intermediary roles that the JWFI has attempted to play in creating employer voice in this complicated environment. The first is the *impannatore*, individuals who have brokered relationships among firms in Italy's textile industry since medieval times. The *impannatore* manage relationships and facilitate deal making among customers, fabric designers, fashion houses, finishers, shippers, and financial institutions. Highly knowledgeable about the industry and extremely trustworthy, their purpose is to help promote the growth of the industry overall while maintaining the independence of individual firms in the network (Jaikumar, 1986). The JWFI has played a kind of *impannatore* role among employers and providers, in part by collecting information from employers and brokering it with providers to help them align their programing with company needs.

The importance of this information brokering function is explained through a second metaphor drawn from network theory. According to Ken-ichi Imai (1989), a scholar of industrial systems, one outcome from networks is the production of information that must be "edited" in order to be useful. While some kind of structure initially controls and sets direction of the network, the structure gradually evolves from designing itself to "editing the network." He adds that this editing function is an entrepreneurial role and provides a milieu whereby, through employing, combining, and assembling various actors and by introducing entirely new elements, a new synergy can be developed. Unexplored opportunities, both on the demand side in creating new business opportunities and on the supply side in coordinating new network combinations, are the result. The many program and system reform initiatives described earlier in this chapter are examples of how the JWFI played this entrepreneurial role of "editing the workforce network."

The Entrepreneurial Role of the JWFI: Tactics and Tools for Creating Voice

The networking editing function played by the JWFI involved the intentional use of a range of tools and tactics that helped create and communicate the employer voice.

Quality Information. The JWFI organizers believed that collecting, interpreting, and distributing current information about employer workforce needs would result in positive change. The initial agenda was driven in large part by a detailed survey of the workforce needs of 1,200 employers representative of the area's economic structure. This was supplemented with surveys and focus groups that assisted with design of specific initiatives and continues with detailed workforce assessments in targeted industry clusters.

Segmentation. As discussed earlier, employers often do not sing from the same hymnal when they voice their workforce concerns. From the start, the JWFI attempted to sort the employer community into coherent segments by organizing efforts that responded to the workforce needs of groups of companies with common needs. This approach has become even more prevalent in the JWFI's effort to link workforce development with economic development where sectoral and industry cluster initiatives have proven useful in organizing sections of the employer choir.

Marketing and Media. The media were and continue to be an important ally in ensuring that the voice of employers was and is heard. To ensure a structural connection, the Growth Association organizers included media representatives in the JWFI advisory board. Focusing events, such as the regional workforce forum, supplemented with press releases, media briefings, and invitations to media representatives, were important tools in attracting media attention and support that raised the credibility of the JWFI within the community.

Positive Infiltration. Business leaders drawn from the JWFI have assumed positions of influence within the public sector systems, including membership on the state and local Workforce Investment Boards, the Cleveland Municipal School District's School to Career Advisory Board, and the Empowerment Zone Citizens Advisory Committee. The JWFI focus on developing a cadre of business leaders to participate in these bodies has helped ensure that an articulate voice that can speak on behalf of employers is present in key policy-making circles.

Strategic Alliances. Although the Growth Association represents a large and broad segment of companies though its membership, it cannot speak with authority on behalf of all of the 80,000 companies in northeast Ohio. For this reason, the association was careful to develop alliances with other business-serving organizations on specific JWFI initiatives. These included human resource organizations such as the Employers Resource Council and the Cleveland Society of Human Resource Managers, trade associations like the Cleveland chapter of the National Tooling and Machining Association, the Precision Metalforming Association, other membership organizations such as the Greater Cleveland Hospital Association, and community based employer organizations such as the West-side Retention and Expansion Network. The alliances with these groups extended the reach of the JWFI, enhanced its credibility, and enabled it to speak more authoritatively on behalf of employers.

Trusted Partners. It was not the intent of the JWFI to develop a new workforce service infrastructure or to compete with others in the community for limited resources. Rather the goal was to work with like-minded organizations to advance a shared agenda. The JWFI organizers recognized the need for allies who could do the actual work, heeding the advice of noted systems theorist Herbert Simon (1969) who has said, "A system must have windows on the world so that it can adjust to its outer environment, but it also must have hands so that it can act to change that environment." Examples of this approach were described under each of the five objectives. Most recently, the Growth Association has structured an arrangement with Cuyahoga Community College whereby its Corporate College will provide customized training services to member companies and support the association's business attraction and retention efforts.

The Internet. The worldwide web represents an enormous potential for communicating the employer voice that the JWFI has only begun to tap. Early in the process, JWFI representatives began meeting with representatives of the Northeast Ohio Council on Higher Education and representatives from other private sector workforce initiatives in the region. One product that resulted from this collaboration was NOWDirectory.com, an on-line inventory of training resources across the region that has been modified recently to accept feedback from employers and individuals on the quality of the training experience.

Limits of the JWFI Intermediary Functions

Even with the availability of these tools and tactics, there are both theoretical and practical limits to what intermediaries can accomplish. Systems theorists argue that there is an important distinction between complicated and complex mechanisms. The French sociologist Bruno LaTour (1996), for example, says that complicated mechanisms need *intermediary* functions within them, while complex systems need *mediators* among their elements. Employers are a *complicated* group, and intermediary functions like the JWFI can be helpful in creating a coherent voice. However, the workforce system, comprised as it is of many stakeholders—schools, jobseekers, students, training groups, and government, along with employers—is a *complex* mechanism that requires mediators among its elements.

Moving from theory back to practice, the JWFI has been effective in performing intermediary functions but unable to play the mediating role that is needed to align the interests of many stakeholders in the workforce system. In part, this happens because the employer voice is only one among many voices that are heard in dialogues about workforce systems or issues. At times, the employer voice is unpopular and disregarded, as was the case when the Growth Association took the lead in opposing passage of a living wage ordinance in Cleveland in 2001. Although the association was representing its members' interests in opposing the legislation, it was strongly endorsed by organized labor, and the city council eventually passed it by a 21–0 vote.

The Workforce Investment Boards, at the policy level, and the One Stop systems, at the service delivery level, were intended to play the important,

mediating function among the various stakeholder voices. The absence of
effective mediating institutions in northeast Ohio has clearly inhibited
responsiveness to the voice of employers. Creating such mechanisms
requires committed political leadership. As the Workforce Strategy Center
noted in its assessment of New York City's workforce development experience: "No city has been able to meet the twin goals of coordinating scattered
training programs and obtaining buy-in from the business community without committed and persistent leadership at the highest levels of city government and the business sector" (Fischer et al., 2002).

THE NEXT PHASE

The JWFI has seeded important efforts that have added permanent capacity to the region's workforce development capability. It has supported many
other important efforts through advocacy and achieved some important
system reforms. Millions of dollars have been invested through the resulting initiatives, and thousands of individuals and hundreds of companies
have benefited. Even so, the JWFI clearly fell short of achieving some of its
major system reform goals, and some of its achievements remain fragile. In
this context, recalibration of strategies and tactics is necessary and underway. In charting the JWFI's future, the business leaders have suggested a
six-point agenda to the Growth Association.

1. *Continue advocacy for broad system reform.* No one else is pursuing this
   agenda on behalf of employers. Although the political environment
   has not been conducive to city-county collaboration at the systems
   level, the Growth Association should continue to work toward this
   goal. It should support the efforts of business representatives on the
   State Workforce Policy Board and the city and county Workforce
   Investment Boards to push for effective One Stop systems and
   employer leadership in the system. The hope is that these boards
   ultimately can play the mediating functions among stakeholders that
   are necessary to achieve meaningful systems change.
2. *Seize the moment.* The bright side in the current difficult economic
   times is that it may well represent an opportunity for reform that
   was diluted by the strong economy of the late 1990s. Companies in
   desperate need of workers during the JWFI's early years were willing to work with nearly any educational and training institution, and
   the providers were not motivated to address long-term fundamental change in such an environment. With many training organiza-

tions now struggling to place their graduates because of the economic climate, they are much more responsive to suggestions about how to shape more effective ways of approaching employers. The community should act quickly to realize this opportunity.

3. *Develop a clear, consistent theme to both communicate and guide efforts.* As discussed earlier, the breadth and complexity of the workforce agenda has proven to be a complicating factor for the JWFI. It has given at least the appearance of a lack of focus and created difficulties in succinctly communicating the scope and accomplishments. Articulation of a more descriptive theme and vision would enable the JWFI to have a more coherent voice and to be selective about what it is trying to accomplish. This may require rebranding of the JWFI.

4. *Focus on collaboration with training and educational institutions that are ready, willing, and able to work as partners.* The JWFI should avoid operating programs on an ongoing basis and turn over program administration to willing community partners as soon as possible. The practice of working with trusted partners, cited earlier in the examples of Cuyahoga Community College, Youth Opportunities Unlimited, and the Cleveland Scholarship Programs, should be continued and expanded in order to achieve scalability. The many worthwhile efforts underway in the community still do not yet add up to a major impact on the system.

5. *Ensure that past JWFI successes survive and thrive.* The JWFI must consolidate and preserve past gains. The experience indicates that the systems change process is more labor intensive and requires more time than initially anticipated. It requires ongoing management of a portfolio of projects. Taking many of the JWFI efforts from the idea stage to success will take longer than five years, and achieving substantial progress and sustainability will require patience and long-term commitment. Initiatives like the Center for Employment Training, the Business and Education Network, and the State Tax Credit all are fragile. They must be monitored and adapted to changes in political and economic realities and shifts in policy priorities if they are to survive.

6. *Translate broad messages into specific projects that have clear outcomes and time horizons where the JWFI has some measure of control over outcomes.* One example is the ROME initiative, which has translated the general call for improved inner city education to planning and advocacy for a Technology and Advanced Manufacturing Academy. Although this initiative is complex and requires collaboration among the

industry clusters, Cuyahoga Community College, CAMP, WIRE-Net, and the Cleveland Municipal School District, it can be expressed as a specific project that has an end point.

The bottom line for the JWFI is that its intermediary position limited its ability to directly control many of the outcomes that the participating employers had deemed desirable. The JWFI's primary tool was persuasion. Despite the fact that this persuasive power was grounded in the collective voice of a large number of businesses, this alone was not enough to achieve all the recommended system changes—for all the reasons described earlier. Even so, the JWFI's employer voice called for and successfully stimulated actions from a variety of other stakeholders. These provided companies with qualified workers and created career opportunities for many unemployed and low-wage residents.

Today, during the current recession, workforce development is still a higher priority on the Cleveland region's agenda than it was in the beginning. This is due in part to the JWFI's continued emphasis on the importance of addressing the issue. The remaining challenges in Cleveland are to build effective mediating capabilities within the workforce development system where the voices of all stakeholders can be heard and to bridge the gap between listening to their concerns and taking action to address them.

REFERENCES

Berry, Daniel. 1998. "Northeast Ohio Employers Plan for Workforce Development." *Economic Development Quarterly*, Vol. 12, No. 1.

Center for Workforce Preparation. 2002. *Higher Skills: A Chamber Guide to Improving Workplace Literacy.* Washington, DC: U.S. Chamber of Commerce. (Spring).

Center for Workforce Preparation. 2001. *Benchmark Survey Summary Report for Council of Smaller Enterprises.* Washington, DC: U.S. Chamber of Commerce. (May).

Fischer, David J., Neil S. Kleiman, with Julian Alssid. 2002. *Rebuilding Job Training from the Ground Up: Workforce System Reform after 9/11.* New York: Center for an Urban Future and Workforce Strategy Center. (August).

Imai, Ken-ichi. 1989. "Evolution of Japan's Corporate and Industrial Networks." in Bo Carlsson, ed. *Industrial Dynamics: Technological, Organizational and Structural Changes in Industries and Firms.* Boston & Dordrecht: Kluwer Academic Publishers.

Jaikumar, Ramchandran. 1986. *Massimo Manachetti.* Cambridge, MA: Harvard Business School Publishing Division.

Jobs for the Future. 2002. *Survey of Workforce Development Professionals on Role of Employers.* http://www.jff.org/jff/pdfdocuments/WINsSurveypdf.

Judy, Richard, and Carol D'Amico. 1997. *Workforce 2020: Work and Workers in the 21st Century.* Indianapolis, IN: Hudson Institute.

LaTour, Bruno. 1996. *Aramis or the Love of Technology.* Cambridge, MA: Harvard University Press.

Osterman, Paul. 1993. Quoted in Glazer, Nathan. "City Leadership in Human Capital Investment." In Henry G. Cisneros, ed. *Interwoven Destinies: Cities and the Nation.* New York: W.W. Norton.

Simon, Herbert A. 1969. *The Sciences of the Artificial.* Cambridge, MA: MIT Press.

9

Perception vs. Reality: Employer Attitudes and the Rebranding of Workforce Intermediaries

JESSICA K. LAUFER AND SIAN WINSHIP

INTRODUCTION

Looking at Demand

The field of workforce development has now extensively documented the "supply side" of the labor equation, studying best practices and longitudinal outcomes for low-income people who receive training, education, and job placement. Less documented, but no less important, is the demand side of the equation: the needs, attitudes, beliefs, and outcomes for employers. In an effort to close that gap, in 2001 the John D. and Catherine T. MacArthur Foundation commissioned Laufer Green Isaac (LGI), a Los Angeles–headquartered strategic marketing communications firm specializing in social issue marketing and corporate-community partnerships, to research the "demand" side of the workforce development equation.

What we found was surprising. In the process of identifying and understanding the needs of business executives relative to workforce development, the research revealed a complete disconnect between employer perceptions and preferences for workforce programs and the programs themselves. In other words, *the facts of a program's success matter less to employers than the attitudes employers have about the program, what type of institution is running it, and the workers it serves.* This revelation is startling because it flies in the face of the conventional wisdom of funders, advocates, and other thought leaders that says, "If you build a better mousetrap, the world will beat a path to your door."

As many workforce development advocates know, engaging employers in workforce development programs for low-income people and nontraditional labor pools is not an easy task. Despite the presence of many successful models and reports of promising outcomes for individuals, business, and society, developing the partnerships necessary to implement win-win strategies eludes many of the most talented, sophisticated, and successful practitioners in the country.

Understanding the attitudes and preferences expressed by employers is one of the first steps toward effectively responding to the demand side of the labor force equation. Workforce development advocates may utilize the research findings discussed here to better craft appropriate strategies for developing win-win alliances with corporations in their targeted industries.

The Relevance of Branding to Workforce Development

The employer attitudes revealed in our research may be more easily understood if viewed through the lens of social psychology and consumer behavior. Marketers have long known the value of "brand imagery" in affecting behavior. Many people incorrectly associate the term "branding" with icons of commercialism, e.g., Nike and the ubiquitous swoosh. However, according to David A. Aaker (1996), noted author, professor at the University of California, Berkeley, Haas School of Business, and internationally recognized authority on branding, "Brand equity is a set of assets (and liabilities) linked to a brand's name and symbol that adds to (or subtracts from) the value provided by a product or service to a firm and/or that firm's customers." A brand is a relationship. A brand is the emotional connection that a consumer has with a product or service that sometimes causes him to short-circuit a logical process of evaluation, based on the consumer's beliefs. In other words, *a brand is distinct from the functional attributes of a product or service.*

Consumer identification with a brand is primarily based on the emotional connection of trust. The trust a consumer feels for a particular company is transferred to the company's products or services. Brand experts sometimes refer to this as the "halo effect" of a brand. *This same "brand halo effect" applies to different types of labor market intermediaries and to the disadvantaged people they serve.*

Through the research discussed here, LGI found that "brand image" is a surprisingly important challenge for advocates and funders interested in workforce development issues. For workforce development organizations, this means dealing with the realities of the ethnic, social, and cultural stereotypes employers have about disadvantaged and low-income people. This chapter highlights the findings of this research and offers specific recommendations for advocates and funders alike to increase the effectiveness of their programs, their communications, and their funding practices.

RESEARCH BACKGROUND

Objectives and Design

The workforce organizations included in this chapter comprise the broadest array of labor market intermediaries and workforce development organizations—private temporary service firms, nonprofits, and public organizations and colleges. Workforce intermediaries, as defined in this book, are among the organizations and partnerships that are studied. There is, however, no one single term that covers all these types of organizations, so we will use the term labor market intermediaries, as is also done in chapter 13, to capture this breadth. Recommendations are addressed to all these organizations, with specific attention to workforce intermediaries.

The objectives of the research were threefold: 1) identify and understand the needs of business executives from three target industry clusters, relative to the employment of low-wage workers and the issues that affect them; 2) define a pragmatic, actionable solution to those needs; and 3) gauge reactions to labor market intermediaries and, at the same time, measure the current level of interest in the use of intermediaries as a catalyst for addressing employer needs.

Three industrial clusters of interest were identified including: fabricated metals and industrial machinery manufacturing; transportation, distribution, and logistics; and healthcare and biomedical technology. Participants included executives from such esteemed companies as United Parcel Service, Teradyne, Maytag International, Hartmarx, New World Van Lines, Hitachi Transport Systems, Alberto-Culver, Abbot Labs, and United Pharmaceuticals. Lesser known metal and other manufacturing firms and large local hospitals and care-giving facilities were also involved in the study. Overall, over 80 different companies were represented in the focus groups.

The research was conducted in two waves: Wave I (June 26–28, 2001, in the metropolitan and suburban areas of Chicago) and Wave II (July 31–Aug. 1, 2002, in Edison, New Jersey, and in New York City). The elapsed time between the two waves of research is significant to the findings in that Wave II was conducted in a post-September 11 economy. It is also worth noting that Wave II was conducted after the corporate accounting fraud scandals (e.g., Enron, Global Crossing, etc.) of early 2002. Despite a significant downturn in the economy, a surge in unemployment, a dip in durable goods, and plunging consumer confidence, the essential results of Wave I and Wave II of the study were remarkably similar.

Focus Groups

As the late political consultant Lee Atwater once said, the conversations in focus groups "give you a sense of what makes people tick and a sense of what's going on with people's minds and lives that you simply can't get with survey data." For decades, businesses have used focus groups to monitor attitudes, product usage trends, and beliefs among consumers on a national basis.

To provide a forum in which we could probe and understand the complex issues associated with the research objectives relative to labor market intermediaries, a qualitative research methodology (i.e., focus groups) was recommended.

A total of ten two-hour focus groups were conducted across three locations: Chicago, New York City, and Edison. At the close of the session respondents were paid an honorarium of approximately $125 per person.

Groups were segmented by industry with an average of three groups per industry cluster (see Table 9.1).

Each group was composed of senior-level human resources executives with decision-making responsibility for the recruitment and training of entry-level/low-skilled workers at their company. Respondents were recruited according to strict screening criteria and were chosen to represent a mix of large, medium, and small companies (with more than 25 employees).

Focus Group Process

Focus group participants were led through a series of structured and unstructured exercises and projective techniques during the two-hour period. After a brief introduction and warm up, an independent moderator led respondents through a predetermined discussion guide. The facilitated sessions began with an unaided discussion of the challenges associated with filling entry- to mid-level positions.

Table 9.1   Focus Group Research Matrix

	Chicago, IL	New York, NY	Edison, NJ
Metal Manufacturing	1		1
General Manufacturing	1		1
Transportation/Logistics and Warehousing	2	1	
Healthcare/Caregivers	1	1	
Healthcare/Biomedical Technology	1		

Respondents were then exposed to a series of five one-paragraph examples of training and/or recruitment partnerships between companies and labor market intermediaries. One example was provided for each of the following: 1) types of community based nonprofit organizations, 2) for-profit employment agencies, 3) community colleges, 4) trade associations, and 5) union based organizations or coalitions with union involvement. The examples were screened to represent a wide range of industries and to exclude any organizations within the local testing area to prevent bias. After providing their initial reactions, the moderator engaged the participants in a lengthy discussion of the examples. Respondents were then each asked to independently identify the pros and cons associated with the different types, then discuss their choices with the group. Following that exercise, respondents were each asked to craft their "ideal" intermediary and share it with the group.

In a final exercise, respondents were exposed to stimuli listing more than 30 labor market intermediaries from their surrounding area. They were then asked to rate their impressions of these intermediaries as positive or negative, and indicate if they had direct experience with them. Respondents were then asked to share a few examples of organizations they had rated positively and negatively with the group and their reason for that assessment.

The LGI team conducted the analysis of the research. Team members observed each group on site and also conducted extensive review and analysis of recordings of the proceedings. Although qualitative research is inherently not statistically projectable, the scope of the research design and implementation, the rigor of the methodology, and the consistency of respondent comments over time support the research findings as viable trend information for use by a variety of concerned stakeholders.

THE RESEARCH FINDINGS: STEREOTYPES, PREJUDICE, AND PERCEIVED RISK

I'm a Horatio Alger kind of person. The same problems that
put them into their situation come into your organization . . .
theft . . . confrontations . . . then they sue you.
—Metal Manufacturing Employer, Chicago

Employer Attitudes toward Low-Income Workers

The findings from the focus groups revealed that racial and ethnic stereotypes increase the perceived risk associated with the training and employment of low-income people.

Despite the advances in civil rights, diversity, and cultural awareness over the last half-century, racial, ethnic, and social stereotypes still exist in this country. In fact, they are remarkably close to the surface. Focus group respondents were extremely candid about their beliefs as supported by their experiences.

Employer respondents generally associated low-income individuals with crime and substance abuse problems. When exposed to examples of companies who had hired low-income individuals, the initial unaided reactions of the research participants was often to equate low-income people with drug and alcohol problems. As a Chicago employer said, "Do they have a history of substance abuse? Do they have criminal backgrounds? These are some of the things that have to be overcome with my management."

Employer Attitudes toward Former Welfare Recipients

In addition to the perceptions of crime and substance abuse among low-income people, employers also harbor negative stereotypes about former welfare recipients. When exposed to examples of companies that hired people from training programs that work with individuals formerly on public assistance, focus group respondents consistently questioned the motivation, work ethic, and loyalty of these individuals.

The following are verbatim quotes from focus group participants across all industries and regions:

> I was thinking about the types of people that would come out of the backgrounds here [in these examples]. We hired a receptionist coming out of welfare. She was with us six months. They don't have the drive. They don't have the desire. . . .

> The people who are unemployed are unemployed for a reason . . . they are unemployable.

> I'm a Horatio Alger kind of person. The same problems that put them into their situation come into your organization . . . theft . . . confrontations . . . then they sue you.

> [People from public assistance] . . . that's where drug testing is a problem. They fail.

> Many don't report that they are employed and they still get the food stamps. How can you trust a worker like that?

You tend to get the welfare-to-work types . . . their only motivation is because they have to get a job. They are my terminates. They're coming to fill out the applications to tell people they were looking for a job.

[Employees we hired from public assistance] were doing an okay job . . . but they feel like you owe them something. There is a pervasive attitude like that in that pool.

There is a stigma associated with [examples of hiring from public assistance]. Why would you want to stick them in a room with 300 people who have always worked hard for a living?

I did have some success [with hiring people from public assistance], but they were not stereotypical welfare recipients . . . multigenerational welfare recipients.

The realities are that it is difficult to sell to the managers. People from public assistance are difficult for people with Harvard educations to deal with. It's a class issue. My managers think it's their own fault what happened to them—why they are on welfare or in jail.

As can be seen from these comments, individuals formerly on welfare face serious prejudices in breaking into the workplace. These stereotypes transcend participation in training programs and even, in some cases, satisfactory on-the-job performance. Embracing these individuals into a workplace increases the perceived risk of higher turnover, more shrinkage (theft), decreased productivity, and employee morale.

At the root of these negative perceptions is the idea that the individuals in question are inherently to blame for their need for public assistance. As one employer framed it, "Forgive me for being blunt . . . but 'second chancers' shouldn't be taking jobs away from the kids." The framing of public assistance recipients as "second chancers" implies that they have failed their first chance and are, in essence, damaged goods to employers.

Additionally, because of their need for public assistance, welfare recipients are erroneously framed as "dependent" individuals to employers. This flies in the face of the cultural norms of business that value and reward independence and self-reliance. This manifests itself in dysfunctional employer/employee relationships. Focus group respondents, for example, framed their welfare-to-work hires as dependent children (e.g., the perceived need to "baby sit" these individuals with respect to dealing with dress code violations and transportation needs). As the first quote above shows, employers also tend to frame welfare as a *place* not a condition (i.e., "coming *out* of welfare")—a place very likely associated with the inner city, with failed housing projects and many of the negative images associated with those places.

The LGI research findings are consistent with historical research in this arena.

Generally, two main theories are thought to explain labor market discrimination. One, known as taste based discrimination, posits that employers and/or customers, co-workers, or supervisors have a preference against hiring minority applicants, even if they know they are equally productive. The other, known as statistical discrimination, assumes that employers personally harbor no racial animus but cannot perfectly predict a worker's productivity. For example, an employer assessing an applicant's resume would assign some weight to the average performance of the person's racial group, instead of basing the judgment solely on the individual's merits (Krueger, 2002).

According to the 1996 book *When Work Disappears* by Harvard University sociology professor William Julius Wilson, the 1998 Urban Poverty and Family Life Study found that 74 percent of the 179 Chicago employers surveyed expressed views of inner city blacks that were coded as "negative." The view of inner city blacks, specifically males, was that they were uneducated, unstable, uncooperative, and dishonest. Even among the 15 survey respondents who were African American, 12 expressed views of inner city blacks that were negative. The reasons most often cited for this lack of confidence were poor work ethic, poor attitude, and poor interpersonal skills.

Employer Attitudes toward Cultural Differences

Sadly, in addition to the stigmas associated with socioeconomic conditions, traditional racial and ethnic stereotypes still create barriers for millions of Americans in the workplace. This is manifesting itself in a new kind of racism. Recent waves of white immigrant populations from Eastern Europe and Russia, as well as a significant increase in the number of Asian immigrants, have stimulated employer preferences for workers from these populations vs. African American and Hispanic individuals. The general perceptions are that these recent immigrants are often more skilled, willing to work harder, or willing to take on difficult or unglamorous jobs than their counterparts who have established themselves in this country. The following representative comments span all industries and regions of the research:

Immigrants who have just come to the country work harder. Their work ethic is better than the typical American who has been unemployed.

The Polish are more motivated to work . . . they have machining skills.

African Americans tend to be unreliable . . . immigrant Hispanics are more reliable. They don't take it for granted . . . Americans take it for granted.

The ones that are schooled in this country don't want to work those kinds of jobs, even if they are Hispanic.

Immigrants are here to work because their families need them. If it wasn't for the Mexicans and the Ecuadorians, 98 percent of our jobs would go unfilled.

Employer respondents in the Chicago focus groups were particularly vocal about their negative perceptions of the Hispanic population. Such prejudice was not witnessed in other areas. Specifically, Chicago participants attributed sub-standard work ethic and cultural norms to the Hispanic population. Hispanics were generally characterized as lazy, violent, disrespectful, and unreliable:

My workforce is 85 percent Hispanic from a rural setting. They don't know in a lot of cases . . . they don't know they have to get up in the morning for work.

In the rudest sense, they don't know . . . you don't know how many times I have had to paint the bathroom walls. I don't know what the sanitation conditions are like in Mexico, but I don't think they are like [the conditions] here. We've had people piss on the walls . . . piss in the trucks. . . .

You want to keep the gang bangers out. You can tell them by looking at them. We've had to go as far as eliminating an entire shift because of gang activities.

It is an upward mobility thing. If they leave for a better job, then it's good you put in the time [to hire and train them]. But that's not it. They just go home to Latin America.

It gets cold here and people like to go back to Mexico.

People want to leave for two months to visit their families. Supervisors say, 'I don't want to hire any more of those people.'

EMPLOYER ATTITUDES AND RISK PERCEPTION

Regardless of the nature of the stereotype held, the net effect is to increase the perceived risk employers associate with hiring low-income people from training programs. By definition, business is about risk mitigation. Executives are trained to weigh decisions in terms of associated risk. Downward trends in economic and business cycles increase the importance of risk measurement and mitigation, as company resources become inherently more precious and the fear of personal failure and job loss more prevalent.

Analysis of the responses from employers in these focus groups identified three main types of increased risk: 1) fear or personal discomfort in interacting with poor people, 2) difficulty in selling such programs to upper management, and 3) the need to frame such hires as a "secret."

The Risk of Personal Discomfort

Employer respondents in these focus groups often articulated either personal discomfort in interacting with poor people or expressed concern about the effect of integrating a nontraditional workforce into the current social dynamic of their organization. In the words of one human resources executive from Chicago, "You can give them all of the training, but you don't know if they are going to fit in socially. Since they are coming from welfare, it might be hard to tell them about going on a cruise last summer." Alternatively, an executive from New York feared backlash from current employees: "What? You want me to work next to a crook?" And finally, when one executive was exposed to the example of Salomon Smith Barney's welfare-to-work program with Wildcat Services in New York, the individual's initial unaided reaction was most telling: "That surprised me. Salomon Smith Barney? Makes me wonder who is handling my account."

The Risk of Management Resistance

The negative social and ethnic stereotypes identified in this research also make selling these programs to upper management extremely challenging. Among the few executive respondents who had implemented programs or hired from these nontraditional populations, each expressed significant push back from management. "The guys in Memphis looked at me like I was bringing in derelicts," reported one executive.

Another focus group participant had tried and failed, "I put a whole package together with Wildcat and management wouldn't buy it."

The Risk of Concealment

Some respondents described the stigma of hiring from nontraditional labor pools as so damaging that they think of it as a *secret*: "I could never get my colleagues to buy-off on one of these programs," said one Chicago executive, "They are middle-aged white men with blinders on. We actually hired some [people from nontraditional populations] . . . if only they knew. . . ." In further discussion, one participant posed the question to the group, "Well, how would the general employee population know that [they were former welfare recipients]?" A fellow participant remarked, "There's no such thing as a secret."

MITIGATING RISK FACTORS FOR EMPLOYERS

As these findings show, ethnic stereotypes and negative perception of low-income populations and individuals on public assistance create significant barriers to the adoption of workforce development programs among employers. Specifically, they increase the perceived risk employers associate with getting involved in these kinds of programs. Knowing that business executives are looking to reduce risk, how do intermediary organizations navigate these perceptions effectively?

The Cultural Gap between Nonprofit and For-Profit Organizations

First, these organizations need to identify the specific needs and issues of a particular company. Then you can put together the whole value proposition. Go in and say, "For you, Mr. Employer, we've done our research, we know that you need trained employees in this area . . . you have trouble filling the slots in the second shift . . . there's subsidies, tax credits, you can test drive the employees, there's visibility, and, by the way, there's a lot of good press that goes with this. The participants get something out of this too: they will become self sufficient, productive, you'll reduce crime, reduce welfare, etc. In our experience, these employees will become very loyal, long-term employees."
—Transportation Employer, Chicago

The perceptual gaps that exist between corporations and nonprofit organizations amount to profound cultural differences. As documented in the Laufer Green Isaac's 2000 research publication, *Hidden Agendas: Stereotypes and Cultural Barriers to Corporate Community Partnerships*, these cultural differences between nonprofit organizations involved in workforce development and corporations often undermine the trust necessary for effective training and hiring partnerships.

For instance, business culture dictates certain "cost-of-entry" attributes for workforce development organizations if they want to be attractive to employers. Business executives have articulated and demonstrated little interest in learning the ways of nonprofit culture. Therefore, to be effective in engaging with business, nonprofit organizations must approach interactions as a crosscultural issue, with understanding and respect for the cultural differences and without judgment. These cost-of-entry items include:

- Leading with the business benefit and following with the community benefit when attempting to engage with corporations.
- Doing the homework; understanding the needs of that specific company prior to engaging them on the merits of a particular workforce development program.
- Demonstrating respect for "time is money"—emphasizing punctuality, streamlining meetings, and focusing on outcomes, not embracing process.
- Speaking the language of business; creating brief, pithy verbal and written communications that quickly and efficiently substitute substantive bullet points for lengthy prose, and a two- to three-minute elevator speech for long diatribes on key issues.
- Using language like "win-win" that communicates clearly with executives and counters negative perceptions of nonprofit organizations as partners.
- Eliminating nonprofit jargon from communications that is both confusing and exclusionary in nature.

By adopting a crosscultural approach, nonprofits can build confidence among employers and avoid unknowingly reinforcing the negative perceptions that undermine the trust needed for partnership.

The Workforce Development Organization as a Buffer for Employers

My impression [of the examples] is that every one of these companies has a third party taking on the risk . . . my biggest concern with people from public assistance

is that they are late . . . they don't have a car . . . and these
groups are taking in the risk. Why wouldn't I do this?
—Health Care Employer, Chicago

These organizations provide a buffer; they really manage
these marginal employees. From the company standpoint,
it doesn't seem like there is much risk . . .
—Manufacturing Employer, Chicago

According to the recent LGI focus groups with human resources executives, labor market intermediaries play a unique role in corporate-community partnerships. Among those executive respondents who were interested in tapping into low-income communities and nontraditional labor pools, intermediary organizations were seen as vehicles for reducing the high personal and company risk associated with the failure of such programs.

Despite the economic shift that occurred between the first and second waves of research, the intermediary's greatest value-add was defined by executives in both waves as risk absorption. Whether it was providing a pool of trained and screened workers during economic boom times, or screening the large pool of available trained workers when supply exceeds demand, workforce development intermediaries reduce the risks associated with hiring low-income people and bridge the distance between the company and nontraditional populations.

THE RESEARCH FINDINGS: PERCEPTIONS OF WORKFORCE DEVELOPMENT ORGANIZATIONS

The Chamber of Commerce might be good for a luncheon, but what
would they know about training and screening employees for me?
—Manufacturing Employer, New York

Different Types of Labor Market Intermediaries Mean Different Things to Employers

Focus group respondents identified a series of distinctive "brand attributes" for each type of organization discussed: community based nonprofit organizations, trade organizations, community colleges, vocational colleges, for-profit employment agencies, government agencies, and labor unions. These attributes transcended any one geographical area, industry, or time period and appear to be the foundational assumptions that employers bring to the table about different types of intermediaries.

These perceptions are the result of a wide variety of stimuli and information obtained over the course of a human resources executive's career. They are likely the result of such diverse drivers as personal experience, company experience, word of mouth, and exposure to the media.

It is important to note that during discussions of the examples and their ideal programs, respondents focused little or no discussion on the methodology of the program or comparison of the results. All of the examples presented in the stimulus materials included comparable and substantive business and community benefits (either real or fictional for purposes of eliminating bias). Respondents were clearly more swayed by the "brand" image of the program supplier than they were by the program itself. A summary of the positive and negative brand perceptions by intermediary type are listed in Table 9.2.

Community Based Nonprofits. Employer respondents generally perceived the greatest strength associated with using a nonprofit workforce intermediary to be low cost. The importance of this factor increased during Wave Two of the research when economic pressures increased. In addition to equating nonprofit with lower cost, some respondents also identified a potential community relations benefit from working with a community based organization.

The negatives associated with community based nonprofits involved in workforce development mirrored the more general findings of the LGI *Hidden Agendas* research cited earlier—specifically citing slow turnaround and "lack of professionalism." As described by one respondent in Chicago, "Nonprofits are usually pretty low-staffed and stressed out."

Additionally, respondents expressed some concern about the sustainability of a community based organization, and lack of commitment with workforce and training being the "flavor or the month." Employer perceptions of training quality varied among respondents and can be attributed to the diversity of organizations in this category. Among all respondents, there was a general preference that the nonprofits have close ties to their industry (e.g., industry-specific workforce development training programs).

Most importantly, employer respondents expressed concern that community based organizations would not sufficiently screen applicants for substance abuse, criminal history, etc. Juxtaposed with employer needs for risk mitigation and buffering, this presents the biggest challenge for community based organizations.

Community Colleges/Vocational Colleges. Among respondents, community and vocational colleges were associated primarily with high-quality training

Table 9.2   Summary of Brand Attributes by Intermediary Type

	Positive Brand Attributes	Negative Brand Attributes
Community Based Nonprofits	1) Low Cost 2) Community Relations	1) Insufficient Screening 2) Transitory 3) Slow 4) Lack of Accountability/ Professionalism
Community Colleges/ Vocational Colleges	1) More Professional 2) Training expertise 3) Local to company/facility	1) No pool of unskilled labor
Trade Organizations	1) Industry Knowledge	1) Lack of training expertise/curricula
For-Profit Companies/ Employment Agencies	1) Fast turnaround 2) Ability to try before hiring 3) Well known	1) Expensive
State or Federal Agencies	1) Large pool of applicants 2) Tax credits	1) Not discriminating; no match w/ employer needs 2) Inefficient 3) Bureaucratic
Unions		1) Cost Escalation at Company 2) Loss of Employer Control

(both hard and soft skills), reflecting their mission and core competency of education. Community colleges and vocational schools were generally considered by respondents, therefore, to be the most credible teaching/training entities. Community colleges carried the additional perception that they would be geographically proximate to the company or facility location.

Community colleges were also observed to have the greatest top-of-mind awareness among all types of workforce development organizations. Focus group respondents were observed to have spontaneously mentioned community colleges far more often than any other type of intermediary organization during the initial warm-up and general discussion of workforce challenges and solutions. It should be noted, however, that many of these mentions failed to distinguish passive "bulletin board" placement activities from more aggressive training programs.

Trade Organizations. Executives in the focus groups generally acknowledged the value of trade organizations but not relative to workforce development issues. Although respondents generally believed that these organizations would bring deep knowledge of the industry, most human resource executives from the groups did not perceive them to be credible training or teaching entities and, rather, saw them as having deep deficiencies in curricula development. This was especially true with respect to the large amount of soft skills training associated with disadvantaged or nontraditional labor pools.

For-Profit Companies/Employment Agencies. Employment and temporary agencies were frequently used by respondents in these focus groups to address a variety of human resources challenges. Respondents generally associated fast turnaround and the ability to "try before you buy" with organizations such as these. "If you deal with Manpower, they are not your employee," said one respondent in New York, "you can just call up your account manager and never see them again." Generally, employers had associations with multiple agencies.

The primary negative associated with for-profit employment agencies was high cost.

State or Federal Agencies. Perceptions of state and federal agencies as workforce development intermediaries were generally negative. Government (perhaps one of the biggest brands of all) tended to color perceptions of the Department of Labor (DOL) or more local agencies, overwhelming the perceived positive of a large pool of applicants.

Generally, federal agencies were seen as bureaucratic, non-service oriented entities with little screening or training capacity. "Welfare placement people are interested in sending people out on job interviews, not on what you are looking for," said one respondent from New Jersey. "Often they are wasting my time. Also with DOL, if that person doesn't work out, then you have to answer all these questions about the individual that you wouldn't have to worry about otherwise." This point of view was corroborated by an executive from New York: "State or federal agencies don't screen very well. That's a problem."

Despite efforts by some agencies to be more responsive to the needs of business, more work needs to be done. "In the last few years, I've had better experiences with some government bodies that are really getting their act together," remarked one executive from Chicago. "By and large, though, they are still inefficient."

Unions. Generally, the brand perceptions associated with union partnerships in workforce development and training were overwhelmingly negative. Few, if any, respondents were able to articulate a positive attribute, other than unionized companies having to keep good relations with organized labor. Executive respondents feared a lack of control and flexibility, plus the potential for company cost-escalation as a result of union partnerships for training and development. While all three cities in which the research was conducted have strong union histories, one executive summed up the discussion nicely: "That's like someone saying 'I'm from the IRS and I'm here to help you.'"

It is interesting to note the consistency of these findings with the work and observations of William Julius Wilson (1996). The Urban Poverty and Family Life Study survey revealed that employers favored graduates of private schools to graduates of the mostly black public schools in Chicago. Moreover, in addition to having disdain for public high school graduates, employers were also found to dislike recruiting from welfare programs and state employment service programs. The survey revealed that only 16 percent of employers from city firms recruited from welfare agencies, and only one-third recruited from state employment agencies. These programs, which mainly serve blacks from the inner city, were disliked because employers felt that they sent applicants who were unqualified or inappropriate. Wilson's correlation between employer attitudes and behaviors in Chicago suggests potential negative implications for the behavioral realization of the LGI research findings, as well.

The Brand "Halo Effect" on Employer Perceptions of Low-Income People and Individuals from Nontraditional Labor Pools

The first barrier is the stigma. If [a person] is in a program
of this nature, they are not qualified. If you stigmatize
them as a candidate from this kind of program
you can't sell them to upper management.
—Health Care Employer, New York

In the most startling finding of all, the research determined that the perceived attributes (positive and negative) from the type of intermediary organization are often "inherited by" or "transferred to" the low-income individuals participating in the workforce development program. In essence, the training participants carry the "brand" associated with the intermediary regardless of the nature of the program itself.

People from a community nonprofit are more unskilled, the professionalism isn't there, and the life skills are not there.

With schools they are there to learn a trade. Nonprofit trainees would have the least skills and the most transportation problems.

Community based nonprofits—like welfare-to-work people—these people also have to prove that they've been out looking for work. They don't come prepared . . . the last thing they want is for you to offer them the position.

My concern would be to get a partnership going. The organization would need to show that a manager is devoting personal time to it and that it can be an ongoing concern. So actually, my preference would be to deal with something that is stable . . . a community college.

Nonprofits say 'Can you help this person?' It tends to be a one-off that you have to put your name/job on the line for . . . nonprofits locally have lacked the resources to provide volume/quality.

When considering the negative ethnic and social stereotypes, the role of the workforce intermediary as a risk mitigator and buffer, the relative "brand" attributes associated with different types of workforce development organizations, and the tendency to overlay those attributes on low-income people and individuals from nontraditional labor pools who move through these workforce development programs, the reasons employers are positively predisposed to community colleges as partners becomes clear. The brand associated with the type of intermediary organization has a halo effect that positively affects employer perceptions of the workers themselves.

These findings also have specific implications for how different types of workforce development organizations can "compete" more effectively for employer partnerships. These and other implications will be discussed at the close of this chapter.

COMMUNITY COLLEGES' BRAND ATTRIBUTES BEST FIT EMPLOYERS' RISK MITIGATION FRAME

We've had great success with community colleges.
It is a win-win situation. We're getting the labor and
these underprivileged kids are getting an education.
—Transportation Employer, New York

In totality, among all the labor market intermediary types discussed, community colleges carried the best mix of brand attributes, characteristics, and positive experience needed to limit the risk associated with these programs and add value to their businesses.

When asked which of the intermediary types they would be most likely to consider working with, the majority of executive respondents indicated the community colleges or vocational schools. This was corroborated in a second exercise in which respondents were asked which of the workforce examples they found most interesting, and a majority of respondents gravitated to the example using the community college. Lastly, when asked to rate their perceptions of a list of over 20 actual workforce intermediaries in their general area, respondents rated more community colleges positively than any other intermediary type.

Across all groups, industries, geographic locations, and time periods, community colleges/vocational schools were generally perceived to be the most attractive source of workforce development programs for low-income people and nontraditional labor pools. Graduates from community colleges and vocational schools were assumed to be more ambitious, motivated, disciplined, physically accessible, and literate. Representative comments supporting this finding include:

> Anyone who goes to school is motivated—they took the effort to enroll, they are motivated and they are willing to learn.

> The vocational trade school people have paid. They chose a school. They (for the most part) are dedicated and looking to improve their situations. Therefore, they are good employees.

> The perception is that from the community college they are educated people—they are a higher level on the food chain than someone coming off work from a prison. Although that is not always the reality.

> Taking people from the trade school that are already interested in this kind of work . . . maybe that has something to do with it.

> They must be able to read if they are in a community college.

During discussion, a number of focus group respondents indicated that a community college would be an easier sell to supervisors and management than some of the other types of programs. Some executives were even willing to believe that community college training and curricula would be more effective than in-house training.

Industry-Specific Insights on Employer Perceptions

*I need to get people on the floor fast. I don't have a lot
of lead time. I have to have people at their machines within
three or four days. Our business is driven by big orders.
When I need them, I need them right away. They have to
pass a reading test, a math test, and the drug screen. I need
trained people fast. A lot of the social services just don't
move as fast as I need them to. By the time they
get back to me, I've already hired the people.*
—Metal Manufacturing Employer, Chicago

Because individual focus groups were recruited to reflect the industry clusters of greatest interest to funders, it is also possible to draw several conclusions about some of the nuances relating to the recruitment and training of low-income people and nontraditional labor pools for each of the industries studied.

With regard to specific industries, awareness, need, and interest in such programs vary dramatically by industry cluster and sub-segment. Metal manufacturing and healthcare (direct care/caregivers) show the most potential. Transportation/warehousing shows mid-range potential, with the segments of transportation (drivers) and biotechnology showing the least potential.

Key factors correlating with interest in industry-specific training for low-wage workers as facilitated by a community college included:

- Unique skills/technical skills required.
- Lack of in-house capacity at companies to provide worker training.
- Mission-critical nature of the job description relative to independent tasks (i.e., a production line job).

Among metal manufacturers, filling entry-level jobs is often marked by short lead time and quick placement of individuals with machine-specific skills. In keeping with the overall findings of this research, executive respondents from metal manufacturing companies felt these attributes were most likely to come from community college training and placements.

Among transportation companies, interest in workforce development programs for low-income individuals and people from nontraditional labor pools was far higher among those companies with warehouse workers than those with drivers, logistics, or customer service workers. Hiring individuals who may be considered "high risk" for substance abuse, violence, or theft is untenable.

In the healthcare industry, caregivers were more receptive to workforce development programs than biotechnology companies. However, hospitals present unique challenges as they are not collaborative, contain line managers with additional prejudices, and rarely are proactive or interested in "investing" in low-wage staff.

RECONCILING REALITY
WITH EMPLOYER PERCEPTIONS

While the methodology of this study cannot be used to verify a causal relationship between employer perceptions and employer behavior, employer workforce development practices (or the lack thereof) do positively correlate with this behavior.

A December 2002 study by Marianne Bertrand of the University of Chicago and Senhil Mullainathan of M.I.T. indicated that resumes with names that were perceived to be Caucasian were 50 percent more likely to be called back by employers than resumes with black-sounding names. Nearly 5,000 applications were submitted to 1,300 help wanted ads from newspapers in Chicago and Boston. Their most alarming finding, perhaps, was that the likelihood of being called for an interview rises sharply with an applicant's credentials (e.g., experience and honors) for applicants with names perceived to be white sounding, but much less so for those with names perceived to be black sounding (Krueger, 2002).

As the University of Chicago/M.I.T. study indicates, employer perceptions do correlate with action, and therefore should be considered as one potentially serious barrier to the engagement of business and the sustainability of these partnerships.

The reality is that successful models for recruitment and training programs for disadvantaged populations come in all shapes and sizes, and are not necessarily correlated with one type of intermediary organization. If the goal of advocates and funders is to influence the adoption and diffusion of workable models for workforce development, then employer perceptions must be factored into the equation.

Although the logical response to this issue may be to simply "educate employers about what the important issues and factors really are," research, experience, and history tell us that this is a slow and extremely difficult process that has very little to do with logic, and everything to do with the emotional and intangible components of decision making. It is far more difficult to *change* someone's fundamental beliefs than it is to work *within* those existing beliefs to effect behavioral change.

Potential Course of Action

With this in mind, the research implies the following potential courses of action for consideration by advocates and funders.

- Encourage the adoption of best/leadership training practices by community colleges. That is, match the highest level training models and training products with the distribution channel that employers are most positively predisposed to. Encourage the sharing of best practices among community colleges and vocational schools as well as across all types of workforce development organizations.
- Build the capacity of all labor market intermediaries and workforce development organizations to master all of the cost-of-entry criteria associated with respectfully navigating the culture of business mentioned earlier in this chapter. From learning to research and respond to employer needs, and speaking the language of business, to efficiency training and streamlining externally focused organizational behavior, executives and staff of intermediaries need crosscultural training to effectively engage employers.
- Build the marketing/communications capacity of non-community college based intermediaries to "rebrand" themselves (e.g., provide information specifically designed to counter negative perceptions and to help them compete more effectively in the marketplace). Based on employer perceptions about strengths and weaknesses, organizations can use communications to leverage their strengths and negate their perceived weaknesses, thereby creating a new and more appealing value equation.

  For community based nonprofits, this means creating programs that are low priced and communicating this to employers. Secondly, it means emphasizing screening capabilities, commitment, and accountability in all communications (written and verbal). Lastly, it means lowering perceived risk by allowing employers to "try before they buy," leverage tax benefits, and utilize employer peers as testimonials for the organization.

  For trade organizations, this means developing local partnerships with credible partners like community and vocational colleges, and potentially local community based nonprofits for the unskilled labor component of the service offering. Additional differentiating value could be created by promoting assistance with tax credits and other bureaucratic barriers. Of all the intermediary types, trade organizations have the greatest credibility for proffering management advice and services.

For-profit companies generally have few barriers, but may expand their share of the employer market by reducing price or communicating the low cost of already available programs. Creating broad awareness of these programs will also serve to grow this segment of their business.

State and federal government agencies need to communicate their business driven approach and offer experiences that positively reinforce this promise. Rebranding government is likely to be one of the most difficult branding challenges imagined in the for-profit or nonprofit arena. Consistency and integration are key to making strides in this area.

Unions face the difficult challenge of having no positive brand attributes to leverage. Their low-hanging fruit is obviously those companies that are already unionized. Unions or coalitions with union involvement probably face increased opportunity during times of economic boom or in cases where the demand for workers far exceeds the supply. Concerns about cost escalation and loss of employer control may be insurmountable during recessionary times or cost cutting.

All this points to the importance of building capacity among intermediary organizations and, specifically, the marketing/communications capacity that has long been considered a luxury. This research shows that to widely disseminate these practices, marketing/communications capacity is key to success. While building capacity within the field from the onset would have been ideal, this capacity may well be the tipping point that takes the field to the next level.

- Advocates, funders, and organizations may also want to consider joining forces or building strategic alliances to credibly leverage the strengths of each and counter the perceived weaknesses. The field has already experienced some success with this in partnerships between community based nonprofits and community colleges or the development of coalitions with union involvement. These are examples of what this book calls workforce intermediaries. However, practitioners sometimes think of these alliances as strengthening the program or service offerings, rather than as "co-branded" marketing partnerships that symbiotically create compelling messaging for employers.

- As part of a long-term solution, advocates and funders may also want to consider some version of a "public awareness" campaign among employers to build the credibility of all types of intermediaries and help employers make an informed decision about the available options and their key value propositions.

SUMMARY AND CONCLUSION

Like all people, employers operate within a framework of beliefs, values, stereotypes, and assumptions that influence their decisions about training and hiring a workforce. The research discussed here provides a useful, innovative framework for viewing employer perceptions about low-income workers and workforce development intermediaries. For instance, while the idea of a "brand halo" was never meant to be applied to people, the insights from the research conducted with employers tells us that is exactly what happens when employers consider workforce development intermediaries, their programs, and the low-income people they serve. The understanding of consumer psychology and the assignment of attributes to people and organizations can, therefore, be of assistance in finding solutions to employer resistance to workforce development approaches.

The research also reveals that it is possible to learn, not only from negative employer perceptions, but that employers' *favorable perceptions* about workforce development also provide clues to working with the demand side of the labor force equation. For instance, our research revealed that employers highly value community colleges among the various types of workforce development intermediaries. Employers are far more likely to believe that a trainee or graduate has shed the traits attributable to stereotypes if they have participated in a program provided by a community college or vocational school.

As one focus group participant's remarks suggest, the Horatio Alger archetype is a vital part of the employer value system. But it is also possible to argue that the mythic characteristic of "reinventing oneself" speaks to the fundamental American psyche. Admiration for willfully rising from rags to riches is shared on some level by corporate employers and low-income workers who undertake the gargantuan effort of meeting the challenges in a shifting labor market. This attitude found among employers might be an essential cultural link between companies and workforce development intermediaries that are both reinforcing the independence and self-reliance that is a core value of American society.

This essential, unspoken cultural link cannot be forged or strengthened without intervention. Workforce development intermediaries must understand employers' needs, perceptions, risks, and fears—no matter how erroneous—in order to respond to them. Intervention, as we've seen, may take many forms: from building the capacity of individual intermediaries to crosspollination among organizations within the field. The demand side of the labor force equation is here to stay. It is a significant factor in the enabling environment for workforce development programs for low-income people and needs to be continuously factored into the work of funders, advocates, policy makers, and thought leaders around the country.

REFERENCES

Aaker, David A. 1996. *Building Strong Brands.* New York: The Free Press.
Krueger, Alan B. 2002. "What's in a Name? Perhaps Plenty if You're a Job Seeker."
    New York Times, December 12, 2002.
Wilson, William Julius. 1996. *When Work Disappears: The World of the New Urban Poor.* New York: Knopf.

10

How Do Workers See Advancement?

ROBERTA REHNER IVERSEN

L IFE DEALS DIFFERENT HANDS TO DIFFERENT PEOPLE. MANY FAMILIES
whose lives were disadvantaged by past mistakes or incarceration,
immigrant or refugee dislocation, too little education, domestic violence,
interspersed periods of welfare and work, or workplace racism have persistent difficulty advancing through work. Historically, stand-alone workforce
development organizations have been the main source of training and help
for jobseekers trying to overcome challenged pasts and gain productive
employment, but often with mixed success. In the more recent labor and
policy environment, new *interorganizational partnerships* have emerged,
generally linked under the auspices of an umbrella organization or entity,
to address the needs of an increasingly broad swath of disadvantaged jobseekers. Such partnerships or networks are sometimes called workforce
intermediaries.

These new partnerships may take the form of tight and highly developed linkages between unions, employers, and projects; expansive collaborations between community based organizations, community colleges,
development organizations, and employers; or more traditional, linear
alliances of workforce programs, temporary agencies, and employers.
These forms are among those found in the Annie E. Casey Foundation's
Jobs Initiative (JI), a national workforce demonstration targeting jobseekers from impoverished inner city neighborhoods. In the Jobs Initiative, new
partnerships were forged to move jobseekers beyond "any job" to a "good
job." At the same time, the partnerships were designed to help employers
get "good workers," not just "any worker."

In this chapter, family heads who participated in the Jobs Initiative tell
real stories of what it takes to advance. They tell us how they got jobs with
significantly higher wages than ever before, non-wage benefits for the first

time, new career options, and greater family stability. They show us that strategic and sustained work supports increase the odds of retention and advancement. At the same time, the work experiences of these men and women, for over five years after re-entering the work world, illuminate that advancement is not a simple, linear story of wanting work, getting a "good job," and then automatically being in position to move up. These workers show us that advancement is very complicated, takes a long time, is beset by many challenges along the way, and thus must involve "players" *both* in and outside of the new networks.

In particular, the experiences of these jobseekers illustrate that a work-force consists of *families*, not individuals. Closely related, they show us that families are embedded in influential *social systems* that intersect with family and work life, for good and ill. Not only do parents' lives and work affect children's welfare, children's well being and schools affect parents' work. Not only do employer practices affect worker advancement, but worker supports and subsidies affect employers' profits.

The families in this chapter are "exemplars" of over 6,000 Jobs Initiative participants, and likely thousands of other low-wage jobseekers and workers across the country as well. The "family stories," excerpted here, are a result of repeated contact with low-income working parents and their educators and trainers, employers, children and children's schools, and people in other organizations and institutions in their communities. Essentially, these narratives tell "the whole story" of families trying to move forward through work.[1]

Each story first lays out the history that the jobseeker has previously not been able to overcome, despite his or her notable strengths. The stories then tell how families want to move forward, look for programs that can help, and what roles they see for themselves and their programs. The stories next show how the family heads get "good jobs" but encounter new challenges as they try to keep job and family intact. Finally, the stories show how workers perceive and pursue advancement in the context of the lives of other family members and the systems that affect them all. The chapter concludes with what else can help the family advance. Family names are pseudonyms chosen by the family members; other pseudonyms were chosen by the author.

"WITHOUT A START, THERE'S NO FINISH"

The Kevin McDonalds Family Story[2]

"My felony background froze me out of the 'good job' I needed to provide for my family." As a 29-year-old African American male who had been incarcerated twice, Kevin McDonalds knew that his employment prospects were

poor. He graduated from high school with little confidence, as no guide-posts were available to cultivate his talents. He lamented the absence of information and opportunity for urban people of color:

> When I grew up, for Blacks and Latinos there were only two things pumped—college and the armed forces. We were not told about different apprenticeships, different skilled trades. We were just told if you didn't have college, you couldn't succeed. If the high schools had information about the trades, a lot more people would do it. They could introduce us to what was going on. We could have seen more things we could do. If we didn't want to go to college, or to the armed services, we had the sense that there was nothing else we could do. With information about these other possibilities, it would not have seemed just like a dead end.

Instead, faced with young adulthood, dreams of owning a music club for African Americans outside the violent inner city where "nice people can come to talk and dance," and no knowledge of options, Kevin had turned to the quickest way to make money that he saw available to him: selling drugs. As a result, Kevin was incarcerated twice: initially for eight months and then for three years. While Kevin found both periods of incarceration difficult, the second period was more so; by this time he had small children to support and few job prospects upon his release from prison. By the time Kevin was introduced to the Milwaukee Jobs Initiative (MJI), he had identified a strong reason to resist the financial allure of selling drugs—the freedom to provide for and raise his three young children:

> I go through occasional withdrawals when I look at my small paycheck sometimes. The paycheck goes fast. But I want to see my children grow up. I'm lucky they were young when I was in prison. They knew I was gone, but they couldn't feel it like they would now. Now is a critical point in their life.

Kevin's family became the chief motivating factor in his efforts to excel at training and work. A printing project affiliated with MJI gave Kevin an opportunity to define himself outside of his status as felon, legitimately support his family, and be a full-fledged parent to his children.

"High-quality skill training and supportive staff kept me in the training program." When Kevin was first introduced to the Milwaukee Jobs Initiative, he was skeptical of training programs because an earlier, stand-alone plumbing program had not provided a network of potential employers to contact:

I was in a plumbing course before MJI. It was different from this one. You
had to go to look for a job yourself. If there had been more help job searching—like this program [MJI printing project], it would have been a nice
program. At the time I didn't know what I was looking for. I didn't have my
driver's license. I was a felon, and that was looked at negatively. I was into
the program, the classes, and figured they'd help me find a job. We were a
team. I was thrown for a loop when they didn't. I never went for the final
aptitude test. We were supposed to take it together [everyone in the class].
But the teacher left. If people would have cut the yellow tape—sent us to
meet Bob, Joe, Lou—it would have helped. Like the MJI program did.

For Kevin, "cutting the tape" meant more than simply developing contacts; it also meant helping to overcome his prison record. In the two years
between prison release and his connection with MJI, Kevin cycled through
a series of low-wage jobs. In one year, Kevin worked at two jobs for 40
weeks earning a total income of $6,000. A subsequent job paid $6.50/hour,
for a potential annual income of $13,500, and offered no non-wage bene-
fits. This job, at the hospital where his fiancée, Lynn, worked, held opportunities for advancement until a new law prohibiting the employment of
felons forced the hospital to fire him: "[Eventually] they changed the law
back, so that felons can work in hospitals as long as they don't have direct
contact with the patients, [but] it was too late for me."

With understandable apprehension, Kevin attended an information
session at the printing project and met its program manager and employer
liaison. They encouraged Kevin to enroll in their eight-week skills training
program that was customized to industry needs through project-employer
partnerships. Kevin's reflection about training and subsequent employment
made it clear that without the support of the two staff persons who "work
beyond their job," he would not have persevered. When the program manager, who described herself as "half case manager," left the project, Kevin's
response illuminated the relationship between personal support and program retention:

> When I learned that Program Manager was gone—I was shocked! She was
> the one that really got me motivated and started—her and Employer Liai-
> son. Program Manager *really* put me out there. I hated it when she left.
> Seeing her and talking to her helped keep me motivated and uplifted.

"The project's partnerships with employers led to a 'good job' for me."
Through the printing project's employer connections, Kevin began work
in April 1999 as a floor person in the "Bindery" pressroom where he made

$9.76 per hour with full non-wage benefits. According to the program manager, the company's wages were good but advancement was uncertain: "Bindery moved into the city to access the population—they are flexible with personal situations, but there is no clear path for advancement."

Kevin soon realized this. After six months at Bindery, a period that Clymer, Roberts, and Strawn identified as common for job change in their 2001 publication *States of Change*, Kevin recontacted the printing project for re-employment advice. Importantly for Kevin's future, the project offered post employment services that facilitated a move to another of its broad array of industry partners, "Printing & Bindery." Although his initial wage as a floor person at Printing & Bindery remained $9.76/hour, Kevin did not view this as a lateral move. He saw Printing & Bindery as a union position with room for advancement, including further education that he wanted to pursue:

> There's room to move around. You're not stuck in tunnels. I could even move to an advertising agency to check colors, do desktop publishing. It's not a dead end. At a bindery you can only do so much—there's a fixed number of machines. Now I also go to school through my worksite. I work on different machines. It pays about the same, but I can do a lot more.

Although Printing & Bindery had a strict tardiness/absentee system, characteristic of many manufacturing firms, Kevin had missed only two days of work at the six-month mark. His supervisor wished he could "clone" Kevin based upon his record of consistently showing up to work and getting the job done. Kevin responded to the supervisor's commendation with loyalty and new understanding that his printing skills might be transferable to his future business goal.

After six months, Kevin was promoted to jogger at $11.51 per hour, which included a 90-cents/hour bonus for third shift. In addition, Kevin worked with a team that was diverse in age and experience, which helped him stay motivated and satisfied with his job:

> For a convicted felon, it was hard to find a job. MJI made it easier. In my new position as jogger—I'm motivated at work. You work as a *team* on the press: two joggers, a compensator, roll tender, first and second pressmen—we work together to keep the press running or get it started back running. I learn from them. I hope we stay a team.

Kevin was the only African American on his team, but as with other challenges, he was comforted by the knowledge that there was a procedure he could follow to redress racial grievances:

I know it's there, but people stagnate themselves if they let it eat at them. They end up the victim. If racial problems occur, I go to my union. If I don't get help there, I go over their head. There is always something I can do to combat it.

"My employer's clear, supportive advancement path helped me move forward, but my family still struggles with debt and problems at the children's school." Kevin felt that his ability to stay focused and motivated was because he perceived opportunity for advancement: "In my job now, I can go all places . . . otherwise I'd get discouraged." Opportunity for advancement was a central part of the printing project's job preparation and ongoing support, what they called "career laddering." As Kevin noted: "If you don't know what's behind the door, you don't go in. It's too 'iffy.'"

According to the program manager, the project's basic mission was *both* employer and advancement oriented:

> To serve contributing employers—not become an entry-level training school. Serve *incumbent* workers—expand skills and finish apprenticeships. We are a printing industry school—"the union school"—versus the technical college. We have an apprenticeship program here—the technical college does not.

Kevin thrived under the project's mission. First, affordable upgrade education was available at a familiar location. He attended three-hour classes for the next step of "press operator" at the project one to two mornings a week after his shift, even though this meant working for 12 hours straight (11 P.M. to 11 A.M.). He paid for the classes up front, but course grades of "As and Bs" qualified him for full and near-full employer reimbursement. When finished with the press operator classes, he hoped to take computer classes for the press, viewing the skill classes as critical to advancement, whether in printing or elsewhere:

> You can really get ahead in this business. There is a lot of opportunity to do that. You can just keep moving up by taking classes. I don't know if I want to stay in it, but you learn a lot of things that will help. The classes are easy. Except going there after work.

Second, although the career path at Printing & Bindery was not fast, it was at least visible. Kevin knew that his ability to advance was contingent upon open slots and that it could be several years before he achieved a higher paying position such as pressman or foreman, but it was important to him that guideposts existed: "I'm something like 27 now on the list for the next promotion. It will probably take three to four years until the next position, five at most."

Despite having entrepreneurial aims, he viewed a printing career with growing interest and dedication, gradually learning about the nature of the career ladder: "I'd like to own my own bar or club. I'd like to stay in the printing industry for some years. Finish school and get some experience."

At the time of his first year anniversary at Printing & Bindery, Kevin earned $12.09 an hour ($11.19 plus 90 cents for third shift) and had taken on a second, part-time job at "Fast Food," adding 15 hours of work to his already full week. With a second job he could provide more for his family, save a little, help the friend who asked him to work there, and have a little extra spending money. While he remained positive about work, he was tired, despite claims that he only needed three to four hours of sleep per night.

Kevin's two-month stint at Fast Food raised important "red flags" about the potential tension between income advancement and children's welfare. Kevin and Lynn's overtime and his second job meant that neither parent was home on Saturdays, which severely limited "family time" for this newly reunited family. Kevin's six-year-old daughter had been held back after first grade, and his kindergartener was also threatened with grade retention, largely due to what teachers characterized as "behavior" rather than academic problems. Teacher and administrator comments at this carefully selected school reflected that the school did not understand or value the demands on two working parents:

> We have a full calendar of events for the students, families, and teachers to join in. We take trips to the museum. We went to the Shedd Aquarium in Chicago, and to the apple farm. We are having an ethnic potluck this coming Wednesday. We have Sock-Hops, and a sleigh ride during the winter holidays. We have a Black History program in February. I have never seen the family here.

Compounding this stress, the family's subsidy for their three-year-old son's childcare was in danger of being cut off because the eligibility worker calculated Lynn's occasional overtime as regular. These predicaments exacted time, energy, and hours of unpaid consultation and negotiation with schools and subsidy offices.

Not surprisingly then, after 18 months' work at Printing & Bindery, Kevin spoke again of needing two jobs, despite pressures created by overtime from one: "Last week I worked 24 overtime hours. It was a hardship on my family. Lynn needed a break. The kids needed to see me."

Kevin needed extra overtime to pay off a tax debt that he just learned about. Eight years earlier, he had filed income taxes incorrectly and as a result owed the IRS $9,000. The original sum was smaller, but unknown to him, the debt accrued interest while he was in prison. Kevin's wages were now garnisheed, which left very little money for his family. Worse yet, even punishing overtime was eliminated by his company's financial downturn:

> They garnish my wages 15 percent; that leaves me with nothing. I got $120 last paycheck without overtime. To make up for this, I worked two 12-hour shifts and Friday and Saturday last week. There I am, doing the right thing, and whoa! Here I am in another hole that I've got to fill up. Before the tax problem, I was bringing home $400–500 a week; $1200–1600 a month. How do they expect a person to make it without overtime?

These simultaneous burdens left Kevin frustrated. He had almost reached the ceiling wage for his position, and advancement was contingent on two additional factors outside his control: a union contract under negotiation and the company's economic survival:

> The ceiling may change, depending on the contract and whether the company stays in business. A lot of people have quit, so I may get a promotion earlier. If taxes hadn't eaten into my income, my current income could have sustained me. It [taxes] threw me for a loop.

The "loop" presented a significant challenge to Kevin's staying power. Illustrating the importance of post employment support, a staff person at the printing project helped Kevin lower the tax debt, countering his discouragement somewhat. Kevin explained: "I'm not where I want to be—feel I should be—not a failure all around, but not enough accomplishment either."

After two and a half years of steady work, Kevin recognized that economic mobility would require more than the wage increases he anticipated, yet he felt he did not have access to the full array of tools that would help him. MJI had offered him a critical start in the labor market, but he now perceived the limitations of that market, of his specific industry and employer, of his children's school, of post incarceration legalities, and of policies affecting subsidies that the family needed. These challenges will require continued resilience, determination, and support as Kevin labors for his family's welfare.

"RESPONSIBILITY . . . WORK AND HOME"

The Maya Vanderhand Family Story[3]

"I did not have an education credential, so I was stuck in dead-end jobs." Maya
Vanderhand, a 32-year-old Latina wife and mother of four children aged
seven to 13, had high standards for her work and home life that she
expressed as "responsibility." Maya's job at home was "to raise children who
will be responsible," and her idea of a good employee was "someone who
is responsible." Maya's ethos of responsibility, together with training,
placement, and case management from organizations affiliated with the
Seattle Jobs Initiative (SJI), helped to compensate for the absence of a high
school diploma or GED.

Maya had long known that too little education prevented her from
achieving the success she wanted and needed in order to support her family. Before she enrolled in SJI's office training project, Maya worked for two
years as a lead cashier in a military office. Her top wage there was $8/hour
for a 20-hour week that yielded an annual income of about $8,000. Her hus-
band's full-time job raised the family income to about $30,000, 150 percent
of the federal poverty level (FPL) for a family of six. However, Maya's husband suffered frequent layoffs, so hers was often the only family income.
Maya's dream was to work for the Immigration Department, to help other
immigrants overcome the obstacles she had overcome, but she knew that
this goal was out of reach without an education credential.

"I got a lot from the office training project, but I also suggested improvements."
Spurred by the family's precarious income situation and the needs of four
growing children, Maya responded to a community based organization's
(CBO) outreach flyer about a new program that she hoped would help her
get a GED and a better job. The CBO referred Maya to a 12-week office
skills training program developed in conjunction with a local community
college partner under SJI's auspices. Maya's classes included hard-skill
instruction in spreadsheets, word processing, keyboarding, business writing, and customer service skills. The classes also included "softer" instruction in resume production and interview skills. Significantly, Maya's was the
first cohort through the office project. As such, she suggested improvements that the industry, CBO, and community college partners of
SJI implemented over time, illustrating the synergistic potential of such
partnerships.

For example, Maya felt that the project's entry standards should be
more stringent and the quality of instruction enriched: "They are spending

too much money on people who don't want to be there." Project staff confirmed that Maya's assessment was accurate:

> Maya's office training was still in very formative stages. Maya's class was not a good class. There was no training supervisor—no one monitoring the trainees day to day. Slackers got through. Trainees went from class to class without any overarching supervision.

In response, the project instituted a training supervisory process whereby a specialist on location monitored all trainees and liaised regularly with CBO case managers. The project also helped its CBO affiliates conduct more thorough assessments of general work preparation skills before referring an applicant to formal training.

Second, Maya had desperately wanted intensive GED preparation. During office training, she had attended newly developed prevocational ABE classes and worked on her GED, but did not finish it at that time, unfortunately, as GED attainment would have significantly improved her advancement potential. Maya stopped attending because of the teacher's demeanor, highlighting that it is critical to have sensitive and competent teachers in compensatory programs:

> I started going to some classes for GED, but then it got to the point where the lady that was teaching it, the way she was teaching it, it wasn't very professional. She was kind of rude, and so I decided not to go again.

An SJI staff member concurred with Maya: "Maya was the first to expose the fact that we should be preparing individuals for the GED. Then we expanded this section a lot." The office project later teamed with the community college on the federally funded ABE/ESL (Adult Basic Education/English as a Second Language) program to offer jobseekers more inclusive prevocational preparation in reading, math, and language before formal office training.

Increasing the overall length of the training was a suggestion as well. Maya believed that a three-month course followed by one to two months of internship would have prepared trainees even better. This call for longer training was universal among Jobs Initiative participants, in stark contrast to the proliferation of "rapid attachment" programs under the 1996 welfare reform legislation and reduced funding for workforce development under the Workforce Investment Act (WIA) of 1998.

"The new skills, sustained support, and 'legitimization' I got from the project catapulted me past education deficits into a 'good job.'" After completing office training, Maya received job offers from two employer partners of her office

project whose curricular input and relationships with staff at several partner organizations gave them confidence in the project's graduates. Maya
chose "Insurance Company" and began work there in January 1999 as a
personal lines operator at an annual income of $24,000 (approximately
$11.50/hour) with benefits. This salary was $16,000 higher than that of her
pre-JI job and fortunately covered her medical needs.

When the research team first met the Vanderhand family, Maya had
worked at Insurance Company for just over one year, and her annual salary
of $25,800 reflected a generous 7´ percent increase. Maya felt that the office
project's skill training had prepared her well: "I use them [the skills I learned
at SJI] every day. Because of the computer skills and stuff like that, now I
am having to help other people with that, how they even get into Word."

Maya also felt that case management helped her succeed on the job.
The first year of case management was provided by the CBO affiliate, and
the second year was provided by a retention counselor in the SJI office.
Although Maya had three different case managers during the first year,
their regular outreach encouraged her to use their support: "They call me
like once in a while, 'how are you doing? Do you need anything?' and that
is when I started getting help, after I started talking to them more." Given
cultural and other differences in individuals' readiness to ask for and accept
help from formal organizations, persistent outreach may be necessary for a
portion of workforce program participants.

Particularly critical to her ability to remain on the job, Maya's third and
most tenacious case manager called just at the point Maya needed help with
moving expenses and a rental deposit, having secured a new and safer apart-
ment for her family because of her new income. Importantly, this point was
after the shift to the SJI retention specialist should have taken place. Maya's
CBO case manager perceptively recognized that the one-year employment
anniversary was often one of particular vulnerability, and thus continued
with her customers through the transition. Maya's improvement efforts had
been economically feasible until her husband lost his job in the middle of
the residential change.

Maya's case manager also helped with gas vouchers and clothing
expenses such as shoes for work—expenses that helped Maya feel comfortable and appropriate in her new professional environment, but ones that
she regularly subsumed in order to meet the children's needs:

> You need a pair of shoes, because with kids it is really hard. I buy the kids'
> first, but then when you really, really need it, it is like geez . . . you got to
> squeeze things here and there. They help me with some shoes and I made
> it work where I could get some tights and shoes and get some sales out there.

The personal and employment challenges that Maya anticipated after her first anniversary on the job graphically illustrate that even competent new workers may need periodic project support over time to stay on a forward course:

> My husband is not working. I probably have to have surgery on my hands. My hands are going numb. I'm having a hard time. I'll have an MRI on March 15. The nerves are bad. My supervisor says he'll do anything he can do—100 percent. I can delegate my job duties. I'll need to train someone. [And the new supervisor?] The new guy, we just don't know yet. He's been there only one week so far. My hands are no good; my workload is cut in half. But he says "Just let me know—we'll go from there." This puts pressure on my co-workers, and there's less money for the house.

"I needed extra time before I felt ready to accept a promotion, particularly after my injury and while my children adjusted to better quality, but harder schools." Maya's excellent job performance was noticed by superiors, even though she did not actively seek career advancement. Advancement opportunities included on-job training, but also involved changing departments or office locations. Maya was one of many families we encountered who *refused* an initial promotion opportunity. She knew what her job required and hesitated to move into another position where she might feel less competent:

> I don't want to change departments any time; there is a lot going on. I have so much on my plate that I don't want to screw that up. I can go to another department, but I want to get to know my job better where I am at. There is claims or underwriting or there is other things and they will train you, but I don't want to jump from one group to another. Plus because my hands are not well, I would rather stay where I am.

She also did not consider firm change as an advancement strategy, in part because she feared that her increasingly severe case of tendinitis would affect performance and attendance at a new job: "I know I am very smart and capable, and I do not like to work places where I am not sure I will succeed."

Because Maya's injury occurred before the Supreme Court decision declassified tendinitis and carpal tunnel syndrome as "workplace injuries," rendering them ineligible for employer initiated disability benefits and adjustments, Insurance Company implemented ergonomic improvements that enabled Maya to remain on the job—and in position for eventual advancement.

Maya knew that education also complicated her advancement process. While the quality of her project's skill training and employer connections compensated for too little education in *getting* a job, the absence of an education credential severely limited her long-range advancement opportunities:

> I want my GED. There was a time when I did need a GED to get a job, but this job offers more than what I was offered before, particularly without the GED. Because of the GED I can't really go forward outside the company, but now there isn't time to study for the GED after work. I would like to get a job in immigration; they do require a GED.

Even though Insurance Company reimbursed GED pursuit, Maya anticipated a several-year delay in taking this advancement step. Helping her children adjust to new schools took all her extra time, and lack of time might jeopardize her success:

> That could be maybe next year's goal to get my GED, to really focus on that because I can't really do two things at a time. It is hard, and then with the four kids, no I am not going to even try to do that because I might fail. So I found out that through the job that they might even pay for it. [Time off to do it too?] No they won't give me time off, but I am going to have to work my schedule so that I can go to school and then work at the same time.

"I am finally taking active steps toward advancement; I am pursuing a GED." After two and a half years at Insurance Company, Maya's children were proceeding smoothly in school, and she finally felt the confidence to actively pursue advancement. She enrolled in a GED class that met twice a week from 6:30 to 8:45 P.M., was a mile from home, and free. Maya described growing amenability to change, yet noted also that competing family responsibilities persisted:

> It was hard. I couldn't remember what I'd learned before. But now it's coming back. It's interesting. It's cool to find out about perimeters. And I see others who are worse than me—they don't know how to add, subtract, do division. The schedule was also hard in the beginning—it was a new schedule; I had to leave home by 6.

Maya was encouraged by a passing pre-test score and a supportive teacher who said she "only needed a little more work." Together with citizenship attainment several years earlier, GED acquisition would establish a base from which Maya could parlay her SJI training and Insurance Company competencies into significant career advancement: "Training is here today, but not tomorrow. With a GED, I can go higher and higher."

Maya's story illustrates that program and workplace supports are *both* important for job retention and advancement. Case management provided transitional instrumental aids, and her workplace provided structural consideration of health and family needs such that Maya could "responsibly" attend to both. Her story also underscores that further education is critical for advancement, particularly for an immigrant, but that it is difficult for working parents to take time away from their children's educational needs for their own. Considering that Maya's children have already benefited from her work accomplishments, through moving to a safer neighborhood and shifting to carefully researched, higher quality schools, further advancement could help Maya's family realize their goals of home ownership and asset accumulation for a more secure future.

"I WAS BLESSED TO FIND EMPLOYMENT I AM ABLE TO GROW IN"

The Ayesha Muhammad Family Story[4]

"An injury on my old job meant a period on welfare and the need to change careers in mid-life." Reflecting a long history of caretaking, Ayesha Muhammad was a 45-year-old African American mother of three young adults aged 18 to 23, a 12-year-old son, and 10-year-old twins. She was also grandmother to her older daughter's two children. Ayesha left her Georgia home at age 11 when her father moved to Philadelphia "to make a better life for his family." After her mother died when Ayesha was 15, she raised her sisters and brothers, which gave her considerable practice in family maintenance.

Despite these demands, Ayesha completed high school and two post secondary healthcare certifications en route to a nursing assistant career path. She married, bore four of her six children, and worked as a Certified Nursing Assistant (CNA), generally at ill-paid positions in nursing homes. She eventually divorced her husband because of domestic violence and partnered with the father of her twin boys until he became unfaithful. On her own then, with little financial help from the children's fathers, Ayesha struggled to support her growing family.

In the late 1990s, Ayesha's nursing career came to an abrupt end. She was injured on the job such that paralysis could result from further heavy lifting or long hours of standing: "Lifting and having someone fall on me, I hurt my shoulder and back. I can't lift anything more than 10 pounds now or I'm at risk for permanent paralysis." She took one year to recuperate, supported her family with modest income from unemployment insurance and welfare, and then actively sought to change her career direction.

"A 'rapid attachment' welfare-to-work program did not give me the skills I needed." Referred by her welfare caseworker, Ayesha attended a one-month welfare-to-work program in fall 2000 at a vocational center partner of the Philadelphia Jobs Initiative (PJI). Consistent with its "rapid attachment" format, Ayesha felt she got a drop of office training and an ocean of "job readiness" instruction. Having been a steady worker for the past 20 years, Ayesha vehemently critiqued the program's "Work First" emphasis: "I wish they'd had more training. Especially computers. My company has a training lab. The welfare-to-work program was like an assembly line. Four weeks and you're out the door."

Once employed, she was even more vocal about how longer pre-employment training could have prepared her better for the demands of the new, more highly skilled workforce, and how it could have sped career advancement:

> There are people out [there] who end up in offices and deal with computers and things like that, and they are not giving them enough training. Really, truly, they are not giving them enough time to get what they necessarily need to deal with the workforce. To be honest with you, I was not skilled. The skills that I picked up are from the learning centers that my job had. I learned about everything I had to do to deal with computers, how to print out spreadsheets, how to do logs. If they [welfare-to-work program] was to make their computer classes more intense, you could easily move ahead faster. They show you how to do some Microsoft, how to do some Excel, and basically that's it. It's just so you can get your feet wet and you won't get too lost. But when you get on job site, you do get lost. You really and truly get lost. It just so happened, my supervisor, she is the type of person [who says], "If you don't know, call me and I will come over and help you. I will take you step by step and help you get where you got to get." She is fantastic because I had help with all the stuff I know now.

Despite helpful supervision, Ayesha knew that she was still "behind" others who learned such skills in community college or a longer skill training program. She was frustrated that advancement would take longer as a result.

One year later Ayesha's welfare-to-work program amplified its computer component, as the research team observed during a site visit. Program flexibility is one of the potential strengths of interorganizational partnerships, even though funding requirements may impose restrictions at the same time.

"I held out for a 'good job' and eventually got one through the program's place-ment network." Although Ayesha was more than eligible for many jobs that the welfare-to-work program suggested, such as restaurant waitress, she held out for a "good job," a kind of "job matching" orientation that wel-fare-to-work funding mandates strongly discourage:

> They stay with you until you find employment—or until they find you employment. [How long did it take you?] It took a while before—I just didn't want just anything. The job coach [eventually] got me in touch with a temp agency and set me up with an appointment. I went in and I talked with the lady there. She said she liked my image. Also, she said, "Don't worry, I'll have you something very soon," and the next morning, she calls me with the job for here. I told her. "Okay, how do I get there?" No ifs, ands, or buts, and I was here at Financial Insurance Company. I began in February 2001 as a temp, and I was hired on permanently in May.

Thus, although Ayehsa's PJI affiliate had few direct connections with employers, it collaborated with a quality temporary agency that did. Ayesha's work supervisor described the partnership between "Financial Insurance Company" (FIC) and the temp agency that placed Ayesha with them in a way that highlights the synergy that is possible when organiza-tions are purposefully linked:

> It is a temporary service that we use when we have peak periods or project work. We contact our temp service to have someone come in just to help us out with our larger than normal workload. So, she [Ayesha] started working for us to help us out, and after several months, we were very impressed with her quality and the quantity of the work that she produced. She had already expressed to us her interest in becoming a Financial Insur-ance Company employee, so we kept that in mind, and eventually her posi-tion became available. We extended an offer of employment to her.

At the same time, the supervisor's comments vividly illustrate the increas-ingly typical hiring practices of the "new labor market" that make "good jobs" harder to attain for jobseekers in workforce programs, as Paul Oster-man described in his 1999 book *Securing Prosperity*.

Three months of searching ultimately paid off for Ayesha. As a temp she earned $8.25/hour; as a full-time worker her entry wage was $10.50. After six months of full employment, she received a $2/hour raise to $12.50/hour. Ayesha's motivation was strong, as evidenced by the trans-portation challenges she battled daily:

I get up at 4:00 a.m. and I start. I take the same three busses back unless I work overtime. Then I take four busses. It takes about one hour in the morning. If I work overtime, it takes one and a half hours to one hour 45 minutes. You do what you have to do.

"My company's advancement path was clear, supported, and family friendly." Financial Insurance Company's clear, supported advancement path was a critical step for Ayesha's future. Although she began with the company as an assistant in bill distribution in the long-term care division, her goal was to become an underwriter/caseworker in the company's health insurance division:

I am being trained to take any position that is opened in our company. I want to go take some courses to become an underwriter because my boss is supervisor of the underwriters, and with my medical background, she wants me to get some business courses, and she wants me to oversee the nursing homes.

Ayesha's supervisor outlined clear company advancement practices, but at the same time, illustrated a phenomenon we found regularly in the family heads' advancement experiences: that a number of lateral moves were necessary prerequisites to a vertical move:

As far as progression within the company is concerned, we offer a couple things. One thing that she has been educated on and is aware of and has looked at is our posting board. It is on the computer. Accessible to all employees. It is web based, so all they have to do is type in their personal identification information and it launches them into all of the postings that FIC has for positions available, not only in this site but all of FIC's sites. You can search for positions through salary, through interest, through locations. And if you were just interested in seeing everything that FIC had to offer in this location, then you would just type in the city, and it would bring up all of the jobs that are posted that week. If you are interested in posting, you just submit your posting on line. This position handles both responsibilities, and as a result, when we got a vacancy in this area, she expressed her interest. We had posted the job, but we had also told Human Resources that she was interested in the position, so they asked her to submit her paperwork, and because I worked with her, an interview wasn't needed. All other employees that were interested in the position had to go through an interview process with Human Resources. Ayesha was the best qualified, and so we selected her to move over from that position into this one. [Would that be a pay increase?] Not at the time. No. It will be a lateral move for her.

Family oriented policies and practices at Ayesha's company were another significant boost to her advancement goals. Because the jobsite was so far from home, Ayesha had to forego work at times to confer with her children's teachers. One such time was when one of her fourth-grade twins was threatened at gunpoint by a child at school. Ayesha's response was to move both twins *immediately* into another school, which took several days' time from work. Compounding matters, one twin had been scheduled for learning disability testing, but even after six months in the new school, his orders had not been transferred. Tracking down the paperwork and arranging for testing at the new school also took several days of work time. Importantly, Ayesha's was the *only* workplace out of over 50 in this research that offered flexible time. Flextime enabled Ayesha to handle her children's serious needs *and* remain firmly on an advancement path at work:

> My supervisor there is very flexible because she knows I have children. Something might come up where I have to take off a day, or I might come home and something happens and I can't go to work the next day; I just call in and let her know. [Do you make up that time?] Sure. I just stay extra hours and make it up.

The company's official "mentor" program was another boost to Ayesha's advancement goals. Mentorship included not only encouragement, but concrete guidance and financial support toward a specific career path. Although the program was voluntary, Ayesha's supervisor described it as structured, rich, and occurring *on company time*:

> Ayesha has already utilized the mentor program. She expressed an interest to me to have a mentor identified for her, and I had always known of her medical interests and went to the manager of our long-term care division that still deals with medical information and explained her background and what her interest was for the future. They were able to identify a person in their division who was interested in being a mentor, and we hooked up that individual with Ayesha, and they try to meet on a weekly basis. If they are not able to meet once a week, then they meet every other week and just get together for about an hour on company time and talk about things; what's going on, what she can do, areas that she can improve in, that sort of thing.

A final "plus" was the fact that the company's advancement structure included further education, both off- and on-the-job. Ayesha creatively solved the common problem of providing upfront funding for courses that were eventually reimbursable by using her Earned Income Tax Credit (EITC) refund:

> I can go to any college I want to. The courses will cost me anywhere from $300 to $500 a course. [And how difficult is that going to be to get the upfront money?] It's not going to be difficult at all because I am going to use my income tax [EITC refund].

However, company reimbursement was not total. Ayesha's supervisor reported that "80 percent of your college education can be paid for by FIC if the courses are job related or work related in the future." At Ayesha's income level and family demands, even 20 percent could be forbidding.

Ayesha's company also offered unusually rich on-job training, *during company time*, that aimed to enhance employees' longer term goals. Her supervisor explained:

> And we have a lot of "lunch and learn" sessions at lunchtime where you bring your lunch and you sit down and you learn information about health items or items that are interesting to women, like heart disease or joining a walking club. The nurse comes down and talks to us about different health related items, and I have seen her [Ayesha] take advantage of a lot of those sessions as well. She has also become a member of what we call our activity committee, and as a member of that committee, she gets to say exactly what's going to be offered to employees in the future. And she has also taken advantage of some of the classes that we had *during company time*, which we definitely encourage. We ask all employees to go to at least 40 hours during work sessions.

"At the same time, systems outside of work made my advancement aims more difficult." The first systemic impediment to Ayesha's advancement was her inability to receive vital subsidy supports because of outdated eligibility criteria. Despite her "good job," Ayesha had serious problems making ends meet. Her $26,000 annual income left her at 147 percent of poverty level, yet she was not eligible for food or housing assistance because *occasional* overtime was calculated as *regular* by eligibility workers, and *only* her three younger children were counted in family composition:

> My caseworker there said I didn't qualify for Food Stamps. How can that be? It costs a lot to feed this big family, and I don't make that much money. [Do you think they counted overtime in your eligibility?] Definitely. And

I can't always count on having overtime. [Do you have any housing sub-sidy?] No; that would be good too, if I did. [How much rent do you pay?] $525 a month [one-quarter of her gross income].

Subsidy ineligibility thwarted many Jobs Initiative workers, as Iversen's 2002 monograph, *Moving Up Is a Steep Climb*, illuminated. In response, because interorganizational networks represent multiple constituencies, they could powerfully advocate for new "basic needs" standards that are based on local costs and the reality that even children over age 18 may be "dependent," particularly if they are in training themselves, as Ayesha explained:

It's not really the fact that making $13.00 an hour is not good, making $12.75 an hour is not good. It *is* good. But it's according to where you live. That's right. Like if I was in Georgia making that amount of money. Yes, I would be doing fine. But no, I'm up north and the degree of living here is much, much higher. And neither of my [over age 18] kids is working right now, since they're going to the construction training. All they get at training is carfare.

Irrational expectations from other systems also obstructed Ayesha's advancement efforts. Just as Kevin McDonalds's children's school did not adjust its schedule and demands to the needs of working parents, Ayesha's public assistance office did not adjust its schedule and demands either:

[My caseworker told me] "I need to see you before Friday." Now this is like on a Wednesday, and they call me and tell me, "oh, I need to see you before Friday." You know, leave a message on my machine. So I will call them back and I'll get the person. "As you well know, I work. Just like you. I can-not just up and come into your office or into the school the next day or the day after. I have to give my supervisor ample time so she can find some-body to replace me just like you would have to give your boss ample time. You just can't go in there and tell me this. No, if there is something we can talk about over the phone, we can do that now. If not, send me a letter." They are making it very difficult for single parents that are working. They say, okay, get off of welfare. You get off of welfare. Then you're working but they are not helping. They are not helping at all. Are new workers just going to lose out on a whole day's pay just for a couple of hours?

In sum however, Ayesha felt that workplace supports outweighed system obstructions. Despite the particularly burdensome worries of the dangers and lack of special learning help in her younger children's urban schools, Ayesha felt firmly on course for significant advancement in the near future.

CONCLUSION: WHAT ELSE
CAN HELP FAMILIES ADVANCE?

What do these stories tell us? First, jobseekers with histories of labor market disadvantage *want* to work hard to support their families. To a one, family is paramount in advancement decisions and actions. Second, the systems involved in worker advancement far exceed those traditionally associated with worker skill building, to include children's schools and public policies. Third, helping men and women *get* a job is far simpler and less expensive than helping them *keep* and *advance* through work. Last, interorganizational networks, such as those in the Jobs Initiative, play a unique and crucial role in helping such families advance. At the same time, additional players are needed to cement these "good starts."

Kevin's family still needs help navigating inhospitable children's schools, a punitive legal system, and essential subsidies. Both parents need guidance for further career development. Maya's family still needs help managing work, health, and home demands, navigating educational systems, and learning about financial management and asset development. Helping Maya's husband find work that would be less subject to layoff would significantly forward this family's goals. Ayesha's family still needs help negotiating the best possible education for the younger children, finding education and training support for the older children, and navigating elusive housing and food supports to extend her still-inadequate income.

Stand-alone workforce organizations did not have the capacity to satisfy these needs earlier in the families' work lives, and despite the fact that synergistic partnerships in the Jobs Initiative reduced some of the difficulty of advancement, they could not satisfy all the families' needs either. Workforce organizations and networks are simply not funded adequately to address the complete array of advancing families' needs. Two partial solutions come to mind: referral and political advocacy.

Referral is a common solution to resource gaps, although it is often not successfully transacted. Service providers and families alike emphasize that "the person you go to first is the person you stay with." However, if workforce organizations are funded sufficiently to be able to assess the needs of *all* family members, identify and nurture relationships with quality resource providers, and provide individualized linkage and active follow up, referrals are likely to be more strategic, effective, and permanent.

Second, interorganizational networks may constitute a unique and powerful platform for political influence. Partnerships between education and service providers, employers, policy makers, and funders, crafted and guided by a mission driven umbrella organization or entity, yield webs of constituents with the cumulative leverage needed to shift employers and public policy makers to a family and systems agenda. Workplace outcomes such as reduced turnover, less absenteeism, and improved climate—outcomes that result from partners' pre-employment training and post employment support of new workers—may stimulate employers to expand incentives such as release and flextime for school or family issues and on-job GED or skill building. These webs of constituents may also be able to wield significant leverage, particularly at the state level, toward the unification of funding streams and the enactment of more relevant subsidy eligibility standards. Essentially, families and organizations *together* can show employers and public policy makers that systematic investment in workers pays dividends to all parties, *if* such investment is extensive enough and long enough.

NOTES

The author wishes to acknowledge Annie Laurie Armstrong's many contributions to this chapter.

1. See Iversen (2002) for details about the Annie E. Casey Foundation's Jobs Initiative and the ethnographic research design.

2. Kathe Johnson and Michele Belliveau contributed significantly to the original Kevin McDonalds family story (see Iversen, 2002).

3. Annie Laurie Armstrong and Mona Basta contributed significantly to the original Maya Vanderhand family story (see Iversen, 2002).

4. Cynthia Saltzman and Michele Belliveau contributed significantly to the original Ayesha Muhammad family story (report to the Annie E. Casey Foundation).

REFERENCES

Clymer, C., B. Roberts, and J. Strawn. (2001). *States of Change*. Philadelphia: Public/Private Ventures.

Iversen, Roberta R. (2002). *Moving Up Is a Steep Climb*. Baltimore: Annie E. Casey Foundation.

Osterman, Paul. (1999). *Securing Prosperity*. Princeton, NJ: Princeton University Press.

11

Labor Market Intermediaries in the Old and New Economies: A Survey of Worker Experiences in Milwaukee and Silicon Valley

LAURA LEETE, CHRIS BENNER,
MANUEL PASTOR JR., AND SARAH ZIMMERMAN

INTRODUCTION

Labor market intermediaries (LMIs) are not a new phenomenon. Public sector employment services for unemployed workers, union hiring halls in the building trades, and for-profit temporary agencies have existed for a long time. What seem to be new, however, are the number and variety of LMIs, and the extensive roles they are playing in the restructuring of the U.S. labor market. To date there is little comprehensive quantitative work documenting who uses intermediaries, why they use them, and what their impacts are on labor market outcomes. In this chapter, we attempt to begin filling this gap by reporting on a recently completed phone survey of 1,300 workers in the Silicon Valley region of California and the Milwaukee, Wisconsin, metropolitan area. We particularly focus on the labor market experiences of disadvantaged workers and document the incidence of use and range of activities of a broad group of labor market intermediaries, including temporary agencies; head hunters; community based, church based, and government agencies; labor unions; community and vocational colleges; private vocational schools; and membership organizations.

The coverage of our survey includes a broader range of labor market intermediaries than is typically included in the category of workforce intermediaries that are the central focus of this volume. This is why we use the term labor market intermediary. We included a variety of organizations that work at all levels of the labor market, offering a variety of job placement, training, and support services. Studying labor market intermediaries in two regions of the U.S. allows us to compare findings across two very different economic contexts: the quintessential high tech economy driven by information technology and a more traditional manufacturing based economy. We chose these two regions, in part, in order to examine whether the much reported volatility and short product cycles of the high tech industry of Silicon Valley has fostered a more widespread use of intermediary organizations, as workers try to navigate the constant flux of the labor market there.

Our survey work was informed by focus groups conducted with representatives of numerous intermediaries in both regions and a total of 146 interviews with staff and clients (both workers and employers) of 23 different intermediary organizations we profiled in-depth. On the basis of this qualitative work, we developed a typology of intermediaries according to their role in the market and some correspondence between that typology and organizational form (Benner, et al., 2001; Bernhardt, et al., 2001). While some authors have attributed the rise in LMIs to external conditions—for instance, the increasingly volatile demand for products that gives firms an incentive to downsize the core or permanent labor force (Scott, 1999), or the improvements in communication and information technologies that allow for more fluid boundaries between firms (Benner, 2002; Castells, 1996; Storper, 1997; Saxenian, 1994)[1]—our typology goes beyond the view that LMIs are essentially "meeting the market." Instead, in our qualitative work we found some LMIs to be actively involved in "making" the market—that is, working to restructure the labor market on both supply and demand sides. This can be either a positive or a negative force for workers. For example, temporary agencies are increasingly being contracted to run whole aspects of the personnel process for some sections of a company's labor force, often driving down costs and standards in the process. There is a high road as well, however: organizations such as the Wisconsin Regional Training Partnership (WRTP) are trying to place and train workers even as they raise standards and productivity in the industries in which they work. Of course, LMIs do not come defining themselves as market "makers" or "meeters." Instead they are generally categorized by organizational form, including for-profit temporary agencies, public agencies (such as welfare-to-work agencies and Private Industry Councils, now Workforce Investment Boards), not-for-profit placement agencies, community/technical colleges, and membership based organizations (such as unions and professional groups), which is how we organized our survey questions. Nonetheless, the survey results provide important insights into the nature of intervention in the labor market. In turn, this information can provide important clues into how policy can help foster institutions that specifically focus on the needs of low-skill, low-income workers and are motivated to help these workers successfully navigate the increasingly fragmented labor markets that they face.

In the overview of intermediary use and services that follows, we organize the discussion in the following way. First is a brief section describing in more detail the methodology of the survey. This is followed by a section describing the levels of intermediary use and services across the labor market. The subsequent section focuses more specifically on the experiences of disadvantaged workers in using intermediaries. We then briefly explore the relationship between use of labor market intermediaries and the depth of social networks that individuals have available to them. The concluding section discusses areas of further research and the policy implications of our survey findings.

METHODOLOGY

The findings reported here come from a random-digit-dialing phone survey of workers in the Silicon Valley region of Northern California and the Milwaukee, Wisconsin, metropolitan area.[2] The survey was conducted between August 2001 and June 2002 and was administered to individuals between the ages of 25 and 65 who had worked sometime in the past three years. In order to collect detailed information on intermediary use we oversampled those who had used some kind of intermediary to obtain a job that they had held in the last three years. We collected responses from 1,348 individuals (659 in Milwaukee and 689 in Silicon Valley), of which 739 were from LMI users (373 in Milwaukee and 366 in Silicon Valley). By collecting comparable information from both LMI and non-LMI users, we are able to compare the characteristics and outcomes of the two groups. Low-income phone prefixes were over-sampled in order to ensure adequate representation of low-income individuals in the sample.[3] The survey was conducted in both English and Spanish as needed. The overall survey response rate was 39.9 percent.

It should be noted that our survey reports specifically on intermediary use that resulted in obtaining a job that was held sometime in the three years prior to the survey. As a result, the contact with the intermediary itself could have occurred at any time, and by necessity we are not reporting on intermediary experiences that did not result in employment. These sample limitations were introduced in order to improve the accuracy of the survey responses that we received. Through the use of focus groups and pre-testing in the development of our survey instrument we found it to be quite difficult to elicit information from random respondents about experiences they had had with LMIs. While intermediaries are becoming more and more ubiquitous in our economic landscape, it is not yet a well-defined concept in the popular consciousness. Through repeated drafting and testing we found that individuals were most accurately able to recount experiences with LMIs if those experiences were connected to a job they had actually held. To increase the accuracy of this accounting, we limited the inquiry to jobs that were held (although not necessarily obtained) in the three years prior to the interview.

In the survey we identify and categorize the intermediaries used by workers to find jobs into five distinct groupings—temporary placement agencies and head hunters; unions; community based, nonprofit, and governmental organizations and agencies; community and technical colleges and private vocational schools; and membership based professional associations. We limit the sample to those who are 25 years old and older and so deliberately curtail our observation of early labor market experiences and job churning that exist among the youngest members of the labor market as they are getting a foothold in the workforce. We also do not include job placement functions of regular academic institutions such as high schools and four-year colleges and universities, in an effort to focus the discussion on organizations that make job matching and vocationally oriented training their primary focus.

CHARACTERISTICS OF INTERMEDIARY USE IN TWO REGIONS

In order to understand the role that intermediaries are now playing in our labor markets, we first turn to looking at the overall incidence of intermediary use in two regions. While one might expect the volatility of the high tech industry in Silicon Valley to have fostered greater use of intermediary organizations, in looking at the percent of current jobs held that were obtained through an intermediary we find the surprising result that intermediary use in Milwaukee is higher than that in Silicon Valley. In Milwaukee, we found that 22.3 percent of currently held jobs were obtained through an LMI, compared to 15.6 percent in Silicon Valley. Similarly, a broader measure of intermediary use, counting LMI use to obtain any job held in the last three years, yields similar results. By this measure, 29.8 percent of Milwaukee workers had held a job in the last three years that they had obtained through an LMI, compared to 26.3 percent in Silicon Valley.

A detailed analysis of the survey data suggests two broad reasons why intermediary use might be higher in Milwaukee than Silicon Valley. One explanation may be that workers in Silicon Valley have stronger social networks, since in Milwaukee 19.8 percent reported finding their current job through friends, compared to 25.4 percent in Silicon Valley. A second factor may be that people in Silicon Valley use the Internet more, since only 1.6 percent in Milwaukee reported finding a job through the Internet, compared to 4.3 percent in Silicon Valley. In both cases, workers in Silicon Valley may have somewhat less need of intermediaries to help them find work.

Whatever the reasons for the difference in overall incidence rate in the two regions, the level is quite high, with more than a quarter of the labor force having held a job in the last three years that they got through an LMI. Beyond the overall incidence rate, there are many similarities in LMI use in both regions, and some interesting differences. In what follows, we summarize the key findings of the survey, highlighting the similarities and differences between the two regions.

Types of Intermediaries

Temporary and for-profit job placement agencies clearly dominate the intermediary landscape. As shown in Table 11.1, more than half of intermediary use is through such agencies, and their presence is comparable in both regions studied, with 15.1 percent of workers in Milwaukee and 15.3 percent of workers in Silicon Valley having gotten a job they'd held in the last three years through a temporary agency. Community colleges and vocational schools play a somewhat larger role in Milwaukee than in Silicon Valley (6.3 compared to 4.4 percent), as did nonprofit or government agencies (4.4 versus 2.7 percent) and unions (2.7 percent versus 2.4 percent), while Silicon Valley had a higher use of professional associations (1.6 versus 1.3 percent).

Who Is Using Intermediaries?

Intermediary users differ along a number of lines from non-users. Furthermore there are significant differences between those who use temporary agencies, nonprofit or government agencies, and other LMIs. An overview of this comparison for both regions and by type of intermediary is shown in Table 11.2. In both regions, all LMI users tend to be younger and are more likely to be ethnic minorities than non-LMI users, although these

**Table 11.1   Percent of Those Working in the Last 3 Years
in Jobs Obtained through an Intermediary,
Ages 25–65, by Type of Intermediary**

LMI Type		Milwaukee	Silicon Valley
Temporary Help Agency		15.1%	15.3%
Community College		6.3%	4.4%
Nonprofit/government agency		4.4%	2.7%
Union		2.7%	2.4%
Professional association		1.3%	1.6%
	Total	29.8%	26.3%

differences tend to be more pronounced in Milwaukee than Silicon Valley. In Milwaukee, 88.6 percent of non-LMI users were white compared to only 58.4 percent of temp agency users, 62.4 percent of nonprofit agency users, and 83.8 percent of other LMI users. In Silicon Valley, 51.8 percent of non-LMI users were white, the same as the percentage of temp agency users, but more than the 40.1 percent of nonprofit agency users and the 50.3 percent of other LMI users who were white. However, the pattern of use of inter-mediaries by Hispanics varies dramatically between the two regions. There is a disproportionately high use of temp agencies by Hispanics in Milwaukee and disproportionately low use of temp agencies in Silicon Valley (this is dis-cussed in more detail in the following section under disadvantaged workers).

Regional differences also emerge when looking at the education level of LMI users. In Milwaukee, LMI users tend to have less education than non-LMI users (averaging 14.3 years of schooling for non-LMI users, com-pared to 13.9 years for temp agency users and 13.0 years for nonprofit agency users and 13.7 for other LMI users). In Silicon Valley, there is a dif-ferent pattern. As in Milwaukee, users of nonprofit agencies have less edu-cation than non-LMI users (13.8 and 14.8 years, respectively), but temp agency users and users of other LMIs have higher levels of education (15.0 and 16.0 years respectively). The difference is even more striking when comparing use of temporary agencies by workers in the two regions by the highest level of schooling attained. In Milwaukee, there is a large concen-tration of temporary agency users who have less than a high school degree, accounting for 11.3 percent of all temporary agency users, more than 3 times the percentage of non-LMI users without a high school degree. In Silicon Valley, by contrast, less than 1 percent of temporary agency users had less than a high school degree, compared to 3.7 percent of non-LMI users. At the top end of the workforce, the contrasts are just as stark. In

Table 11.2 Demographic Characteristics of Workers, Employed in Past 3 Years, by LMI Use

	Milwaukee				Silicon Valley			
Characteristic	Non-LMI	Temp Agency	Nonprofit/ Govt	Other LMI*	Non-LMI	Temp Agency	Nonprofit/ Govt	Other LMI*
Average age (years)	44.6	37.8	44.4	41.0	40.8	38.3	36.8	39.7
Female (percent)	56.8%	45.9%	60.3%	53.9%	52.0%	50.7%	68.8%	32.4%
Ethnicity (percent)								
Non-Hispanic White	88.6%	58.4%	62.4%	83.8%	51.8%	51.8%	40.1%	50.3%
Hispanic	3.9%	17.1%	5.8%	3.6%	28.8%	9.7%	39.5%	26.7%
Black	5.3%	17.7%	24.5%	12.2%	2.6%	13.1%	10.0%	2.7%
Asian/Pacific Islander	0.8%	4.2%	0.0%	0.1%	12.8%	20.6%	1.9%	13.4%
Other	1.3%	2.7%	7.2%	0.2%	3.5%	4.6%	8.5%	6.5%
Highest level of schooling (%)								
Less than High School	3.6%	11.3%	8.2%	2.2%	3.7%	0.5%	6.3%	0.2%
High School or GED	38.0%	36.2%	69.0%	30.7%	35.8%	26.8%	42.3%	28.1%
Associate Degree	14.1%	8.8%	7.7%	32.3%	9.0%	16.4%	18.8%	13.0%
Bachelor's Degree	26.6%	35.4%	7.9%	16.4%	30.8%	29.3%	26.1%	29.0%
Advanced degree	15.1%	6.4%	6.7%	4.5%	20.7%	22.8%	1.0%	25.4%
Certificate or License	2.7%	2.0%	0.5%	13.8%	0.0%	4.1%	5.6%	3.2%
Total years of schooling								
Average # of Years	14.3	13.9	13.0	13.7	14.8	15.0	13.8	16.0

*Includes unions, professional associations, and community/vocational college placements

Silicon Valley, 22.8 percent of temporary agency users have an advanced degree (master's, Ph.D., or professional degree), slightly more than the percentage of non-LMI users. In Milwaukee, in contrast, only 6.4 percent of temporary agency users had an advanced degree, compared to 15.1 percent of non-LMI users. Clearly, there is a group of temporary agencies in Silicon Valley that cater to a more highly educated workforce. It is here that the hypothesized connection between the "new economy" and use of intermediaries emerges. Thus it is apparent that there are both regional commonalities and differences in the populations served by this broad array of intermediaries and that the populations served vary dramatically by type of intermediary as well.

Why Are People Using Intermediaries?

In our survey, we also asked our LMI sample about the circumstances under which they sought intermediary service. These results are shown in Table 11.3. Here further differences between the two regions also emerge. In both regions, the largest group of LMI users were those who were currently not working and looking for a job (Group 1), including those either unemployed or (re)entering the labor market (coming out of school, moving into the area, previously keeping house, or coming off of welfare). In both regions, this group made up half of those who used temporary agencies. For those using nonprofit agencies, however, this group accounted for 61.8 percent in Milwaukee and only 48.0 percent in Silicon Valley.

Even greater differences between the two regions emerge in looking at a second group of workers—those who went to an LMI because they hoped it would get them a better job, or better career (Group 2). In Silicon Valley, this group accounted for another 31.8 percent of temporary agency users, and 55.8 percent of other LMI users (though only 16.9 percent of nonprofit agency users, suggesting that people using nonprofit agencies have low expectations about the quality of jobs to which they provide access). In Milwaukee, by contrast, only 18.8 percent of temporary agency users and 38.5 percent of other LMI users went to the LMI because they thought it would be able to get them a better job (and 20.8 percent of nonprofit agency users).

What Services Are People
Getting from Intermediaries?

In addition to simply helping people get a job, LMIs of different kinds provide a range of supplementary services. These can range from simple advice

Table 11.3   Reasons for Going to an LMI, by Type of LMI and Region

	Milwaukee			Silicon Valley		
Reason for going to LMI	Temp Agency	Non-profit/ Govt	Other LMI*	Temp Agency	Non-profit/ Govt	Other LMI*
Group 1: Getting a job	54.9%	61.8%	33.4%	50.3%	48.0%	27.6%
Group 2: Getting a better job	18.8%	20.8%	38.5%	31.8%	16.9%	55.8%
Group 3: Other reasons	26.3%	17.4%	28.1%	17.9%	35.1%	16.5%

*Includes unions, professional associations, and community/vocational college placements

on job hunting and networking skills, to help with writing a resume, to more in-depth assistance like training, and assistance with transportation and childcare. Table 11.4 shows the percentage of people who said that they received additional services from the LMI that got them their job. The clearest picture that emerges is that individuals got significantly less additional assistance from temporary help agencies than they did from nonprofit agencies or other LMIs. This is consistent across the two regions. In every category, the percentage of nonprofit agency users and other LMI users reporting other assistance is much higher than the percentage of temporary agency users. This is an important finding, given that more than half of all LMI users are using temporary agencies, the vast majority of whom are getting no additional assistance beyond job placement.

There are some interesting differences between the two regions that emerge in examining the services provided. Some temporary agencies in Silicon Valley, for instance, seem to be providing more assistance in training, since twice the percentage of temp users in Silicon Valley report that they had received some kind of computer or advanced training, compared to Milwaukee. The other major difference between the two regions that appears is in the area of transportation assistance; 13 percent of temporary agency users in Milwaukee reported receiving transportation assistance, compared to only 2 percent in Silicon Valley. It is also interesting to note that a significantly higher percentage of nonprofit agency users in Silicon Valley than in Milwaukee report receiving additional assistance in many categories, most strikingly in networking skills (55 percent versus 36 percent), advanced training (35 percent versus 16 percent), and mentoring (36 percent versus 18 percent).

Table 11.4 Type of Assistance Received from LMI, by Type of LMI and Region

Type of Assistance	Milwaukee			Silicon Valley		
	Temp Agency	Nonprofit/ Govt	Other LMI*	Temp Agency	Nonprofit/ Govt	Other LMI*
Job finding skills						
Job hunting advice	32%	62%	67%	31%	63%	69%
Networking skills	19%	36%	47%	18%	56%	48%
Help with resume	14%	46%	36%	20%	58%	40%
Training						
Computer training	4%	32%	35%	7%	33%	38%
Advanced training	2%	16%	36%	4%	35%	41%
GED/ESL classes	0%	7%	37%	0%	24%	22%
Other assistance						
Mentoring	0%	18%	40%	3%	34%	41%
Legal help	1%	11%	27%	2%	35%	18%
Transportation	13%	25%	8%	2%	38%	6%
Childcare help	0%	12%	7%	1%	33%	4%
Health insurance	15%	18%	28%	12%	36%	26%
Pension plan	4%	18%	26%	10%	25%	27%

*Includes unions, professional associations, and community/vocational college placements

Satisfaction with Intermediary Assistance

Beyond the services provided, different intermediaries also vary considerably on the nature and quality of jobs to which they provide access. These results are shown in Table 11.5. Consistently across both regions, more people who used LMIs other than temp agencies felt the LMI had helped them get a better work situation. In not a single category were temporary agency users more satisfied with the quality of job they had received than the users of other LMIs. Nonetheless, a significant minority (between 31 and 50 percent) of temporary agency users in each region said that the agency had helped them get a job with higher wages, better career opportunities, better working conditions, or a job that they enjoy more. For people who used nonprofit agencies, roughly half or more in both regions felt the LMI had helped them get a job with better career opportunities, a more stable job, or one that they enjoyed more. In most categories, however, it is users of other LMIs (unions, community colleges, and professional associations) who are the most satisfied with the jobs they have received.

Again, however, there appear to be differences in the role of temporary agencies in Silicon Valley as compared with Milwaukee. Temp agency users in Silicon Valley report a higher satisfaction level than those in Milwaukee, or at least less dissatisfaction. In Silicon Valley 50 percent of temp agency users felt the agency had gotten them a job they enjoy more, versus 45 percent in Milwaukee. Forty-two percent thought the agency had gotten them a job with higher wages and better career opportunities, compared to 31 percent in Milwaukee. Still, the most significant finding is that for people using LMIs, in most categories the majority of people felt the assistance the LMI gave them did not help them get a better job or improved employment situation.

The basic story that emerges is this: intermediary use is quite widespread, with more than a quarter of all workers in both regions having held a job in the last three years that they got through an intermediary. Unfortunately, however, the majority of intermediary users are using the types of LMIs—temporary agencies—that provide the least additional assistance, and whose clients are least likely to have reported that they got a better job. In both regions, it is clear that intermediary users are disproportionately from disadvantaged sectors of the labor market—with lower education, minority status, or unemployed looking for work. This is most pronounced among nonprofit agencies, but temporary agencies are also disproportionately used by disadvantaged workers. In comparing the two regions, it is clear that there is no simple relationship between LMI use and the higher levels of employment volatility in Silicon Valley. What Silicon Valley does

Table 11.5 Satisfaction with Assistance Provided by Intermediaries, by Type of LMI and Region

Percent who agreed with statement that the assistance from LMI helped them get:

	Milwaukee			Silicon Valley		
	Temp Agency	Nonprofit/ Govt	Other LMI*	Temp Agency	Nonprofit/ Govt	Other LMI*
Job they enjoy more	45%	53%	67%	50%	59%	70%
Job that is more stable	39%	75%	59%	32%	54%	54%
Job with better working conditions	33%	46%	60%	32%	50%	47%
Job with better career opportunities	33%	49%	64%	41%	44%	62%
Job with higher wages	31%	31%	48%	42%	49%	48%
Job with better schedule	26%	35%	39%	21%	56%	31%
Job with better medical coverage	24%	47%	47%	20%	33%	38%
Job with better pension	23%	54%	46%	18%	34%	41%
Better commute	17%	23%	17%	11%	46%	23%
Better childcare	4%	12%	11%	2%	50%	10%
Something else	7%	9%	23%	10%	23%	25%

*Includes unions, professional associations, and community/vocational college placements

appear to have, however, is a significant group of more highly educated workers who are using intermediaries as a way of finding better employment. This group seems to be minimal in Milwaukee.

LABOR MARKET INTERMEDIARIES
AND DISADVANTAGED WORKERS

Recent labor market developments have resulted in problematic and volatile outcomes for workers with low levels of education and skills. Wage and hours distributions have become polarized, involuntary un- and under-employment has risen, and work has become increasingly temporary and contingent in recent decades. Disadvantage in today's market is often a constellation made up of varying parts of low pay, low skill, and racial and ethnic discrimination. Workforce intermediaries often aim to restructure the labor market—meeting the needs of both the supply and demand side—in order to ameliorate these conditions. In this section, we look explicitly at the relationship of disadvantaged workers to the full range of labor market intermediaries. Rather than explicitly defining "disadvantage," we explore it along three different dimensions, looking at individuals living in households with low incomes, individuals with low-education levels, and those who are non-white racial or ethnic minorities.

First, the pattern of intermediary usage varies for those who do and do not have some level of disadvantage. Table 11.6 compares the incidence of intermediary use of low-income, low-education workers with their higher income and more highly educated counterparts and for all workers by race. Low-income workers are those who live in households with incomes in the bottom one-third of the regional distribution of household income;[4] low education is defined as a high school diploma or less. The patterns of intermediary use vary markedly across regions by income and education, and to some extent by race. In Milwaukee, for instance, those with low household incomes or low levels of education have strikingly higher usage of temporary agencies and nonprofit and government agencies but somewhat lower usage of community/vocational colleges and schools, unions, and professional associations. In contrast, in Silicon Valley workers from low-income households or with low levels of education are less likely to use temporary agencies than their higher income, more educated counterparts, and are more likely to use unions. As in Milwaukee, however, the disadvantaged groups are more likely to receive assistance from nonprofit and government organizations and community colleges and less likely to work with professional associations.

Table 11.6 Use of Labor Market Intermediaries to Obtain Job Held in the Past 3 Years, by Income, Education, Race, and Region

Milwaukee

	All	Household Income		Education Level		Race			
		Bottom 33%	Top 67%	HS Grad or Less	Some College or More	Black	Hispanic	Asian and Other	White
Used an Intermediary	29.9	40.7	26.7	32.4	27.8	57.9	54.1	32.6	24.9
Temp Agencies	15.0	26.7	11.6	16.5	13.9	31.0	43.4	22.7	10.9
Community Colleges	6.3	2.3	7.2	4.4	7.7	9.5	2.1	0.5	6.6
Nonprofit, Government	4.5	9.4	2.9	8.0	1.8	12.6	4.4	7.5	3.4
Unions	2.7	2.0	3.4	2.6	2.8	1.3	3.4	1.9	2.8
Professional Associations	1.3	0.3	1.6	0.9	1.6	3.5	0.9	0.0	1.2
N	659	279	280	345	311	172	62	39	386

Silicon Valley

	All	Household Income		Education Level		Race			
		Bottom 33%	Top 67%	HS Grad or Less	Some College or More	Black	Hispanic	Asian and Other	White
Used an Intermediary	26.3	28.6	26.2	21.5	29.3	57.7	18.8	29.2	26.3
Temp Agencies	15.3	12.6	15.3	11.5	17.8	46.0	5.7	19.9	15.6
Community Colleges	4.4	3.7	5.6	3.0	5.1	2.4	3.8	6.2	4.1
Nonprofit, Government	2.7	6.0	1.2	3.6	2.3	6.4	4.2	1.4	2.2
Unions	2.4	6.2	1.4	3.5	1.6	3.0	3.5	0.1	2.7
Professional Associations	1.6	0.3	2.7	0.0	2.5	0.0	1.5	1.7	1.7
N	689	218	361	264	417	32	177	135	345

Turning to race and ethnicity, we divide the population into four groups—African American, Hispanic (of any race), Asian and other races, and white. The use of intermediaries across different races is similar in both regions. Non-whites generally use all types of intermediaries, except professional associations, with higher frequency than whites. This is especially true of temporary agency usage, which is far higher for non-whites than whites. For instance, in Milwaukee 43 percent of Hispanics and 31 percent of African Americans report having obtained a job they held in the last three years through a temporary agency, as compared with only 11 percent of whites. Similarly, in Silicon Valley 47 percent of African Americans and 20 percent of Asians (and those of other races) used temporary agencies, compared with only 15.6 percent of whites. There is one striking exception to the regional similarities in racial patterns, however. Hispanics in Silicon Valley use intermediaries at a far lower rate than any other racial/ethnic group, and at a rate lower than whites in either Milwaukee or Silicon Valley. Furthermore, where the other groups of non-whites report obtaining jobs through temporary agencies at extremely high rates (ranging from 20.2 to 47 percent), only 5.5 percent of Hispanics in Silicon Valley reported using a temporary agency.

From the previous discussion, we know that temporary agencies provide a considerably different, and less rich, mix of services than other intermediaries. We have also seen that disadvantaged workers are far more likely to receive job search assistance from temporary agencies than from other intermediaries. We now turn to comparing the mix of services received by disadvantaged workers and non-disadvantaged workers. Data are presented in Table 11.7 showing the percentage of individuals receiving particular types of services (help with job search, support while working, benefits, or training) again by levels of household income, education, and race. Overall, however, there is no clear pattern that disadvantaged workers disproportionately receive (or do not receive) certain services in either region. Similarly, among those who use temporary agencies, there are also no clear patterns. In some cases, those with low household incomes, low-education levels, or those who are non-white report a higher level of assistance from temporary agencies, but many times this is not the case, particularly in Silicon Valley.

Among users of other kinds of intermediaries, however, the patterns are much clearer; the disadvantaged groups using these other intermediaries generally report higher levels of support and assistance than those who are not disadvantaged. In some cases, the differences are substantial. This suggests that in addition to being far more likely to offer support services,

Table 11.7   Types of Intermediary Services Provided, by Income, Education, Race, and Region

| | | Milwaukee | | | | | |
| | | Household | | Education Level | | Race | |
	All	Bottom 33%	Top 67%	HS Grad or Less	Some College or More	Non-White	White
Percent of All LMI Users Receiving:							
Help with job search[1]	58.6	53.1	67.8	54.9	56.3	51.4	61.9
Support while working[2]	39.1	45.0	40.2	40.5	37.6	46.1	35.5
Benefits[3]	22.8	23.9	24.1	25.7	20.4	29.1	19.4
Training[4]	31.6	23.0	34.8	28.9	34.2	24.3	34.7
Percent of Temp Agency Users Receiving:							
Help with job search[1]	39.9	36.2	49.4	42.1	37.1	31.8	45.8
Support while working[2]	23.8	32.4	21.0	30.8	16.6	33.7	16.7
Benefits[3]	15.6	14.2	20.1	16.5	14.9	25.2	8.7
Training[4]	5.2	1.8	4.6	2.2	7.9	4.5	5.6
Percent of Other LMI Users Receiving:							
Help with job search[1]	77.5	86.9	77.5	80.8	74.6	88.5	74.1
Support while working[2]	55.2	70.1	55.4	50.7	59.0	69.8	50.7
Benefits[3]	30.8	43.7	28.1	35.4	26.9	37.0	28.4
Training[4]	59.2	65.3	58.3	57.2	60.9	62.1	57.9
N	364	134	183	136	225	177	182

| | | Silicon Valley | | | | | |
| | | Household | | Education Level | | Race | |
	All	Bottom 33%	Top 67%	HS Grad or Less	Some College or More	Non-White	White
Percent of All LMI Users Receiving:							
Help with job search[1]	62.5	56.6	70.1	67.0	57.7	59.5	60.7
Support while working[2]	35.6	38.0	32.9	34.9	35.8	38.8	31.8
Benefits[3]	20.6	33.1	17.4	25.8	17.9	18.9	23.0
Training[4]	27.4	27.0	28.2	35.7	23.0	26.7	28.4
Percent of Temp Agency Users Receiving:							
Help with job search[1]	46.8	28.7	61.0	50.0	45.3	40.9	50.8
Support while working[2]	21.3	14.9	20.3	18.2	22.6	23.9	17.7
Benefits[3]	14.5	18.2	18.1	14.8	14.5	12.1	17.6
Training[4]	8.5	9.7	6.5	18.4	4.8	4.1	13.0
Percent of Other LMI Users Receiving:							
Help with job search[1]	79.7	78.3	82.9	86.3	77.1	83.4	75.2
Support while working[2]	55.9	56.0	51.2	53.9	56.9	58.4	52.3
Benefits[3]	29.6	44.7	17.8	38.4	24.4	29.0	30.9
Training[4]	54.0	40.6	59.0	55.3	52.0	56.2	50.8
N	369	164	154	193	174	167	198

[1] "Help with job search" includes advice on job hunting, help with resume, and networking skills.
[2] "Support while working" includes childcare help, transportation help, legal help, mentoring, and help with problems after.
[3] "Benefits" includes health insurance and pension plans.
[4] "Training" includes GED, ESL and computer classes, and advanced training.

LMIs that are not temporary agencies as a group are far more responsive to the needs of disadvantaged workers than are temporary agencies. For example, in Milwaukee, of those in low-income households who went to other LMIs, 65.3 percent received training and 43.7 percent received benefits, as compared with only 58.3 percent and 28.1 percent of their counterparts in higher income households, respectively. In contrast, among those from low-income households who received assistance from temporary agencies, only 1.8 percent received training and 14.2 percent received benefits, rates that are lower than those for individuals from higher income households (of whom 4.6 percent received training and 20.1 percent received benefits).

We also look at another dimension of contact with intermediaries—the intensity or length of that contact. We have a number of measures of this, including the length of time during which individuals had ongoing contact with the organization, and among those who received various types of classes or training, whether the training led to some kind of certificate or diploma, whether the training was helpful in finding a job, and the amount of time spent in GED, computer, or advanced training classes. These measures are minimal for those who used temporary agencies but are quite rich for those who had contact with other types of intermediaries. The results for intermediaries other than temp agencies are presented in Table 11.8. We look here to see whether disadvantaged workers seem to have more intensive contact with non-temp agency intermediaries along any of these lines. However, the patterns are not particularly clear. While disadvantaged workers were more likely to report that intermediary provided training was helpful in their finding a job, it is generally the more advantaged groups that consistently report receiving training that led to a diploma or certificate and spending more time in training or classes.

Finally, we also look at the kinds of job outcomes that are attained by disadvantaged and other workers, according to the kind of intermediary through which they obtained their job. Of course, it should be noted that these simple comparisons do not account for the myriad of underlying factors that determine labor market outcomes for individuals, such as education, work experience, race, and gender. Thus while the comparison of wages and other outcomes across intermediary types is descriptive, it cannot be considered to be indicative of causality. Instead, these differences can be due to differences in the mix of type of workers who use each intermediary as well as differences in the efficacy of the intermediaries themselves. Future research will delineate these differences further.

Table 11.8 Intensity of Intermediary Contact by Income, Education, Race, and Region

Milwaukee

	All	Household		Education Level		Race	
		Bottom 33%	Top 67%	HS Grad or Less	Some College or More	Non-White	White
Length of Contact with LMI (days)	395	325	475	311	487	213	473
Among those Who Received Training or Classes:							
LMI Training Led to Diploma	0.60	0.53	0.68	0.40	0.66	0.59	0.53
LMI Training Helped Find Job	0.75	0.77	0.63	0.74	0.68	0.70	0.71
Time Spent in GED Classes with LMI (days)	282	349	308	334	307	164	407
Time Spent in Computer Classes with LMI (days)	170	171	122	93	181	101	167
Time Spent in Advanced Training with LMI (days)	237	167	190	386	214	136	316

Silicon Valley

	All	Household		Education Level		Race	
		Bottom 33%	Top 67%	HS Grad or Less	Some College or More	Non-White	White
Length of Contact with LMI (days)	401	386	394	265	451	337	458
Among those Who Received Training or Classes:							
LMI Training Led to Diploma	0.56	0.72	0.50	0.56	0.60	0.56	0.62
LMI Training Helped Find Job	0.74	0.92	0.70	0.85	0.76	0.80	0.78
Time Spent in GED Classes with LMI (days)	279	142	313	217	234	229	232
Time Spent in Computer Classes with LMI (days)	165	134	224	128	224	144	242
Time Spent in Advanced Training with LMI (days)	277	339	247	89	369	172	458

In Figures 11.1 and 11.2 we show median hourly wages for those who did not obtain their job through an intermediary, for those who used a temporary agency, and for those who used some other kind of intermediary. In each case, we distinguish between those from low-income households and others, those with lower and higher levels of education, and members of white and non-white racial and ethnic groups. The results are quite striking. In both Milwaukee and Silicon Valley, disadvantaged workers who use a non-temp agency intermediary have a significant wage advantage over those using temp agencies or no agency at all, but this same pattern does not hold among more advantaged workers. Similarly, in Figures 11.3 through 11.8, we use the same format to display differences in obtaining employer provided health insurance, pension plans, and job training. The results are quite similar. In these cases, those who obtained a job through an LMI that is not a temporary agency have better outcomes than those who obtained a job through a temporary agency, and in some cases than those who obtained jobs without using LMIs. Interestingly, these results hold for both the relatively disadvantaged and advantaged. However, the extent of the gain among non-temp agency LMI users is generally much greater for the disadvantaged population than for others. In other words, the difference between those who use temporary agencies and those who use some other kind of intermediary is far greater among disadvantaged workers than among others. Unfortunately, disadvantaged workers who have the most to gain from the use of other kinds of intermediaries are precisely the group that relies most heavily on temporary agencies to find work.

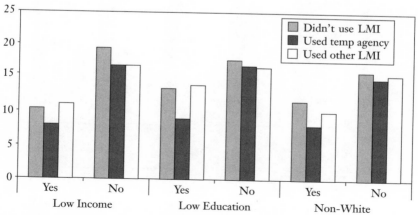

FIGURE 11.1   Median Hourly Wage by Type of Intermediary Used, Milwaukee

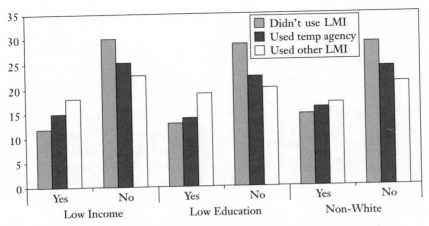

FIGURE 11.2   Median Hourly Wage by Type of Intermediary Used, Silicon Valley

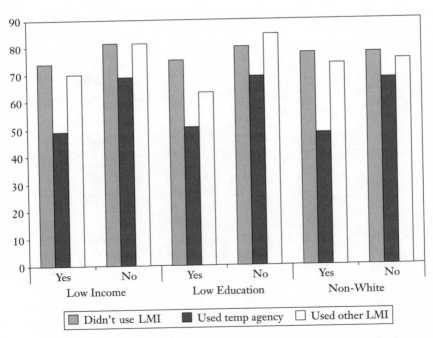

FIGURE 11.3   Percent Receiving Employer Provided Health Benefits by Type of Intermediary Used, Milwaukee

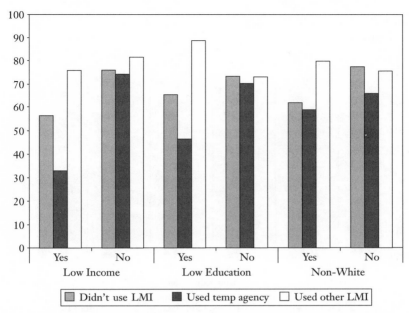

FIGURE 11.4   Percent Receiving Employer Provided Health Benefits by Type of Intermediary Used, Silicon Valley

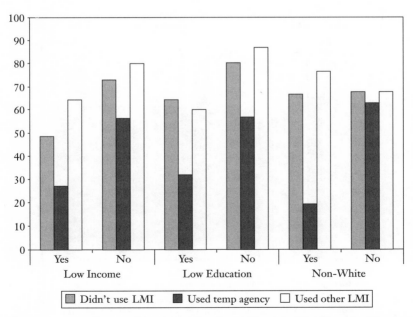

FIGURE 11.5   Percent Receiving Employer Provided Pensions by Type of Intermediary Used, Milwaukee

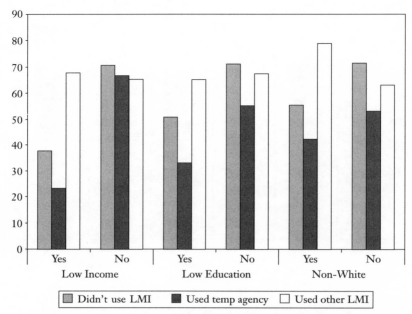

FIGURE 11.6   Percent Receiving Employer Provided Pensions by Type of Intermediary Used, Silicon Valley

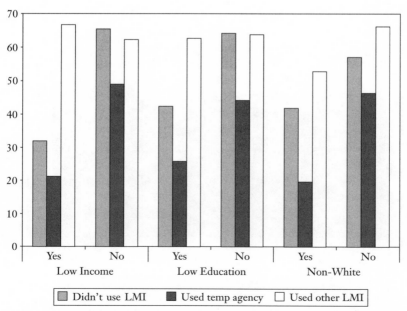

FIGURE 11.7   Percent Receiving Employer Provided Job Training by Type of Intermediary Used, Milwaukee

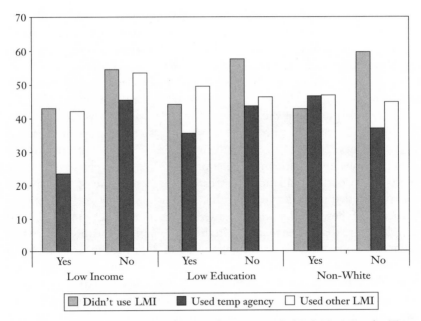

FIGURE 11.8   Percent Receiving Employer Provided Job Training by Type of Intermediary Used, Silicon Valley

JOB SEARCH, INTERMEDIARIES, AND SOCIAL NETWORKS

Finally, we also take a look at the relationship between intermediary use and one final important element of labor market navigation—social networks. It has now become common wisdom that many workers solve the dual problems of job seeking—simultaneously collecting information about jobs and signaling reliability to employers via referrals—through the use of social networks (Granovetter, 1995; Fernandez and Weinberg, 1998). Of course, not all networks are equally up to the task, particularly when social circles are constrained by living in conditions of concentrated poverty (Jargowsky, 1997; Pastor and Adams, 1996). Indeed, one of the reasons for the growing policy interest in the potential of LMIs by those concerned about low-income individuals is exactly to help those jobseekers who have weaker or less effective social networks (see Harrison and Weiss, 1998; Johnson, Bienenstock, and Farrell, 1999; Massey and Shibuya, 1995; Pastor and Marcelli, 2000). In short, there is ample reason to assume that differing levels of social capital may have an impact on the probability of using or not using an LMI.

In this section, we explore the relationship between social networks and intermediary use. Within our survey, we asked a battery of traditional social connection questions, including attendance at various meetings (such as neighborhood watch groups, school organizations, professional groups, political organizations, or religious groups) and the number of friends or close relatives with whom the respondent talked and how often. We also asked respondents about the number of friends that they would feel comfortable asking for help with a job search and also asked a set of questions regarding Internet access, to reflect the increasing use of the Internet in both obtaining jobs and maintaining relationships. We then put together the results in various combinations to create a single measure of "social connectedness" that might stand in for the extent of social networks. The least restrictive of these combinations focused on whether or not the respondent attended more than three meetings in the previous year; the most restrictive required high levels of contact on all measures. Our final measure includes all four dimensions, but not at the highest level of contact: three or more meetings in the previous year, communication with close relatives or friends at least once a week, one to two individuals who could be approached for help with a job search, and Internet access of some sort.[5]

As can be seen in Figure 11.9, there is a dramatic difference in the likelihood of using an LMI depending on whether one is considered socially connected by this measure or not. Considering both regions, those who are categorized as socially connected have an incidence of LMI use of 20 percent; for those who are not socially connected, the incidence rate rises to 31 percent. The patterns are quite similar in each region. We are currently exploring this issue further, including an investigation of whether the gaps revealed in this simple comparison hold up in a more complicated analysis in which we use other variables to predict the likelihood of LMI use; preliminary results suggest that social connectedness is still an important explanatory factor. We are also exploring whether social connectedness plays any role in steering individuals to "good" or "bad" intermediaries, with the merit of each type based on the outcomes for wages and career paths. Results here also suggest that this may be the case, perhaps because friends, relatives, and acquaintances provide advice in negotiating the LMI landscape.

Those who have suggested that LMIs may be useful to those with weak social networks seem to be right in at least one sense: the weaker the social network, the more likely one is to use a substitute (that is, an LMI) to obtain employment. However, whether this is a useful strategy or not depends on the wage and other outcomes, and our initial analysis both for disadvantaged workers and the general respondent pool suggests that it is only a

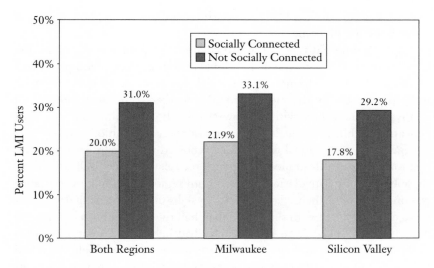

FIGURE 11.9   Percent LMI Users by Socially Connected

small group of LMIs—and definitely not the most common variant, temporary agencies—that will yield positive results on worker well being.

CONCLUDING COMMENTS

Our regional comparison of workers' experiences navigating the labor market confirm some qualitative observations that have been made about labor market intermediaries and unveil some surprising new patterns. Data from the survey indicate widespread intermediary use, with both interesting similarities and striking differences between Silicon Valley and Milwaukee, as well as between less-skilled, more disadvantaged workers and their more advantaged counterparts.

Unequivocally, we find considerable incidence of intermediary use—over a quarter of workers in both Milwaukee and Silicon Valley have used an LMI to obtain a job that they held in the last three years. In both regions, the incidence of LMI use was highest for temporary agencies and was comparable across regions. In Silicon Valley, use of community colleges and nonprofit/government organizations to secure employment is less prevalent than in Milwaukee, probably due to greater use of the Internet and social networks and the higher overall levels of education in Silicon Valley. In Milwaukee, users of all types of LMIs have slightly less education than non-LMI users, are less likely to be white, and are more likely to have a lower household income.

Among different types of intermediaries, temporary agencies are the least likely to offer any type of additional assistance beyond job placement services. This is troubling, considering that temporary agencies are most utilized precisely by the most vulnerable workers—the unemployed and disadvantaged workers with the lowest household incomes and the least education. While individuals obtaining assistance from unions, community colleges, and professional associations reported more help with training, mentoring, health insurance, and pensions, relatively few individuals use these types of intermediaries. Thus in both regions, the bulk of assistance is more likely to be focused on job finding skills than on training or support services. Coincident with this, more than half the users in both regions felt their involvement with an intermediary had helped them get a job with more stability and that they enjoyed more, but less than half believed it had helped them to get better wages or career opportunities. There is little evidence that the typical agency is assisting individuals in building careers or improving their long-term economic security.

These findings suggest to us that more needs to be done to alter the incentive structures facing labor market intermediaries. Policies should have two main goals. First, they should encourage intermediaries to meet the immediate economic needs of low-income people. Such policies would reward job placement agencies for identifying jobs with higher wages and gearing training programs to place workers in those jobs. To clarify the outcomes, they might set self-sufficiency wages as targets for LMI users, and policies might attach public funding to programs that result in such placements. We found models of such in the qualitative work associated with this project, including Working Partnerships Staffing Service, a high-road staffing agency in San Jose, California. Second, policies should design and nurture intermediaries that can offer workers services that improve long-term employment outcomes. Unfortunately, the LMIs currently offering such services are among the least accessible to and least used by workers, particularly disadvantaged workers. The WRTP program in Wisconsin is one of the most successful examples of a partnership that meets both employer needs for improved worker training and insures quality employment for worker participants.

At present workers in both regions studied here are currently most likely to make use of temporary agencies and frequently make use of nonprofit or public agencies that are passively acting as market "meeters." This most likely results from public policies that encourage a Work First model without emphasizing quality training, and in part from the immediate needs of unemployed individuals to simply gain employment. The policy recommendations suggested here could begin to provide incentives for the development of more worker centered market "maker" intermediaries.

NOTES

Acknowledgments: This research was conducted under the organizational auspices of Working Partnerships USA, San Jose, California, and the Center for Wisconsin Strategy at the University of Wisconsin. The Ford, Rockefeller, and Russell Sage Foundations generously provided funding.

1. Another aspect of this view is the rise in project oriented work that necessarily requires the composition of work teams for different projects and leads to independent contractors, temporary hiring, and the like. See the discussion in Christopherson (2001).

2. For these purposes Silicon Valley was defined as phone prefix ranges that encompassed all of Santa Clara County as well as bordering areas of San Mateo County, Alameda County, and Santa Cruz County. The Milwaukee metropolitan area is defined as Milwaukee, Ozaukee, Washington, and Waukesha counties.

3. Low-income prefixes were defined as those in which average household income was in the lower 30 percent of the distribution specific to each region. This criterion led to an income cutoff of $30,000 in the Milwaukee area and $50,000 in the Silicon Valley.

4. Annual household income cutoffs of $40,000 and $60,000, respectively, were used for the Milwaukee area and the Silicon Valley area.

5. It is important to stress that all the measures we constructed performed similarly and that measures that captured only one dimension were often very similar as well; we chose this measure primarily because it was consistent with our prior belief that all four dimensions might be important.

REFERENCES

Benner, Chris. 2002. *Work in the New Economy: Flexible Labor Markets in Silicon Valley.* Cambridge, MA: Blackwell Publishers.

Benner, Chris, Bob Brownstein, Laura Dresser, and Laura Leete. 2001. "Staircases and Treadmills: The Role of Labor Market Intermediaries in Placing Workers and Fostering Upward Mobility." *Industrial Relations Research Association, Proceedings of the Annual Meeting.*

Bernhardt, Annette, Erin Hatton, Manuel Pastor Jr., and Sarah Zimmerman. 2001. "Moving the Demand Side: Intermediaries in a Changing Labor Market." *Industrial Relations Research Association, Proceedings of the Annual Meeting.*

Castells, Manuel. 1996. *The Rise of the Network Society.* Cambridge, MA: Blackwell Publishers.

Christopherson, Susan. 2001. "Does Innovation Require Trust? Risk and Work-force Strategies in Media Work." Ithaca, NY: Department of City and Regional Planning, Cornell University.

Fernandez, Roberto, and Nancy Weinberg. 1998. "Sifting and Sorting: Personal Contacts and Hiring in a Retail Bank." *American Sociological Review*, Vol. 62.

Granovetter, Mark. 1995. *Getting a Job: A Study of Contacts and Careers*. 2nd Edition. Chicago: University of Chicago Press.

Harrison, Bennett, and Marcus Weiss. 1998. *Workforce Development Networks: Community-Based Organizations and Regional Alliances*. Thousand Oaks, CA: Sage Publications.

Jargowsky, Paul. 1997. *Poverty and Place: Ghettos, Barrios, and the American City*. New York: Russell Sage Foundation.

Johnson, James H. Jr., Elisa Jayne Bienenstock, and Walter C. Farrell, Jr. 1999. "Bridging Social Networks and Female Labor-force Participation in a Multi-ethnic Metropolis." *Urban Geography*, Vol. 20, No. 1.

Massey, Douglas, and K. Shibuya, 1995. "Unraveling the Tangle of Pathology: The Effect of Spatially Concentrated Joblessness on the Well-being of African-Americans." *Social Science Research*, Vol. 24, No. 4. (December).

Pastor, Manuel Jr., and Ana Robinson Adams. 1996. "Keeping Down With the Joneses: Neighbors, Networks, and Wages." *Review of Regional Economics*, Vol. 26, No. 2.

Pastor, Manuel Jr., and Enrico Marcelli. 2000. "Men N The Hood: Spatial, Skill, and Social Mismatch for Male Workers in Los Angeles." *Urban Geography*, Vol. 21, No. 6.

Scott, Allen, 1999. *Regions and the World Economy: The Coming Shape of Global Production Competition and Political Order*. New York: Oxford University Press.

Saxenian, Anna Lee. 1994. *Regional advantage: culture and competition in Silicon Valley and Route 128*. Cambridge, MA: Harvard University Press.

Storper, Michael. 1997. *The Regional World: Territorial Development in a Global Economy*. New York: Guilford Press.

V

BUILDING WORKFORCE INTERMEDIARIES

12

Financing Workforce Intermediaries

JERRY RUBIN, MARLENE B. SELTZER,
AND JACK MILLS

INTRODUCTION

Workforce intermediaries are a critical component of any national effort to advance low-skilled, low-income workers to family-sustaining careers. To achieve this ambitious goal, though, workforce intermediaries must gain substantially greater scale and have the stable resources and support infrastructure that make such scale possible.

This chapter explores challenges and strategies for creating a sustainable, efficient, and scaleable financing system for workforce intermediaries. First, we offer a rationale for public (and private) investment in intermediaries. Second, we present data from recent surveys and interviews on how they are currently financed, and we identify significant gaps that restrict their ability to promote advancement. The chapter concludes with an assessment of several financing options that address these gaps and can support the valuable work of workforce intermediaries as organizations, along with the advancement agenda that motivates them.

The past two decades have seen substantial growth of new organizations and initiatives to improve labor market outcomes for both low-skill, low-wage job- and skillseekers and employers. The reasons for the rapid and seemingly spontaneous growth of these organizations are discussed elsewhere in this volume (chapters 3, 4, and 6).

The proliferation of workforce intermediaries, although receiving some financial support from foundations and federal and state governments, and gaining some national attention from policy makers and analysts, has primarily been a local, grassroots phenomenon. However, as some of these organizations have grown and achieved significant outcomes, they have attracted increased attention, spawned additional organizations, and created stronger regional partnerships and networks. They have begun to look and behave like leaders of a newly emerging field of practice. With growth and the ambition it brings have come questions of sustainability as workforce intermediaries seek the influence necessary to substantially improve fragmented labor markets.

Today, workforce intermediaries are at a stage of development not unlike that of the Community Development Corporation (CDC) movement in the mid-1960s, when CDCs emerged to address the failures of market forces and public investment to promote inner city development (chapter 12). From 150 CDCs founded in the 1960s and 1970s, the field has grown to more than 2,000 such organizations (Halpern, 1995) and programs.

Achieving its current level of financial sustainability took the CDC movement nearly 40 years, extensive local and national political mobilization, a reasonably clear definition of their roles in low-income communities, and a sophisticated set of arguments to support their quest for private and public investment. For workforce intermediaries to achieve growth and sustainability comparable to that of CDCs, they, too, will need to better define their roles in the labor market and to develop a clear argument for investing limited private and public dollars.

RATIONALE FOR FUNDING
WORKFORCE INTERMEDIARIES

There are two primary arguments for substantially increased and reliable private and public financing of workforce intermediaries. The first is the role of intermediaries in addressing serious problems in local labor markets as a result of global economic changes over the past few decades. The second is an argument about the value of intermediaries to the publicly funded workforce development system as it now exists.

Responding to a More Volatile
and Challenging Labor Market

Workforce intermediaries emerged in the 1980s and 1990s in response to powerful changes in the U.S. and world economies, labor markets, and internal firm structures that have generated significant inefficiencies and economic losses for both employers and job- and skillseekers (chapters 6 and 7).

In local labor markets around the country, innovative and entrepreneurial organizations and partnerships have emerged in response to these challenges, trying to help meet the changing labor market needs of both employers and workers. Many of these—the workforce intermediaries that are the focus of this volume—are particularly concerned about advancement paths and opportunities for low-wage workers whose mobility is limited.

These intermediaries are committed to strengthening or reconstructing the components of an efficient and equitable labor market. In a more volatile and difficult market for qualified entry-level and lower skilled workers, they help address obstacles that keep employers from getting workers they need and workers from gaining skills and job opportunities they want. They organize key stakeholders in the labor market and help employers and others plan and work together to improve how the labor market serves low-skill, low-wage workers and their employers. These organizations also broker or deliver quality workforce development services—including job matching, training, and career management—that both promote low-wage workers' advancement to family-sustaining wages and meet employers' human resource requirements.

Workforce intermediaries are the "glue" holding together players in a complex and fragmented labor market. They are also active drivers for innovation in workforce development, advocating for ways to overcome the limitations of existing practice and policy through new partnerships, programs, and priorities.

Enhancing the Performance of the Publicly Funded Workforce Development System

A second rationale for funding workforce intermediaries is their important role in filling gaps in the publicly funded workforce system and enhancing the system's ability to achieve its goals. The nation currently invests significant resources in adult workforce development services, primarily job matching and training. Workforce intermediaries can improve the outcomes from that investment for employers and low-skill workers.

Workforce intermediaries play several roles that the public workforce development system typically does not. First, they focus on promoting advancement, not just placement in entry-level jobs. In the face of public policy that stresses work first and universal access to services, intermediaries focus their attention and resources on the advancement of low-income job- and skillseekers to family-sustaining careers and incomes. This focus on advancement, particularly in the context of the workplace, has begun to generate outcomes for low-income individuals far more effectively than traditional publicly funded workforce development programs (Aspen Institute, 2002).

Second, in contrast to the one-to-one approach of the public workforce development system, intermediaries aggregate the interests and demand of employers, job- and skillseekers, and providers to help ensure better labor market outcomes for both workers and employers (chapter 3). Finally, because they link together a variety of public and private resources, they can frequently design and deliver programs and services that are more flexible, more intensive, and better targeted toward advancement than categorical public funding from one agency can permit.

According to Ellen O'Brien Saunders, executive director of Washington's Workforce Training and Education Coordinating Board, intermediaries can help the public system be more creative, responsive, and effective:

> We need an R&D/experimentation capacity. We want to use state discretionary money and drive economic vitality and opportunity. We try to seed innovation by strong, local leadership from which exciting partnerships and innovation will emerge. We know we have to create high quality services and build connections and relationships so employers see and experience the value of these services. Additionally, we're creating these alternatives because we want to use them to change the behavior of public systems.

There is great variation in the relationship of local intermediaries to the publicly funded workforce development system. Some workforce intermediaries are operated directly by particularly entrepreneurial Workforce Investment Boards. Others have close ties to local boards and have effectively sorted out respective roles. While some perceived and actual competition between workforce intermediaries and Workforce Investment Boards and One Stop Centers can be found, there is little enthusiasm for duplicating services or creating a parallel workforce development system. "We don't want two separate systems," notes George Coulter of the Greater Cleveland Growth Association, an intermediary led by an employer association:

> We want to have our members gain access to the public system, and to be a conduit through which that can happen. We want to make sure our members are linked and are provided with the most detailed and current information around workforce services within our community and how that effectively links to the public system and any proprietary interests.

HOW INTERMEDIARIES FINANCE THEIR ACTIVITIES AND WHERE THEY SEE THE GREATEST GAPS

Workforce Intermediary Roles and Activities

Workforce intermediaries play a wide range of complex and challenging roles in improving the effectiveness of their local labor markets and promoting the advancement of low-skill, low-wage workers. Many of these roles require different kinds of financial resources, with variations in timing, use restrictions, and outcome requirements.

The findings below on how workforce intermediaries finance their activities is based on in-depth interviews that Jobs for the Future (JFF) conducted with eight leading workforce intermediaries and a survey of 243 workforce intermediaries done by the National Network of Sector Partners (NNSP) in August 2002 (chapter 4). The organizations surveyed and interviewed for this chapter undertake three major kinds of activities: services to advance low-income workers, labor market services to employers, and the planning and development of advancement programs. While these activities require different types of financing, they are closely linked and synergistic for most intermediaries.

According to NNSP's survey, the most often noted service is placement of individuals in jobs, for which 56 percent of those intermediaries surveyed receive funding. Other low-income worker advancement services for which most intermediaries are most often funded are occupational training (55 percent), aptitude testing (54 percent), career counseling (48 percent), ESL services (47 percent), job readiness services (46 percent), and supportive services (45 percent).[1] Post employment services that are critical to advancement are funded much less commonly. For example, only 37 percent of survey respondents received funding for training for incumbent workers, and only 36 percent received funding for post placement career advancement services.

JFF's interviews, as well as the NNSP survey, suggest that labor market services for employers are much more difficult to fund than advancement services. Several interviewees noted that incumbent worker training funds are difficult to secure, but that employer services beyond training are even more difficult to come by. For example, services that examine how to restructure jobs, create internal career ladders, or enhance internal human resource practices to support retention and advancement are very difficult to fund.

Workforce intermediaries interviewed by JFF and NNSP survey respondents undertake a number of planning and program development activities to design advancement programs, but these activities tend to be more difficult to fund than advancement activities. The most commonly identified planning and program development activities are industry/labor market research and analysis, coordination of stakeholders, and policy development and advocacy. (For a more comprehensive description of these roles and activities see chapter 3.)

Current Financing of Workforce Intermediary Roles and Activities

The NNSP survey data and interviews undertaken by JFF suggest that the primary source of financing for intermediary activities is various public funds under the federal Workforce Investment Act (WIA), including WIA Governors' Discretionary 15 percent funds, Dislocated Worker funds, and WIA Individual Learning Accounts (ILAs) or vouchers. Secondary public sources of financing are Temporary Assistance for Needy Families (TANF) and state Department of Labor and Education funds.

Some workforce intermediaries demonstrate an impressive ability to gain operating efficiencies from bundling public funding for direct training services to pay for a range of planning and program development activities, such as identifying and aggregating employer demand. One excellent example of this kind of leveraging is the Wisconsin Regional Training Partnership, which covers some of its R&D activities by running a broad array of training offerings.

Several important sources of private financing support intermediary activities, with foundation funding playing a particularly important role. According to Margaret Berger Bradley, director of the workforce services division at The Reinvestment Fund (TRF), "Private foundation funding is flexible. It's critical for leveraging public funding. The strategy of TRF, an intermediary that serves as a community development financial institution and workforce intermediary, is to go to the public system as a co-investor."

Westside Industrial Retention & Expansion Network (WIRE-Net), an intermediary in Cleveland, also relies on flexible foundation funding. John Colm, director of WIRE-Net, says, "Mott and several local foundations provided the funding in 1998 for pay for the development of our precision machinist program, including networking, strategic planning, and institution building. Now, we receive $100,000 annually of member dues, and we also have $1.2 million Department of Labor funding over two years."

Many workforce intermediaries raise substantial corporate funding through fee-for-service and corporate contributions, though this tends to represent a small share of their overall funding. Corporate funding is motivated by a number of different factors, including membership in employer led intermediaries like Greater Cleveland Growth Association, proven return on investment, as in the case of Shoreline Community College in Seattle, or collective bargaining agreements, as in the case of labor/management partnerships such as those between AFSCME District 1199C Training and Upgrading Fund and Philadelphia hospitals.

At Shoreline Community College, for example, employer fees play an important role in paying tuition for their career ladder programs. According to Shoreline's Joe Renouard, hospitals are developing career ladders, but they can't provide the training themselves. "They've committed to paying tuition for students. They send the employees to Shoreline, and it's a win-win. *That's huge.* Those dollars can then be used to support organizing, planning, and development of new resources."

Other fee-for-service activities are being explored by intermediaries. To achieve long-term sustainability, several interviewees from intermediaries noted that they are considering, or actively engaged in, developing for-profit placement firms. These businesses, which would focus on temporary or permanent placements, or both, would generate income to help support the intermediaries' other advancement activities.

Workforce intermediaries excel in utilizing private dollars to leverage public investments. Private dollars allow them to develop deep knowledge of their customers, bring stakeholders together, aggregate and clarify demand for workforce services, and design those services. Private funding can support the policy advocacy that unlocks the door to more effective use of public funds. In addition, private funding can support employer services that make the difference between marginal and substantial impact, by creating jobs that are structured as steps on career paths, by supporting advancement, and by making it easier for employees to balance responsibilities for work, their families, and learning.

Financing Gaps

JFF's interviews and NNSP's survey identified major gaps in financing in all three areas of workforce intermediary activities: services to advance low-income workers, labor market services to employers, and planning and program development.

Services to Advance Low-Income Workers. The survey and interviews strongly suggest that the full range of advancement services, particularly post employment services that are delivered at the workplace, are very difficult to fund. In the NNSP survey 69 percent of respondents found it difficult to secure sufficient funding for post placement career advancement services; 66 percent found it difficult to secure sufficient funding for occupational training; 65 percent found it difficult to secure sufficient funding for supportive services; and 56 percent found it difficult to secure sufficient funding for incumbent worker training. Several interviewees noted that restrictions on employee eligibility often hinder their best efforts at providing advancement services, particularly when it comes to incumbent worker training, on-the-job coaching, and mentor programs where activities must be closely tied to the operations of participating employers.

There is often a mismatch between the requirements of public funding and the requirements of advancement activities. For example, the Wisconsin Regional Training Partnership (WRTP) was able to influence state legislators to redirect some TANF funding to employer based advancement activities, but the eligibility restrictions made for a very narrow and awkward set of services. According to Eric Parker of WRTP:

> Funding streams are driven by individual eligibility.... When you're working with employers, you want to address the needs of the enterprise; you don't want to provide training based on TANF eligibility. You need to approach it from a workplace standpoint, not an eligibility standpoint.... Employers don't make decisions about training or other programs based on the eligibility of their workers. Some of them agreed to do projects based on the understanding that some of their employees would be eligible and they could recoup some of the costs. But we would have no way of knowing in advance what this would be, and therefore it was impossible to know the actual cost to the firm up front, which makes it hard to close a deal.

Other interviewees noted that the fragmentation of public funding, including reporting requirements and differences in eligibility criteria, allowable uses, and performance standards, makes most public funds difficult to use to develop a continuum of services that support advancement. Moreover, this fragmentation creates an overly burdensome administrative and coordination challenge, particularly when employers are involved.

Labor Market Services to Employers. Providing services to employers is another set of services that is both critical for advancement and difficult to fund. According to the NNSP survey, 66 percent of those surveyed found it difficult to secure sufficient funding to identify employer needs, such as skills, specific training, and curriculum; 66 percent of those surveyed found it difficult to secure sufficient funding to provide human resource services for employers, such as supervisory and mentoring training.

Several interviewees reported that direct work with employers is hard to support. "Nobody on the public side has [sector work] as something they want to pay for," says John Colm of WIRE-Net. "They all want to see it result in a placement. Putting six months into building a relationship or a set of relationships with other industry associations so that their members' training needs could be met isn't really in the cards."

Planning and Program Development. Intermediaries play several important planning and program development roles, including researching labor market and skills issues, organizing the necessary stakeholders, identifying their needs, negotiating the design of programs that meet a wide range of needs for both employees and employers, piloting those programs, and identifying resources to sustain the operation of those programs at scale and continuously improve programs based on experience and changes in the environment. They can play these roles because they stay very close to and have deep credibility with both workers and employers. Yet they find it very challenging to secure financing for these activities. According to the NNSP, 67 percent of those surveyed found it difficult to secure sufficient funding to coordinate key stakeholders, and 51 percent found it difficult to secure sufficient funding to undertake labor market research and analysis.

Several interviewees also stressed the difficulty of securing planning and program development funding, even though intermediaries add enormous value to training at the program development stage as brokers, providers, or contractors of services. "The public resource streams are tied to outcome measures for individual clients—wage gains, placement rates, and advancement," says Dan Berry of the Greater Cleveland Growth Association. "While those are very important, the Individual Training Accounts and performance indicators don't allow for a lot of flexibility in creating capacity, because you generally can't recapture the development costs in the training."

Almost every intermediary interviewed stressed the difficulty of maintaining funding throughout the different planning and program development stages. In many cases, foundation funding has provided intermediaries with the time and support needed to research and develop and even pilot a program. Some of the sites pointed to Casey and Mott Foundations' multiyear support as critical in these early phases. "Casey was critical in terms of start up," says the WRTP's Eric Parker. "The trial and error, helping us establish a track record, trust, etc. That organizing work is really tough to fund. Foundation money is critical." And John Colm notes that the environment created through Mott's initiative allowed WIRE-Net to troubleshoot and problem solve with peer organizations experiencing similar problems.

However, for the most part, foundations do not have sufficient resources to support program operation at scale, nor do they see that as their role. By providing early development support, they have enabled workforce development intermediaries to gain access to state and federal funding for demonstration grants and different types of training programs. Yet some organizations report that full-scale implementation and sustainability is the most serious challenge. "It's fairly easy to get the pilot money," notes the director of Shoreline Community College's career ladder program. "But then the funding dries up," even in cases when an intervention has proven effective.

A NEW FINANCING MODEL FOR WORKFORCE INTERMEDIARIES AND LOW-WAGE WORKER ADVANCEMENT

Existing strategies for financing workforce intermediaries and their advancement activities are limited, incomplete, and insufficient. New approaches will be needed if workforce intermediaries are to expand to the level of sustainability and support akin to that of the nation's Community Development Corporations. We propose financing approaches to promote two distinct priorities: 1) Expanding and sustaining workforce intermediary organizations as stable, local institutions; and 2) Expanding and strengthening workforce intermediaries' and the workforce system's ability to support advancement activities for low-wage workers and their employers.

We identify un- or underfunded gaps in institutional infrastructure and services. We propose financing mechanisms to address the most serious of these gaps and encourage the expansion of and a deeper role for workforce intermediaries in their regional labor markets.

There is no dominant workforce intermediary model in the United States today. This is a period of great experimentation and trail-and-error in the design and organization of these organizations and the services they provide to their dual customers—employers and job- and skillseekers. For this reason, a "one size fits all" approach to financing workforce intermediaries is impractical. Moreover, too standardized a set of expectations and design specifications, while administratively attractive, runs the risk of undermining the flexibility, rapid response, and mission driven character of the best intermediaries.

As the blue-ribbon MIT Working in America Project concluded: "[The] federal government should foster experimentation, evaluate and disseminate the results, support the development of sustainable funding strategies and review the emergent institutional structure to ensure the coherence of the system as a whole" (Osterman et al., 2001).

Financing of workforce intermediaries should focus not on the organizational form or structure, but rather on specific outcomes that those who receive public funding should strive to achieve. Financing rules and mechanisms should articulate desired outcomes of program activities but then encourage flexible application of resources to activities that achieve those outcomes.

Financing strategies should also acknowledge that outcomes might need to be different in different phases of organizational and program development. For example, in its sectoral initiative, the Mott Foundation provided workforce intermediaries with planning grants. The outcome measured for the planning grant was the quality of the analysis of the regional labor market and the industry. Metrics included the number and size of employers in an industry and the types, number, and quality of jobs in those industries. Success during the planning grant stage led to a 36-month implementation grant. Midway through that grant period, the foundation required a second analysis of the regional labor market and the industry to determine whether conditions changed and if the program should follow suit.

Drawing lessons from innovative venture philanthropy, foundations might need to supplement public funding to help support the strengthening of capacity among emerging intermediary organizations. They might want to act as investors do in a venture capital model, engaging intensively with the financing recipient to support their development. The Annie E. Casey Foundation, for example, used this investment model in its Jobs Initiative, combining flexible dollars and tight outcomes with capacity building and coaching (Dewar, 2002).

Expand and Strengthen the Organizational Capacity of Workforce Intermediaries

The NNSP surveys and JFF interviews with intermediary staff members suggest the need for dedicated, predictable, and long-term financing if workforce intermediaries are to expand their capacity, achieve significant scale, and generate solid advancement outcomes for low-income job- and skillseekers. Recent financing innovations in several states point to vehicles that can help provide such financing. So, too, does recent experimentation by the U.S. Department of Labor with innovation financing for workforce partnerships that play intermediary roles. California, Washington, Massachusetts, and several other states have turned to varied funding sources, including direct appropriations, Governors' Discretionary 15 percent funds under WIA, and unemployment insurance diversion funds to support inter-mediary functions and activities. The U.S. Department of Labor demon-stration programs, including the sectoral initiative ($3.8 million), the Faith Based Intermediaries initiative ($5 million to intermediaries, $11.9 million for states), and the Skills Gap Panel initiative ($10,272,838) have provided program and operating support for a number of intermediaries.

We propose three mechanisms for financing an increase in the num-ber of and capacity of workforce intermediaries during the next few years:

- Expand and regularize existing federal and state demonstration projects.
- Use federal resources to match state incumbent worker training dol-lars that fund advancement services for less-skilled workers.
- Create a new, competitive, demonstration program that would pro-vide operating and program support for effective workforce inter-mediaries within a subset of states that want to move in this direction.

Expand and Regularize Existing Federal Demonstration Programs. A common complaint among leading workforce intermediaries is the episodic and fleeting nature of federal pilot or demonstration projects. While they appreciated being able to tap demonstration programs for funds, these resources disappear after one or two years. As a first step toward ensuring more predictable and stable funding for building the capacity of interme-diaries, the U.S. Department of Labor could take two important actions. First, it could build on the model of existing pilots, such as the Sectoral Ini-tiative and the Skills Gap Panels, and create a longer term or permanent annual competitive program to support intermediaries undertaking sec-torally focused activities. Secondly, the department could strengthen lan-guage in this program to target resources and activities for the advancement of low-income workers.

Provide a Federal Match to State Incumbent Worker Training Funds. The 1990s brought about significant increases in state investments in employer focused incumbent worker training and skills development programs. By 1998 over 47 states had invested over $575 million.[2] States have financed these programs primarily in two ways, either an unemployment insurance diversion or a general state appropriation.

Recognizing that a highly skilled workforce contributes significantly to business productivity and expansion, these programs have primarily focused on increasing the skills of newly hired or already employed workers. Of the wide range of publicly funded programs, these are fairly closely aligned with the types of activities and services workforce intermediaries provide. In general, these programs are employer focused, provide both generic and technical skills training that are transferable across firms, focus on skills upgrading, and are starting to invest in activities that help employers change their human resource practices. However, these programs generally lack an organized way to aggregate employer demand within a region, they do not generally fund what we have described as intermediary capacity, and they do not fund building a state network of workforce intermediaries.

To leverage these dollars, a federal appropriation could be authorized that would match state investments in employer focused training programs at some percentage and require that these dollars be used to fund research and development of new programs, employer services, and post employment advancement services provided by WIs. The goal would be to increase the number of organizations that are high-functioning intermediaries as well as to fund the gaps in service identified above.

Create a Voluntary State Run Workforce Intermediary Investment Fund. One potential approach to financing intermediary capacity would be for states to create a Workforce Intermediary Investment Fund. This fund would make available, on a competitive basis, operating support for effective workforce intermediaries. The federal government, through the U.S. Department of Labor, could provide an incentive to states that wanted to create such a fund and make matching funds available to states for capitalizing it.

Federal funds could require a dollar-for-dollar state match, which states could meet through a combination of direct appropriations and private resources, including regional foundation funds and corporate support. For example, if the federal government supported 10 pilot states willing and able to match its resources, and each state supported an average of five regional or local intermediaries at a $1.5 million operating budget, the program would cost the U.S. government $37.5 million a year. If expanded to all 50 states, the program would cost the federal government approximately $375 million a year. One possible source of federal funding might be federal WIA discretionary funds.

Each state would need to raise $3.75 million in some combination of appropriations and private match. The fund could be enhanced by a state tax credit for nonprofit workforce intermediary capacity building. State governments that operated intermediary investment funds might consider contracting with a particularly entrepreneurial quasi-public corporation, as exists in many states, or even a private contractor to minimize political pressures that frequently arise in the management and distribution of resources from such funds. And the federal government would want to include a research and evaluation component to ensure quality and learning if the investment fund model were expanded.

Role of Foundations. As noted earlier in this chapter, national foundations have played a crucial and pivotal role in developing workforce intermediaries by providing the necessary flexible venture capital needed to build the infrastructure and develop the service strategies needed to serve businesses and low-income individuals. Foundation dollars typically are used to leverage public sources of money, fund activities not currently funded through other sources, and for organizational start up costs. Because this field is in its infancy, it is important that foundations continue to provide this type of seed funding. In addition, it is important that foundations continue to support a wide range of national research and policy activities and peer convenings that promote best practices and identify and advocate for necessary policy changes.

However, as practitioners and policy makers grapple with the challenges of how to scale up and sustain workforce intermediaries, foundations need to consider different financing models that support these objectives. What can foundations do to sustain this emerging field? There are a number of collaborative investor models that foundations might consider. One approach would be to establish a no-interest revolving loan fund to help a number of high-performing intermediaries build their capacity to expand their models to other cities or locations. Another option for foundations is to explicitly support, in each of their multisite community-wide initiatives, the development/enhancement of local workforce intermediaries to support each community's workforce effort. In addition, foundations might also consider pooling resources to provide venture capital to states that are willing to invest in building a strong intermediary capacity. These dollars might support some field building activities, convening of the key stakeholders, the development of the statewide plan, and/or the development of performance measures and self-assessment processes to continually judge success.

Over the long term, it is important that foundations support a wide range of activities that continues to build public demand and a public policy agenda and financing system for the advancement of low-income workers. These activities might range from public surveys, public forums and convening of key stakeholders, and so forth.

Long-Term Financing of Advancement for Low-Wage Workers

Creating or adapting state and federal funding streams to promote, through competitive grants, the creation or growth of effective intermediary organizations is necessary at this stage in the development of this field of practice. At the same time, new financing strategies are needed that can make it easier for workforce intermediaries and others to undertake advancement activities that engage both low-wage workers and their employers. In the long run, advancement will require greater attention to post employment services, workplace based training and supports, and education and training credentials that are portable and have meaning in the labor market across firms and industries.

The traditional public system's financing mechanisms and rules often make it hard for advancement initiatives undertaken by workforce intermediaries and others to secure adequate public resources. Eligibility requirements often limit access to needed services as workers successfully climb career ladders to higher income. Advancement strategies that are workplace based, where payoff can be significant, can be difficult to finance and deliver, because employers want to provide similar services to whole classes of employees, not a subset eligible for public services. Fragmented and poorly aligned public funding streams are not easily pooled to create larger, more flexible sources of resources for training, supports, and other services that might be more likely to promote advancement for low-wage workers. Performance measures in WIA and TANF tend to promote placement over advancement, short-term labor market gains over long-term success.

In the end, advancement in today's economy depends upon the ability to keep learning and earning valued credentials over time. For this reason, our recommendations regarding financing of advancement activities and services addresses two related but distinct challenges:

- Revisiting current workforce laws and regulations so they are more "advancement friendly."
- Addressing the challenge of supporting lifelong learning and skill development with long-term financing that is portable, is more readily available to low-skill adult workers, and targets significant new resources to the educational and skill development needs of low-skilled workers.

Adapt Existing Federal Workforce Related Funding Streams to Promote Advancement More Aggressively. A number of changes to existing workforce development programs could provide incentives to substantially improve advancement outcomes. These changes primarily involve the Workforce Investment Act and Temporary Assistance to Needy Families.

Both WIA and TANF missions should emphasize advancement toward family-supporting wages for low-income adults. To achieve this goal requires easier and broader access to intensive, job-specific education and training services. For reasons noted above, WIA implementation has limited the provision of training. At the same time, current TANF policy makes it difficult to provide training services and skill development to those who need them to move up in the labor market. Worse, legislative reauthorization proposals under consideration in Congress could make access to training for individuals eligible for both TANF and WIA services even more difficult to secure. This would be a step backwards for communities that want to integrate WIA and TANF funds for services that promote self-sufficiency and advancement, not simply entry-level employment.

WIA could promote greater attention to advancement by eliminating the strict requirement of sequential services and enabling communities to develop individualized service plans that mix core, intensive, and training services as needed for particular jobseekers and low-income workers. This flexibility must still be guided by the broad goal of helping jobseekers and low-income workers advance toward an income that allows for self-sufficiency, and the services should be tied closely to employer needs.

WIA and TANF performance standards should be aligned with each other and emphasize advancement. WIA performance measures emphasize employment, retention, and earnings gains. This was a deliberate effort by Congress to begin to redirect the workforce system toward retention and advancement goals and outcomes. A more aggressive improvement on current performance goals would include a measure that captures the progress of those served by WIA toward self-sufficiency. This must be done carefully, both to avoid penalizing states for economic changes beyond the power of the workforce system to affect and to make it possible to track progress over time. Still, some quantifiable guide to progress toward the stated goal of the act is needed.

TANF should replace caseload reduction and participation rates with performance measures similar to those used in WIA. This would focus states and localities on employment and wage advancement as goals for TANF recipients. It would also make it easier for agencies working with both WIA and TANF funding to simplify their data collection and reporting and to pool funding from different agencies to serve those in need.

Financing Lifelong Learning for Low-Income Adults. Ultimately, advancement along career pathways to family-supporting income requires skill development and the acquisition of credentials that employers value and reward. Three distinct financing approaches for lifelong learning are discussed below: Lifelong Learning Accounts (LLAs), unemployment insurance (UI) reform, and improved access for working adults to higher education student aid.

These are ambitious and controversial proposals. What they have in common is the recognition that advancement for most workers will require learning on the job and the earning of educational credentials—and that financing for this kind of system must be portable, compatible with learning that takes place at the worksite, and relatively free from the income eligibility requirements that keep less-skilled adults from qualifying for needed public supports and services as they start to climb their career ladders.

Our proposals have something else in common. They are financing mechanisms—strategies for making more money available for advancement services. Financing mechanisms and steadier funding streams are critical—but they do not eliminate the need for workforce intermediaries. In fact, adequate funding for advancement services would put new demands upon intermediaries to do the laborious and difficult work of bringing employers, educational institutions, service providers, and government leaders together to design, assess, improve, and manage training and advancement programs that work for low-wage workers and their employers.

Lifelong Learning Accounts are individual asset accounts held by workers over the course of their working life (Osterman et al., 2001). They are financed by employee and employer contributions with the potential for public subsidy, and they allow the account holder to draw down resources to pay for eligible education and skill development services. Most LLA models are designed to be universally available to all workers, funded by both employees and employers, with any public subsidies highly leveraged by private contributions through such mechanisms as tax deductibility of contributions. Some models propose to steer tax subsidies to lower income workers by allowing Earned Income Tax Credit (EITC)–eligible employees to finance their accounts exclusively through employer contributions.

LLAs are portable, traveling with the employee, regardless of income, employer, or job category. They are an efficient way for employers to promote training and skill development. For example, employers can arrange customized training and organize their employees to use their LLAs for such training in return for certification and advancement opportunities. LLAs can leverage other public workforce training and education resources: WIA Individual Training Account vouchers could be linked, for example, as could incumbent worker training funds funded by many states from UI diversion funds.

The Council on Adult and Experiential Learning (CAEL) is currently piloting an LLA model in several states and has helped to draft federal legislation to create a national LLA demonstration project. CAEL's experience with LLAs has led them to several key design principles: make LLA's universally available to all workers, leverage private dollars by requiring employer contributions, make the account tax deductible, and develop an accompanying career transcript to record an individual's skills progression and education for portability.

LLAs require substantial marketing and promotion to ensure a high rate of take-up. Workforce intermediaries can organize training providers to offer "bulk" discounts if employers agree to training financed through employee LLAs. Intermediaries can provide critical career counseling services to workers, enabling them to make good choices about how to use their LLA assets for career advancement. State Workforce Intermediary Investment funds should consider supporting the provision of career management services by workforce intermediaries to overcome the information challenges facing workers not used to making their own learning purchase decisions. Alternatively, or in addition, LLAs might be structured to treat career management as an allowable tax exempt expense for some limited proportion of an individual's account.

Unemployment insurance has always been viewed as the primary vehicle for providing temporary income support to workers who lose their jobs due to cyclical or temporary layoffs. Recent debates about UI have centered on the serious problem of declining coverage of workers and the need for changes that can help low-wage workers stay attached to the labor market in times of economic hardship. These changes, which expand eligibility and make benefits portable, are necessary but not sufficient. Given the need for continuous skill upgrading to be able to secure a job that pays a family-supporting wage, it may be time to broaden the purpose of UI from an income-support system to one that would help eligible workers adjust to and succeed in the new economy by supporting investments in training and skills upgrading.

There may be a few ways to tackle this issue. Currently, the federal government uses the $15 billion in the Employment Security Administrative Account to offset the deficit. At a minimum, a portion of these funds reserved for administration of workforce programs and UI benefits could be returned to states through a Reed Act distribution (a law that authorizes periodic redistribution of these funds back to the states) to encourage states to fund workforce services that help the advancement of low-income, eligible workers. In addition, incentives could encourage states to use these dollars to support labor market services to employers and planning and program development services, in addition to advancement services provided by workforce intermediaries.

Another option for the federal government to consider is adopting the policy and financing model of a few states, such as California, New Jersey, Indiana, and Texas, that invest significantly in a wide range of employer focused incumbent worker training programs through a UI tax diversion. These states primarily assess a per-employee tax on employers covered by the UI system and simultaneously reduce the unemployment tax burden by the same amount, therefore avoiding a tax increase on employers.

Federal policy, through an amendment to the Federal Unemployment Tax Account, could support a similar funding mechanism to leverage and increase state spending by providing matching funds to states that support training and advancement through UI diversions. Federal policies guiding the use of these funds should encourage investments in advancement and retention activities that build the skills and knowledge of low-skilled individuals, support employers at the workplace, and support the services and operations of workforce intermediaries.

However, over the long run, far-reaching changes in UI law may be needed if the nation is to have a sustainable system that enhances the skills of our workforce and meets the needs of businesses in our knowledge based economy. A permanent percentage of UI funds (for example, one tenth of 1 percent) could be returned to each state for the sole purpose of upgrading the skills of their workforce. Because the UI system is funded through an employer tax, employers want to be assured that these dollars are used to meet the skill requirements of business. Most states have an oversight board for their incumbent worker UI funded programs that includes business representatives and other stakeholders, and this should be a required feature.

Moreover, as a nation, we should consider broadening the responsibility for skill upgrading and advancement beyond just the employer. Support for skills upgrading could include not only an employer assessment but also a small but meaningful contribution by the employee. For example, New Jersey requires an annual employee contribution of $4.83, compared to an employer contribution of approximately $19.83.

Finally, the federal government should provide a match for those most in need of basic skills upgrading. In this way, support of lifelong learning would be a tripartite responsibility of employers, employees, and government.

Student financial aid for higher education, particularly at the federal level, is perhaps the most significant potential public source of advancement financing. Total federal adult workforce training in 2001 consisted of $950 million for adult employment and training and $1.6 billion for dislocated workers under the Workforce Investment Act, combined with $561 million in Adult Basic Education funding. By comparison, federal student financial assistance through the Higher Education Act, including grants and loans, totaled nearly $50 billion (Bosworth and Choitz, 2002).

Despite the rising number of adults finding their way toward further education, access to financial aid for low-income working adults is difficult to secure. While in 1999, 28 percent of working adults who were enrolled in higher education less than half time were among the working poor, only 7.7 percent of all working parents received *any* federal, state, or institutional aid.

Limited access to financial resources remains perhaps the largest obstacle to, and federal higher education funding may be the largest untapped source of, potential advancement financing. Strategies to make Pell Grants, Hope and Lifelong Learning Tax Credits, and other student loans and grants easier for working adults to access and use could be a powerful lever for lifelong learning and educational advancement that is now all but closed off to many low-skill working adults (Choitz and Bosworth, 2002).

In a recent study, FutureWorks recommended four policy changes that could expand federal financial support for the advancement of low-income workers in higher education:

- Amend the Hope and Lifetime Learning Tax Credits so they provide better opportunities for working adults to pursue skill development. Modifications would include allowing students enrolled less than half time to participate and expanding the amount of the tax credit from 20 to 50 percent of qualified educational expenses.
- Make less than half-time students eligible for some government guaranteed loans.
- Modify eligibility barriers for less than half-time working adult students with dependents within the Pell Grant program.
- Revisit financial aid eligibility barriers to shorter term and more flexible educational programs.

Expanding access to student financial aid will not in and of itself ensure that higher education is accessible to low-income, working adults. Programs that fit the needs, time constraints, and academic deficiencies facing many working adults are not readily available in post secondary institutions. Proposals to widen eligibility for student aid also run into significant political resistance from higher education advocates who see opening up opportunities for poor, working adults as a "zero-sum game" that diverts resources from needy students already competing for limited funds. Despite these obstacles, expanded access to higher education financing for low-wage working adults (combined with supports to ensure success in post secondary programs) has to be part of any long-term strategy for advancement and lifelong learning.

As many observers of public policy point out, throwing dollars at social problems does not solve them. Clearly, adequate financing for the range of services necessary for advancing low-income adults to family self-sufficiency will not, by itself, propel working adults out of poverty. Many hurdles outside the control of even the best workforce intermediaries and financing systems stand between poor adults and the skills and careers they need to support their families. Yet there are few other major national challenges that offer a greater gap between the high risk if the problem is not solved and the low level of public spending. Helping working Americans attain the skills and supports they need to thrive and contribute to their communities remains a great national challenge. Failing to address the challenge puts our families, our communities, and our nation's economy at great risk.

NOTES

Acknowledgments: The authors acknowledge the important research for this chapter by Claudia Green and Heath Prince, as well as Richard Kazis's important contributions in framing the issues and reviewing and editing the text.

1. The NNSP survey asked respondents to identify which activities they receive funding to perform and may not include unfunded activities.

2. A 1999 survey of state incumbent worker training programs determined that about one-third of such programs target specific groups of workers, but the study did not determine what dollar amount of incumbent worker training funds was targeted to low-wage workers.

REFERENCES

Aspen Institute. 2002. *Measuring Up and Weighing In: Industry-Based Workforce Development Training Results in Strong Employment Outcomes.* Washington, DC: The Aspen Institute. (March).

Bosworth, Brian, and Victoria Choitz. 2001. *Held Back: How Student Aid Programs Fail Working Adults.* Belmont, MA: Futureworks. (April).

Center For Workforce Preparation. 2002. *Completing the Workforce Puzzle.* Washington, DC: U.S. Chamber of Commerce, Center for Workforce Preparation. (Spring).

Dewar, Tom. 2002. *Using an Investment Approach to Grantmaking.* Baltimore: Annie E. Casey Foundation.

Halpern, Robert. 1995. *Re-Building the Inner City.* New York: Columbia University Press.

Osterman, Paul, et al. 2001. *Working in America: A Blueprint for the New Labor Market.* Cambridge, MA: MIT Press.

13

The Final Act:
The Challenges of Implementing
Workforce Development Policy
via Nonprofit Organizations

WILLIAM P. RYAN

IN THE DRAMA OF POLICY MAKING, THE FIRST TWO ACTS — GETTING the right policy, and getting public money for that policy—tend to capture all our attention. The third act—in which the right policy with the necessary money is actually implemented is presumed to be a foregone conclusion, a tale of public administration that's hardly worth staying to watch. As a new round of workforce development policy unfolds, our attention span conforms to these expectations. In conferences and policy papers, we worry about getting the policy right and focus on questions of funding, presuming that implementation is the inevitable result of the two. But in this case, the plot will turn in large part on implementation.

THE IMPLEMENTATION CHALLENGE

For several reasons, this story of implementation will be high stakes. First, public assistance is now granted mostly to those who are working or training to work, and is generally terminated after five years. This policy makes job training and placement an urgent matter. Second, job training is not enough help for some clients. Many also need help with childcare, transportation, health problems, or substance abuse; without addressing these, the chances of finding and keeping a job are slim. Third, the growing desire within the field not only to train and place people in jobs, but to support them after placement to encourage job retention and advancement only raises the bar higher. Finally, these are large-scale challenges. As Anthony P. Carnevale and Donna Desrochers estimate in chapter 7, there are more than 20 million low-wage, low-skilled workers who could benefit from these "second chance" workforce development services.

If the stakes are high, so are some of the obstacles posed by our approach to the delivery of public services. Because of the American preference for government decentralization, this implementation will not be the work of one or a few federal departments, but will involve scores of state and county agencies. And because those agencies in turn are often convinced of the benefits of contracting out service delivery, a large share of the implementation will ultimately rest with an array of government funded nonprofit organizations (Donahue, 1989).

Analysts have long argued that nonprofit organizations have important comparative advantages over government agencies. Freed from the strictures of large bureaucracies, nonprofits are thought to be more capable of innovation. And unlike public agencies, community based nonprofits can often target the needs of particular, marginalized populations. For example, they can use specialized outreach or services to gain access to and the trust of ethnic and linguistic minorities. Beyond improving service delivery, some argue that nonprofits encourage citizens to become directly involved—as volunteers, active donors, or trustees—in public work. This involvement—goes the argument—strengthens our civil society, the space where citizens pursue the public good outside of formal government systems (Alexander et al., 1999).

Along with these benefits, however, nonprofits bring some disadvantages. Their organizational competence—to create stable enterprises capable of delivering quality services over time—is widely questioned. The past 10 years have seen the rise of an "organizational effectiveness" movement within the nonprofit sector. Funders, educators, consultants, and researchers have attempted to define and build the competencies needed for high-performing nonprofits—in large part because the organizational deficits of nonprofits are judged to be so troubling. Especially in the human services, even the most innovative and effective nonprofit organizations are often fragile. They face a hostile funding environment, where money is not only hard to get, but comes with restrictions and reporting requirements that make it difficult to use (Ryan, 2001). Perhaps more troubling are doubts about nonprofits' programmatic efficacy. Even the most loyal philanthropic supporters of nonprofits are establishing and documenting outcomes as a way of holding nonprofits accountable. They are no longer taking on faith that good intentions and hard work produce good results (Walker and Grossman, 1999).

The other player in this implementation system—the government agencies that contract with nonprofits—has struggled with its own role. As a growing literature attests, managing an outsourced service delivery system is not necessarily any easier for government agencies than delivering the services themselves (Donahue, 1989; Behn and Kahn, 1999). Many of today's contract administrators are yesterday's frontline workers. They have moved with little training from working directly with clients to designing, managing, and overseeing complex contracts. The systems for administering these contracts are often crude. Outcomes can be difficult to define. Incentives can have perverse effects. And while the case for outsourcing often hinges on the benefits of efficiency and innovation that emerge as providers compete for contracts, the reality in many locales is that there are not enough providers to generate competition (Smith and Lipsky, 1993).

Given this environment, any assumption that smooth implementation will follow inevitably from policy development is misplaced.

UNDERSTANDING THE CAPACITY CHALLENGE OF IMPLEMENTATION

This chapter focuses on what is often the last link in the service delivery chain—nonprofit organizations. Several types of organizations provide job training and placement assistance. Temp and staffing firms help companies find workers for short-term assignments. Proprietary schools offer training in a variety of trades and occupations—from "beauty academies" to truck-driving "institutes." Labor-management partnerships jointly fund and operate apprenticeship training programs. But it is usually nonprofit human service organizations that provide services for those who were not well served by mainstream educational systems, or who need more than staffing and training schools alone can offer. Of the nonprofits that offer these second chance services, we are especially interested in the emerging "workforce intermediary." This type of organization aims to serve the needs of individual jobseekers by offering not just training but a package of training, placement, and support services that will equip workers *and* connect them to local employers whose recruitment needs the intermediary is also committed to filling. As we will see later, and as several other chapters suggest, this is complex work.

We will explore two questions about the workforce intermediary that are not normally central to policy development. What kind of capacity do we need to build in these nonprofits that our public service delivery system relies on? And how do we go about building it? The fact that these questions are not often discussed, much less debated, should not be mistaken as evidence of a clear or consensus vision. To the contrary, assumptions about organizational capacity are usually unexamined, often unfounded, and sometimes in conflict. My aim is not so much to prevail in a debate about these issues as to provoke that debate.

Toward that end, I will make three arguments. First, we have distinguished different types of capacity only implicitly, if at all, and the implicit model of capacity that has been most influential is also the most flawed. It locates capacity in the wrong place, and therefore leads us to invest in the wrong things. Second, this implicit approach is especially incompatible with the workforce intermediary, which we can appreciate after laying out the special characteristics of this type of nonprofit. Third, even if we understand what kind of capacity we need—and are willing to invest in it—the particular demands of the workforce intermediary will again complicate things. They are almost certain to defy the most prevalent approaches to capacity building.

To put the challenge for policy makers another way: we need to make the implicit, conventional wisdom on capacity building explicit, and then challenge it.

An Organizational Capacity Framework

Organizational capacity attracts little debate in part because it is both a vague and banal seeming concept. To begin uncovering the choices these attributes tend to mask, I propose here an organizational capacity framework in which effective nonprofits rely on three types of capacity.[1]

Programmatic capacity is needed for effective delivery of a social program, defined here as a formalized approach to serving clients or constituents. In cases where nonprofits are implementing programs they did not develop, they will import programmatic capacity in the form of a "model program" or "best practice," sometimes with technical assistance from the original program designers.

Administrative capacity is needed to keep the organization running and to demonstrate accountability to its stakeholders. Most of this capacity concerns money and takes the forms of fundraising, budgeting, accounting, and reporting on expenditures to funders. It is helpful to think of these as hygiene functions. Neglecting them can have disastrous consequences, but tending to them only keeps the organization alive; it cannot guarantee effective service or community impact. In that sense, they are like flossing: it can fend off bacterial infection that can lead to serious illness or death, but it will not confer the benefits of aerobic exercise, much less personal happiness.

Adaptive capacity lies in the higher order intellectual processes—of learning, planning, or innovating, for example—that organizations need in order to attain their mission. While programmatic capacity helps organizations understand *how* to implement programs effectively, adaptive capacity enables an organization to decide *which* programs to implement in the first place, to evaluate *how well* those programs are working, and to determine when to modify or improve them.

We can think of adaptive capacity as having four elements that raise important questions for nonprofit managers:

1. *Learning.* Do we have an approach—formal or informal—to learning about our work? Do we know what explains our best work and what accounts for our worst work? Do we have some idea of what to do differently if we want to improve?

2. *Quality.* Do we have a way to assess and improve not only the efficacy of our programs but also the quality of our program delivery? Even a highly codified technical program—for example, a medical service—can be both efficacious and low quality. A specific medical intervention might work, but might also be inaccessible, or the treatment of clients unwelcoming or disrespectful. These failures might conflict with the organization's values and aspirations and could undermine its impact by alienating clients and reducing the number who seek help.

3. *Innovativeness.* Do we promote innovation within the organization, so that we can modify or create programs to respond to new needs? For nonprofits, the distinction between *innovations* and *innovativeness* is especially important (Light, 1998). An organization that supports its own capacity for innovativeness might have important advantages over one that relies heavily on the innovations of others. Innovating organizations can be more responsive to changes they see in their own environment, and organizations that develop their own programs may have more success in implementing them effectively.

4. *Motivation.* Do we have a way to attract, retain, and develop staff and volunteers committed to enthusiastically delivering our services? Nonprofit leaders tend to approach this question by manipulating two variables: mission and money. If their mission is compelling enough, they hope they will attract people willing to put up with the low salaries and gritty work conditions that many nonprofit organizations cannot afford to improve. But leaders could also consider other variables in motivation, particularly whether staff are equipped and whether jobs are designed to enable workers to achieve and see results.

These adaptive capacities do not reside in programs but in organizations. Indeed, since these are capacities that enable organizations to make the best use of programs in advancing their missions, they *cannot* reside within the programs themselves. And although these capacities require organizational processes, they do not require MBA-certified managers or management consultants. Any number of approaches—as long as they are intentional and thoughtful—will enable nonprofit leaders to develop these adaptive capacities.[2] Consequently, adaptive capacity is not a resource only for large or well-funded organizations. It is essential for any effective organization.

In sum, this three-part framework argues that effectiveness is the product not just of good program design and faithful implementation, supported by administrative competence, but also of an organization's capacity for learning, improving, innovating, and motivating. The challenge for capacity building is to consider how to allocate our investments across these capacities. How much of which capacity do we need in order to improve the prospects for enabling the sustained delivery of effective services at a large scale?

Prevalent Allocations of Capacity Investment and Their Consequences

The typical response to these allocation choices has been to invest heavily in programmatic capacity, starve administrative capacity, and ignore adaptive capacity. These choices reflect a set of assumptions—I will argue, misguided assumptions—about where the capacity for effective service delivery resides.

It is not surprising that we believe that the capacity for effectiveness resides largely in the design of programs. Programs do matter. If we can conclude that adult mentoring relationships with children really do promote academic achievement and desirable social behavior, we are right to support and promote them. Or if we learn that an approach to discouraging drug use among youth does not appear effective, we are right to look for an alternative. Following this logic, the nonprofit social service world has been organized around the development and dissemination of programs. Foundation grants typically fund the development, evaluation, or replication of programs. Research often focuses on programs, as we study their effects through program evaluation. Technical assistance aimed at helping nonprofits improve their effectiveness often amounts to assistance in implementing a model program. And we locate innovation itself in programs. The breakthroughs we talk about tend to be programs—not organizations, leaders, or movements.

It is also not surprising that we tend to starve administrative capacity. Most administrative functions—budgeting, accounting, or personnel procedures, for example—are considered regrettable but necessary overhead expenses. And considering how scarce resources are, every dollar spent on overhead is considered a dollar diverted from programs and clients. This is a deeply held conviction. It explains why nearly every nonprofit organization's annual report will feature a pie chart showing that the vast majority of its revenue goes to support programs and services, and not administration or overhead. The thinner the overhead wedge, the better the organization.

The only problem with these intuitive assumptions is that they often lead to disappointing results, especially when they are put to the test of program replication. According to the theory implicit in this prevalent understanding of capacity, replication should work as follows: a promising program attracts the attention of funders or other nonprofits, and is carefully studied to determine if its outcomes are as significant as they seem. If a program evaluation confirms that the outcomes are indeed significant, the researchers or program originators codify the program, determining which elements are essential and specifying how the program should be delivered. Either the original program designers or a third party then helps other organizations implement the program, in effect disseminating the capacity needed to create the desired impact. In reality, however, we often find a different result: programs that produce impressive results in their original site often produce highly mixed and disappointing results when replicated.

Workforce development provides a notable example in the story of the Center for Employment Training (CET). CET was one of several job training and placement approaches studied in two evaluations in the early 1990s. Researchers found that it offered striking results. CET helped clients prepare for and find jobs faster than other providers; the jobs CET found its clients paid better; and CET clients tended to keep their jobs longer. The Department of Labor responded with funding for the replication of the program to other locations. And as has happened with other replication efforts, the second generation of programs was, on the whole, inferior to the original, in some cases markedly so (Berkeley Policy Associates, 2000).

Puzzling situations like these have not prompted a reassessment of replication's implicit, program centered theory of capacity. Instead of questioning whether the capacity for effectiveness can be disseminated as a program in the first place, program designers and researchers tend to conclude that their program has simply not been codified explicitly enough to enable effective replication. Or they suspect the problem is one of fidelity, caused when second-generation program operators start tampering with the model. This approach can lead to questionable attempts to reduce implementers' influence, as in the highly rigid education programs that practitioners ridicule as "teacher-proof curricula."

Alternatively, we could conclude that all the knowledge needed for effective implementation does not reside in the program itself, but in the interplay between the program and the program implementer's knowledge or capacity. And this interplay might be far subtler than we have imagined. Organizational theorists call such knowledge—decisive to results yet hard to locate or describe—tacit knowledge. Michael Polanyi, a chemist turned philosopher, coined this term to explain a number of mundane puzzles of performance. We know how to ride a bike, but don't know how to explain how to ride a bike. Even some manufacturing processes—which we expect to be invariably precise—rely on tacit knowledge. Polanyi (1974) notes the problem of a light bulb manufacturer that could produce good quality light bulbs in one factory, but not in another, despite using the same equipment and procedures.

While we have had considerable success in standardizing manufacturing processes, tacit knowledge remains a challenge in complex, knowledge driven endeavors. Even when professions rely on highly technical, well-codified knowledge—as in specialized medicine or tax law—the performance of different practitioners varies widely. This is because the capacity for effectiveness does not lie entirely in those codified programs. Different practitioners are bringing different capacities to their use of the same program, although it can be difficult to locate or explain these capacities.

Social programs tend to be especially complex. They often involve trying to help clients both with learning and behavior change. Given their nature, the expectation of "practitioner-proof" programs that can simply be scaled up with money and technical assistance seems especially naïve. The capacity for effectiveness in such cases almost certainly resides in both the program and the program implementer or, where programs involve the support of an organization, in the program and the implementing organization.

The story of CET looks different in light of this understanding of capacity. Instead of codifying the program as if it alone accounted for CET's initial success, champions of CET could have analyzed both the program and the organization that proved capable of designing and operating it effectively for many years. Certainly, CET's program was important, and departed from more prevalent practice in significant ways. But CET the organization—and the way it developed and implemented the program—surely accounts for some part of the success.

A visit to the original CET training school, in fact, is most striking for what it suggests about effective implementation of the program. The instructors are uniformly enthusiastic, not just when interacting with visitors, but with students. The program is highly responsive to, and embedded in the culture of, its clients. (I happened to visit on Cesar Chavez Day, and witnessed a ceremony in which staff and clients, many of them Latinos raised by farm workers, memorialized him in song and speech.) And to hear staff describe their relationships with the local employers who hire CET graduates is to understand that the simple program injunction "develop employer relations" does not begin to suggest how this is done effectively.

If we studied the formal and informal, implicit and explicit organizational processes and assets that CET brings to bear on its work, instead of studying its program design alone, we would start looking at the prospects for large-scale impact as a function of supporting those organizational capacities among the second-generation program sites.[3] To use the framework introduced earlier, we would locate some of CET's capacity in its program design; some in its administration (which enabled the organization to survive); and a good deal in its adaptive processes for promoting quality, responsiveness, innovation, and motivation.

The prevalent conception of capacity would discourage this account. And the problem is not only that it overlooks the role of adaptive capacity. Worse, it conflates adaptive and administrative capacities. It treats the higher order organizational processes—which promote learning, innovating, and responsiveness—the same as overhead costs like rent and utilities: both get jammed into the thinnest possible wedge in the expenditure pie chart and are starved of investment. But adaptive capacity is arguably as important as programmatic capacity, and should not be treated like overhead. The challenge for policy makers is to understand that difference, and to develop a more refined theory of capacity to take account of it.

Understanding Workforce Development Capacity Needs

Two recent accounts of capacity needs—one from policy analysts and one from the leaders of workforce nonprofits—can help develop a more refined theory of capacity for workforce development organizations. The two accounts are not only consistent, but sharply contradict the prevalent, implicit theory of capacity.

In the first account, policy analysts attempt to define the characteristics of an emerging class of workforce development organization that is increasingly favored within the field. The new organization is built on the premise of a dual customer. In this approach, providers attend equally to the needs of individual jobseeking clients on the one hand and their prospective employers on the other. As uncontroversial as this dual customer focus might seem, it represents a significant shift in workforce development. Historically, providers have tended to focus on training clients first and then engaging second, if at all, in helping them find jobs. Understanding and responding to employer needs was helpful to this approach, but not central. To distinguish that earlier type of provider from those using the new approach, some have begun using the term workforce development "intermediary," which emphasizes the provider's role in linking the needs of their two clients.

Chapters 5 and 12 in this volume elaborate on this approach and its implications for providers. These accounts are consistent with earlier work by Jobs for the Future (JFF), which we will use here as an overview of the critical characteristics of the effective intermediary (Liebowitz et al., 2000). Based on their analysis, workforce intermediaries should:

1. Understand the labor market well.
2. Know particular employers and their needs.
3. Know jobseekers and their needs.
4. Be entrepreneurial and customer driven.
5. Keep employment the primary focus,
6. But also develop ties to nonemployment service providers.
7. Use data to improve performance.
8. Focus not just on access to employment but on retention and career advancement.

In later analysis, presented in this volume, JFF underscores two additional characteristics: intermediaries must be *trusted*—by both employers and jobseekers—and be *stable*, perceived by employers as a reliable supplier with whom they can develop productive relationships.

A series of interviews with leaders of workforce development nonprofits and close observers of their work in seven cities[4] provides a second account of capacity needs (Ryan and Human Service Solutions, 1998). Those interviewed identified seven organizational needs as most pressing:

1. *Capital.* The nonprofit leaders said they lacked working capital to help them deal with chronic cash flow problems, which often result from slow payments on government contracts. Many also needed funding for facilities and equipment—either additional space, or equipment that clients must know how to operate in order to compete for jobs. Some also cited the need for venture capital to develop and launch new programs.

2. *Information technology.* Almost all the providers, faced with contracts that require complicated billing and case management, regarded themselves as technological laggards, making do with second-rate or obsolete technology that limited their administrative capacity, as well as their ability to analyze their own performance.

3. *Cost accounting.* Most nonprofit leaders felt that they lacked the knowledge and tools to determine their true costs, making it difficult for them to challenge public funding levels that they often deemed inadequate.

4. *Human resources.* Compared to government and private sector employers, many nonprofit providers felt that their low salaries put them at a disadvantage in recruiting and retaining employees. Others were frustrated that they could not offer training and development opportunities, particularly where the organization is shifting to a dual customer approach that demands new skills and methods from workers.

5. *Marketing.* Many providers and other observers felt that nonprofits often did not understand the needs of employers well enough to provide appropriate worker preparation and referral. Others felt that even strong providers lacked the resources and knowledge to market their services effectively to employers.

6. *General management.* Many providers traced their problems to the simple fact that they have too few people doing too much work, which leaves too little time for planning and learning.

7. *Research and development.* Providers regretted that they could not develop better data about the outcomes of their efforts, which they would like to use in refining and developing programs.

Both the policy analysts' and the practitioners' accounts suggest that instead of investing heavily in programmatic capacity, starving administrative capacity, and ignoring adaptive capacity, an effective approach to intermediaries is more likely to invest heavily in adaptive capacities, moderately in administrative capacities, and modestly in programmatic capacities.

JFF's characterization especially implies heavy investment in adaptive capacity. It is striking that its unit of analysis is the intermediary as organization. Instead of calling for dual customer job training and placement programs, it emphasizes the need for "entrepreneurial and customer driven" organizations. And by describing an organization that understands its labor market and knows the needs of employers and clients, it implies the need for organizational learning processes: there is no understanding and knowledge without learning. It also suggests a role for some sort of quality improvement process by pointing out that effective intermediaries "use data to improve performance." Finally, in noting the activities that effective intermediaries focus on—employment preparation, support for retention and advancement, and coordination with nonemployment services—it suggests a programmatic direction, but stops well short of prescribing a programmatic solution.

The accounts of nonprofit executive directors provide a consistent but broader picture of capacity needs—emphasizing the need to build both administrative and adaptive capacities, often simultaneously. For example, they emphasize their need for two forms of capital. A supply of working capital would build their administrative capacity, by protecting them from chronically slow payments on government contracts. But they also want what some called venture capital—funds to help them develop and experiment with new programs. Similarly, when they emphasize their need for improved information technology, it serves both capacities. It would help them administratively, managing their billing and reporting on government contracts. But it would also enable them to collect and use data on client outcomes, which they feel would help them improve their services. Many of the directors emphasized their need to attract and develop employees who would be suitable to the work of cultivating and responding to the intermediary's dual customer. They need to redesign jobs, look for ways to motivate employees, and shift their cultures away from the mono-client approach of social work to the dual client, customer driven approach of the intermediary—all of which entails not administrative personnel practices but strategic, adaptive human resource development capacities.

In a recent survey by the National Network of Sector Partners (presented in chapter 4), the leaders of workforce intermediaries described similar capacity challenges. While about two-thirds of the respondents said they needed help with programmatic capacity (referred to as "best practices information" in the survey), over 80 percent identified "strengthening organizational capacity" as a critical need. If we consider the other needs they identified—for assistance with "strategic planning," "research and education," and "building relationships with employers"—these practitioner accounts point us again toward a combination of adaptive and administrative capacity.

In locating the capacity for effectiveness in administrative and adaptive organizational processes, the practitioners' and policy analysts' accounts pose a challenge for policy makers. We know how to replicate programs (though perhaps not reliably). But how can policy makers replicate or build these adaptive and administrative capacities at a large scale?

UNDERSTANDING CAPACITY BUILDING

Just as current conceptions of capacity do not fit well with the challenges facing workforce development policy makers, current approaches to capacity *building* are unlikely to serve them well either. The two most prevalent capacity building approaches involve risks that are especially unappealing given all that is at stake for individual jobseekers in need of high-quality services. In this section, I will review those two approaches—one that relies on inputs and the other, outcomes—and then describe the advantages of an alternative, integrated approach that relies on inputs and outcome strategies together. Finally, I will propose a set of principles for workforce development capacity building.

Prevalent Capacity Building Approaches and Problems for Workforce Development

Some capacity building approaches invest in the development of nonprofit organizations by offering them an array of inputs. Foundations have invested in training, education, individual and group consultation, conferences, peer learning networks, and documentation of best practices and model programs for their grantees. Some of these are aimed at improving programmatic capacity. But especially in recent years, with more attention focused on the organizational needs of nonprofits, funders have offered resources to improve strategic planning, board development, fundraising, budgeting, and accounting.

However deserving nonprofits may be of these resources, focusing primarily on input approaches like these is a dubious strategy for building the capacity of workforce development organizations. Under any circumstances, this is a risky approach. Many nonprofits will simply prove unable to convert these capacity building resources into performance. And while this is an honorable risk to run in advancing the long-term goal of building a stronger field of nonprofits, the stakes may be too high for workforce development. If investment in capacity resources does not bear fruit, the price will be paid not by the nonprofit and funder alone, but by clients as well.

Even if there were no time pressure, an input-dominant approach would still be a poor fit for workforce development organizations. Offering capacity building resources is most suitable for meeting technical capacity needs. When the challenge at hand is technical, the gap from input to performance is manageable. Organizations that need to know how to implement a given program or how to handle an administrative function like accounting can begin applying new technical knowledge in these tasks relatively quickly.

In contrast, if the challenge is to build *adaptive* capacity, the gap from input to performance becomes much wider. Consider the claims of policy analysts and nonprofit practitioners that intermediaries should "use data to improve performance." Offering inputs—in the form of data collection training and tools—might help nonprofits produce the data, but using the data to improve performance is beyond the reach of training and tools. To improve performance, a nonprofit needs to make many judgments about the use of data collection processes: which performance issues should we focus on? Which type of data will help us understand these issues? Once we know where we want to improve performance, how will we go about it? What sense can we make of the data? It takes a data collection system and an effective organization—not just the former—to answer these questions. And focusing on inputs alone is not sufficient to get both.

A similar gap between capacity and performance emerges when we consider the interorganizational character ascribed to the effective workforce intermediary. Jobs for the Future notes the importance of collaborating with other organizations—to provide the sometimes complex packages of supports a jobseeker needs. Others suggest that in addition to formal collaboration, effective intermediaries benefit from rich informal social networks (Harrison and Weiss, 1998). Whether formal or informal, this collaborative, networked activity is likely to demand adaptive capacity. Determining with whom the organization should collaborate and which networks best reflect its values, aspirations, and constituencies requires the kind of reflective and strategic thinking that cannot be prescribed programmatically.

An outcome-dominant capacity building approach sidesteps these input problems entirely. Government funders are most apt to take this approach. By spurring competition and paying for performance, they demand that nonprofits develop whatever capacity they may need to attain the outcomes they have committed to. The funders themselves need not get involved in supplying the inputs for that capacity, nor worry about how to convert those inputs into performance. Under the classic pay-for-performance contract, for example, a government agency specifies the outcomes it desires, invites providers to bid for the contract, selects winning providers, and then pays them for performance. High performers who exceed the contract goals might get bonuses. Good performers will recover all their costs. Low performers will suffer financial losses, and will be less likely to win additional contracts. Each of the providers decides how best to go about getting the job done for the agreed upon price and deals with its own capacity challenges.

The logic of the competitive, outcomes focused approach is appealing but the practice is often disappointing. The accounts of the nonprofit leaders in our seven-city survey suggest that even where there is a large enough supply of providers to enable competition for contracts, nonprofits sometimes inhibit that competition. Some smaller providers—fearing the hassle and risks imposed by large performance based contracts—simply opted out of the competition, sometimes by becoming subcontractors to larger providers. In one county, several of the largest nonprofits informally divided up the service regions put to bid so that no one of them would be competing against the others for contracts.

In most places, instead of seeing their contracts as incentives to innovate and build appropriate capacities for the goals they sought, the nonprofit providers saw them as threatening and punitive. Many claimed that the base prices of the contracts did not even cover their basic costs, let alone leave a surplus that would provide working capital to fund improvements in their organizations. When a slow economy or a difficult client caseload led to low placement rates, the providers felt they were punished for conditions they could not control. With the exception of a few who had negotiated start up advances on new contracts, the providers generally felt that outcome focused contracts were complicating their prospects for building better organizations.

The solution to the imperfections of outcome-dominant and input-dominant approaches is, of course, to combine the two. But doing so radically changes the character of the capacity building. Instead of *programing* capacity building by designing and offering inputs, or *purchasing* capacity building by specifying and rewarding outcomes, an integrated approach entails a *capacity building relationship*, in which the capacity builder provides inputs while also working to convert them to outcomes.

The emergence in recent years of what are sometimes called "high-engagement" funders provides an example. While traditional funders rely on grantmaking to advance their mission, and some funders provide technical assistance for their grantees to complement their grants, Christine Letts and I learned in a recent study of six high-engagement funders that combining the two shifts the nature of capacity building from input providing or outcome seeking to an accountability relationship (Letts and Ryan, forthcoming).

As described by grantees, these relationships were less important for improving technical management skills than for improving strategic thinking. Funder and grantee, through ongoing communication, asked together: what kind of capacity do we need given the challenges we face? And which of our capacity needs is most important to work on first? The funders then provided both the support and pressure needed to answer these questions over the course of their relationships, which were generally long term. Support took the form of capacity building inputs: funds for consultants, training, professional education, or help on these matters directly from a funder (if the funder was qualified). It also came in the form of encouragement and commitment: funders expressed their confidence and backed it with funds. But equally striking in these relationships is the use of pressure. Funders joined with grantees in setting "stretch" goals, made judgments with the grantees about their progress in meeting those goals, and pushed them to deliver. This use of funder power and accountability is obviously a complicated proposition for nonprofits. Yet most grantees valued this relationship highly, even when it amounted to a "kick in the butt."

A parallel development in government funding of nonprofits provides another example. While many government funders are increasingly drawn to the appeal of performance based, outcome focused contracting, one class of government funder may be moving in another direction. Government funding agencies that have been chartered exclusively to fund and monitor third-party service delivery often have reason to combine input and outcome oriented approaches. These special-purpose entities are given a mission (for example, improving services for children within a county, or managing substance abuse services). But they are prohibited from delivering services themselves. Entirely dependent on outside providers (almost always nonprofit organizations), these agencies often discover that engineering competition and paying for performance are not enough to improve service. Instead, they develop capacity building relationships with the nonprofits they fund: investing in information technology improvements, upgrading accounting systems, exposing providers to model programs, or, particularly when organizations are in crisis, troubleshooting along with their executives and boards to solve critical problems. Like high-engagement funders, these public funders do not rely on inputs alone, or on incentives or sanctions for outcomes. They create relationships to build capacity.[5]

Principles for Workforce Development Capacity

What are the implications for policy makers who might want to encourage more, and more appropriate, capacity building to improve the workforce development field? The integrated, relationship driven approach to capacity building suggests four guiding principles.

Resist Standardization. A commitment to large-scale results often leads policy makers to favor highly standardized approaches. But in workforce development, the capacity for effectiveness is not encoded in a simple, standard program that can be mass produced. The capacity lies not only in nonprofit organizations, but also in the more complex adaptive capacities that support learning, innovating, and quality improvement that require a relationship driven capacity building approach. None of this lends itself to standardized approaches. And nonprofits themselves may not value a standardized approach. The study of high-engagement funders mentioned earlier found that grantees were consistently dissatisfied when their funders attempted to economize by standardizing their approach to capacity building. They insisted that a group workshop that offers training is not the same as a one-on-one relationship that uses pressure and support to improve performance. The efficiency of standardization should not trump the impact of customization.

Provide Choice to Nonprofits. The integrated, relationship driven approach recommended here understandably raises concerns about autonomy for nonprofit organizations. As much as they might value the support of such a relationship, they worry about the way it might influence their choices and priorities. The most important protection for nonprofits, then, is to provide choice. Instead of designating a single capacity provider and forcing nonprofits to decide between no assistance and assistance from one approved source, both private and public funders can build choice into their approaches.

Supply Working Capital. Both public and private funding systems have created a hostile environment for nonprofit managers to work on capacity building. Public contracts are often underpriced, and private funds are often tightly restricted to program development and delivery. As a result, managers often have little or no funds to support the type of planning, learning, and evaluating they need to improve their performance. Any credible capacity program will have to supply some flexible funding to allow such work to take place.

Be Willing to Target Resources. Many capacity building efforts seek to strengthen an entire field of players by dispensing funds, training, and technical assistance to an array of organizations. But those seeking to build adaptive capacity with a relationship driven approach will need to target their resources. Generally, they should look for good organizations that are eager to get stronger and improve their performance. Chronically unstable and underperforming organizations—especially if they lack a keen eagerness to improve—are poor prospects. Others will simply not be interested in the intense work and accountability that would be involved. They, too, should be avoided. Additional considerations—such as finding organizations that can reach underserved and marginalized populations—are certainly valid, but a capacity building program that ends up serving every organization is likely to serve none of them effectively.

Many funders and policy makers will be averse to this targeted approach. To them, working intensively with a handful or organizations seems to fall far short of the type of field building and system improvement required for large-scale progress. But in the end an effective field needs effective organizations. Someone, somewhere has to invest in particular organizations as if their performance mattered. And unless we're willing to leave that work entirely in the hands of nonprofits themselves, capacity builders will have to take an almost proprietary interest in a very few organizations.[6]

Envisioning a Capacity Building Approach for Intermediaries

How could federal and state policy makers—along with private funders and nonprofit intermediaries themselves—convert these principles into an effective capacity building approach? Here is one scenario.

Federal policy makers would end the benign neglect that is undermining many nonprofits by putting capacity building high on the policy agenda and appropriating funds for the states to develop capacity building programs. While federal budget outlays will be critical, federal acknowledgement of the challenge can be decisive as well. In its overseas development work, for example, the federal government has consistently supported building the capacity of effective nongovernmental organizations. The policy rationale—that these organizations can do what government often cannot, by promoting innovation, citizen engagement, and a pluralistic approach to development work—has been influential in shaping overseas development funding. We need an equally compelling policy rationale for building the capacity of nonprofits at home—one that shifts our appreciation of capacity from "overhead" to a critical resource that drives social outcomes.

Consistent with our devolved policy making and service delivery system, each state would be eligible for some of these federal capacity building funds. States would propose a program that demonstrates how improved capacity of providers will lead to improved outcomes for jobseekers, and then outline steps to support the development of capacity. We might expect the states to develop, at minimum, a three-part approach.

First, the states should commit to a policy of "do no harm," under which they would commit to identify funding, contracting, and regulatory practices that undermine the effectiveness of nonprofits. A series of unglamorous, administrative reforms could enable nonprofits to function more effectively, including: improving the turnaround time on contract payments, easing unnecessary bureaucratic reporting requirements, and developing fair contract prices that allow nonprofits to build up some working capital. Although they do not build new capacity, measures like these at least allow nonprofits to conserve what capacity they have.

Second, notwithstanding the earlier recommendation for targeting, state policy makers could identify the most prevalent capacity needs and fund or deliver generic capacity building programs open to all nonprofits. These might focus on widespread problems like access to information technology needed to administer contracts and report on caseloads. States could also improve understanding of trends in the regional and state labor markets through briefings and workshops. Although intermediaries still need to understand the particular needs of local employers, this type of economic information can be useful as well, and can be made accessible to groups of nonprofits.

Third, and central to the states' capacity building programs, would be frameworks and funding to enable the relationship driven approaches needed to develop adaptive capacity. The challenge here is to determine which players would be best suited to work with nonprofits on their capacity building needs. Workforce Investment Boards (WIBs) would certainly have a role in shaping an approach to capacity building, but it seems unlikely that most of them would be suited to do the work themselves. The customized, intensive, proprietary-like stance of effective capacity building partners would be a hard one for WIBs—concerned with all providers and local employers—to assume. More plausible for WIBs is the role of capacity building gatekeeper. The WIB could disburse funds to individual intermediaries for capacity building initiatives and monitor their performance to ensure the investments are paying off.

Here they would face a final design choice—about whether to anoint a single capacity builder, or to enable nonprofits to find their own. State tax credits for charitable giving suggest how nonprofits could find their own partner. Sixteen states offer tax credits to corporations participating in Neighborhood Assistance Plans. To get the credits, participating corporations must agree to make large grants over a long period of time to selected nonprofits. Most of the programs require the businesses to work with the nonprofits on strategy development or organizational capacity building, sometimes mandating plans that outline the major objectives and expected milestones. The result is a long-term capacity building relationship that supplies flexible working capital and a partner willing to work with a non-profit. Importantly, nonprofits are not compelled to work with any one funder—nor with any funder at all.

A similar approach might serve workforce development nonprofits well. While tax credits tilt the choice of capacity builder toward businesses, a government grants program could extend the choice, allowing nonprofits to develop capacity partnerships with one of a number of institutions—local foundations, nonprofit management support organizations, or even local public funders. This approach would avoid the risks of an input-only approach, in which we have to gamble that capacity resources will be converted into performance. And it avoids the problems of relying on outcomes alone—which often deprives nonprofits of the resources they need.

Alternatively, WIBs might consider the experience of community development capacity building programs, and fund a consortium to provide capacity building assistance. In community development "operating support collaboratives," funders who know the field join together—with resources and expertise—to select a limited number of nonprofits to participate in an intensive capacity building program. The small staff of the collaboratives are chosen for their ability to engage intensively with nonprofits on their capacity building agendas, providing the kind of pressure, support, and resources that characterizes the high-engagement funders described earlier.

At every level in this system—the federal, state, and regional—another important variation might be appealing: enlisting private philanthropic funders to underwrite some of the costs of capacity building, and to bring to bear on these questions their own experiences with nonprofit providers. The result might be a critical new resource for nonprofits that have been called on to do large-scale, high-stakes work in an environment that offers them little support.

CONCLUSION

Funding, encouraging, and monitoring the development of customized, relationship driven capacity approaches may seem implausible to those attracted to the convenience and efficiency of standardized, program centered approaches. But based on what we know about the characteristics of the emerging workforce intermediary and the type of capacity it will require, it may be the short cuts of standardized approaches that prove implausible. A policy debate that takes up the challenges of implementation should weigh these choices.

NOTES

1. This framework is adapted from the one developed with my colleagues earlier (Letts, Ryan, and Grossman, 1999). The concept of adaptive organizational capacity is inspired by the adaptive leadership concepts of Ronald A. Heifitz (1994).

2. See Letts, Ryan, and Grossman (1999). When we brought managers from for-profit and nonprofit organizations together in a series of seminars to discuss broad organizational topics like "quality improvement" or "organizational learning," we found that the nonprofits had often improvised their own versions of the for-profits' highly formalized organizational processes. Where the two differed was in their environments: whereas the businesses were supported and encouraged in using these processes, the nonprofits were highly discouraged from "diverting" limited resources to this work.

3. The Berkeley Policy Associates (2000) evaluation makes the critical connection between effective program implementation and organizational capacity. It stresses the administrative capacity of the implementing organizations (to explain the fact that only five of the 12 replication sties it studied were highly stable) but also takes note of CET's highly committed staff.

4. These interviews were conducted before the construct of the workforce intermediary was in use, and not all of the organizations interviewed work under that construct. Both to update the interview findings and to focus specifically on the perceptions of intermediaries, follow up interviews were conducted in 2002 with some of the organizations originally interviewed in 1998.

5. For a corporate analog in which purchasers and suppliers favor a relationship built on joint problem solving over one that is arm's length and strictly outcomes focus, see Womack, Jones, and Roos (1990).

6. Of course, broader field building and this more targeted approach are not mutually exclusive. Funders or policy makers could distribute funds and support to all players, and focus intensively on those few with strong appetites and prospects for improving their organizations.

REFERENCES

Alexander, Jennifer, Renee Nank, and Camilla Stivers. 1999. "Implications of Welfare Reform: Do Nonprofit Survival Strategies Threaten Civil Society?" *Nonprofit and Voluntary Sector Quarterly*.

Behn, Robert D., and Peter A. Kahn. 1999. "Strategies for Avoiding the Pitfalls of Performance Contracting." *Public Productivity & Management Review*, Vol. 22, No. 4.

Berkeley Policy Associates. 2000. *Evaluation of the Center for Employment Training Replication Sites*. Oakland, CA: Berkeley Policy Associates. (June).

Donahue, John D. 1989. *The Privatization Decision: Public Means, Private Ends*. New York: Basic Books.

Harrison, Bennett, and Marcus Weiss. 1998. *Workforce Development Networks: Community-Based Organizations and Regional Alliances.* Thousand Oaks, CA: Sage Publications.

Heifitz, Ronald A. 1994. *Leadership Without Easy Answers.* Cambridge, MA: The Belknap Press of Harvard University.

Letts, Christine W., and William P. Ryan. Forthcoming. "High-Engagement Funding: Filling the Performance Gap." *Stanford Review of Social Innovation.*

Letts, Christine W., William P. Ryan, and Allen Grossman. 1999. *High Performance Nonprofit Organizations: Managing Upstream for Greater Impact.* New York: John Wiley & Sons.

Liebowitz, Marty, Marlene Selzer, and Richard Kazis. 2000. *Building Organizational and System Capacity: How Government Can Support 'Demand-Led' Reform.* Report prepared for "Welfare to Work: New Solutions for the New Economy UK/US Symposium."

Light, Paul C. 1998. *Sustaining Innovation: Creating Nonprofit and Government Organizations That Innovate Naturally.* San Francisco: Jossey-Bass.

Polanyi, Michael. 1974. *Personal Knowledge: Toward a Post-Critical Philosophy.* Chicago: University of Chicago Press.

Ryan, William P. 2001. *Nonprofit Capital: A Review of Problems and Strategies.* Prepared for Fannie Mae and Rockefeller Foundations.

Ryan, William P. and Human Service Solutions. 1998. *Challenges Facing Nonprofit Workforce Development Organizations: Review and Analysis.* Report prepared for The Rockefeller Foundation.

Smith, Steven Rathgeb, and Michael Lipsky. 1993. *Nonprofits for Hire: The Welfare State in the Age of Contracting.* Cambridge, MA: Harvard University Press.

Walker, Gary, and Jean Grossman. 1999. "Philanthropy and Outcomes: Dilemmas in the Quest for Accountability." In Charles T. Clotfelter and Thomas Ehrlich, eds. *Philanthropy and the Nonprofit Sector in a Changing America.* Bloomington, IN: Indiana University Press.

Womack, James P., Daniel T. Jones, and Daniel Roos. 1990. *The Machine that Changed the World.* New York: HarperPerennial.

14

Community Development Intermediation and Its Lessons for the Workforce Field

CHRISTOPHER WALKER
AND JOHN FOSTER-BEY

O VER THE 1990S, COMMUNITY DEVELOPMENT INTERMEDIATION HAS come into its own as an important contributor to the ongoing work of improving America's neighborhoods. Established to help the community based portion of the community development industry solve some of its chronic financial, technical, and political difficulties, community development intermediaries have filled major gaps in the array of funding, capacity building, and policy activities that compose community development systems. They have done so in increasing numbers of cities, drawing on growing government, corporate, and private foundation support.

This chapter assesses the experience of community development intermediation to determine whether creation of new institutions might help the workforce development field solve some of its own chronic problems. It finds that the workforce system, indeed, shares some basic features with the community development field, arguing for the potential value of intermediaries in the workforce development arena. But it also finds that participants in the workforce field may lack sufficient incentives to create and sustain effective intermediary organizations.

The following discussion relies heavily on recent Urban Institute work on community development systems and the role of Community Development Corporations (CDCs) and intermediaries in those systems.[1] Conducted over seven years, this research tracked the evolution of community development systems in 23 cities, including most of the largest cities in the country. The extended discussion of community development in the pages to follow reflects this point of departure—from the community development system that is by now well understood to the workforce system, which is once again shifting, in perhaps fundamental ways, due to changes wrought by new national legislation.

Intermediation in the workforce arena, as understood in this chapter, refers to *system* intermediation, and not to the intermediary role between jobseekers and employers frequently played by many workforce intermediaries as discussed in this book. Rather, intermediation refers to activities that broker relationships among providers, government, foundations, employers, and other institutional participants in the workforce system, to support workforce intermediaries in specific regions.

NEIGHBORHOODS AS MARKETS AND COMMUNITIES

Since the 1960s, the challenge of deteriorating urban neighborhoods has occupied the attention of public policy makers in and out of government. Each year, billions of dollars of federal funding, as well as substantial sums of private and foundation funding, goes to support efforts to improve the quality of these communities.[2] But efforts to improve distressed urban neighborhoods have run up against endemic challenges that make community development among the most difficult of all areas of public endeavor (O'Conner, 1999).

To understand community development, its accomplishments, and its challenges, it is useful to think about urban neighborhoods as markets and as communities, consisting of multiple institutions, tied to one another in complex ways, and linked to city-wide sources of money and power. To be successful, community development activities must: 1) meet a market test by responding to, and creating, opportunities for profitable investment; 2) meet a test of community acceptance by encouraging participation in neighborhood planning, projects, and institutions; 3) respond to the unique challenges and opportunities of individual neighborhoods by blending multiple types of financial and programmatic resources; and 4) attract the support of external actors who command financial, technical, and political resources.

First, as markets, neighborhoods consist of profit motivated buyers and sellers of land, real property, and goods and services, including labor services. Profit motivated, private sector banks provide the bulk of new investment in housing and business enterprise. To influence market performance—to increase the value of goods and services produced—community development efforts must induce new investments from a myriad of neighborhood and city-wide actors. Potential investors respond favorably to improvements in neighborhood quality, requiring coordinated efforts to upgrade the physical, social, and economic characteristics that influence the perceived desirability of neighborhoods.

Second, community improvement efforts require the participation of those who live there, in view of the substantial assets they command. From the beginning, community development has emphasized citizen participation in the design and sometimes implementation of solutions to community problems. Community development agencies (and some local governments) created structures of participation to advise development of housing and economic development programs, public safety, education, and neighborhood zoning and land use issues.

Third, although the structural features of neighborhoods are the same across neighborhoods, each contains a different mix of institutions, of varying strengths. For example, some housing markets are dominated by a few large owners of rental properties; others by many individual homeowners. But the resources on which neighborhoods depend are largely provided by city-wide, regional, and even national institutions that are indifferent to these unique features of each neighborhood. For example, local government services are provided by specialized agencies, each with its own sources of funding, program technologies, and standards of effective performance. These specialized agencies rarely work together effectively, even at the city level. But at the neighborhood level, inefficiencies of multiple agency services are compounded by the mismatch between the volume and quality of these services and the unique needs of individual neighborhoods.

Fourth, because few neighborhoods are self-contained, successful revitalization requires engagement of powerful external actors in the hard work of neighborhood change. These external actors can include banks and major corporations; unions and large institutional investors; local and state government; local, regional, and national foundations; religious bodies; and others. What's needed are institutions able to negotiate successfully with external actors on behalf of neighborhood interests, broker some relationships among neighborhood stakeholders, and act effectively in the marketplace while responding to community interests. Community Development Corporations were created, and have grown as an industry, to accomplish these tasks.

THE ROLE OF COMMUNITY DEVELOPMENT CORPORATIONS IN RESPONDING TO COMMUNITY DEVELOPMENT CHALLENGES

One of the signal developments in the evolution of community development policy and practice in the five decades since the Housing Act of 1949 created a national program of urban renewal is emergence of community based, nonprofit institutions to meet basic community development challenges. Known as Community Development Corporations, these institutions engage in market transactions, but do so on behalf of, and are partially controlled by, community representatives. Unlike some other community based institutions, they attempt to establish and maintain connections with powerful external actors. And as they mature as organizations, they tend to take on an array of programs intended to respond to multiple neighborhood problems across a broad front.

CDCs as Alternative to Government and to For-Profits

In the 1990s, and in most major U.S. cities, CDCs emerged as a relatively stable partial solution to core problems of market and community. By 1997 there were an estimated 3,600 CDCs nationwide, roughly double the number from the beginning of the decade, this from a relative handful of CDCs at their inception in the mid-1960s (National Congress for Community Economic Development, 1998). This growth was attributable to their comparative advantages relative to government and for-profit business.[3] As a rule, government agencies tend not to be sensitive to the market consequences of the decisions they make on the scale of services they provide, their allocation across neighborhoods, or the efficiency with which they are provided. Service delivery is endemically fragmented. Private developers are quite good at investments that take advantage of market opportunities, but they have little interest in bundling multiple programs into a coherent investment program, and they are notably intolerant of community process, which extends development timeframes and drives up costs.

Unlike government, but like private business, CDCs make investments and deliver programs that are responsive to the marketplace. Unlike both government and for-profit business, CDCs are willing and able to adopt, revise, combine, and discontinue programs that respond to neighborhood conditions. And like government, but unlike private business, CDCs regard community participation as an integral part of their public purpose. CDCs stake their claims on community and external support based on their ability to make market-sensitive investments, respond effectively to community concerns, and assemble and deliver a package of community improvement programs.

CDC Responses to Community Development Challenges

As market-responsive agencies, CDCs have produced thousands of units of affordable housing for renters and new homeowners; national figures show a cumulative housing unit production of 245,000 units through 1997. In addition, CDCs had developed some 71 million square feet of commercial and industrial space, and invested nearly $2 billion in loans to business (National Congress for Community Economic Development, 1998). All of these investments almost always involve some kind of private finance, which is supplied only on the condition that CDC investments meet basic tests of market acceptance and financial stability. But further, CDCs aim to influence the behavior of neighborhood markets by making high-cost and high-risk investments and by creating community programs that absorb some of the risk that private investors might otherwise face. For example, some CDCs operate community-wide rehabilitation programs that encourage homeowners throughout the neighborhood to invest in the upgrade of their homes.

To engage and sustain citizen support, CDCs make direct investments in "community" programs, affordable housing, and other projects that directly benefit community residents. They also shape development projects to meet community demands on the size, location, and character of buildings. These community benefits are secured, in theory, by creation of governing boards consisting of community representatives, adoption of community participation structures that advise CDC directors on the pace and direction of investments, and adherence to a community minded vision of neighborhood quality.

To help solve the problems of "bundling" community programs into effective, community-responsive investments, CDCs rely on both the direct provision of city and foundation funded programs and advocacy with elected representatives and city agency staff to provide or influence a range of human service, physical infrastructure, public safety, and housing and commercial development programs. Increasingly, CDCs have relied on formal and informal partnership arrangements with other neighborhood based organizations to help achieve a better fit among public programs and community needs.

To help attract the participation of external agents in neighborhood improvement, CDCs maintain ties with financial institutions, foundations, politicians, government agency staff, and others in a position to direct resources to neighborhoods. A track record of effective project development, coupled with demonstrated community support, is critical to CDC ability to stake an effective claim on these resources. In turn, CDC ability to secure funding from outside the neighborhood is an important demonstration to community residents that support for CDC strategies and programs is worthwhile.

THE CDC CONNECTION TO COMMUNITY DEVELOPMENT SYSTEMS

To do their job effectively, CDCs must draw down resources from city-wide repositories of financial, technical, and political capital. It is helpful to think about these capital stocks as controlled and allocated by three related subsystems within an overall community development system (Walker, 2002). *Community development systems are comprised of the relationships among neighborhood leaders and organizations and city-wide institutions to mobilize, allocate, and wield finance, expertise, and political influence to accomplish community development goals.* (To simplify the following discussion, these systems are defined primarily in terms of the allocation of resources for affordable housing development, the most common CDC activity.) The three subsystems that channel the flow of these forms of capital are: production systems, which allocate financial capital; capacity building systems, which allocate human capital; and leadership systems, which allocate political capital.

Production systems consist of the relationships among private sector firms and government agencies to provide public subsidy and private finance for development projects, regulate allowable land uses and establish rules for development project approvals, and monitor project compliance with local, state, and federal statutes. These systems originate and channel the flow of funds, from sources of investment capital, through project development, and back to investors in the form of financial payments to private investors or public benefits to public investors. As an example, a typical rental housing development project will rely on investor equity generated through the low-income housing tax credit program (operated by state agencies), additional project grants supplied by local government from the Federal Community Development Block Grant Program, and loan funds provided by a bank. Contributors of private equity and loan capital expect a market return on their investments.

Capacity building systems consist of the relationships among entities that support creation of organizational capacity, as indicated by strength of leadership (including director and board), staff quality, internal management systems, and public programs and the quality standards to which they adhere. Some organizational development is built by carrying out community programs, and is paid for out of program funding, e.g., the fees earned through real estate project development or payments on government service contracts. Other organizational development costs are covered by contributions from individual, corporate, and foundation donors, who value CDCs' community roles.

Leadership systems consist of relationships among holders of political power and influence, which can be wielded to increase, decrease, and otherwise shape the flow of resources to neighborhoods for community development purposes. CDC ability to accumulate community development assets and sustain the flow of production and capacity building funding depends in part on their ability to participate effectively in the political arena. The political clout CDCs may accumulate stems from the support they command from community residents and from stakeholders in the broader system. Community support rests in part on CDC ability to deliver concrete benefits to residents, which depends on broader system support, which depends on their ability to attract community support.

Generally speaking, there is a direct relationship between the quality of local systems and the ability of CDCs to carry out their community development roles.

CHRONIC CHALLENGES FACING CDCS AND COMMUNITY DEVELOPMENT SYSTEMS

This preceding portrait of CDCs is an idealized one, drawing on the best examples of their contribution to neighborhood change in the past. In reality, the evolution of CDCs as a part of community development industries has been marked throughout by financial, technical, and political "undercapitalization." Shortfalls in needed financial, technical, and political capital stemmed from the stresses caused by the twin demands of markets on the one hand and communities on the other. These chronic difficulties were aggravated where financial, capacity building, and leadership systems performed poorly.

CDC Financial, Technical, and Political Undercapitalization

As socially motivated developers, CDCs often wind up without adequate capital to carry out and manage development projects effectively. To ensure that lower income people can afford to rent the units they develop, CDCs sometimes plow project earnings back into developments to allow reduced rents. This same financial tactic has been used to fund costly but desirable development projects, for example, renovation of historic properties. Moreover, CDCs lack the option to diversify project investments, instead limiting their efforts to single neighborhoods. Project development pipelines also are unpredictable, reliant on availability of city subsidies that are sometimes in short supply. These constraints undermine project financial health, which over the long term may deteriorate if financial reserves are inadequate. Finally, the relatively meager returns from project investments means that CDCs cannot accumulate financial reserves needed to seize future development opportunities.

These shortfalls of financial capital translate into an inability to make adequate investments in leadership development, staff training, management systems, or new program development. Aggravating this organization or technical undercapitalization is community pressure to adopt an open-ended revitalization agenda, risking adoption of a full slate of ultimately unsupportable program commitments. Finally, embrace of a community process to guide development and implementation of revitalization plans is, at the same time, an acceptance of the higher costs and longer development periods that community involvement necessarily imposes. At worst, this community role may embroil CDCs in fractious community politics that undermines its ability to carry out program tasks effectively.

The balancing act of development on the one hand and community on the other, if unsuccessful, can result in several kinds of political undercapitalization. If CDCs fail to bring projects on line or deliver community development programs relatively effectively, they may lose the community support upon which their claim on agency support in part depends. They also lose political power conveyed by ownership of property and their ability to participate effectively in neighborhood land use decisions. At worst, CDCs become captive to political leadership interested in using their organizations as sources of patronage and votes. On the other hand, excessive attention to delivery of projects and programs at the expense of community interests produces a kind of opportunism that also risks the loss of community support. Under these circumstances, poor community reputations can undermine CDC claims on external support from city and philanthropic funders.

In most cities, the twin challenges of development and community virtually guaranteed that few CDCs would become organizations that were financially strong, technically adept, and politically well established. Before the advent of system intermediation, most CDC industries were marked by extreme concentration of capacity, and overall, the sector was not competitive with for-profits in the fight for scarce public subsidies, or even with some public agencies, in its ability to carry out physical revitalization activities.[4] But despite this overall record of underachievement, some CDCs were able to do well, particularly those with strong executive directors, able to forge close ties to systemic sources of financial, philanthropic, and political support. The success of these organizations was due to the extraordinary political and leadership skills of executive directors and their ability to forge a network of personal relationships throughout the community development system.

How Community Development Systems
Aggravate Chronic CDC Problems

These chronic problems were aggravated by *systemic* ills afflicting the production, capacity building, and leadership components of the community development systems upon which neighborhoods depended. The excessive costs and high risks confronting individual CDCs were matched by the excessive costs and risks faced by participants in the broader system. As a result, solving the problems of frontline organizations in neighborhoods required solutions to "systems-level" problems facing other actors in the community development system.

Production systems typically consisted of multiple and disconnected streams of project funding, provided by state and local (and sometimes directly by federal) government agencies with little coordination of project financing, occupancy, application, or other requirements. Regulatory and administrative barriers to efficient development of projects drove up costs and introduced considerable uncertainty into construction schedules (Stegman, 1991). Financial institutions lacked information about inner city market prospects, and were skeptical (often rightly) of the "bankability" of CDC projects. Bank avoidance of high-risk early project phases produced chronic shortfalls of the predevelopment finance needed to seize development opportunities.

Fragmentation and gaps in production systems imposed additional costs on already cash-short CDCs, as they sought information on subsidy opportunities and the conditions under which project finance was available, assembled as many as seven or eight different sources of financing for a single project, and complied with reporting and other requirements for each of these sources. Because of uncertainties in the availability of project subsidies, as well as uncertain bank acceptance of proposed financing packages, CDCs ran the risk of investing hard-earned cash in land acquisition, early design, financial feasibility, and financial packaging, without assurance of reimbursement from project proceeds. Where CDCs had no retained earnings, few lenders were willing to extend financing for these early project phases.

For their part, banks lacked information about the quality of CDC products and their ability to deliver on development projects, and lacked the incentive to acquire such information for all but the largest prospective development deals. In the absence of solid information about CDC performance, banks were loath to accept the downstream credit risk that projects would fail to repay due to poor CDC management or unwillingness or ability to maintain adequate reserves for repair and replacement of major building systems. Finally, without the assurance that initial public subsidies would be followed by other supporting community development investments, banks would increase their perceived risk of project investments and limit their own participation accordingly.

To acquire the resources needed to supplement the limited revenues generated by project development and government contracts, CDCs relied heavily on contributions from corporations and foundations. Foundations sometimes awarded funds in modest amounts—from $50,000 to $100,000—through social and community programs to accomplish specific, foundation defined purposes. More often, foundations and corporations supplied grants for general operating support in small amounts, ranging from $3,000 to $15,000, much as United Way funds typically are distributed. Government supplied operating support usually took the form of contracts for performance of community planning and other services. These general support grants—often labeled as "capacity building"—were hardly ever linked to specific organizational development activities. Even when they were, few foundations or corporations looked behind grantees' final reports to determine whether genuine improvements had taken place, or sought to help organizations find capable providers of technical support services.

This system of piecemeal grant support required CDC directors to assemble a workable operating budget from dozens of separate financing sources, and by doing so, incur substantial transactions costs. These costs included the time and attention directors and their development officers (if they had them) devoted to identifying funding sources, assessing funding chances, developing funding applications, and filing project reports. These costs were accompanied by a considerable risk that funding commitments made in one year, and on which program budgets were built, would not be forthcoming in a subsequent year, thereby complicating program planning.

For their part, foundation and corporate donors were not in a position to acquire information on the needs, capacities, and past performance of recent or prospective grantees, nor to coordinate their giving with one another. Absent the payoff from leveraging the investments of others, and the ability to distinguish among the respective merits of multiple supplicants, foundations and corporations ran considerable risks of making bad investments.

Political systems that mobilize support for neighborhood interests among influential financial, philanthropic, and political elites are not as easily characterized as the production and capacity building systems just discussed. Moreover, the features of these systems appear to be more enduring, less amenable to change, than those primarily involving banks and foundations. Important to the community development system are the place of neighborhoods on the urban agenda and the role of CDCs as mechanisms for the delivery of community development services.

Where leadership systems break down is in disconnects between neighborhood leadership and city political leadership, between government and private sector supporters of community development, and in the lack of deliberative bodies able to formulate and advocate for a neighborhood agenda. In some communities, the urban political leadership is committed to a vision for neighborhood change, but has not sought to engage private sector supporters in pursuit of community improvement. In other communities, private sector leaders have declared an interest in neighborhood improvement, but have not been backed by concrete public policies that favor neighborhoods relative to downtown or industrial area improvements. Except in a few cities, historically, political and civic leadership have rarely been committed to a common agenda for community based solutions to community development problems.

In systems without mechanisms to surface, debate, and advocate for neighborhoods outside of the political arena (councilmanic and executive bodies), CDCs incur some costs as the price of participating in the political arena. Costs of advocacy have traditionally been borne by coalitions formed to advocate for neighborhoods, and CDCs, on an ongoing basis. These coalitions typically are limited to CDCs and other nonprofits, and lack ability to bridge to sources of corporate support. Moreover, systems without institutionalized support for community development outside the political apparatus face considerable risk of policy reversals that undermine the value of investments already made in organizational capacity (to develop rental housing, for example). These policy reversals also pose costs to banks and foundations that have adopted lending and philanthropic policies with an eye to supporting, or taking advantage of, government policies.

As these three systems—production, capacity building, and leadership—are interrelated, so too are their dysfunctions. Problems in one system produce problems in another; investments in correcting problems in one system work best if supported by complementary investments in another. For example, the excessive costs of production system inefficiencies, if borne by CDCs, can offset otherwise productive investments in CDC capacity to fundraise effectively. Similarly, investments in capacity building make sense only if government production subsidies are available to make use of capacity to build community projects.

HOW INTERMEDIATION HELPS SOLVE PROBLEMS OF HIGH COST AND EXCESSIVE RISK

The job of intermediation is to help solve endemic problems of community development systems and, by doing so, advance CDCs' ability to carry out community programs successfully (von Hoffman, 2001). By enabling more productive ties among elements of these systems, and filling resource gaps, intermediaries absorbed excess costs and risks to induce more active participation in community development.

By definition, intermediation makes productive exchanges possible where they would not otherwise take place. The most well-known form of intermediation—in the creation of secondary mortgage markets—connects the originators of home mortgages seeking to generate new capital to make loans with investors seeking relatively low-risk investments. Intermediation helps reduce the cost of these transactions by creating a marketplace where transactions can occur. Intermediation helps reduce the risks by providing information about buyers and sellers and setting and enforcing standards.

Activities of Community Development Intermediaries

Similarly, community development intermediaries accumulate funding from investors and philanthropic donors and channel it to community organizations, thereby lowering transactions costs for each. They also acquire and disseminate information about funders and grantees, and set and monitor performance standards. In intermediated systems, banks, foundations, and government gain assurances that investments in CDCs and their activities are well spent, thereby inducing additional contributions. As a result, CDCs gain access to larger and more reliably available amounts of project and operating support.

Two national community development intermediary organizations are most prominent in the field: the Local Initiatives Support Corporation (LISC) and the Enterprise Foundation. Founded in 1979, LISC now works in 38 cities and 66 rural areas, with annual expenditures for programs and operating costs of $94 million (2001). In 2001 LISC made $550 million in loans, grants, and equity contributions. Founded in 1982, the Enterprise Foundation operates in 26 cities on an annual budget of $54 million (2001). Although there are differences across localities and between the two organizations, local field offices provide a common bundle of services that includes five basic elements (Walker, 2002):

1. Participation in development project financing by such means as loans to CDC sponsored projects, syndication of low-income housing tax credits, and provision of financial packaging services.
2. Creation of funding pools for operating support, drawing on national sources of support and funds raised from local corporations and foundations, and allocated to individual groups, with funding policies and requirements established and overseen by a funders "board."
3. Design of new community development programs, including new packages of funding and organizational development for such activities as homeowner down-payment assistance, community crime patrols, construction or renovation of community facilities.
4. Arrangement or direct provision of technical assistance to CDCs, including contracted consulting assistance, seminars and workshops, distance learning programs, project development, financial management, and property management software.
5. Research and advocacy for public and foundation policies that favor neighborhoods and CDCs.

Intermediary activities are funded through a combination of philanthropic support, earned income from financial transactions, and in some cases, government contracts to provide technical assistance to CDCs and other actors within community development systems. Arguably, the most important source of support for operations comes from their role as financiers, even though this may not represent the largest source of revenue. Intermediaries earn syndication fees from tax-credit supported projects (and nationally, manage funding pools for such investments), financial packaging fees for these same (and other) development projects, and interest on loans they originate. So long as the federal low-income rental housing tax credit program continues, and state governments allocate credits to CDC sponsored projects, intermediaries can count on a continuing source of operating capital.

Other intermediary support comes from corporate and foundation contributions, both as general support to intermediary offices and as defined contributions to CDC operating support pools, technical assistance activities, and advocacy efforts. Important to corporate contributors is the intermediary role in stimulating the growth of neighborhood markets, which creates demand for home mortgages, insurance products, and other financial services.

Intermediary activities fill in the patchwork of existing activities within production, capacity building, and leadership systems. Further, by coordinating their investments across systems, intermediary organizations aim to achieve synergies not otherwise possible in nonintermediated systems. Intermediation helps encourage new funding for community development by bearing extraordinary costs and absorbing risks that otherwise would deter investment.

Intermediary Reduction of Costs and Risks in Community Development Production, Capacity Building, and Leadership Systems

In production systems, intermediary financing reduces the extraordinary costs CDCs incurred to obtain funds for the up-front costs of project development, and allows banks and other investors to concentrate on lower risk, downstream aspects of projects. Financial packaging services reduce CDC, government, and financial institution costs of bundling multiple sources of project funding. Design of new programs based on models from other cities reduces both the costs and risks to government and CDCs of crafting wholly new programs to respond to community problems.

In capacity building systems, pooled operating support reduces the costs to CDCs of seeking out and obtaining the general support funding critical to continued operations. These funds allow CDCs to invest in internal systems and to hire people with experience in property development, financing, and management. Technical assistance provided by independent consultants, local intermediary staff, and national intermediary training programs further builds staff capacity for organizations that take advantage of it. In the best intermediated systems, operating support and technical assistance funding are provided only to those CDCs that agree to carry out an organizational development program and meet project and program performance goals.

In "leadership" systems, intermediaries help organize the support for CDCs in particular and the community development agenda in general. Funders of general operating support programs create, in effect, a platform for surfacing and debating issues of neighborhood change, which is in addition to the advisory boards created by local intermediaries. Furthermore, the transparency of funding collaboratives helps stabilize the financial, operating support, and political commitments of multiple players, who cannot withdraw their participation without offering reasons to others who expect a continued commitment. Local office connections to national sources of financing add some legitimacy to CDCs, especially in communities without a long tradition of community based activism. Research sponsored by national and local intermediary offices helps document the value of supportive public policies, thereby encouraging their adoption locally. These activities help legitimize community development and CDCs, thereby helping them and the community development field compete for financial support and political attention with other policy domains.

The Role of Community Development Intermediaries in Setting and Monitoring Performance Standards

System investments interact with one another in beneficial ways. Of special importance is the emphasis on performance that intermediaries bring. Although projects are underwritten in the past by government and private funders, intermediary predevelopment lending provides an early review of project quality that helps ensure that the development projects proposed downstream meet industry standards. Operating support tied to concrete benchmarks of project quality (e.g., the production of a certain number of units) or of organizational development (e.g., hiring staff, training board members, or converting to an approved financial management system) helps introduce and sustain a performance ethos. Establishing performance standards also ensures a public promulgation of concrete markers of organizational success known to all funders.

Improvements to the quality of CDC organizations as measured by commonly accepted standards of performance contribute to a more smoothly functioning production system. In several cities, intermediaries have extended letters of credit to CDCs that meet several tests of financial health and have a demonstrated track record of successful performance. CDCs can draw down these funds without lengthy application and approvals, thereby seizing fleeting development opportunities more effectively. Furthermore, operating support investments in CDC ability to develop and manage projects backstops, in effect, the investments made in CDC projects by banks, local government, and other investors, further reducing risks to investors.

Intermediation does not squeeze all of the risks out of local community development systems. Some risks and costs attend pursuit of public policy goals. But as a way of organizing community development systems, it formalizes the system of personal ties between CDC directors and foundation, corporate, and government funders (although these one-to-one relationships survive in all systems to varying degrees). Intermediation can't and shouldn't completely disrupt previous relationships or inhibit innovation outside formal structure. But a portion of the rationale for intermediated systems is recognition that problems due to specialization of agencies and functions can't be solved at a government level, and that oft-decried "stovepipes" are more or less permanent feature of the institutional landscape.

FACTORS INFLUENCING INTERMEDIARY SUCCESS IN COMMUNITY DEVELOPMENT

Throughout the 1990s, intermediation has helped CDCs increase production and strengthen their ability to carry out community development programs. In more advanced community development industries, those with a track record of accomplishment dating back several decades, capacity has become more evenly distributed, as previously lagging CDCs have begun to catch up with the industry leaders. In less advanced community developments systems, intermediation has helped create rudimentary CDC industries, helping narrow the gap between most cities of the South and West and the traditional centers of CDC strength in the Midwest and Northeast. And in nearly all cities, intermediary support has helped CDCs diversify their activities, branching out from housing or commercial development to a broader slate of community development activities.

But intermediaries have not been equally successful in generating new resources for community development. They have been most successful where production funding favors projects that CDCs are apt to be good at, where local philanthropic funding is relatively plentiful, and where local intermediary offices are able to take full advantage of the flexibility a national intermediary structure offers.

First, intermediaries have benefited enormously from the availability of a continuing source of federal funding that fuels project development and allows intermediaries to earn revenues from project transactions. This direct role in project finance gives local intermediaries a legitimate and informed voice within community development systems, allowing an independent, critical stance toward government, banks, and CDCs. The strong intermediary growth throughout the 1990s was fueled by increases in the flow of project funding, particularly as the low-income housing tax credit gained market acceptance and private financial markets had evolved a relatively efficient system for syndicating credits and investing the proceeds (Cummings and DiPasquale, 1999). At about the same time, Congress created a major new housing program—operated through state and local governments—that supplied subsidies for affordable housing development. Changes in financial markets throughout the 1990s eased the flow of capital to affordable housing projects and other investments in low-income neighborhoods, further reinforcing the financial health of CDC industries and the intermediaries that supported them.

But these and other community development resources have not always been allocated in ways that favor CDC projects. They have traditionally invested in rental housing and some forms of owner-occupied housing, but some government agencies choose not to invest housing and other community development resources in ways favorable to CDC project participation or that call on the special sources of capital supplied by intermediaries. Some states, responsible for tax credit program administration, have devised targeting rules and program cost limits that effectively steer program funds to suburban and rural jurisdictions where CDCs lack strength. Some conservatively administered local governments continue to favor for-profit enterprise as a matter of policy, or regard community based organizations with suspicion.

Second, intermediaries have benefited from a continuing private foundation and corporate willingness to support community development, and to recognize the value of institution building in the community development industry. This new money on the production side was complemented by new national support for CDCs on both the capacity building and production side. (For example, the National Community Development Initiative, supported by a consortium of national corporations and foundations, provides support for LISC and enterprise investments in national intermediary activities and local system building.) However, with the exception of some West Coast communities, many western and southern cities have only shallow pools of philanthropic money from which to draw funds to support CDC capacity building.

Third, the national "architecture" of community development intermediation—with national offices at the hub of a network of field offices—produces a number of local benefits. Local office connections to national practice through affiliation with national offices provide a conduit for information about best practice national foundation opportunities and policies. It offers a career ladder for local staff who aspire to prominence within the field. It has helped confer legitimacy on CDCs in particular jurisdictions, diffuse program innovation across multiple jurisdictions, and establish a national role in advocating for community development and CDCs in Congress and the administration. But the decentralized structure of national intermediaries places great weight on the entrepreneurial and other skills of local office directors, who are not equally talented across cities.

But generally speaking, intermediation in community development appears to rely on a number of elements that have made it a relatively rare example of successful system building. Perhaps most importantly, the "spine" of national tax credit gives intermediaries a core financial role in production systems, around which a number of ancillary functions can be attached. Intermediary financial involvement in CDC projects allows them to partially support their own operations based on fees earned from their project participation, creates a continuing financial interest in the capacity of CDCs to carry out and manage development projects successfully, and allows them to claim a voice in the community development system based on the importance of their own financial contributions to it.

CONTINUING CHALLENGES OF INTERMEDIATED COMMUNITY DEVELOPMENT SYSTEMS

Intermediation cannot pretend to have solved all of the problems that afflict CDC industries. Even under the best circumstances, community based development remains an inherently difficult enterprise, in which success depends primarily on a continuing balancing act between community expectations on the one hand and market demands on the other. Moreover, successful community development requires the cooperation of many actors, only some of whom can be influenced by the activities of CDCs and their supporters. As a result, even the best intermediated systems remain vulnerable to shifts in government community development policy, episodes of state and local fiscal crisis, and changes in foundation policy. That said, successful intermediation breeds a series of new challenges, some of which are just beginning to be addressed.

Given the dearth of capable community institutions in poor neighborhoods, CDCs have become increasingly recognized by government and private foundations as useful platforms for delivery of a range of community services. Intermediaries have supported this development by adopting programs to provide funding and technical support for such programs as public safety, community facilities, and workforce development. On the one hand, this expansion matches up well with CDC interests and their competitive advantages over government and for-profit parties. On the other hand, intermediaries run the risk of overburdening the very institutions they were established to support.

Ironically, the increasing ability of CDC industries to pursue community development goals effectively has sharply increased competition among CDCs in some systems for a limited supply of project subsidies. And because project subsidies are limited, as is capacity funding, community development systems have found it difficult to accommodate the emergence of new Community Development Corporations, most troubling where these represent growing immigrant populations.

Most troubling overall for the future of community development intermediation is the continuing dysfunction of many municipal and county government agencies, on which much of the community development industry relies for project funding, permitting, land use decision making, and other core public tasks. The costs of these inefficiencies fall most heavily on small development organizations, like CDCs.

Finally, in some of the newer systems, and in several older ones as well, intermediaries continue to face resistance from old-line CDCs that had established their own relationships with funders and local government, and feared that these would be disrupted by creation of pooled funding arrangements. And even within the top tier of CDC industries, organizational capacity problems remain chronic. In addition, in some cities, local government allocation of operating support to unproductive CDCs constitutes a politicized, "capacity building" system, operating in parallel to the newer merit based operating support programs.

THE COMMUNITY DEVELOPMENT EXPERIENCE AND WORKFORCE DEVELOPMENT

The story of community development intermediation has been one of on-the-ground challenges faced by a portion of the community development industry most suited to respond to the twin challenges of community and market. Chronic organizational problems—finanical, technical, and political "undercapitalization"—were aggravated historically by gaps in the support systems from which money and technical and political support flows. By closing gaps, bearing costs, and absorbing risk, intermediaries help induce new funding into community development systems and increase the ability of CDCs to pursue community change effectively. It would appear that workforce development system challenges resemble, in important ways, those of community development systems. The remainder of this chapter discusses whether there, too, intermediation would be both valuable and feasible.

It is important to re-emphasize that intermediation in the workforce arena, as understood in this chapter, refers to *system* intermediation, and not to the intermediary role between jobseekers and employers frequently played by many workforce intermediaries as discussed in this book. Rather, intermediation refers to activities that broker relationships among providers, government, foundations, employers, and other institutional participants, in the workforce system analogous to the role that a handful of community development intermediaries play for CDCs.

CHARACTERISTICS OF WORKFORCE DEVELOPMENT

The current publicly supported workforce development system grew out of the nation's attempts to wrestle with the issues of poverty and economic dislocation. The foundation for the system grows out of the social legislation of the 1960s,[5] although from 1954 to 1964, several federal laws were passed that began to establish the character of the modern workforce development system as one aimed at providing a *second chance* to individuals who were not successful in mainstream education and labor market institutions, including the disabled, displaced workers, unemployed youth, and minority workers.[6]

Starting in 1965, the emerging workforce development system moved decisively toward becoming a principal tool in breaking down economic and social inequality—especially inequality grounded in racial bias. In 1965 the Vocational Rehabilitation Act was amended to change the definition of disability to include vocational education, social, cultural, and environmental (neighborhood) disadvantages, as well as other factors. That same year, the Higher Education Act and the Elementary and Secondary Education Act provided compensatory education for individuals from deprived homes or economically and socially distressed neighborhoods. In 1966 subsidies were provided to employers to encourage hiring economically disadvantaged workers, and the Job Corp was established to provide residential job training for economically disadvantaged youth. From roughly 1966 on there was a series of other legislation and programs—such as the Neighborhood Youth Corp and the Work Incentive Program—that provided employment and training services to socially and economically disadvantaged individuals and groups.

The funding and administration of these programs were generally handled directly through the federal government, but starting with the 1973 Comprehensive Employment and Training Act (CETA), federal policy moved to a decentralized model in which control of service delivery passed increasingly to local communities—cities, counties, and state governments. As a result, some level of local control has become an important defining feature of the current workforce system.

The evolving workforce system was designed to provide services to the disadvantaged not to meet the labor market needs of employers. The Job Training Partnership Act (JTPA), passed in 1982, was an attempt to connect training programs to the needs of the labor market by mandating the participation of private employers as members of Private Industry Council (PIC) boards of directors. It also tied workforce programs even more closely to local government. Program funds were delivered to local cities, counties, and consortia to provide services. Each local community had to establish a service delivery area (SDA) and a PIC to provide policy direction and oversee the administration of local JTPA organizations. The PICs could directly deliver services or contract with local organizations to deliver services.

The most recent attempt to reform the publicly funded workforce development system is the 1998 Workforce Investment Act (WIA). WIA attempts to address several issues that continued to plague the workforce system:

- *The poor connection between program participants and business and employers.* WIA has attempted to address this issue by mandating an even greater participation of employers on the new Workforce Investment Boards (WIB) in each community receiving WIA funds. The WIBs replaced the old JTPA PICs as the recipient and manager of local workforce funding. Each state is expected to establish workforce investment areas that are supposed to represent sub-state labor markets. Each workforce area has to have a WIB to develop and oversee the implementation of a long-term workforce investment strategy. Unlike the old PICs, WIBs are restricted from using staff to directly provide employment services.
- *The fragmentation in funding and service delivery in the workforce system.* WIA attempts to reduce the fragmentation of services and funding by coordinating and consolidating where possible several different federal employment related funding streams. The major vehicle for promoting consolidation and coordination are One Stop Centers where jobseekers can get a full array of workforce services in one place. Each local WIB has the responsibility of designing its own one stop system and determining which services should participate.
- *The perception among employers, program participants, and the public at large that the workforce development system consistently wastes money and*

produces poor results and low-quality services. WIA is attempting to improve the quality of services by providing training vouchers for individual jobseekers rather than service delivery contracts to service providers. Under this new system service providers only receive funds if individuals use their vouchers to purchase services. The hypothesis is that this should force greater competition between service providers. The result should be an increase in the quality of services and the level of innovation and efficiency within the system.

- *The perception that workforce development is really for individuals who failed to succeed in the mainstream.* In order to move away from both the perception and reality that the workforce system is only there to serve the economically disadvantaged, WIA is attempting to provide a more universal system capable of serving the employment and training needs of all jobseekers regardless of income.

While WIA was designed to improve the efficacy of the workforce system, at this writing, it has so far had only modest impacts. To a large extent, most local communities are still in the implementation phase of WIA—they are still struggling with the appropriate role of the local WIB, setting up One Stop Centers, and figuring out how training vouchers and performance contracts are supposed to operate.

INSTITUTIONAL FEATURES OF THE CURRENT SECOND CHANCE WORKFORCE SYSTEM

The cumulative result of the public policy decisions of the 1960s through the late 1990s is a workforce system designed primarily to meet the needs of individuals who require a second chance—i.e., individuals who have not been successful at gaining the work related training and education through the traditional mainstream educational and labor market institutions used by the vast majority of citizens in the United States. Despite WIA's attempt to move the workforce system toward a more universal system, workforce development continues to primarily serve the needs of those individuals who have failed to succeed in traditional education and training institutions.

This second chance system is delivered primarily through a vast array of nonprofit organizations—some are large, well-run, well-financed, and highly effective institutions, such as workforce intermediaries, while others are small, fragile groups serving the most disadvantaged individuals in the most distressed environments. The services they provide run the gamut from providing jobseekers help in preparing resumes and calling prospective employers to formal education and occupational skill training. While most of the institutions within the second chance system are nonprofits, there is also some overlap with traditional educational institutions, such as community and technical colleges, and for-profit entities, such as temporary employment agencies.

The nonprofit operators can be large national institutions such as Goodwill Industries or small neighborhood based organizations. Because the roots of the modern workforce field emerge from the service delivery approach embodied in the social reform legislation of the 1960s, many of the nonprofits operating workforce programs are currently or former social service organizations. Since poor and economically disadvantaged people tend to be spatially concentrated, many of these nonprofits also have a geographic focus—city, county, or neighborhood. These geographically focused workforce nonprofits often share service boundaries with the types of community development organizations discussed earlier. (Indeed, many CDCs have operated employment programs as part of their larger community change agenda.)

While workforce intermediaries as described in this book have demonstrated how to effectively deliver workforce services by meeting the needs of both employers seeking employees and disadvantaged jobseekers and workers, most nonprofits lack experience and skill in working on both the supply and demand sides of the labor market. Nevertheless, nonprofits in the second chance system do have some comparative advantage over mainstream educational institutions and for-profit actors aiming to serve the same population. Because many nonprofits are community based, they have an advantage in performing outreach to the residents of a disadvantaged community. Moreover, many of these organizations tend to be committed to reaching the hardest to serve—those with multiple barriers, such as long-term welfare recipients, long-term unemployed, low-income minority youth, and ex-offenders. These are the groups that don't seem to naturally benefit from the rising tide of economic expansion. Program operators who understand—indeed even share—the social and cultural values and norms of a disadvantaged population have a distinct advantage in helping them overcome their obstacles and successfully connect to the mainstream.

Special Challenges to Nonprofits in the New Workforce System

Prior to the introduction of WIA, nonprofits providing employment services to the disadvantaged could depend on grants and contracts from JTPA and other government sources to finance their organizations. While these funds were not always adequate, they were a reasonably reliable source of program financing. But in an effort to improve the quality of services, WIA has shifted to a customer service model. Rather than the WIB deciding which nonprofit will get contracts or grants to deliver employment services, jobseekers, using training vouchers, can now choose which organization they will purchase services from based on the reputation, quality, and features of the service provider. There are a number of implications associated with these changes.

First, this new consumer driven model will require that nonprofits learn to market themselves effectively to the public, an activity in which most have little, if any, experience or expertise. This lack may leave many effective but inexperienced nonprofits without an adequate customer base.

Second, nonprofits will face a more competitive environment, placing a premium on their ability to demonstrate that they can provide services worth paying for. They will compete not only with other nonprofits, but also with mainstream educational institutions and possibly with for-profits. Under JTPA, a good nonprofit grant writer, a politically savvy director, or a strong claim to represent an underserved and disadvantaged constituency could gain the organization access to reliable funding.

Finally, just as in community development, even effective nonprofits are undercapitalized and will be hard-pressed to adjust to new, voucher based reimbursement systems. In short, nonprofits will not get paid until jobseekers use their training vouchers to purchase services. This means that nonprofits in the new system must find a way to finance their operations prior to actually receiving funds. It also means that funds may not come in large payments, as would be the case with grants or contracts, but in small amounts over time. A nonprofit that services 130 individuals a year, in the past would have gotten a grant or contract with a predictable payment stream. Now the same group can serve the same number of individuals over the same period, but the payment stream will probably be much less predictable.

These changes have the potential of having a profound impact on the workforce field, increasing the quality of services throughout the system, but leading to a concentration of capacity to the detriment of the community based, nonprofit portion of the sector. There is every reason to believe that competition will produce a long overdue improvement to services, but coupled with scarcity of funding, it may drive many nonprofits out of the workforce development business. This may be good if what remains are the most effective and most innovative institutions. But there is considerable risk that a shakeout will mean the loss of small but effective community based agencies, serving difficult-to-reach populations not well served by other portions of the workforce system.

PROSPECTS FOR COMMUNITY DEVELOPMENT-LIKE INTERMEDIATION IN THE WORKFORCE SYSTEM

The workforce system continues to be plagued with problems, many of which mirror those in the community development system. First, and most obvious, there are few connected to the workforce field who would argue that existing funds are enough to meet the nation's workforce development needs. Second, the funding stovepipes associated with federal and even some philanthropic funds create huge transaction costs for everyone involved—program operators, clients, employers, and funders. Most observers and program operators see the continued fragmentation of funding as one of the principal stumbling blocks to achieving an effective national workforce system. Third, workforce providers in the second chance system have only weak connections to employers—the demand side of the labor market. And fourth, the capacity and performance of the nonprofits in the second chance system, never strong, may weaken even further under the new voucher based system, which substantially increases costs of marketing, heightens uncertainty of cash flow, and increases demands on service quality.

Intermediation as practiced in community development successfully responded to several of the problems that afflict the workforce system—funding fragmentation, undercapitalization of nonprofit organizations, ineffective services—and the high costs and risk these problems imposed on system participants. Intermediation reduced transaction costs for CDCs and community development funders and investors, increased capacity and production of the CDC industry, established standards of performance, improved the public reputation of the field, and increased the amount of funding available to undertake community development efforts nationwide.

It seems likely that intermediation would also have considerable value in the workforce system, as well. However, potential participants in the workforce system appear not to have strong incentives to create intermediary arrangements.

POTENTIAL VALUE OF INTERMEDIATION

Solving some of these problems is up to workforce providers themselves and the WIBs, but national workforce intermediaries could help bridge financial gaps in the workforce system just as they do in community development, and by doing so, establish themselves as platforms for delivery of capacity building aid to nonprofit providers, makers and monitors of performance standards, and advocates for new funding for the workforce field.

The move toward a competitive, consumer driven model provides a potential opportunity for a financial intermediary. To operate in this new environment, nonprofit providers will require the financial strength to finance program operations absent a predictable funding stream. Most non-profits lack access to bankers able to supply lines of credit to bridge cash flow gaps, which would result from delays in vendor payments. A financial intermediary could provide short-term financing to support working capital, allowing nonprofits to compete in a customer driven delivery system.

Working capital loans or lines of credit would require an intermediary to develop underwriting standards to ensure that providers could repay their loans. These standards could resemble those established in the community development field, where lines of credit secured by organizational assets (in the workforce case, voucher payments-receivable) are available to organizations that pass strict standards for financial management and service quality. These standards would have considerable value in signaling to all organizations which types of program delivery and organizational management capacities would need to be developed. Finally, setting such standards would help allay employer suspicions that graduates of the second chance system fail basic tests of employability, as access to lines of credit and other organizational support would depend on the demonstrated value of the services nonprofit agencies provide.

Once established, intermediaries could take on other roles, as well, just as they do in community development—as conduits for the supply of operating support, as providers or arrangers of technical assistance, and as advocates for increased funding for the field. Intermediary ability to carry out these tasks over the long haul, however, would appear to rest on their successful performance of a financial role in the workforce system, which, as in community development, would give them the needed credibility among system players and knowledge of the problems and challenges providers face.

FEASIBILITY ISSUES FOR WORKFORCE INTERMEDIATION

The key to the success of financial intermediaries in community development is their business model. It seems likely that replicating this model will prove far more difficult in the workforce field than in community development, where the low-income housing tax credit provided a tailor-made source of intermediary revenue, and a firm rationale for system participation.

A financial intermediary in the workforce field would have to develop a sustainable financing model that would allow it to at least partially fund its own operations. One source of financing for the intermediary might be the fees and interest charged to nonprofits for loans. Another source might be investment earnings on idle funds. A third source might be the syndication fees from organizing investment pools using existing job related tax credits.

But support from other sources is required to support an intermediary's own operations and the range of services it provides. However, a basic incentive to corporate contributions to community development intermediary funding would also appear to be lacking in the workforce field. In community development, relatively few banks account for most of real estate finance transactions, and further, a small number of successful investments by CDCs, if they are large and targeted, can help generate spin-off demand for home mortgages, home rehab loans, commercial loans, and so on. Federal law requiring bank community reinvestment adds a regulatory incentive to participate actively in CDC projects or in lending in low-income neighborhoods. The upshot is a clear connection between bank participation in intermediary sponsored programs and ultimate financial benefits to banks.

In workforce, no single employer or small group of employers would appear to have a strong interest in the overall quality of the second chance system. None have as large a share of their respective markets as do banks; without spin-offs to the overall labor market, graduates from the second chance system would appear to be a rather small portion of their overall hiring. Industry associations and unions might take on this role, e.g., a hotel industry association or the Service Employees International Union would appear to be logical participants in an intermediated workforce system. An intermediary with clearly defined standards for financing high-performing programs just might be able to convince employers that programs funded by the intermediary are capable of producing the high-quality employees they seek. For its part, the public sector economic development community has increasingly embraced the role of workforce development as an economic development tool. State and local publicly funded economic development programs might be willing to invest in such an intermediary if it strengthens the local institutions that help to provide a skilled workforce, but the size of these contributions is likely to be very modest.

The philanthropic community, which supported start up of community development intermediaries, displays comparatively modest interest in workforce issues, although there are several large foundations funding workforce development. If the employer community, as suggested here, lacks strong incentives to participate in intermediary supported activities, creation of an intermediated system would rest almost solely on philanthropic contributions, which funders may have insufficient interest, or ability, to provide.

NOTES

1. This research was supported by Living Cities: The National Community Development Initiative. Two major summary reports on the Initiative were published in 2002, and cited in the references as Walker (2002) and Walker, Gustafson, and Snow (2002).

2. These investments generally reflect a basic premise that an individual's life chances are shaped by the support available from family and community on the one hand, and the availability of social and economic opportunities on the other. To the degree that neighborhoods provide little support or afford few opportunities, the educational, social, and economic promise is diminished thereby. This means that investments in community development help people directly, but also help others who are not their primary beneficiaries. For example, better quality and more affordable housing benefits those who reside there, but also helps improve the overall quality of urban neighborhoods, a benefit to everyone.

3. The value of CDCs in their role of community based market participants active in the delivery of coordinated programs tailored to neighborhood circumstances appears greatest where neighborhoods have clear social, economic, and political relevance. Particularly in the Northeast and Midwest, it is meaningful for investors to speak in terms of neighborhood residential and commercial markets, residents tend to recognize their allegiance to a neighborhood with distinct social characteristics, and political participation and representation tend to reflect distinct neighborhood interests, and city politics is driven, in large part, by these interests.

4. It's essential to point out that some CDC industries remain afflicted by these problems despite the best efforts of local intermediaries and their supporters.

5. The roots of workforce development go back to a much earlier period. From 1862 to 1945, there were several pieces of key legislation that helped to establish a government role in supporting workforce development. In particular, during this span of time, Congress passed four laws that helped establish government support for worker training. In 1862 the Morrill Land Grant College Act was passed to encourage the development of a competitive farm workforce. The second piece of legislation was the Smith-Hughes Act of 1917. It provided federal funding for vocational education as a strategy for promoting a skilled workforce. In 1933 the Wagner-Peyser Act established a nationwide employment service to assist dislocated workers and to provide an economic safety net. Finally, in 1944 the Congress passed the GI bill, which provided support for returning soldiers to continue their education.

6. These included the 1954 Vocational Rehabilitation Act, concentrated on the rehabilitation and employment of the disabled; the 1962 Manpower Development Training Act, intended to support the retraining of workers who had been displaced

due to technological changes; the 1963 Youth Unemployment Act that set up the Youth Conservation Corps; and the 1964 Civil Rights Act that assisted minority individuals to enter occupations that had been closed to them because of racial and ethnic discrimination.

REFERENCES

Cummings, Jean, and Denise DiPasquale. 1999. "The Low Income Housing Tax Credit: An Analysis of the First Ten Years." *Housing Policy Debate*, Vol. 10, No. 2.

National Congress for Community Economic Development. 1998. *Coming of Age: Trends and Achievements of Community-Based Development Organizations*. Washington, DC: NCCED.

O'Conner, Alice. 1999. "Swimming Against the Tide: A Brief History of Federal Policy in Poor Communities." In Ronald Ferguson and William Dickens, eds. *Urban Problems and Community Development*. Washington, DC: Brookings Institution Press.

Stegman, Michael. 1991. "The Excessive Costs of Creative Finance: Growing Inefficiencies in the Production of Low Income Housing." *Housing Policy Debate*, Vol. 2, No. 2.

von Hoffman, Alexander. 2001. *Fuel Lines for the Urban Revival Engine*. Washington, DC: Fannie Mae Foundation.

Walker, Christopher, Jeremy Gustafson, and Chris Snow. 2002. *National Support for Local Systems Change: The Effect of the National Community Development Initiative on Community Development Systems*. Washington, DC: Urban Institute.

Walker, Christopher. 2002. *Community Development Corporations and Their Changing Support Systems*. Washington, DC: Urban Institute.

VI
CONCLUSION

15

Conclusion: A Future for Workforce Intermediaries

ROBERT P. GILOTH

O N THE WEEKEND OF FEB. 6–9, 2003, 70 WORKFORCE DEVELOPMENT professionals brought an advance draft of this volume to a mountain-top retreat for the 102nd American Assembly on the future of workforce intermediaries. Arriving by buses and cars, the participants included business leaders, workforce practitioners, policy makers, academics, journalists, public sector officials, and foundation program officers. Over the next four days, they broke into three discussion groups that considered a set of questions about workforce intermediaries, listened to plenary speakers David Ellwood of the Kennedy School and Jeremy Nowak of The Reinvestment Fund, and participated in panel discussions on the relationship between workforce intermediaries and the public workforce development system.

A distinguishing quality of each American Assembly is that delegates ultimately produce a policy report that is collectively edited. To arrive at this destination, discussion groups each considered common questions about the definition and characteristics of workforce intermediaries, the role of the business sector, and relevant partnerships, policies, and investments that would advance the practice and results of workforce intermediaries. Then, the Assembly's co-directors, group facilitators, and documenters pulled an all-nighter to draft a report they slipped under delegate doors at 4:00 A.M. The report included a problem statement, strategic approach, and specific recommendations for expanding the practice of workforce intermediaries.

On Sunday morning, everyone gathered for a three-hour editing session that clarified recommendations, added new ideas, and deleted unpopular concepts. By noon, to everyone's surprise, a document that represented the spirit of the Assembly had emerged. This report, "Keeping America in

Business: Advancing Workers, Businesses, and Economic Growth," was published and disseminated in March 2003 and is included in this volume.

The concluding chapter of this volume of research and perspectives on workforce intermediaries seeks to accomplish four objectives:

- Revisit the workforce intermediary premise in light of Assembly discussions.
- Summarize salient research findings and policy recommendations contained in this book.
- Describe overarching Assembly strategies to expand workforce intermediaries.
- Discuss more specific Assembly recommendations to expand workforce intermediaries.

THE WORKFORCE INTERMEDIARY
PREMISE AND DISCUSSIONS

Although participants revised and amended the report, they generally endorsed the Assembly's framing premise about the importance of workforce intermediaries. That agreement served as a foundation for developing specific recommendations and an overall strategy to expand workforce intermediaries.

The framing premise of the Assembly argued that a new set of workforce practices and organizations has emerged in the past decade, named workforce intermediaries, that are producing new and important results for business and for workers/jobseekers, especially the opportunity for low-income workers to experience real career advancement. These intermediaries are eclectic in origin and sponsorship, but they play similar roles in being dual customer, brokering partnerships and relationships, integrating a variety of resources, and developing new occupations, workplace tools, and policy agendas.

Although the number of these intermediaries is growing, their prevalence is still narrow, and their effectiveness is promising but still unproven by the most rigorous standards. To fulfill their promise and advance their workforce innovations, Assembly sponsors believe, requires more ambitious and targeted policies.

While general agreement existed on this overall premise, important debates and amendments occurred during the four days of the Assembly. Not every debate was fully resolved or captured in the Assembly's Final Report. Five of the most important debates are summarized.

Workforce Crisis

During a first-evening plenary session, David Ellwood of the Kennedy School discussed the recently published *Grow Faster Together Or Grow Slowly Apart* report produced by the Domestic Strategy Group of the Aspen Institute (2003). (Ellwood was director of the Domestic Strategy Group during the preparation of this report.)

The report and Ellwood's talk clearly placed the workforce development challenge in the context of the U.S. economy's long-term health. He argued that the declining supply of new workers, lack of skills growth, and wage stagnation present severe challenges for the U.S. economy, whose growth in the past decades depended upon a rapidly expanding labor force and a growth in skills and productivity. Among many solutions offered, Ellwood and the Domestic Strategy Group spotlighted the practices of workforce intermediaries, especially sector based workforce efforts, and the Earned Income Tax Credit.

The Assembly adopted two rallying cries—promote economic prosperity and meet the looming workforce crisis—to spur discussions about workforce intermediaries.

Approach versus Organization

The introduction of a relatively new term—workforce intermediary—produced a considerable amount of discussion at the Assembly. And the shortening of workforce intermediary into "WI" aggravated concerns even more, as though introducing an acronym was akin to moving in the direction of a short-term, policy fashion.

There were three parts to these discussions, not of equal importance. The first worried that legislators, the media, advocates, and investors can easily pick up new terms and phrases without paying attention to the substance behind the phrasing. The result may be more confusion and acronyms that businesses and jobseekers do not understand.

Moreover, the aim of using the workforce intermediary language was to provide a common umbrella term to include sector partnerships, employer intermediaries, labor/management partnerships, and the like. But the umbrella banner of workforce intermediaries could diminish the identity and efficacy of intermediary organizations and networks in these specific niches, thus potentially undermining their ability to advocate effectively for their members.

Second, some participants believed that the intermediary language created a "them and us" feeling—that is, an elite, high-performing set of groups, and the rest of the system and workforce providers. This notion could cause several problems.

On one hand, building an effective coalition to advocate for the disrespected and underfunded workforce development field is more difficult if some groups are valued more—and more likely to receive funding—than others. Bowing to this fear, the majority of the Assembly voted to exclude from the report a sidebar about one well-known workforce intermediary.

On the other hand, the fundamental premise of the workforce intermediary discussion is that a small but growing number of partnerships are obtaining worker and business results that differ from those achieved in the workforce field in general. By definition, workforce intermediary equals outstanding results. Creating a level playing field may be good for politics and egos but not for making a more effective argument that workforce development in general can make a difference.

Most Assembly participants vividly remembered the saga of the Center for Employment Training, which became CET. It was adopted by the U.S. Department of Labor as a panacea and replicated around the country. A program with strong results was dumbed down and replicated too quickly, in the process losing the key ingredients that made it effective in the first place.

The third concern in some ways most influenced the writing of the Assembly's report and its overall strategy for expanding workforce intermediaries. As noted in the introductory chapter, workforce intermediaries include two components: a strategy and role, and a set of organizational characteristics. The strategy and role consist of the dual customer workforce model, brokering services and partnerships, integrating a variety of resources, and generating workforce innovations for workers, employers, partners, and policy makers. Organizational characteristics include entrepreneurship, focus on results, and adaptive learning—that is, the ability to learn from ongoing practices and changes in the environment. Both components need to be in place for workforce intermediaries to produce results. It is dangerously easy to conclude from the workforce intermediary discussion that a new class of organizations should be launched to achieve career advancement and employer results. In fact, many new workforce intermediaries started up because no one else was focusing on these promising strategies. For better or worse, insufficient public and private resources exist to create new organizations to perform functions that many other organizations feel they are mandated to pursue.

But the alternative approach of encouraging existing organizations, such as community colleges or Chambers of Commerce, to adopt workforce intermediary strategies presents its own challenges. This strategy is discussed in more detail below. The danger is that these organizations will rename their programs as workforce intermediaries while remaining the same program driven, bureaucratic institutions, or organizations devoted to only one of the key customers. Strong program elements languishing in a non-dynamic, non-learning organization will wither.

A larger problem for workforce intermediaries, as well as for other workforce organizations, is that employers maintain a negative perception of many workforce organizations, in part derived from negative attitudes about the welfare-to-work population, especially communities of color. These attitudes are transferred to organizations that advocate for low-income populations, though not all workforce organizations are considered the same. Employers rate community colleges as most reliably meeting their needs. A significant challenge for workforce intermediaries is to change business perceptions.

Business and Economic Development

Many workforce development gatherings, such as The American Assembly, attract the usual policy, practice, advocacy, and academic suspects. While Assembly organizers emphasized the importance of business participation in the meeting, few representatives of business showed up. Even the language surrounding business became dicey. Some delegates felt using the word *employer* only partially represented the role and interests of business in workforce development. Their bottom line purpose as profit-making entities that produce goods and services consists of more than the employer function. They are businesses.

While emphasizing the dual customer focus of workforce intermediaries, the outcomes framed most strongly at the outset of the Assembly related to career advancement for low-income, low-skilled workers. Assembly discussions, however, emphasized that increasing the economic productivity of businesses, and their ability to grow and thrive, as the real selling point for workforce intermediaries. This is the argument that had not been made to date with significant force, but that provided the most compelling rationale for long-term public and private investment in workforce development. Ultimately, the title and recommendations of The American Assembly report, "Keeping America in Business: Advancing Workers, Business, and Economic Growth," tried to communicate the right balance.

The challenge of adequately recognizing the role of business in workforce development is also a question of measuring outcomes and benefits. Unfortunately, measurement problems exist for both business and worker customers. Nonetheless, more attention is being paid to measuring retention and advancement for workers than to the benefits for businesses, such as reduced recruitment costs, turnover, and higher productivity. Although the phrase "return on investment" is regularly invoked to describe business benefits, the measurement tools for capturing business benefits at the level of workforce projects are inadequate and seldom used.

This imbalance is further complicated by evaluation challenges. On the jobseeker side, workforce intermediaries are under fire for not having their impacts confirmed by the "gold standard," rigorous, random assignment evaluation models. For firms and industries, almost no good way to evaluate business and sector effects exists. Paradoxically, paying more attention to improving the evaluation measures for one customer may undercut the ability to evaluate the impacts on the other customer. For example, a random assignment evaluation model for examining impacts on workers might make it more difficult to capture industry or policy effects because of the focused attention on a more narrow program intervention.

Who Is the Worker Customer?

An estimated 15 to 50 million people need workforce services in the United States. The American Assembly began its discussions by using the term "low-income workers" and ultimately adopted the phrase "low-wage, low-skilled workers" in its Final Report. The point delegates tried to make is that not all low-wage workers are low-skilled, and not all low-skilled workers are low-wage. An emphasis on career advancement almost by definition requires this broader definition of workers.

This debate and compromise are not new. Many employers and unions, for example, do not want to focus only on the low-income and low-skilled. They either want to promote the continued livelihoods of their existing membership or ensure that they get the best-qualified employees. Many employers and unions do not want to subdivide their workers by social service eligibility requirements. Businesses, moreover, often maintain negative perceptions of hardest to employ workers, and they rarely acknowledge that any job is low wage or dead end. So focusing just on the hardest to employ worker is a framework too narrow for action.

Discussions about these phrases and their meanings are part of a broader policy and politics debate. The Workforce Investment Act (WIA), for example, with its One Stop Career Centers, provides universal access to all requiring employment services. This approach partially has been guided by the understanding that everyone needs to invest in lifelong learning.

Moreover, workforce development needs to escape the past perception that it represents only a second chance system that delivers second-rate services.

Not all low-income jobseekers and workers find this universal service approach welcoming, supportive, and comprehensible. They have voted with their feet and are not taking advantage of many work supports and post employment services. This trend is exacerbated by the rigid performance requirements applied by WIA that focus services on the easier to employ, just as its predecessor, the Job Training Partnership Act (JTPA), did.

The larger political issue is: how do we make workforce development a priority for more Americans? Many believe that this can only be accomplished if we build a broader coalition of workers, businesses, unions, and communities to advocate for more sensible, effective, and better funded workforce investments. Such an agenda will not go very far, however, if it is perceived as only an issue for the poor.

Summary

The above debates demonstrate that American Assembly participants seriously grappled with the workforce intermediary premise, producing a more nuanced definition and laying the groundwork for a viable strategy for increasing the scale and impact of workforce intermediaries. Ongoing discussions will be required to incorporate all implications of these debates.

FINDINGS AND POLICY RECOMMENDATIONS FROM CHAPTERS

This volume represents a unique resource about the emerging theory and practice of workforce intermediaries from a number of perspectives. The richness of these perspectives is so important at this early stage because we are trying to understand the workforce intermediary role and practice. Moreover, from a policy point of view, it is important to develop approaches for expanding these workforce innovations that are anchored in this understanding of their roles, capacities, performance, and constraints.

Two types of information about workforce intermediaries presented in the chapters are summarized below: research findings and interpretation, and policy recommendations. This selective review does not capture the breadth and depth of the chapters, but it does help set the context for subsequent discussions on the Assembly's workforce intermediary strategies and recommendations.

Research Findings

The chapters in this volume use key informant interviews, surveys, focus groups, ethnographies, meta-analysis, participant observation, and economic, demographic, and policy analysis to shed light on the role, rationale, and performance of workforce intermediaries. These findings comprise information about the definition, characteristics, and capacities of workforce intermediaries.

A number of chapters added nuance to our definition of workforce intermediary, especially related to the intermediary role. Several chapters argue that workforce intermediaries are "market makers" not "market meeters" that work with business to create economic development, such as expanded market opportunities, career ladders, and improved job quality. The implication is that intermediaries are highly market oriented and have close relationships with business.

Chapters also emphasize the mediating role that workforce intermediaries play in the labor market, connecting frequently disparate elements for the benefit of business and workers. One author described the role as being an "information broker" that translates data into usable and strategic information.

A survey of workforce intermediaries by the National Network of Sector Partners showed that 20 percent of the respondents were Workforce Investment Boards, and more than half were less than 10 years old. Sixty-six percent served fewer than 500 workers per year, and more than 82 percent served more than 11 employers. Fifty-five percent placed jobseekers in jobs with an average starting wage of $9.50 per hour.

Another chapter interviewed nonprofit organizations about capacity building. The key finding was that respondents saw their capacity needs as related to core organizational functions, like finance and human resources, and to the capacity to make changes and course corrections, or what has been named adaptive capacity. The priority was not on what is most often provided—principles case studies, and tool kits about effective strategies.

Policy Recommendations

Although chapter authors were not asked to produce policy and program recommendations, they could not help themselves. The year 2003 is the time for federal legislative reauthorizations; getting good ideas on the table is important and irresistible. In the end, the authors' attention to policy provided a foundation of ideas and proposals that informed Assembly discussions and the Final Report.

Several chapters provided conceptual advice. In the finance chapter, for example, the authors divided their attention between policies supporting workforce intermediaries and policies supporting career advancement for low-skilled workers. The authors related financing gaps related to career advancement, services to employers, planning/program development, and state level initiatives. The chapter that compared workforce development and community development, however, cautioned that no workforce financing mechanism exists (such as the low-income housing tax credit) to organize the workforce industry and production.

Authors offered many recommendations about how to reorganize federal welfare and workforce legislation. These recommendations advocated for increased training resources, easier access to training, greater flexibility in work requirements, greater funding for employer organizing, and more sector/employer demonstrations. Also much attention was paid to improving and integrating systems that measure workforce and welfare performance.

In the finance arena, authors advocated for changes in Pell Grants and student aid loans to help working adults move ahead. They also suggested the need for new financing mechanisms, such as Lifelong Learning Accounts. The finance chapter offers several scenarios in which state/federal/philanthropic venture funds can invest in workforce intermediaries.

Building the learning and adaptive capacity of workforce intermediaries requires both new resources and high-engagement grantmaking (investor) approaches. Local foundation consortia, similar to community development support collaboratives, working in conjunction with Workforce Investment Boards, could be mechanisms to build this local capacity.

Finally, an expanded research and evaluation agenda on workforce intermediaries is important to build the public policy case to support their work. In particular, much can be learned about the benefits of workforce intermediaries for individual businesses, industries, and local workforce systems. Also the impact of the economic downturn on the role, behavior, and performance of workforce intermediaries needs to be understood in greater detail.

THE ASSEMBLY WORKFORCE INTERMEDIARY STRATEGIES

The report drafting committee, and ultimately the whole Assembly, had to distill from the readings, plenary speakers, panels, and discussion groups a set of strategies and recommendations. The key strategic problem they faced was how to expand dramatically the promising practices of workforce intermediaries to reach more firms and workers, preserve the potency of the intermediary role, stay cost-effective in the context of limited resources, and contribute to promoting economic development and solving the impending workforce crisis.

Paradoxically, the evolutionary path of the current population of workforce intermediaries may not be the appropriate model for future development if scale is important. Over the past 30 years, workforce intermediaries emerged in a haphazard, entrepreneurial manner, promoted by a unique group of social innovators, frequently in spite of public workforce systems, although they drew upon a range of public and private resources. Not surprisingly, relatively few workforce intermediaries have matured and achieved impressive results, probably a smaller group of the 243 intermediaries identified by the National Network of Sector Partners.

The question is whether public policy, supplemented by private and philanthropic investments, fosters these unique, entrepreneur dependent partnerships.

Well, maybe one overall policy won't help because:

- Workforce intermediaries are built one by one, not in cookie cutter fashion.
- Insufficient resources exist to build a new class of organizations.
- A new set of organizations at scale is disadvantageous because they will produce increased fragmentation, duplication, and confusion within the already fragmented and uncoordinated workforce non-system.

Perhaps scaling up workforce intermediaries will require anointing one high-performing example and replicating it. The U.S. Department of Labor adopted such a strategy in the early 1990s regarding the Center for Employment Training, which stood out in multiple rigorous evaluations as producing substantial income effects for participants. The mantra became "1,000 CETs" throughout the land. Unfortunately, the very ingredients that made it work in the first place—deep relationships with communities and businesses, flexibility, and the ability to change—were lost in attempts to scale up.

Other attempts to expand the number of workforce intermediaries have been tried by the Jobs Initiative of the Annie E. Casey Foundation. Three principles of this six-city, eight-year, $30 million effort are relevant for this discussion.

1. The initiative tried to replicate effective programs by extracting key design features (such as dual customer, integrated services, results orientation) and then tried to grow these programs in different economic and institutional atmospheres.

2. Regional investors must be enlisted to assemble the appropriate partnerships and resources while defining and being accountable for results.

3. Building adaptive capacity requires a multi-year investment, support of data collection and reflection, peer learning, and accountability for results.

The drawback of the Jobs Initiative approach to expanding workforce intermediaries is twofold. First, initial stages of this work sometimes bypassed the public workforce development system, choosing instead to work with a diverse set of investors that ranged from union/employer partnerships to community development financial institutions. This lack of engagement with workforce systems, including Private Industry Councils, had several short-run negative effects: it created rivalries, failed to enlist and leverage public support, and fostered the idea that the Jobs Initiative was simply a "boutique" foundation project.

Second, the Jobs Initiative depended upon a large and long-term investment of flexible foundation dollars. The foundation required sites to obtain matching funds that were also flexible. This created a damned-if-you-do and damned-if-you-don't situation. Flexible, long-term money is scarce in many metropolitan and rural regions; but without such flexible funds, workforce intermediaries cannot pay for industry organizing, brokering services, data systems, and start up costs.

With these possible approaches in mind, and considering debates about intermediary approaches and organizations, The American Assembly broadly agreed upon a three-part strategy to expand workforce intermediaries in the future.

- The primary strategy for expanding workforce intermediaries is to encourage the existing infrastructure of community colleges, Workforce Investment Boards, union/management funds, and employer organizations to adopt the entrepreneurial and results oriented characteristics of the workforce intermediary approach. This infrastructure represents thousands of organizations with resources, membership, interest in workforce development, and civic relationships to build upon. They represent a diversity of strategic and organizational starting points.

- This intermediary strategy will only work if financing for intermediaries and career advancement projects is increased, is made more accessible, is flexible, and is related to the most effective practices. The belief was that if options within the workforce arena are increased, both the role of and resources for workforce intermediaries is enhanced. In short, if the pieces of the puzzle are present, entrepreneurs will build workforce intermediaries to assemble them.

- These strategies will only be successful, however, if the business community and a broader constituency are built to confront the coming workforce crisis and to create the leadership needed to expand the resources and practices of workforce intermediaries.

SPECIFIC AMERICAN
ASSEMBLY RECOMMENDATIONS

The recommendations contained in The American Assembly report offer concrete suggestions on how to implement these strategies to expand workforce intermediaries. The report does not delve into ways to spread the intermediary role; rather, it focuses on identifying some of the most important building blocks. This section briefly presents the key ideas and suggestions for each of the five recommendation areas in the report. More details and suggestions are included in the Final Report.

- *Raise the Nation's Awareness.* The coming workforce crisis—a shortfall of workers and skills—threatens U.S. economic prosperity. The business community must take the lead in convincing policy makers and the public that this crisis is looming and can be solved. A national commission or public awareness campaign is needed, along the lines of earlier calls to action, such as *A Nation at Risk* or *America's Choice: High Skills or Low Wages*, which focused national attention on our need to invest in skills to remain globally competitive.
- *Integrate Effective Policy.* The country needs an integrated set of financing tools for career advancement and work supports, plus performance tests that measure benefits to employers and workers and do not distort the workforce system. Some of the best examples of these integrated policy frameworks exist at the state level, frequently focusing on specific industries or employer/worker partnerships.
- *Create Smarter Financing.* Long-term, predictable financing is required to support important intermediary roles, such as employer organizing, brokering services, and labor market innovation. The low-income housing tax credit has supported affordable housing and community development, although tax incentives have proven less effective in the workforce development arena. A workforce intermediary fund, financed by the federal government, the private sector, and foundations, should be a long-term goal.

- *Build Capacity.* The adaptive learning capacity of workforce intermediaries is a distinguishing feature, allowing them to be as nimble as the most high-performing firms. Investments in technical assistance, peer networks, human capital, and high performance must be made if the field of workforce intermediaries is to grow and retain its most powerful features.
- *Build a Constituency for Action.* Responding to the workforce crisis and building the workforce intermediary field is not a one-time investment of leadership and political capital. It is a long-run campaign. Business, labor, community organizations, workforce intermediaries, and a host of others must invest in public awareness, leadership, new coalitions of unlikely allies, and an agenda for action.

THINKING ABOUT INSTITUTIONAL CHANGE AND NEXT STEPS

American Assembly dialogues are effective if they promote a better understanding of important social problems and offer practical solutions. From the vantage point of early 2003, it is difficult to be optimistic about whether business leadership and policy makers will be willing to put aside preoccupations with war, budget deficits, and tax cuts to focus on the workforce crisis. And yet they should. The workforce crisis arguably portends an even greater threat to U.S prosperity, stability, and security.

Sponsors of this American Assembly on workforce intermediaries met to map out a three-year strategy even before the Final Report was published in March 2003. In fact, implementation caucuses met at the Assembly itself. They talked of short-term opportunities to influence the multiple workforce reauthorizations in 2003, but they also agreed that they needed to keep their eyes on a long-term goal, such as creating a $100 million fund for spreading the workforce intermediary role.

The American Assembly produced some immediate impacts, including actionable policy ideas, foundation proposals, forums, more buzz about the workforce crisis, and individual organizations taking up the call to action. Another important challenge for the group of sponsors was how to enlist many voices and perspectives while staying on course and maintaining consistency about the vision and practice of workforce intermediaries.

It is therefore worth suggesting that this group of workforce intermediary advocates consider several questions and opportunities as they map strategies and make various investments. These suggestions go to the heart of a question that The American Assembly posed: how do we encourage institutions, such as community colleges and Workforce Investment Boards, not only to adopt ideas and visions, but to transform themselves into entrepreneurial and results oriented partnerships? Much can be learned from other organizational systems that have tried to transform themselves, whether they are school systems or private sector firms. There will always be "early adopters." The challenge is to go far beyond this group. Five approaches, discussed at the Assembly, provide a starting point.

- *Change the Rules.* Public policy rules and organizational incentives that govern community colleges and the workforce system need to be changed to emphasize employer partnerships, career advancement, innovation, and integration of funding streams.
- *Enrich the Environment.* A supportive policy environment is needed to provide the resources and flexibility required for career advancement strategies and sector or industry based organizing. This could be accomplished on a state and/or industry basis.
- *Find Entrepreneurs.* Leaders who are willing to take risks must lead the process of transforming their institutions (or parts of their institutions) into workforce intermediaries. This will not happen without unusual leadership and commitment.
- *Reward Performance.* Performance of the workforce system has been unsatisfactory. Workforce intermediaries, by definition, are high performing. High performance must be defined, identified, and rewarded as one method of spurring leadership and innovation. Groups must resist the urge to lower standards in order to create a "big tent" movement for workforce intermediaries.
- *Build a Movement.* Ultimately, high performers banding together to share best practices, compare costs and impacts, and advocate will build the workforce intermediary movement. Their performance and leadership will convince others to undertake the challenging endeavor of becoming a workforce intermediary.

Some labor economists say that tight labor markets make everything possible in workforce development. The boom of the 1990s demonstrated the truth of this insight as business embraced workforce development as its top priority and changed many of its employment practices related to front-line workers. Economic development was at stake.

We are at a crossroads in workforce development. In the future, a dwindling supply of domestic labor and diminishing skills will make tight labor markets a way of life. On the other hand, an emerging and expanding group of workforce intermediaries has shown that workforce development can deliver important benefits for workers and businesses. Their work is mirrored, in part, by slow but steady improvements in the public workforce development systems to become more demand and results oriented.

The question is: will we use this unprecedented crisis and depth of economic incentives to build a world-class workforce development system, one that is entrepreneurial, nimble, and partnership based? Now is the time to begin this process if we are to avoid a future of slower economic growth and widening disparities in wealth and quality of life.

REFERENCE

Aspen Institute, Domestic Strategy Group. 2002. *Grow Faster Together or Grow Slowly Apart.* Washington, DC: The Aspen Institute.

APPENDIX

Final Report of the
102nd American Assembly

Steering Committee

About The American Assembly

Final Report of the 102nd American Assembly

PREFACE

On Feb. 6, 2003, 75 men and women representing business, labor, academia, government, workforce intermediaries, nonprofit organizations, and the media gathered at Arden House in Harriman, N.Y., for the 102nd American Assembly entitled "Achieving Worker Success and Business Prosperity: The New Role for Workforce Intermediaries." For three days, participants examined policies, approaches, and actions that need to be taken to assure that workers have access to economic opportunity and to assure that employers have access to the skilled workforce required for them to be globally competitive.

This project was directed by Robert Giloth, director of family economic success, the Annie E. Casey Foundation; John Colborn, deputy director, Economic Development Unit, the Ford Foundation; and Betsy Biemann, associate director, Working Communities, the Rockefeller Foundation. The project was also ably assisted by a steering committee of distinguished leaders from around the country, whose names and affiliations are listed in this report.

Background papers were prepared for participants under the editorial supervision of Robert Giloth. During the Assembly, participants heard formal addresses by David Ellwood, Lucius N. Littauer Professor of Political Science, John F. Kennedy School of Government, Harvard University; and Jeremy Nowak, president/CEO, The Reinvestment Fund. Richard M. McGahey, managing vice president, Abt Associates Inc., moderated a panel of Timothy M. Barnicle, co-director, Workforce Development Program, National Center on Education and the Economy; Steve Crawford, director, Employment and Social Services Policy Studies, National Governors' Association; and Jackie Edens, commissioner, Mayor's Office of Workforce Development, Chicago. Mr. Giloth also moderated an introductory panel that included Cynthia E. Marano, director, National Network of Sector Partners, National Economic Development and Law Center; Marlene Seltzer, president, Jobs for the Future; and Julie Strawn, senior policy analyst, Center for Law and Social Policy.

Following their discussions, participants issued this report on Feb. 9, 2003. It contains both their findings and recommendations.

The text of this report is available on both The American Assembly's website (www.americanassembly.com) and the project's webpage (www.opportunitiesatwork.org), which also contains links to many of the organizations involved in this project.

We gratefully acknowledge the support of the Annie E. Casey Foundation, the Ford Foundation, the Rockefeller Foundation, the John D. and Catherine T. MacArthur Foundation, and the Open Society Institute, Baltimore.

The American Assembly takes no positions on any subjects presented here for public discussion. In addition, it should be noted that participants took part in this meeting as individuals and spoke for themselves rather than for their affiliated organizations and institutions.

We would like to express special appreciation for the fine work of the discussion leaders, rapporteurs, and advisors in helping to prepare the final draft of this report: Daniel Berry, Paul Brophy, Terri Feeley, Lisa Kaplan Gordon, Ed Hatcher, Cynthia Marano, Richard McGahey, Julie Strawn, and Orson Watson.

DAVID H. MORTIMER
The American Assembly

FOREWORD

Over the past decade, a set of workforce development policies and strategies has emerged to meet the needs of both businesses and low-wage, low-skilled workers. In some cases, the results have been nothing less than remarkable: employers are finding a well-trained competitive workforce while at the same time workers are being placed in jobs that can sustain their families.

The opportunity exists to spread this workforce intermediary approach, as this Assembly has named it, to a wider array of existing institutions in order to achieve greater impact. Achieving this impact will not be easy. Employers and job training providers adopting "promising workforce practices" won't get the job done.

The challenge ahead is about transforming workforce development practices in a variety of institutional settings, such as community colleges, workforce boards, labor unions, employer associations, and community organizations. It is about creating and sustaining entrepreneurial organizations that have the commitment and capacity for innovation and to build partnerships, learn, change directions, and relentlessly pursue results.

Transforming workforce development practices, however, will only occur if there is top-level leadership committed to this agenda. Public and private workforce development resources must lay the groundwork to support the pursuit and achievement of substantial results.

The report of this American Assembly provides hope and, most importantly, direction for a broad spectrum of workforce practitioners, business organizations, and advocates who are ready to take on this challenge. Given the current and impending workforce crises that threaten the future of America's families and businesses, the time is right.

We are proud to have supported and participated in this important civic dialogue. But this is just the beginning. We look forward to working in collaboration with our workforce development colleagues to advance this critical agenda in the months and years to come.

Betsy Biemann	John Colborn	Robert Giloth
Co-director	Co-director	Co-director
The 102nd American Assembly	The 102nd American Assembly	The 102nd American Assembly

KEEPING AMERICA IN BUSINESS: ADVANCING WORKERS, BUSINESSES, AND ECONOMIC GROWTH

At the close of their discussions, the participants in the 102nd American Assembly on "Achieving Worker Success and Business Prosperity: The New Role for Workforce Intermediaries," at Arden House, Harriman, New York, February 6–9, 2003, reviewed as a group the following statement. The statement represents general agreement; however, no one was asked to sign it. Furthermore, it should be understood that not everyone agreed with all of it.

INTRODUCTION

As the twenty-first century begins, the prosperity of the United States depends increasingly on the strength of its workforce. The world is becoming one economy, and nations that fully utilize their workers are more likely to thrive than those that do not.

There is a crisis emerging in America: workforce. The future worker shortage in the United States, the lack of worker skills, the increasing wage gaps, the disjointed public programs, and the absence of business participation all contribute to the crisis. But most importantly, it is the failure of our nation to recognize and respond to these challenges that presents the greatest risk.

Over the past 20 years, a dramatic increase in the size and skill of America's labor force has driven its economic growth. Baby boomers were in their prime employment years, and large numbers of women entered the labor force. New workers emerged far more educated than those they replaced. The number of college educated workers more than doubled.

These trends have ended. More than one-third of the nation's current workforce lack the basic skills needed to succeed in today's labor market. During the next 20 years, the American workforce is expected to grow by only half of its earlier pace: there will be no growth of native-born workers in their prime working years; the percentage of the labor force composed of four-year college graduates is predicted to stagnate over the next two decades; the number of workers with two-year degrees and skill certificates will fall far short of the economy's needs.

These labor force trends are exacerbated by globalizing competition and accelerating technological requirements in both domestic and export sectors. Taken together, these trends will lead to severe consequences for the vibrancy of the American economy and businesses. Problems on the horizon include:

- Unfilled jobs and productivity.
- Skill shortages.
- A decrease in regional economic competitiveness for some of the nation's cities and rural communities.
- A loss of jobs to overseas workers.

However, these problems can create opportunities to better involve overlooked labor market pools in the U.S.

A strong economy depends on labor force growth and increased productivity. But if the nation's labor force does not grow, then we must find ways to increase the productivity of all American workers to meet the demands of future jobs.

Today, U.S. tax dollars support workforce development through a fragmented and underfunded patchwork system. In many communities, employers indicate that the workforce development system does not meet their needs, and their engagement in workforce development programs has been superficial; publicly funded workforce programs have been constrained by funding that follows individual personal eligibility and political boundaries rather than regional economies; and systems improvements have proved elusive. As a result, employers still struggle to find workers who can help their businesses succeed, and workers still struggle to find and keep jobs that can sustain their families.

A new strategy—what this Assembly calls a "workforce intermediary" strategy—seeks to help workers advance, help businesses fill critical job shortages, and, ultimately, change systems to bolster regional and national economic development. This approach does not require creating a new category of organization or overhauling public systems, but it does require the transformation of existing policies and programs so that they are more adaptable to the local labor markets. It challenges existing organizations and systems to redefine whom they serve and how they do business through the forging of new partnerships and building the capacity to do so.

Workforce intermediary approaches are practiced by a variety of organizations—including community colleges, federally mandated Workforce Investment Boards (WIBs), state and local government agencies, unions, employer organizations, Community Development Corporations, community development financial institutions, faith based organizations, and community based organizations. Groups using workforce intermediary approaches have these goals:

1. *To bring workers into the American mainstream.* Success for these organizations means that workers are employed in jobs that offer the promise of financial stability.
2. *To increase business efficiency and productivity.* They are equally concerned with serving employers' needs and helping businesses become increasingly productive. They realize that business and worker success are interdependent.
3. *To enhance regional competitiveness.* These groups understand that the health of regional economies affects the ability to advance workers and strengthen business.

This intermediary approach is results driven, entrepreneurial and flexible, trusted by employers and workers, and collaborative.

A PROMISING START

More and more organizations in places as diverse as Wiscasset, Maine and San Francisco are showing encouraging results by using workforce intermediary approaches to help workers and business. But what exactly are these practices?

This approach arose in response to some of the limitations of the present workforce system. The current system is characterized by single customer focus on job applicants; a lack of knowledge of employers and their needs; a focus on limited employability training and initial placement and little post placement retention and advancement services; and the fragmentation of the workforce community and its funding streams.

The "workforce intermediary" approach has several common characteristics. At their core, workforce intermediaries:

- Pursue a "dual customer approach" by serving businesses looking for qualified workers, and by serving jobseekers and workers looking to advance their careers.
- Organize multiple partners and funding streams around common goals, bringing together businesses, labor unions, educational institutions, social service agencies, and other providers to design and implement programs and policies to improve labor market outcomes.
- Provide or broker labor market services that go beyond recruitment and referral by understanding the special needs—and gaining the trust—of firms and industries.
- Reduce turnover and increase economic mobility for workers by assuring continued support and opportunities to upgrade skills.
- Achieve results with innovative approaches and solutions to workforce problems.
- Improve outcomes for firms and their workers by catalyzing improvements in public systems and business employment practices.

Business organizations, labor supported programs, nonprofit community organizations, the public workforce investment system, and community colleges all can pursue workforce intermediary strategies. The number of such efforts has risen from a handful in the early 1990s to several hundred today. *Although they approach their tasks in different ways, successful intermediary organizations bring together key partners and functions to advance careers for all workers—recognizing the special needs of low-skilled, low-wage workers— increase business productivity, and to improve regional competitiveness.* (For descriptions of groups that perform workforce intermediary functions, go to www.opportunitiesatwork.org.)

RESULTS

The workforce intermediary approach promises to improve the economic well being of jobseekers, workers, and their families. Outcomes, where they have been measured, are positive, especially when compared to the impacts of other more traditional workforce development activities.

Early research indicates that businesses reap economic benefits from partnering with workforce intermediary organizations. These benefits include:

- Access to new sources of job applicants.
- Reduced recruitment costs.
- Higher retention rates compared to traditional hires.
- Increased productivity.
- Tax credit savings.
- An enhanced reputation within the community.

By attending to business concerns and increasing productivity, workforce intermediary organizations also bolster regional competitiveness. For example, in New York City, the Garment Industry Development Corporation introduced production changes that enabled area firms to increase profits while maintaining decent wages and benefit packages.

WHAT TYPES OF ORGANIZATIONS USE INTERMEDIARY APPROACHES?

More than 200 organizations in 39 states responded to a recent survey that described their use of workforce intermediary approaches. Most organizations participating in the survey are just a few years old, but two-thirds of them each serve more than 500 jobseekers and workers annually.

While workforce intermediary organizations take many forms, not every education, training, or economic development entity plays this role. Efforts that are single-purpose in character—attend to one particular activity or attend to the needs of a single employer—do not meet the workforce intermediary definition. The power of the workforce intermediary approach is its multifaceted nature, and its potential impact goes beyond the sum of its component parts.

Indeed, many public workforce development agencies—including local Workforce Investment Boards, economic development agencies, and community colleges—act as workforce intermediaries. More often, however, workforce intermediary efforts work to complement these public systems by expanding their reach through new partnerships and adding depth in industry sectors.

Consistent with the mission of the public workforce development systems, workforce intermediary efforts seek to:

- Expand economic opportunity for workers and jobseekers and enhance the competitiveness of firms and regions by identifying the needs of a variety of stakeholders.
- Invite firms, civic institutions, and leaders to address these needs.
- Integrate services and funding streams in ways that enhance effectiveness.
- Leverage new resources.
- Engage in systematic and rigorous assessment of outcomes.

A CALL TO ACTION

A workforce intermediary strategy seeks to help workers advance, businesses fill critical job shortages, and ultimately boost regional and national economic growth and productivity. Such ambitious goals require a "high impact" strategy, one that results in quality services to a greater share of workers and employers and meaningful changes to local and regional labor markets. The challenge is to get beyond what one Assembly participant called "pockets of unreplicable greatness" to a wider scale.

This strategy is an important response to the larger workforce crisis confronting this nation.

The severity of the impending workforce crisis requires nothing less than a major transformation in how the workforce system and workforce organizations go about their business. This change will require that intermediary functions and practices should be widely adopted by thousands of existing organizations—Workforce Investment Boards, community colleges, employer associations, labor programs, community development venture capital funds, and community based organizations. New partnerships between these groups can increase effectiveness in serving employers.

To accomplish this transformation, the system will require:

- An understanding that workforce development is as much an economic policy as a social policy.
- New policies that increase the accountability and impact of programs.
- Decisions by funders to create incentives for the use of dual customer approaches.
- A venture capital orientation on the part of funders, rewarding adaptive capacity and good results over sustained periods.
- Increasing research that demonstrates what works.

- Timely data on local labor markets for mapping labor supply and demand and career opportunities, and identifying job training opportunities and gaps and evaluating the effectiveness of workforce policies and investments.
- Leadership across employer associations, labor groups, community organizations, and community colleges with entrepreneurial vision and the skills to manage these "double bottom line" endeavors.
- Cross-sector sharing of information and most effective practices that advance workers in the American mainstream, increase business productivity, and enhance regional competitiveness.

Implementing the workforce intermediary approach is itself a challenge. For example, finding common ground between business and worker/jobseeker interests is a challenge. At times, these two perspectives have been assumed to be in opposition. However, finding the intersection between these two is essential in order to ensure business productivity, worker advancement, and regional competitiveness in the new skills economy. In addition, intermediary organizations operate in a fragmented policy and institutional environment and must often negotiate new roles and relationships while sidestepping destructive turf battles. This requires trust, credibility, and influence as well as careful diplomacy.

Further, the intermediary approach often faces all the challenges of an emerging business venture. Financial instability, limited resources, strained leadership, and the risks of taking success to scale must be successfully managed.

Many organizations have struggled with the constantly changing landscape of public workforce funding. Public funds have been cut and strict eligibility requirements, short-term timelines, and disparate performance measures have negatively affected outcomes. In general, some level of funding has been available for recruiting and training, but limited funding has been available to help businesses retain new workers and to help workers advance to higher quality jobs. In addition, there is no dedicated public funding for research and planning efforts that bring together stakeholders within specific industries to implement long-term strategies that address changing skill standards and related business needs. More and smarter funding is needed.

Workforce intermediary organizations and employer partners need flexible capital to create innovations in the public or private sector. Several states have created bond financing tools and investment tax strategies to support efforts of intermediary organizations to meet skill shortage demands and wage advancement goals. Other intermediary organizations have created blended financing strategies that include public funding and revenue-generating businesses. Based on the experience of these inter- mediary organizations, flexible financing options are needed to expand the impact of these strategies as well as support their efforts to increase capacity.

In addition to financial challenges, a variety of environmental forces constrain the emerging workforce intermediary efforts. A sometimes rigid policy environment and longstanding practices limit the acceptance of this new approach. Furthermore, slow decision making, inappropriate outcome measures, and cumbersome rules impede the attainment of positive out- comes for workers, firms, and regions.

RECOMMENDATIONS

The crisis facing America's labor market is not widely recognized. This American Assembly recommends the following:

Raise the Nation's Awareness

Faced with the immediate threats of international tensions and economic recession it is easy for the nation to overlook future workforce conditions that threaten the health of our economy. This American Assembly calls on America's civic, education, labor, and business leaders to understand and address this looming crisis, which threatens the nation's prosperity and democratic future.

This Assembly thinks it is especially important for private business to play a leading role in this effort. For more than 30 years, a variety of efforts have attempted to increase support for traditional workforce development activities. Those efforts have experienced, at best, mixed success, in part because the business sector did not perceive that the system met its needs for trained and productive workers and small and medium-sized firms were not organized and supported to participate effectively in the system. If there is one lesson that successful workforce intermediary efforts have taught us, it is that business sector involvement is critical to success. This has been demonstrated by Project QUEST in San Antonio and elsewhere, and will prove true for any national effort to address these issues.

Business leaders, who create jobs, must be actively and immediately approached, invited, and tasked to become key actors in local, state, and national consciousness-raising efforts. This effort could take the form of a national commission, a business led summit, a major public awareness and media campaign, or any and all of these. This Assembly thinks these issues should be immediately debated and made part of the public policy agenda.

At the same time, given the realities of competing pressures that make it hard for this issue to be heard, this Assembly also recommends the following steps.

Develop an Effective Workforce Intermediary Policy for Business, Workers, and Regions

The current disjointed policy environment creates a multifaceted problem, including funding streams that are not aligned, and have difficulty achieving meaningful results. Concerns have been expressed from many fronts, including businesses, community based organizations, educational institutions, unions, and government agencies.

Addressing this workforce development problem will require:

- *Broadening the focus of public workforce development to provide both job applicants and incumbent workers with the skills training needed for competitiveness and career advancement in a technologically driven, globalizing economy.* This requires flexibility, meaningful incentives, and resources for companies, industries, labor, and business organizations to foster and engage in training, growth, and productivity.
- *Incentives aimed at encouraging business investment to hiring, training, and advancing low-wage workers need to be simple to receive, administer, and address the needs of employers and workers.* For example, in Maryland, the state legislature appropriated $2 million for worker advancement training at a coalition of hospitals and other employers, leading to significant wage increases and promotions. In Philadelphia, PA, contributions from 61 employers, belonging to a Taft-Hartley labor management trust fund under the leadership of the District 1199C Training and Upgrading Fund, matched $3 million in federal funds to prepare 1,500 incumbent, dislocated, and new workers for careers in high-skilled nursing and allied health.
- *Supporting industry-specific workforce development strategies, which engage the self-interest of key stakeholders within a particular industry that help to organize a complex web of public and private resources into effective workforce development programs.*
- *Creating strategic economic development initiatives in states, regions, and localities that fully integrate workforce and economic development.* Several states have led the way by developing such plans and integrating funding streams to support them.

- *Redesigning educational financing and regulations to support workforce development. Much of the available student aid and state support for post secondary education does not address the needs of both workers and firms.* Because community colleges and other post secondary education institutions are critical parts of the workforce development system, this needs to change. Policy makers should consider the promising results from Individual Development Accounts and the Lifelong Learning Account demonstration, and important proposals to expand Pell Grant eligibility, adult education supports, and other student aid programs, especially for less than half-time students. Community colleges and other post secondary institutions are critical parts of solving this problem because of the pending need for technical skills, certificates, and portable credentials.

- *Maintaining and enhancing adequate work supports that enable workers to succeed and business to increase retention.* Childcare, transportation, healthcare, the Earned Income Tax Credit, and food stamps are essential to ensuring that no one who works should be in poverty and that workers can succeed and progress on the job. These supports should also be accessible and available for time spent in training.

- *Aligning the performance measures required by diverse funding streams to get real accountability while supporting career advancement goals.* Although a great deal of work must be done to get the measures right, this Assembly commends current efforts to establish consistent outcome measures for diverse federal programs. Congress and the administration should continue with this effort, making sure that their work reflects the real needs of business and workers. For example, many intermediaries, businesses, state and local officials, and others report ongoing difficulties and confusion around conflicting standards among the Workforce Investment Act (WIA), and other publicly funded workforce development programs (e.g., Temporary Assistance for Needy Families [TANF], Perkins). These should be remedied in upcoming reauthorizations. Outcome measures in TANF must be revised to reward employment and advancement outcomes rather than just caseload reduction.

- *Developing new ways to capture the effects of workforce interventions on businesses, workers, and labor markets.* While the current workforce system stresses the importance of actual customer focus, current measures do not adequately capture the benefits that accrue to employers by participating in this system. Several new efforts are under way by the Aspen Institute, National Governors' Association, and others to develop and test new demand-side measures that begin to address this problem.

Promoting Smarter Financing

Although coordinating existing public and private funding will help make progress toward growing the workforce intermediary approach, coordination alone is not enough. There is a need for more resources to help intermediary organizations meet the pressing demands of businesses, especially small businesses and workers. Even the most exemplary organizations, which juggle multiple funding streams and provide high-performing services to businesses and workers, face a daily struggle to finance their work. Because of limited resources, public agencies also face impossible choices between supporting required core activities and intermediary approaches like strategic planning and employer engagement that would strengthen their work and the critical need for training.

Federal, state, business, and philanthropic dollars all need to be expanded, and new types of financing mechanisms should be developed. Specifically, this Assembly recommends the following financing improvements:

- *Expand and target federal, state, business, and philanthropic resources for necessary intermediary functions, such as labor market information, research and development, convening of stakeholders, and business services.* New resources should be identified to support investments in intermediary functions—including business services—that will lead to better outcomes in the broad range of existing workforce funding streams. This includes ensuring that the WIA and TANF are flexible funding streams that allow local actors to design programs that meet local needs. Policy makers should support a proposal to provide new resources for Business Linkage Grants and other employer services in TANF.

- *Develop ways to create long-term capital flows by leveraging relevant employer investments, such as contributions to Taft-Hartley funds and/or tuition reimbursement; existing tax credits; social venture funds; and other financial innovations.* The relevance and applicability for workforce development of a tax credit strategy, such as the Low Income Housing Tax Credit model, should be studied. Financing is an important topic for foundations, and their support of Living Cities, formerly National Community Development, is a model that could be adapted.

- *Connect permanent sources of public financing, such as infrastructure spending, to workforce development.* For example, in several communities, port authorities provide stable investment in workforce development and career advancement tied to their infrastructure spending. Likewise, bond financing for the Pennsylvania Convention Center in

Philadelphia has generated a resource that supported training in the hospitality industry.

- *Implement major comprehensive federal, state, and private sector demonstrations of the workforce intermediaries approach.* This Assembly endorses recent efforts by the Department of Labor to create Regional Skills Alliances, help workforce boards and other workforce intermediaries begin industry-specific workforce development projects, assist healthcare employers address worker shortages, and expand the role of employer associations in providing intermediary services through the Workforce Innovation Networks (WINs) project. These types of demonstrations should be continued and expanded, and include partners from the philanthropic community, as WINs has since its inception.

Build Capacity

Organizations that successfully carry out these strategies conduct a dizzying range of activities to achieve their mission. They coordinate or provide training, work closely with employers, study their local and sectoral economies and labor markets, and link workers with support services like childcare. They do this in an environment where they must constantly seek funds from a variety of sources, each of which has its own demands for accountability and reporting. These demands would challenge the most sophisticated organization. Achieving higher impact, both for the specific organizations and for the system as a whole, will require investments in capacity building, like the following:

- *Invest in the adaptive capacity of organizations to learn, function, and innovate, developing the ability to effectively serve both workers and businesses.* The Annie E. Casey Foundation's Jobs Initiative and the Aspen Institute's Sectoral Employment Development Learning Project (SEDLP) are good examples of building the long-term capacity of workforce organizations to use outcome data to shape their work.
- *Develop technical assistance capacity to help organizations in developing intermediary functions.* Public/Private Ventures' Working Ventures program, a training series for workforce development professionals, has shown both the value of and the unmet demand for this type of service.
- *Help develop the entrepreneurial skills and competencies of workforce development professionals, not only in meeting the needs of their customers, but*

also in running their organizations. National centers in higher education, vocational education, and community development have contributed to the professionalization of those fields, and a similar effort is needed in workforce development.

- *Build the field by linking leading intermediaries into regional and national networks to foster innovation, provide peer learning, and develop a clearinghouse for innovative practice.* Good examples include such efforts as the National Network of Sector Partners, which has created learning forums and a peer technical assistance fund for sector programs around the country, and the AFL-CIO's Working for America Institute, which has successfully stimulated new labor/management partnerships and expanded existing partnerships to serve the interests of low-wage workers and businesses. These networks should distill and disseminate the lessons learned from decades of the nation's investment in the military addressing training and career advancement needs of highly diverse populations.
- *Build marketing and communications capacity of the organizations.* Leaders and staff need to learn to speak the language of business and frame organization-appropriate messages that counter negative employer perceptions and therefore stimulate interest in partnerships.

Build a Constituency for Action

Although it is critical for the nation's future economic success, workforce development has not been a national priority. In part, this is because of competition for public funds and attention, but also because of a perception of poor training results and little understanding or knowledge of the emerging successes. Paradoxically, the broad tasks of advancing workers, increasing business productivity, and enhancing regional competitiveness span so many institutions and stakeholders that they inhibit the necessary attention and public support. As the nation strives to build a more effective workforce development system, the workforce intermediary strategy can serve as an effective way to simplify the system for both business and workers, and foster their long-term advancement. Part of the strategy for achieving this success is building a broad constituency for action. Building that constituency requires:

- *Engaging business as a driving force in support of this effort.*
- *Building new coalitions and alliances across traditional dividing lines, especially in states and regions.* In Massachusetts, the Direct Care Worker Initiative, led by the Paraprofessional Healthcare Institute, brought

together employers, business, consumers, unions, and the workforce training community to advocate for enhanced wages and upgraded training for healthcare workers. These types of alliances will need to be expanded to have the high impact that is necessary.

- *Engaging political leadership at all levels.* The issues raised in this report merit attention from such organizations as the National Governors' Association, the U.S. Conference of Mayors, the National Association of Counties, and others to inform political leaders at all levels about what workforce intermediaries can do.
- *Expanding the voice of the workforce development community.* At the local, state, and national levels, the Workforce Alliance is providing valuable leadership in increasing the presence of the workforce development community in policy and legislative discussions.
- *Emphasizing workforce development as an essential element of economic policy at the federal, state, and local government levels.* This includes forging new alliances that integrate workforce development goals with those of economic development organizations, including the Council on Competitiveness, the Economic Development Administration, the International Economic Development Council, the National Congress on Community and Economic Development, and the Community Development Venture Capital Alliance.
- *Expanding relationships with higher education organizations to create support for these workforce development initiatives.* It is critical that groups such as the American Association for Community Colleges and other members of the American Council on Education, as well as the League for Innovation, engage their members in activities that transform post secondary education in support of the nation's workforce system.
- *Mobilizing a broader spectrum of foundations.* Regional, local, and national foundations that have invested in workforce development should continue their leadership and seek to engage other funders in support of this agenda. One promising start is an emerging group of 60 local and national foundations with an interest in workforce development that have come together under the auspices of the Neighborhood Funders Group. Another is the local funding collaboratives emerging in Baltimore, New York City, and Boston.
- *Strengthening local constituencies.* In the Southwest, community organizations affiliated with the Industrial Areas Foundation not only pioneered one of the early pilots, but then built six more workforce intermediaries in multiple states. These and similar efforts should be supported.

- *Researching and documenting the nature and extent of current investments as well as the return on those investments to employers, workers, and the community.* Expanded support for rigorous research that links outcomes with intermediary practices and documents the return on investment to employers, workers, and the community is needed. This research is essential for addressing misperceptions for documenting cases and context in which training works, and for justifying further public and private investment in these strategies.

CONCLUSION

This report builds upon 20 years of innovation, practice, and research in workforce development. It calls America to action and challenges the nation to use the workforce intermediary approach as a strategy to solve the nation's workforce crisis. There is a great deal at stake. Without aggressive action to expand the labor force in ways that increase productivity for employers, the nation's long-term economic health will be challenged. Workforce intermediary approaches can make a major contribution to meeting this national need.

PARTICIPANTS: THE 102nd AMERICAN ASSEMBLY

David C. Anderson
Human Resource Director
P-K Tool & Manufacturing Co.
Chicago, IL

•Timothy M. Barnicle
Co-Director
Workforce Development Program
National Center on Education and
    the Economy
Washington, DC

Diane L. Bell
President/CEO
Empower Baltimore Management
    Corp.
Baltimore, MD

Henry T. Berg
President
Taction
Waldoboro, ME

**Daniel E. Berry
Vice President
Greater Cleveland Growth
    Association
Cleveland, OH

Betsy Biemann
Associate Director, Working
    Communities
The Rockefeller Foundation
New York, NY

Paul Brophy
Principal
Brophy and Reilly LLC
Columbia, MD

Beth B. Buehlmann
Executive Director
Center for Workforce
    Development
U.S. Chamber of Commerce
Washington, DC

Joy Calkin
Professor Emeritus
University of Calgary
Chester, Nova Scotia

Pamela S. Calloway
Chief of Staff
Workforce Investment San Francisco
    Board
San Francisco, CA

Robert Carmona
President & CEO
STRIVE
New York, NY

Kathy Carney
CEO
Teamworks, Inc.
Park Rapids, MN

Harneen Chernow
Director of Education
    & Training
Massachusetts AFL-CIO
Malden, MA

John Colborn
Deputy Director, Economic
    Development Unit
The Ford Foundation
New York, NY

Carol Conway
Deputy Director
Southern Growth Policies
    Board
Research Triangle Park, NC

•Stephen Crawford
Director
Employment and Social Services
    Policy Studies
National Governors
    Association
Washington DC

Patrice M. Cromwell
Program Development Fellow
Open Society Institute-
    Baltimore
Baltimore, MD

Steven L. Dawson
President
Paraprofessional Healthcare
    Institute (PHI)
Bronx, NY

•Jackie Edens
Commissioner
Mayor's Office of Workforce
    Development
Chicago, IL

Phyllis Eisen
Vice President
The Manufacturing Institute of the
    National Association of
    Manufacturers
Washington, DC

Mark D. Elliott
Executive Vice President
Public/Private Ventures
New York, NY

♦David T. Ellwood
Lucius N. Littauer Professor of
    Political Economy
John F. Kennedy School of
    Government
Harvard University
Cambridge, MA

*Terri Feeley
Executive Director
San Francisco Works
San Francisco, CA

Cheryl G. Feldman
Director
District 1199C Training and
    Upgrading Fund
Philadelphia, PA

Richard A. Feldman
Executive Director
Worker Center- King County Labor
    Council, AFL-CIO
Seattle, WA

Joan Fitzgerald
Professor
Northeastern University
Center for Urban and Regional
    Policy
Boston, MA

Anita C. Flores
Associate Director
Jane Addams Resource
    Corporation
Chicago, IL

Dorian R. Friedman
Vice President, Policy
The Welfare to Work
    Partnership
Washington, DC

Judith Gentry
Program Quality and Operations
    Manager
NOVA
Sunnyvale, CA

Robert Giloth
Director
The Annie E. Casey Foundation
Baltimore, MD

Tamara Gould
Bay Area Video Coalition
Executive Director
San Francisco, CA

Steve Gunderson
The Greystone Group
Arlington, VA

Anne S. Habiby
Co-Executive Director
Initiative for a Competitive
    Inner City
Boston, MA

Ed Hatcher
President
The Hatcher Group LLC
Bethesda, MD

Bruce G. Herman
Director
Center for Workforce and Economic
    Development
New York, NY

Edward (Ned) W. Hill
Professor and Distinguished Scholar
    of Economic Development
Levin College of Urban Affairs
Cleveland State University
Cleveland, OH

Craig A. Howard
Vice President
MDRC
Oakland, CA

Jeffery Jablow
CEO
Origin, Inc.
New York, NY

Steven C. Jackobs
Executive Director
Capital IDEA
Austin, TX

Eleanor Josaitis
CEO and Co-Founder
Focus: Hope
Detroit, MI

Kathleen J. Kearney
Senior Program Officer
Coastal Enterprises, Inc.
Wiscasset, ME

Christopher T. King
Director
Ray Marshall Center, University
    of Texas
Austin, TX

Rebekah Lashman
Special Programs
    Manager
Boston Private Industry
    Council
Boston, MA

Jessica Laufer
CEO
Laufer, Green, Isaac
Los Angeles, CA

*•Cynthia E. Marano
Director
National Network of Sector
    Partners
National Economic Development
    and Law Center
Oakland, CA

**Richard M. McGahey
Managing Vice President
Abt Associates, Inc.
Bethesda, MD

Edwin Melendez
Professor and Director
Community Development Research
    Center
New School University
New York, NY

Mark Melliar-Smith
Partner
Austin Ventures
Austin, TX

Thomas Miller
Low Income Investment Fund
Oakland, CA

Nancy Mills
Executive Director
AFL-CIO Working for America
    Institute
Washington, DC

Holly L. Moore
President
Shoreline Community College
Seattle, WA

Helen Neuborne
Senior Program Officer
The Ford Foundation
New York, NY

Sigurd R. Nilsen
Director
Education, Workforce and
Income Security Issues
General Accounting Office
Washington, DC

♦Jeremy Nowak
President and CEO
The Reinvestment Fund
Philadelphia, PA

Jane Oates
Senior Education Advisor
HELP Committee
Washington, DC

Paul Osterman
Nanyang Professor of Human Resources
Massachusetts Institute of Technology
Cambridge, MA

Eric Parker
Executive Director
Wisconsin Regional Training
  Partnership
Milwaukee, WI

Pamela Paulk
Vice President, Human Resources
The Johns Hopkins Hospital and
  Health System
Baltimore, MD

Mary E. Peña
Executive Director
Project QUEST, Inc.
San Antonio, TX

Ida Rademacher
Senior Research Associate
Workforce Strategies Initiative-
The Aspen Institute
Washington, DC

Judith K. Resnick
Director, Workforce Development
  and Training
CBIA Education Foundation
Hartford, CT

•Marlene Seltzer
President
Jobs for the Future
Boston, MA

Karen B. Shawcross
Senior Vice President
Bank of America
Portland, OR

Rhonda Simmons
Executive Director
Seattle Jobs Initiative
Seattle, WA

Karen L. Sitnick
Director
Mayor's Office of Employment
  Development
Baltimore, MD

**•Julie A. Strawn
Senior Policy Analyst
Center for Law and Social Policy
Washington DC

Pam J. Tate
President and CEO
CAEL
Chicago, IL

James D. Van Erden
Vice President
Membership and Enterprise
  Development
Goodwill Industries
  International, Inc.
Bethesda, MD

Andy Van Kleunen
Executive Director
The Workforce Alliance
Washington DC

Margy Waller
Visiting Fellow
The Brookings Institution
Center on Urban and Metropolitan
    Policy
Washington, DC

*Orson W. Watson
Consultant
Boston, MA

Basil J. Whiting
Senior Fellow
The Manufacturing Institute
Brooklyn, NY

A. William Wiggenhorn
Chief Learning Officer
CIGNA Corporation
Philadelphia, PA

* Discussion Leader
**rapporteur
♦ Delivered Formal Address
•panelist

Steering Committee
Workforce Intermediaries Project

LEADERSHIP

Co-Director
John Colborn
Program Officer
Ford Foundation

Co-Director
Robert Giloth
Director
The Annie E. Casey Foundation

Co-Director
Betsy Biemann
Associate Director
Working Communities
The Rockefeller Foundation

Project Advisor
Paul C. Brophy
Principal
Brophy & Reilly LLC

Project Advisor
Ed Hatcher
President
The Hatcher Group LLC

MEMBERS

Daniel Berry
Vice President
Greater Cleveland Growth Association

Beth Buehlmann
Executive Director
Center for Workforce Preparation
U. S. Chamber of Commerce

Robert Carmona
President and CEO
STRIVE

Patrice Cromwell
Program Development Fellow
Open Society Institute

Emily DeRocco
Assistant Secretary
Employment and Training
U.S. Department of Labor

Phyllis Eisen
Vice President
The Manufacturing Institute
of the National Association
of Manufacturers

Mark D. Elliott
Executive Vice President
Public/ Private Ventures

Joan Fitzgerald
Associate Professor
Center for Urban and Regional
Policy
Northeastern University

Mitch Fromstein
Chairman Emeritus
Manpower International
Headquarters

Paul S. Grogan
President
The Boston Foundation

James Head
President
The National Economic Development
and Law Center

Craig Howard
Vice President
Manpower Demonstration Research
Corporation (MDRC)

Rick McGahey
Managing Vice President
Abt Associates Inc.

Edwin Melendez
Professor and Director
Community Development Research
Center
The New School University

Nancy Mills
Executive Director
AFL-CIO Working for America
Institutes

Manuel Pastor
Professor/Chair
Department of Latin American &
Latino Studies
University of California,
Santa Cruz

Joel Rogers
Professor
Center on Wisconsin Strategy
Dept. of Sociology

Marlene Seltzer
President
Jobs for the Future

Pam Tate
President and CEO
Workforce Chicago/CAEL

About The American Assembly

THE AMERICAN ASSEMBLY WAS ESTABLISHED BY DWIGHT D. EISENhower at Columbia University in 1950. It holds nonpartisan meetings and publishes authoritative books to illuminate issues of United States policy.

An affiliate of Columbia, The Assembly is a national, educational institution incorporated in the state of New York.

The Assembly seeks to provide information, stimulate discussion, and evoke independent conclusions on matters of vital public interest.

American Assembly Sessions

At least two national programs are initiated each year. Authorities are retained to write background papers presenting essential data and defining the main issues of each subject.

A group of men and women representing a broad range of experience, competence, and American leadership meet for several days to discuss the Assembly topic and consider alternatives for national policy.

All Assemblies follow the same procedure. The background papers are sent to participants in advance of the Assembly. The Assembly meets in small groups for four lengthy periods. All groups use the same agenda. At the close of these informal sessions participants adopt in plenary session a final report of findings and recommendations.

Regional, state, and local Assemblies are held following the national session at Arden House. Assemblies have also been held in England, Switzerland, Malaysia, Canada, the Caribbean, South America, Central America, the Philippines, China, and Taiwan. Over 160 institutions have cosponsored one or more Assemblies.

Arden House

The home of The American Assembly and the scene of the national sessions is Arden House, which was given to Columbia University in 1950 by W. Averell Harriman. E. Roland Harriman joined his brother in contributing toward adaptation of the property for conference purposes. The buildings and surrounding land, known as the Harriman Campus of Columbia University, are 50 miles north of New York City.

Arden House is a distinguished conference center. It is self-supporting and operates throughout the year for use by organizations with educational objectives. The American Assembly is a tenant of this Columbia University facility only during Assembly sessions.

THE AMERICAN ASSEMBLY
Columbia University

ABOUT THE CONTRIBUTORS

CHRIS BENNER is an assistant professor of geography at Pennsylvania State University; a research associate at the Center for Justice, Tolerance, and Community at the University of California, Santa Cruz; and a research associate at the Sociology of Work Program at the University of Witwatersrand (South Africa). His work focuses on labor markets and regional development in the information economy, in particular on the relationship between the diffusion of information technologies and transformation of work and employment patterns. His publications have appeared in a range of both academic journals and more popular outlets, and he is the author of *Work in the New Economy*.

DANIEL E. BERRY is vice president for growth strategies and services at the Greater Cleveland Growth Association. He serves on the board of several employment and training organizations in Cleveland, including Vocational Guidance Services; Fenn Educational Fund, Center for Employment Training–Cleveland; and the Workforce Investment Boards of both the city of Cleveland and Cuyahoga County.

ANTHONY P. CARNEVALE is vice president for assessments, equity, and careers at Educational Testing Service and is an internationally recognized authority on education, training, and employment. He was appointed by President Clinton as a commissioner to the White House Advisory Committee on Technology and Adult Education and Training and to chair the National Commission for Employment Policy, while serving as vice president and director of human resource studies at the Committee for Economic Development. Earlier, he had been president of the Institute for Workbased Learning, an applied research center affiliated with the American Society for Training and Development. Dr. Carnevale has held senior staff positions in the U.S. Senate and House of Representatives and the U.S. Department of Health, Education, and Welfare and was director of legislative affairs for the American Federation of State, County, and Municipal Employees (AFSCME). While serving as a research economist with the Syracuse University Research Corporation, he co-authored the principal affidavit in *Rodriguez v. San Antonio*, a U.S. Supreme Court action to remedy unequal tax burdens and educational benefits. This landmark case sparked significant educational equity reforms in a majority of states.

DONNA M. DESROCHERS is a senior economist at Educational Testing Service, where her research informs education and training policy on the need for increased human capital development. She focuses on the role of community colleges, as well as public and private education and job training systems, in preparing students and workers for employment. Previously she served as an economist at the Bureau of Economic Analysis, U.S. Department of Commerce, where she developed long-term employment, earnings, income, and population projections for states and metropolitan areas. She also conducted research at the Center for Labor Market Studies in Boston on the employment and earnings of welfare recipients and Boston public high school students.

JOHN FOSTER-BEY is a senior associate and director of the program for regional economic opportunity at the Urban Institute's Metropolitan Housing and Communities Center. The program focuses on research that examines the factors that improve low-skilled, low-income individuals' and communities' access to employment and economic opportunity, within local regional economies. Previously, he spent 11 years in philanthropy, where he was responsible for leading grant-making programs in economic and workforce development, community development, and youth development. He served as vice president of programs for the Northwest Area Foundation in St. Paul, Minnesota; associate director of the MacArthur Foundation's community initiatives program; and as a program officer in the Ford Foundation's urban poverty program and office of program related investments.

ROBERT P. GILOTH is director of family economic success at the Annie E. Casey Foundation. At the foundation since 1993, he directs its jobs initiative, community building efforts in several cities and ongoing economic opportunity investments for families. Previously, he was executive director of Community Development Corporations in Baltimore and Chicago and served as deputy commissioner of the Department of Economic Development in Chicago. Dr. Giloth is widely published in the areas of economic, workforce, and community development and recently edited *Workforce Development Politics: Civic Capacity and Performance*.

ROBERTA REHNER IVERSEN is assistant professor, clinician educator, and associate dean for academic affairs at the University of Pennsylvania School of Social Work. Her research and publications focus on occupational mobility among low-income urban families. Since January 2000 she has led a longitudinal ethnographic research project among families participating in the Annie E. Casey Foundation's Jobs Initiative, an eight-year workforce demonstration in five U.S. cities. *Moving Up Is a Steep Climb* covers the first study wave in two cities. A book in progress, co-authored with Annie Laurie Armstrong, encompasses more than five years of family advancement efforts in the five cities.

RICHARD KAZIS is senior vice president of Jobs for the Future in Boston. Previously he was research associate for the MIT Commission on Industrial Productivity. A former teacher at a high school for returning dropouts, he also has helped organize fast food workers, supervised a Neighborhood Youth Corps program, managed a cooperative foodstuffs wholesaler, and studied experiential learning in Israel. He is editor of *Low Wage Workers in the New Economy* and author of *Fear at Work* as well as many studies and articles on innovations in education and training.

JESSICA K. LAUFER is the founder and CEO of Laufer Green Isaac, an award-winning strategic marketing/communications firm representing clients in the United States and overseas. A pioneer in social issue marketing, she leads the multidisciplined LGI communications team in the design and implementation of actionable research, media relations strategies, and comprehensive communications campaigns. Her expertise includes global corporate citizenship, community economic development, corporate-community partnerships, consumer product marketing, multicultural campaigns, public health, and social issue marketing. Her firm designs campaigns for Fortune 500 companies, government agencies, entrepreneurial start-ups, and major foundations.

LAURA LEETE is the Fred H. Paulus director of the Public Policy Research Center and associate professor of economics and public policy at Willamette University. She has written and taught on topics relating to low-wage labor markets and occupational mobility; nonprofit labor markets; gender and race discrimination; family/work issues; and welfare reform and labor market access. She has published widely in journals and worked extensively with federal, state, and local government on applied policy issues.

CINDY MARANO is the director of the National Network of Sector Partners where she manages the staff, consultant team, budget, program, and policy agenda for the NNSP and serves as a member of the NEDLC senior management team. Previously, she founded and led Marano & Associates, a small strategic planning firm that specialized in designing and supporting initiatives to reduce poverty, with clients in the foundation and nonprofit sectors. She is also the former executive director and continuing senior program consultant to Wider Opportunities for Women, was named to national advisory commissions of three secretaries of labor, was a five-year appointed member of the DC Private Industry Council, and was awarded the Gloria Steinem Award for Women's Economic Justice. She has developed legislative proposals related to job training, welfare-to-work strategies, and vocational education that have been adopted into federal law.

KARIN MARTINSON is a consultant on welfare and poverty issues for a number of research, advocacy, and public sector organizations, including the Center for Law and Social Policy, the Urban Institute, the Manpower Demonstration Research Corporation, and the U.S. Department of Health and Human Services (HHS). She has over 15 years of experience as both a researcher and a policy analyst on a range of issues related to low-income families—including welfare reform, employment and training programs, child support, and childcare. She was formerly a senior policy analyst at the office of the assistant secretary for planning and evaluation at HHS and at the Center on Budget and Policy Priorities and a researcher at the Manpower Demonstration Research Corporation, playing a lead role on several evaluations of welfare-to-work programs.

RICHARD McGAHEY is a managing vice president at Abt Associates Inc., a research and consulting firm, where he heads the group on education, family support, and workforce development. At the U.S. Department of Labor, he served as assistant secretary for policy and for pension and welfare benefits. In the U.S. Congress, he was executive director of the Joint Economic Committee and economic policy advisor to Senator Edward M. Kennedy. He currently directs research projects on workforce development supported by the Ford, Rockefeller, and MacArthur Foundations.

JACK MILLS, program director for Jobs for the Future, manages research and development, best practices analysis, system change, and policy design related to workforce development institutions' efforts to meet the needs of employers and adults who are underemployed or jobless. His current work includes managing demonstration programs involving employer organizations, Workforce Investments Boards, One Stop Career Centers, and TANF agencies; strategic consultation for state WIA boards; and analysis of policy lessons from large cities' welfare-to-work program experience. He is co-author of *Business Participation in Welfare-to-Work: Lessons from the United States* and *Employer-Led Organizations and Skill Supply Chains: Linking Worker Advancement with the Skill Needs of Employers* and is a member of the National Network of Sector Practitioners Advisory Committee.

PAUL OSTERMAN is the Nanyang Professor of Human Resources at M.I.T.'s Sloan School of Management and Department of Urban Planning and is also area head in the Sloan School Department of Behavioral and Policy Sciences. He is the author of *Securing Prosperity: How the American Labor Market Has Changed and What To Do About It* and *Employment Futures: Reorganization, Dislocation, and Public Policy and Getting Started: The Youth Labor Market*; the co-author of *Working In America*; *A Blueprint for the New Labor Market*; *The Mutual Gains Enterprise*; *Forging a Winning Partnership Among Labor, Management, and Government*; and *Change At Work*; and the editor of two books, *Internal Labor Markets*, and *Broken Ladders; Managerial Careers In The New Economy*. His most recent book is *Gathering Power: The Future of Progressive Politics In America*.

MANUEL PASTOR JR. is professor of Latin American and Latino studies and director of the Center for Justice, Tolerance, and Community at the University of California, Santa Cruz. His research on U.S. urban issues has been published widely and has generally focused on the labor market and social conditions facing low-income urban communities. He is co-author of *Searching for the Uncommon Common Ground: New Dimensions on Race in America*, part of The American Assembly series on "Uniting America."

NAN POPPE has been dean of adult and continuing education at Portland Community College since 1998. In her 20 years of community college administrative experience, her focus has been designing and implementing programs that provide post secondary access to a variety of under serviced populations.

JERRY RUBIN, vice-president of Building Economic Opportunity at Jobs for the Future, has more than 20 years of experience designing and implementing economic development and workforce training initiatives for low-wage workers, low-income individuals and families, municipal and state governments, and private industry. Prior to joining JFF in 2000, he founded and was president of the Greater Boston Manufacturing Partnership, was chief of staff and director of policy and planning for the Economic Development and Industrial Corporation of Boston, and was founder and first executive director of the Coalition for A Better Acre, a Lowell, Massachusetts based Community Development Corporation.

WILLIAM P. RYAN is a research fellow at the Hauser Center for Nonprofit Organizations at Harvard University and a consultant to foundations and nonprofit organizations. His work focuses on nonprofit organizational capacity, primarily among community development and human service organizations. He has written or co-authored several publications, including *High Performance Nonprofit Organizations: Managing Upstream for Greater Impact.*

MARLENE B. SELTZER oversees Jobs for the Future's education transitions and workforce development activities and is responsible for the overall management of JFF's research, model development, policy development, and consulting services. She has more than 20 years of practical experience in workforce development policy and program delivery at the national, state, and local levels. She is the senior advisor for JFF's body of work that focuses on increasing economic opportunity for low-income workers and has provided system design support to a number of workforce development organizations at the state and local levels. Prior to joining JFF, she held a number of positions in the field of workforce development, including commissioner of the Massachusetts Department of Employment and Training. As president of Seltzer Associates, a for-profit consulting firm, she provided policy development assistance to the U.S. Department of Labor on workforce development initiatives. She also served as co-founder and president of Employment Resources, Inc., a nonprofit, community based workforce development organization.

JULIE STRAWN is a senior policy analyst who focuses on workforce development and welfare reform, in particular on job advancement and access to post secondary education for low-income adults. From 1993 to 1996, she developed policy and legislative positions for the National Governors' Association in the areas of workforce development and welfare reform. She has also worked on these issues at the Center on Budget and Policy Priorities, at the U.S. Department of Health and Human Services, and in the U.S. House of Representatives. She has authored numerous publications and provided technical assistance to antipoverty organizations, legislators, and program administrators.

KIM TARR is a program specialist at the National Economic Development and Law Center. She has contributed to the center's work since 2000, supporting myriad projects including the Family Support Program and Californians for Family Economic Self-Sufficiency. Currently, she coordinates the membership services and publications of the National Network of Sector Partners.

CHRISTOPHER WALKER is a senior research associate at the Urban Institute's Metropolitan Housing and Communities Center and director of the community and economic development program. His primary research focus is on public and private initiatives to strengthen low-income communities, with special emphases on the role of community based organizations, intermediary institutions, and partnerships among diverse public and nonprofit agencies. In addition to his research for Living Cities: the National Community Development Initiative, other recently published work includes research on the neighborhood impacts of the Community Development Block Grant Program, the size, characteristics, and performance of economic development loans originated by local governments using CDBG funding, and the relationship between cultural participation and various aspects of community change, including the relationship between traditional arts and economic development and partnerships among museums, public libraries, and public radio and television to promote lifelong learning.

SIAN WINSHIP is a vice president of strategic planning at Laufer Green Isaac and manages strategic development and research for the agency. Recently she spearheaded the firm's groundbreaking research "Hidden Agendas: Stereotypes and Cultural Barriers to Corporate Community Partnerships" for the Ford Foundation's Corporate Involvement Initiative. Prior to joining Laufer Green Isaac, she spent 15 years working on many successful national brand campaigns and corporate product launches, including several during her tenure at Chiat/Day.

SARAH ZIMMERMAN is a senior research associate with Working Partnerships, USA. She co-authored the WPUSA 2001 report on the affordable housing crisis in Silicon Valley, "Everyone's Valley." She has also published two industry reports on hospitality and healthcare in Silicon Valley. Her research interests include affordable housing, gender analysis, accountable development, and building high-road industry partnerships for the labor markets of the new economy.

ACKNOWLEDGMENTS

A NUMBER OF COLLEAGUES ASSISTED ME IN ASSEMBLING THIS VOLUME and in commenting on my introductory and concluding chapters: Paul Brophy, John Colborn, Elisabeth Biemann, Ed Hatcher, Lisa Kaplan Gordon, Richard Kazis, Jerry Rubin, Marlene Seltzer, and Julie Strawn. Jobs for the Future graciously agreed to host an early exchange of ideas among chapter authors, and The American Assembly helped facilitate the scheduling and editing of the volume.

ROBERT P. GILOTH

INDEX